A. PAUL MAHAFFY

THE PRIVATE COMPANY:
A Legal and Business Guide for Owners and Managers

Second Edition

CARSWELL®

A cataloguing record for this publication is available from Library and Archives Canada.

ISBN: 978-0-7798-6068-5

Composition: Computer Composition of Canada

Printed in Canada by Thomson Reuters

 THOMSON REUTERS

CARSWELL, A DIVISION OF THOMSON REUTERS CANADA LIMITED

One Corporate Plaza
2075 Kennedy Road
Toronto, Ontario
M1T 3V4

Customer Relations
Toronto 1-416-609-3800
Elsewhere in Canada/U.S. 1-800-387-5164
Fax: 1-416-298-5082
www.carswell.com
E-mail www.carswell.com/email

To Cynthia

Foreword

When researching and writing the first edition of this book, I was motivated, probably inspired, by many of my clients who owned and operated successful businesses while they were confronted with similar, often recurring problems. They seemed to be in need of a book that described some of the main legal and business issues ordinarily faced by those involved with private companies. I felt they could benefit from a book that provided "one stop shopping", that gave an overview of issues to be aware of, and that served as a guide for preventing problems, not just resolving them.

The aim of the first edition was to make owners and managers more proactive, to be able to plan for their company's future and avoid the many pitfalls along the way, and to be better equipped to deal with their company's many stakeholders and reduce the likelihood of disputes arising.

The first edition covered a number of different topics. Starting up the company, dealing with employees, obtaining debt and equity financing, protecting intellectual property, creditor proofing, director duties and liabilities, dealing with shareholders, business succession and estate freezes, and company governance, all were topics described with a view to assisting owners and managers.

However, after the first edition was released, and while attempting to declutter my basement and find a new home for the long ignored paperbacks and university textbooks residing there, I spied a crinkly old tome entitled the *Everyman's Legal Guide,* which was handed down to me by my late grandfather. After thumbing through the yellowed pages, I realized that a second edition of *The Private Company* would eventually have to happen. The first edition suddenly seemed incomplete.

The *Everyman's Legal Guide* was published in 1920 by McClelland & Stewart, although copyright was attributed to Carswell. It was described as being the sixth edition of *The Canadian Lawyer*, entirely "rewritten" by Edward Meek, K.C., and intended to be "a synopsis of the laws of Canada on many subjects for use in universities, colleges and high schools, and by merchants, bankers, business men, and the public generally".

At 364 pages, its scope is vast when compared to the narrow topics addressed by many of today's legal texts. It favours breadth over depth, although, as I'm often reminded by more senior lawyers, there was less law then. It addressed a number of subjects similar to the courses offered over the years at Canadian law schools.

In his preface dated March 1920, Mr. Meek states that the guide "does not pretend to make its readers lawyers, or to enable them to dispense with the services of the legal profession, but . . . will enable an ordinary student or business man to solve for himself a large proportion of the legal questions which are met with in business, and to do this without the need of applying to a lawyer".

The preface then highlights the advantages of having a basic knowledge of the law:

> *Many persons have neither the time nor the money to apply to a solicitor every day for advice. Cases frequently arise in which the business man must make up his mind and act before he can have an opportunity to consult a solicitor. This book is intended to give him a correct idea, with the least possible trouble or research, of the principles and practical application of the law which every student and every commercial man in the course of a strenuous and busy life, may require to know something about, on each of these subjects. The immense value of this book, with its simple arrangement, cannot be doubted. Wrongs are suffered and money lost every day because people are unacquainted with their legal rights and with the means which the law affords for asserting and enforcing them. Many of the lawsuits which come before the courts have been brought about because some person was ignorant of the law relating to the matter, which he should have learned when at school or at college, as part of the necessary equipment for the struggles of life.*

In short, the *Everyman's Legal Guide* was designed to satisfy the reader's need for legal information without needing a lawyer to obtain it.

While Mr. Meek's reasons for writing a general legal guide in 1920 seem to be equally appropriate today, a modern day version of his guide would likely appear in numerous volumes, if published in paper form at all. Yet however well-intentioned a writer, or more likely team of writers, might be in producing such a synopsis today for the benefit of the non-lawyer public, it would nevertheless be a Herculean task.

This second edition of *The Private Company* has little in common with the *Everyman's Legal Guide* and does not attempt to be its modern day version because of the relatively few topics covered. However, both books, though written almost 100 years apart, share the same goal of giving their readers "a correct idea, with the least possible trouble or research, of the principles and practical application of the law which . . . [they] may require to know something about" on the topics which are covered.

It is in the spirit of the *Everyman's Legal Guide* that this second edition is written.

Many of the chapters in the first edition of *The Private Company* have been updated to reflect changes in the law, and two new chapters, dealing with *Acquiring a Franchise* and *Leasing Commercial Property*, have been added to this edition.

Table of Contents

x

Table of Cases

Introduction

An owner or manager of a private company faces many challenges when establishing, operating and financing the company. Although he may feel that these challenges are unique to the company, they are nonetheless experienced by most owners and managers at some time throughout a company's lifecycle.

Trying to ensure that the company's products and services continue to meet the needs of the company's customers while also addressing the demands of the company's employees, lenders, investors, regulators and other stakeholders can lead to a difficult balancing act. Plotting the overall direction of the company's business is complicated by the many obstacles that often get in the way.

This book describes some of the main legal and business issues ordinarily faced by those who own or manage a private company. It attempts to provide "one stop shopping" for those involved with private companies who want an overview of issues to be aware of, and who want a guide for preventing problems, not just resolving them. It aims to make owners and managers more proactive, to be able to plan for their company's future and avoid the many pitfalls along the way, and to be better equipped to deal with their company's many stakeholders and reduce the likelihood of disputes arising.

A number of different topics are covered. Starting up the company, dealing with employees, obtaining debt and equity financing, protecting intellectual property, creditor proofing, director duties and liabilities, dealing with shareholders, business succession and estate freezes, and company governance, are all described with a view to assist owners and managers.

Because of its general nature, this book does not provide a detailed analysis of the many private company issues which can arise in particular circumstances, and readers may still have to obtain specialized professional advice to guide them through the implications of carrying out specific actions.

Some of the chapters in this book relate to different stages in the company's lifecycle. In addition to the *Starting Up* chapter, those chapters dealing with financing issues reflect the changing relationships the company may have with its shareholders and lenders, especially when new shareholders and lenders arrive on the scene. Growing companies in need of capital continually access additional, possibly institutional, sources of outside money, sources which may impose their own ways of doing business once they arrive. The current owners and managers may feel that they have to do what the newcomers tell them to do as part of the sacrifice to be made for accepting new money.

But the changes which occur aren't necessarily bad, just different, and may well be for the better of everyone concerned, including the current owners and managers. The changes may lead to good company governance, which may simply be good business.

In looking at the private company, this book generally refers to companies incorporated under the *Canada Business Corporations Act*[1], or CBCA, although many private companies in Canada are incorporated under provincial companies legislation. Because most provincial companies acts are modelled after the CBCA, many of the ideas expressed in this book dealing with shareholders, directors, governance and financing apply to most private companies, wherever incorporated in Canada. However, the reader should be aware that minor differences do exist and should consult the provincial act which may govern any particular company. Moreover, as some of the ideas in this book reflect Ontario law, it may be necessary for the reader to consider any differences which may exist between the law of Ontario and the law of any other province in which the company may carry on business.

In order to be gender neutral and in place of he/she, this book will alternate between genders by chapter when referring to an owner, manager or any other individual party.

WHAT IS A PRIVATE COMPANY?

Most corporations in Canada are owned either by a single shareholder or a small number of shareholders. They have traditionally been described as private companies, though more recently have been called "closely-held" companies to differentiate them from other companies with many more shareholders but which are not "public" companies. A public company is usually regarded as a company which issues its securities to the public, whereas a private company does not.

A private company is not specifically defined in the CBCA but is often taken to be a company which is not a "distributing corporation", which is defined in the CBCA.[2] It is also often taken to be a company which has "private company restrictions" in its articles of incorporation or other charter documents as prescribed by provincial securities legislation. These restrictions generally limit the number of shareholders, prevent share transfers without, for example, approval by a majority of directors or shareholders, and prohibit solicitations to the public to subscribe for company securities.[3]

For the purposes of this book, the term private company will be used in its traditional context, as a company which does not offer its securities to the public and which has a relatively small number of shareholders (with a maximum of 50, excluding employees). It will not be a distributing corporation within the meaning of the CBCA. Furthermore, in its references to various income tax implications, this book assumes that the company is a Canadian-controlled private corporation.[4]

Even though a private company may seem "private" because much of its financial information is not publicly available, certain corporate information about the company is far from confidential. For example, the names and addresses of its directors and the location of its head office can be found by searching the records of the Corporations Directorate of Industry Canada.[5] A list of its shareholders, indicating their names, addresses, and the number of shares they each hold, can be requested upon payment of a reasonable fee by not just the shareholders but also by the creditors of the company.[6]

OWNERS VS. MANAGERS

Even though this book is intended to be a guide for both owners and managers of private companies, it recognizes the distinction between the two roles. While many owners are also managers and many managers are, or may become, owners, the CBCA and corporate law in general separates company ownership from company management by ascribing ownership to the company's shareholders and management to the company's directors and officers. Under the CBCA, it is the duty of the directors to "manage, or supervise the management of, the business and affairs" of the company.[7]

Even within ownership and management, there are further distinctions to be made.

Not all shareholders are alike. A shareholder having enough votes through his shares to elect a majority of the company's directors at a meeting of shareholders can control the company. Although all of the shareholders are technically "owners", only the majority shareholder may be regarded in a practical sense as the company's "owner".

When this book refers to a company's owner, it is usually referring to the company's majority shareholder. In many cases, the majority shareholder will be an individual who may have founded the company and was perhaps the company's only shareholder for quite some time, and who may have been the company's only director.

Even though the directors are under a duty to manage the company, the company's management is more likely comprised of certain executive officers appointed by the directors, along with other employees appointed by the officers, who carry out many of the obligations described in this book which are owed by the company to various parties. While some officers may be elected by the shareholders to also serve as directors, many boards of directors consist of individuals who are not also officers. These individuals are often called "outside" directors, and depending upon their lack of other connection with the company and the owner, they may also be called "independent" directors.

Therefore, when this book refers to a manager, it will likely be referring not to a company director but to a company officer or other employee who is regarded as part of the company's management.

WHO IS A SHAREHOLDER?

While the term "shareholder" is not a precise legal term, it is often taken to mean, at least in the private company context, the person who is recorded as the holder of a share on the share register maintained by the issuing company. The share may or may not be evidenced by a tangible share certificate. If it is, the person whose name appears on the face of the certificate is not necessarily the owner, since it may have been endorsed by that person and become a bearer certificate, possibly making the bearer the owner.

The person named as a shareholder in a company's share register will be regarded as a shareholder for the purposes of this book, as is the case under the CBCA.[8]

Often a person becomes a shareholder by first submitting an offer or subscription to the company, followed by an acceptance or allotment by the company. Subject to any pre-emptive rights (described later in the *Shareholder Agreements* chapter), the company's directors are empowered under the CBCA to issue shares at such times, to such persons, and for such consideration as they may determine.[9] Since shares are not to be issued until the consideration is fully paid in money, or an equivalent value in property or past services,[10] a person to whom shares are issued without payment is not a shareholder.

A person may also become a shareholder by way of a transfer of previously issued shares from existing shareholders or their legal successors, including by way of transmission from the estate of a deceased shareholder.

Starting Up the Company

In deciding whether to create a new company, an individual or group of entrepreneurs will likely have already investigated and analyzed a number of issues relating to the intended business of the company long before they decide to arrange for the company's incorporation and organization. They may have determined the size of the potential market for the company's goods or services and identified who the company's customers will probably be, and have assessed what resources they will need to achieve their business plan and what obstacles may be in their way.

In some cases, they may have been carrying on their business as a sole proprietorship[1] or partnership[2] without even considering incorporation. After all, these other forms of business organization have some advantages over a corporation when operating a business that may be losing money. Business losses incurred by a sole proprietorship[3] or partnership[4] may be used to reduce the taxes payable by a proprietor or partner on other sources of income, whereas losses incurred by a corporation can only be offset against corporate profits. However, proprietors and partners (other than limited partners in a limited partnership) face personal liability for the obligations of the business, and thereby place their personal assets at risk when operating the business.

Because a corporation is a separate legal entity, its shareholders are generally not liable for the debts and other obligations of the corporation.[5] Their liability is usually limited to the value of the money or property they have transferred to the corporation in exchange for their shares. If the assets of the corporation are insufficient to fully satisfy the claims of the corporation's creditors, the shares held by the shareholders can become worthless, but the shareholders have no personal liability to make up for the insufficiency of the assets.

In addition to providing its shareholders with limited liability, the corporation provides other advantages. Through the issuance of different classes of shares, different shareholders can be given different levels of control, risk-taking and financial participation in the corporation, and additional funds can be obtained over time by the subsequent issuance of shares. Since a corporation can exist indefinitely, the death or departure of its owners does not necessarily result in its dissolution.

Once the entrepreneurs have decided to incorporate, incorporation can often be accomplished quickly, with only a few simple steps. The incorporating document, called articles of incorporation under the CBCA, together with a name search report and applicable fee, is filed with the appropriate government office. That office will be Corporations Canada in the case of CBCA incorporation.

Although they may choose to incorporate in another Canadian jurisdiction, perhaps under the corporation statute of the province where they reside, there are certain advantages to incorporating under the CBCA. A CBCA corporation may have its head office in any province of Canada, and there can be less of an administrative burden on the corporation should it carry on business in a number of provinces. More importantly, it can use its corporate name in any province.

This right of a CBCA corporation to use its name across Canada, however, creates a certain disadvantage to incorporation under the CBCA. In order for a selected name to be eligible as a corporate name, it must not be similar to the corporate name or trade-mark of another corporation in Canada and must be approved by Corporations Canada. Therefore, the name that the entrepreneurs really want as a corporate name may not be available, and they may have to settle on another less suitable name. By contrast, incorporating under a province's corporation statute usually only requires that the name selected not be the same as the name of another corporation in that province.

CHOOSING THE CAPITAL STRUCTURE

If only one class of shares is chosen for the company, assuming it is incorporated under the CBCA, the holders of such shares must have the right to vote at any meeting of shareholders, along with the right to receive any dividend which may be declared by the company and the right to receive the remaining property of the company upon its dissolution.[6] If more than one class of shares is created, these three rights must attach to at least one class of shares, but they need not all be attached to the same class.[7] Different share classes may be created at the time of incorporation, or later on by filing articles of amendment with Corporations Canada.

Different share classes are often created when there will be different groups of shareholders with different rights, or at least when it is intended that not all of the shareholders will be treated equally. For example, in order to attract outside investment in the company, a separate class of "preferred" shares might be created to provide the investors with a right to receive a specific amount of dividends on a regular basis and a return on their investment before the holders of another class may receive any dividends.

Although such preferred shares are usually created when a financing with the investors actually occurs, they may be created upon incorporation when assets are to be transferred to the company at the outset.[8] In the absence of such an asset transfer, the company will likely be incorporated with only one class of common shares.

ISSUING THE SHARES

The initial shareholders of the company will likely be the entrepreneurs who conceived the idea of the company's business, but may also include some of their family members who will be involved in the business and possibly some friends who are helping along the way. These shareholders are often described as the company's "founders" and are usually expected to have a certain commitment to achieving success for the company, at least during its early stages. The reward for their commitment is sometimes called "sweat equity", since they are more likely to provide the company with labour rather than capital, and are more likely to be compensated in shares, not cash. They may have to wait quite a while before they receive any financial reward for their time and trouble in assisting the company.

Ordinarily their incentive to become and stay involved with the company is provided through their right to subscribe for shares of the company. How many shares each of them is entitled to purchase, usually for a nominal amount since the company will have almost no value at this stage, will depend upon how each of them is perceived by the others as making an essential contribution to the company. Their particular skills, business contacts, work ethic, preparedness to make personal sacrifices for the company, and ability to provide funds to the company when the need arises may be just some of the factors considered in the allocation of shares.

While each founder may regard herself as equally important to the company and entitled to equal treatment, the shares are likely to be allocated unequally when just one or two individuals are regarded as the real driving force behind the business. If one founder acquires more than 50 per cent of the voting shares, she will thereby control the company and be looked at as the "owner" even though there may be other shareholders.

The number of company shares to be issued to each founder is not as important as the respective percentage of shares to be held by each. As the company grows and needs more financing, additional shares may be issued to outside investors, thereby reducing or "diluting" the percentage holdings of the original shareholders.

If a founder intends to transfer certain property to the company, such as equipment or intellectual property, the shares to be issued may not be issued for just a nominal amount. The transfer of the property will be deemed to be made at its fair market value for tax purposes, and if the fair market value exceeds the founder's cost base of such property, she will face a taxable capital gain. To avoid this happening and allow the transfer to be made on a tax-deferred basis, the founder and company will likely elect a value between the fair market value and the founder's cost base, and the founder will receive at least one share in the company as consideration for the transfer.[9]

INCOME SPLITTING

When deciding who the shareholders should be and how many shares they should each hold, the founders may wish that some of the shares allocated to them ought to be issued instead to members of their own family, particularly when there is just one founder. Providing for the issuance of shares to family members allows for "income splitting" among the founder's family for tax purposes.

Income splitting involves the dividing of income which would otherwise be earned by a taxpayer in a higher tax bracket, such as the founder, among taxpayers in a lower tax bracket, perhaps her children. When income is split among a number of family members, the total amount of tax payable by the founder and her family collectively may be considerably lower than the amount of tax payable by just the founder alone, depending upon their respective tax brackets.

By issuing some of the company shares which have been allocated to the founder to the founder's spouse, adult children or other family members who are in a lower tax bracket, or a trust for their benefit, or a corporation which they own, taxable capital gains earned by the family members when the shares are sold, along with certain dividend income received before such a sale, will be taxed at a lower rate than if earned by the founder personally.[10]

Furthermore, assuming the company is a Canadian controlled private corporation as referenced in the *Introduction* and its shares qualify for the individual lifetime capital gains exemption,[11] each family member who realizes a capital gain upon the sale of the shares may be able to take advantage of the exemption and avoid or reduce the tax otherwise payable on the sale. The greater the number of family members who hold company shares, the greater the number of exemptions that may be used by a family collectively to avoid paying capital gains tax.

While issuing shares directly to a founder's family members may have the advantage of income splitting, it may also have the disadvantage of diluting the founder's control over the company. Each family member as a shareholder will have an independent right to elect directors or sell her shares, unless a shareholder agreement is in place which restricts such rights. However, a voting trust agreement among the family members in favour of the founder can be used to give the founder the right to vote all of her family's shares as she sees fit.

These direct share issuances may also be disadvantageous to the other founders, who may not appreciate having a founder's relatives as "partners" in the business, especially when such relatives may be perceived as being uncommitted to the business or unable to contribute to its success.

Issuing shares directly to a founder's family members may also jeopardize the founder's own estate and business succession planning, or deprive her of the flexibility she may need to revise her plans should circumstances change, including her own financial needs. Those children who acquire shares originally allocated to a founder may prove to be unworthy.

USE OF A FAMILY TRUST

Since direct share ownership by a founder's family members may be inappropriate, the shares allocated to a founder might be issued instead to a family trust which could include the founder and some or all of her children as beneficiaries. Family trusts, which are described in greater detail in the *Business Succession and Estate Freezes* chapter, do not give the beneficiaries the same rights they might otherwise have if they held the shares directly. The trustees, not the beneficiaries, exercise the rights attached to the shares held by the trust, including the right to vote.

Furthermore, the trustees are normally given the power to invest the assets of the trust in their complete discretion, including any dividends received on the company's shares held by the trust or any capital gains earned by the trust on the sale of company shares. They are also given the complete discretion to distribute the trust assets to one or more of the beneficiaries, thereby allowing them to favour one beneficiary over another.[12]

Despite this flexibility and control which a family trust provides, there are certain disadvantages to issuing shares to a family trust instead of issuing the shares to the family members directly. Establishing and maintaining a family trust involves additional costs, serving as a trustee can entail certain financial liabilities, and any income retained by the trust will be taxed at the highest marginal rate.[13] Unless all of its assets are distributed before the 21st anniversary of the creation of the trust, the trust will be deemed to have disposed of all of its property at fair market value on that date and be required to pay tax on the accrued capital gains accordingly.[14]

USE OF A HOLDING CORPORATION

Instead of issuing shares directly to a founder's family members or to a trust with such members as beneficiaries, the shares originally allocated to a founder might be issued to a corporation owned by the founder and her family. As with a family trust, a family holding corporation could be the only company shareholder, thereby concentrating control of the company in just one party.

While the costs of establishing and maintaining a holding corporation may be comparable to the costs incurred with a family trust, there may be less flexibility in making distributions to the family shareholders than there would be in making fully discretionary distributions to family beneficiaries under a family trust. After all, shareholders within the same class are supposed to be treated equally. More significantly, the corporation is not eligible to use the lifetime capital gains exemption upon a sale of the company shares which it holds, since such exemption is only available to individuals.[15]

VALUATION AND PAYMENT FOR SHARES

As mentioned above, the shares allocated to a founder will usually be issued for only a nominal amount. But regardless of how low the share price may be, and regardless of whether the shares are to be issued directly to the founder's family members, or to her family trust or family holding corporation, the subscription price for the shares should be paid by those acquiring the shares with their own funds, and not with funds provided by the founder. If the founder pays the subscription price for shares issued to her family, family trust or family corporation, any dividends and capital gains derived from those shares may be attributed back to her and taxed in her hands.[16]

If the company wishes to raise money right away for working capital purposes from outside investors and wishes to receive from them more than just the nominal value paid by the founders and their family, it should allow for some time to pass. If the company sells shares of the same class at the same time to different parties at different prices, a party paying the lower amount may have to pay tax on the difference in the price.[17]

To avoid this result, shares allocated to the founders should be issued at the outset, before any shares are issued to outside investors. If additional shares are to be issued to outside investors around the same time, some effort should be made to create further value in the company before issuing the additional shares, perhaps by producing a comprehensive business plan, signing up a potential customer, hiring a new manager or producing a prototype of an intended product. Alternatively, the class of shares issued to the outside investors might be different from the class already issued to the founders.

SHARE BUY-BACK RIGHTS

In order to avoid the possibility of a founder receiving shares at a nominal price and then leaving the company shortly thereafter while retaining her shares in the expectation that the shares will appreciate owing to the hard work of the other founders staying behind to run the company, founder shares may be subject to buy-back or repurchase rights in favour of the company.

A buy-back schedule, often set out in a share subscription agreement between the company and the founder, or possibly contained in an employment agreement with the founder or a shareholder agreement with all of the founders, attempts to ensure that the founder will "earn" her shares over time and provides the company with the right to purchase the founder's "unearned" shares if the founder leaves the company, either through resignation or termination. The purchase price payable by the company for the founder's shares may be the lower of the original price paid by the founder and their fair market value when the founder leaves.

The buy-back period usually lasts between three to five years, during which the company's right to repurchase the founder's shares may be exercised in declining percentages, depending upon the date of the founder's departure. For example, all of the founder's shares may be repurchased if she leaves within the first year, with the percentage of her shareholding eligible for repurchase being gradually reduced on a quarterly basis to zero over the following four years.

SHAREHOLDER LOANS

Instead of raising money from outside investors for working capital purposes by way of issuing shares, it is not uncommon for private companies, at least those which are closely-held, to receive initial working capital by way of shareholder loans. While the founders may invest only a nominal amount in the company by way of issued share capital as mentioned above, they may advance considerably more to the company as loans, on either a secured or unsecured basis.

Often they will take back security for their loans in order to rank ahead of all unsecured creditors of the company.[18] While they may acquire a security interest over a particular company asset, perhaps specific software which they may have developed or a specific company product which they may have invented, they are more likely to obtain a general security agreement from the company covering all of the company's assets and business.

However, in the event that the company later on borrows from a chartered bank or other outside financier, the general security taken by the shareholders for their loans will usually have to be postponed and subordinated to the security taken by the outside lenders. The requirements imposed upon the company and its shareholders when dealing with these lenders are described in later chapters of this book in greater detail.

Dealing with Employees

Many companies, especially early stage companies, are often unaware of their legal obligations as employers, and thereby expose themselves, as well as their directors and officers, to various liabilities and possible penalties under a number of employment law statutes, in addition to certain obligations imposed by the common law.

Although this chapter will not describe these various statutory duties in any detail, it will attempt to provide an overview of the kinds of employment law issues with which the company's owners and managers should be generally familiar. While it is intended to look at how the company might deal with its employees, it will also touch on how the company might deal with those providing services to the company as consultants or outside contractors.

Part of this chapter is devoted to the hiring process. In order to ensure that its employees are the company's greatest assets, and do not become part of its liabilities, the company should make every effort to properly document its employer/employee relationship from the outset at the hiring stage.

Although the relationship need not be evidenced by a letter of hire or employment agreement to be legally binding, and may well exist only by way of oral agreement, there is still an advantage to having it reduced into written form in the event that a dispute between the company and the employee arises later on. An unwritten agreement may well end up being determined by a court of law which prefers the employee's version of the employment relationship.

EMPLOYMENT CONTRACT
To avoid the uncertainty associated with an undocumented employment relationship, the company should prepare a letter of hire or employment

contract with each of its employees which sets out the employee's job description and responsibilities, term of employment, compensation and benefits. It should also specify the employee's entitlements upon termination, any limitations on the employee's ability to compete with the company or solicit its customers and employees after his termination, a prohibition against disclosing confidential company information to outsiders, and the company's ownership of the employee's work product. It may even indicate how any disputes with the employee might be resolved.

In setting out an employee's salary, some companies are tempted to state a competitive salary for the employee in the employment contract even though they don't intend to pay that salary until a financing is eventually completed, and expect the employee to forego or defer receiving payment of the salary until a later time. Such a practice gives rise to a potential liability for the company and its directors if the deferred payments are not made, and can subject the company to problems under the applicable employment law statute which provides for minimum monetary compensation to employees.[1] It is preferable for the contract to provide for payment of the prescribed minimum wage with a higher salary to become payable when the financing is achieved or other condition satisfied.

A similar caution should be taken when indicating the vacation entitlement in the employment contract, especially since the directors and officers can have personal liability for a certain amount of unpaid vacation pay under the applicable employment law statute.[2] Furthermore, the company has a statutory obligation to ensure each employee takes a minimum amount of vacation each year.[3]

Although it may be awkward addressing the entitlements of the employee upon termination when he may not have even started to work for the company, the employment contact should set out the company's obligations to the employee in the event the employee is terminated. It should out the amount of notice, or pay in lieu of notice, which the employee will be entitled to receive should he be terminated "without cause". This notice period may be limited to the minimum prescribed in the applicable employment law statute.[4]

If the employment contract does not specify the employee's entitlements upon termination, the employee will be entitled to be given the amount of notice, or pay in lieu of notice, upon termination which is calculated using principles established under the common law, and which is considerably more than the applicable statutory minimum. A handy benchmark based upon these principles is one month's notice for each year of employment.[5]

The advantages of quantifying an employee's entitlements upon termination in an employment contract are not just from the certainty gained when dealing with the individual employee later on to avoid a common law claim, but from the collective limit of the company's potential liability to all of its employees. It is not uncommon for a company's financing, or even its sale, to be postponed or cancelled because an outside party is not prepared to finance or buy a company with a significant and uncapped termination liability.

In addition to describing the employee's entitlements upon termination, the employment contract should describe any restrictions upon the employee's conduct upon termination as well. Such restrictions often come in the form of non-disclosure covenants, under which the employee agrees not to disclose the company's confidential information to outsiders, and in the form of non-solicitation covenants, under which the employee agrees not to solicit the company's customers and employees. They may also come in the form of non-competition covenants under which the employee agrees not to compete against the company. However, as discussed in a greater detail in the *Shareholder Agreements* chapter, non-solicitation and non-competition covenants may be difficult to enforce, especially non-competition covenants in the context of employment contracts.

The employment agreement should also contain an assignment by the employee of any intellectual property rights and a waiver of any "moral" rights which he may acquire in the course of his employment with the company. The significance of these rights and of intellectual property rights in general when dealing with employees is described below.

When entering into an employment contract with an employee, it's important that the employee sign the contact before commencing work, and be given sufficient time to review the contract and to consult with a lawyer before signing. An employment contract, like any contract, needs to have consideration in order to be enforceable, and the job itself should be the consideration. If the employee starts the job and is working for the company before the contract is signed, there will be no consideration for any new terms or conditions which may appear in the written contract when it is eventually signed. The employee will, in other words, have been working under an oral contract before then. Any terms in the "later" written contract, such as a restriction on his entitlements upon termination, would therefore require additional consideration, perhaps payable as a salary increase or bonus, in order to be enforceable.

INTELLECTUAL PROPERTY

When the company takes on a new employee, it should keep in mind that it may have a duty to any previous employer of the employee in connection with intellectual property.

For many companies, particularly technology companies, this can represent a recurring problem, since a new employee may be hampered in his ability to carry out his new duties if he is still governed by restrictions imposed by his former employer. Such restrictions may be contained in a hiring letter, employment contract, shareholder agreement, or other form of agreement with his former employer, and may include the assignment of intellectual property along with non-disclosure, non-solicitation, and non-competition obligations.

Any employer should attempt to determine whether a prospective employee might be affected by such restrictions. It's not unusual for a new employee, as well as his new employer, to be subjected to a lawsuit claiming damages or an injunction brought by his former employer for breaching these restrictions. Claims by former employers for infringement of copyright or other intellectual property are commonplace.

When an employee signs an intellectual property assignment agreement, he ordinarily agrees that any of his ideas, inventions, work product or other developments which he has authored or created while working for his employer will be owned by his employer. Even if he doesn't enter into such an agreement, any "copyrightable" work which he authors in the course of his employment will be deemed to be owned by his employer.[6]

However, while his employer many acquire copyright in what he authors, he may nonetheless acquire and retain "moral" rights in his work product.[7] Moral rights protect the integrity of his work even though another party, such as his employer, owns the copyright to it, and can limit the work's use or abuse by the copyright owner. While moral rights cannot be assigned, they may be waived.[8] For this reason, many employment contracts contain a waiver of moral rights as well as an assignment of intellectual property rights in any works produced by the employee in the course of his employment.

Although an employee may not have signed an intellectual property assignment agreement with a previous employer, any confidentiality or non-disclosure agreement he may previously have signed may create problems for his new employer. Even in the absence of such an agreement, he may still be under a legal obligation not to disclose the trade secrets and other confidential information of his previous employer.[9] When the previous employer competes against the new employer, there is often a greater likelihood of the previous employer alleging the employee's breach of his duty of confidentiality.

A new employee may also have previously signed an agreement not to compete with his former employer's business, or to solicit any of his former employer's customers or employees, for a certain period of time after his employment with his former employer ends. Even if he did not sign such an agreement, he may still be under a non-solicitation duty under the common law if he held a relatively senior position with his former employer, perhaps as a director or officer.[10]

If a new employee was planning to move over to his new employer, he should not have used the resources of his previous employer for the benefit of his new employer, and should not have worked on getting business for the new employer during the hours when he was expected to be performing his regular duties for his previous employer.

In light of the foregoing, it's important for the company to address these concerns with prospective employees. But it is also prudent to address these concerns with consultants and other outside contractors, who may be similarly restricted.[11]

OUTSIDE CONTRACTORS

There are some additional concerns to be addressed by the company when engaging outside contractors to perform various services, not the least of which is whether an individual contractor may be regarded as an employee in substance. If an "independent" contractor is held to be an employee, the company could a face a number of statutory and common law obligations as an employer towards that individual.

For example, the company may be required to withhold and remit to the Canada Revenue Agency various employee deductions from the compensation paid to the contractor because of required employment insurance,[12] pension plan[13] and income tax[14] obligations. It may also be required to pay premiums for worker safety and compensation on account of the contractor.[15]

The contractor may also be entitled, as an employee, to the various benefits afforded under the applicable employment law statute.[16] These benefits might include overtime and vacation pay, along with the statutory minimum termination pay. In addition, the contractor may be entitled to receive the notice of termination, or pay in lieu of notice, prescribed by the common law in the event of his termination.

In determining whether an outside contractor is a true contractor and not an employee, government administrators as well as the courts take into consideration a number of factors. The existence of an independent contractor agreement, the contractor's degree of control in setting his own work, the extent to which the company monitors his work, the amount of risk of profit or loss assumed by the contractor, the use of his own workspace and tools, and the extent to which he is integrated into the company's work environment, are all relevant factors to be looked at.[17]

Retaining outside contractors also gives rise to issues over intellectual property. In addition to the concern expressed above that a consultant or other contractor may be restricted in his ability to provide services to the company by reason of his agreement with a previous employer or client which addresses intellectual property rights, he may also pose another problem for the company. Unlike a company employee, an outside contractor typically owns any intellectual property he develops while retained by the company unless he enters into an agreement to the contrary. Therefore the company should obtain a written agreement with the contractor in which his intellectual property rights are assigned to the company.

EQUITY COMPENSATION

Many companies regard equity incentives in the form of stock options, restricted stock grants or stock purchase plans as essential tools in attracting, motivating and retaining key employees. However, equity compensation plans can be quite complicated, and the company will have to address a number of issues when attempting to implement and maintain them.

By introducing these plans for the benefit of its employees, the company will have to recognize that its employees will become company shareholders, having all of the rights ordinarily provided by corporate law. These rights are described in more detail later on this book in the *Shareholder Statutory Rights* chapters. The employees may also come to enjoy the rights, while subject to the various restrictions, provided in the company's shareholder agreement, if such an agreement is in place, as more comprehensively explained in the *Shareholder Agreements* chapter.

The company will have to carefully consider whether the shares to be acquired by the employees under these plans should be of the same class as the class of shares held by its founding shareholders or other outside investors, or whether the employee's shares should even be voting shares.

It will also have to consider whether various rights contained in the company's shareholder agreement should be reduced in respect of those shares issued to employees, or whether various restrictions ought to be expanded in the case of such shares. For example, the company may be given special rights to repurchase an employee's shares in certain circumstances or upon the occurrence of certain events, such as his departure from the company.

In the absence of a shareholder agreement, the company should still consider what contractual restrictions might govern shares issued under its equity compensation plans. It may also consider imposing a "voting trust" upon employee shares, providing for a transfer of the voting power under the shares to a company officer as voting trustee, who would then be authorized to vote in his discretion for company directors and other proposed company actions.

In allowing its employees to participate in one or more equity compensation plans, the company should not require such participation, and any resulting share purchases, as a condition of an employee's initial or continuing employment. The employee's purchase of company shares, or other securities, should be fully voluntary.[18]

When a company implements an employee stock option plan, it often provides for the phased "vesting" of the employee's options over time, permitting the exercise of such options and purchase of company shares only after certain dates or after the achievement of certain conditions or "milestones". It is important for the plan to address what happens to an employee's unvested options if the employee leaves the company. For example, it might state that an employee's options will cease to vest on the date notice of termination or notice of resignation is given.

In the absence of such wording, vesting will continue through an employee's notice period. As discussed above, if a terminated employee is entitled to a notice period determined under common law which may last for a considerable time, the employee may receive additional vesting during that time long after he has ceased working for the company.

A similar concern relates to the exercise of options which have vested prior to an employee's termination but which remain unexercised when he is terminated. The plan may provide for a shortened exercise period in the event of an employee's termination, requiring the exercise period to run from the employee's last day of providing services to the company, and not from the end of his notice period.

CHANGING THE EMPLOYEE RELATIONSHIP

The company may find it necessary from time to time to make certain changes to the terms and conditions governing an employee's employment with the company in order to respond to shifting market demand for the company's products or services or to the prevailing economic climate. However, the company has to be careful if imposing such changes unilaterally, since it may end up facing a lawsuit for constructive dismissal from the employee affected.

Constructive dismissal may be claimed when, in the absence of reasonable notice, a fundamental term or condition of the employment relationship is unilaterally altered by the employer to the detriment of the employee. Any substantial change in compensation, benefits, position, responsibilities, work location or reporting duties can be grounds for constructive dismissal.[19]

However, if the changes requested by the company are not fundamental to the employee / employer relationship, or even if they are fundamental but are notified well in advance of being implemented, the company may be able to avoid a claim for constructive dismissal.

Any amendments made to an employee's written employment agreement should be in writing, with the written consent of the employee. Furthermore, as expressed above in connection with the need to have the employee sign his employment agreement before he starts work, the company should offer additional consideration over and above what it provides under the existing agreement in order to be able to enforce the new terms being added. The mere continuation of employment will not be sufficient to constitute adequate consideration for the contractual amendments.

For example, offering a one-time bonus or other perquisite, however modest, may be sufficient. Alternatively, amending the terms as part of a promotion or salary increase will be sufficient, as will the granting of stock options. But whatever additional consideration is given for the amendments, the amendments must nonetheless be carried out with the full knowledge and consent of the affected employee without any coercion or duress by the company in order to make them enforceable.

TERMINATING THE EMPLOYEE RELATIONSHIP

Although the company may have a written employment contract with each of its employees setting out, among other things, the employee's entitlements upon termination, many times it will not. Often smaller companies lack employment contracts with their most senior employees, who in many cases are the company's directors, officers and perhaps founding shareholders. The absence of employment contracts with these senior, longer term employees can have significant financial implications for the company in the event the employment of any of these employees is terminated.

But the absence of a written employment contract with any employee can have adverse consequences for the company upon termination of the employee. As mentioned above, the application of common law principles to determine the amount of notice to be given, or pay in lieu of notice, may provide much greater entitlements on termination than the employee might receive under a written employment contract or under the applicable employment law statute.

Regardless of whether an employment contract is in place for an employee who is terminated, the minimum standards imposed by the statute must still be met when a termination occurs. The statute has specific minimum requirements relating to the amount of pay in lieu of notice of termination, severance pay, unpaid overtime, "mass terminations"[20] and the continuation of employee benefits during the notice period.[21]

The continuation of the employee's group insurance benefits during the statutory notice period deserves special attention. If the employee's insurance benefits are not continued, whether due to the insurer's refusal or to the company's termination of coverage, the company will not only be liable for violating the statute, it may also be liable to pay the equivalent of the insurance proceeds that would have been payable in the event the employee dies or becomes disabled during the notice period.

For this reason, it is important for the company to obtain written confirmation from the insurance provider that the employee's coverage will continue after the employee's termination or that such coverage may be converted from the group policy to an individual policy within a reasonable time after termination. The company should also advise the employee in writing of the expiry date of his group insurance benefits, any time limits for conversion, and the need to investigate alternative coverage.

In certain circumstances, the company may be entitled to terminate an employment relationship "for cause". Although a termination for cause may relieve the company from any obligation to provide the employee with reasonable notice or pay in lieu of notice, it is usually quite difficult for the company to support an allegation of cause except in the case of extreme misconduct by the employee.[22] Such misconduct might include serious theft or fraud, blatant and gross negligence, or a fundamental breach of a specific, critical term of the employee's employment contract.

If the company is concerned about an employee's performance or misconduct, it should warn the employee in writing of those concerns requiring attention, and grant the employee a reasonable opportunity to improve his performance or remedy his misconduct. If no improvement or change can be demonstrated after a prolonged period and repeated warnings, the company may consider obtaining legal advice on whether sufficient grounds are present to support the employee's termination for cause. In some circumstances, the company may have lawful grounds to take reasonable disciplinary steps such as short suspensions to redress employee misconduct.

However, even a well-documented process of warnings and diligent investigation by the company, along with ample opportunity for improvement by the employee, may be insufficient to justify an employee's termination for cause. In such circumstances, reasonable notice or pay in lieu of notice must be provided to the employee if the company then decides that termination is necessary.

WORK ENVIRONMENT

In dealing with its employees, the company must continually monitor its compliance with various statutes and regulations relating to the workplace and the company's obligation to maintain a healthy and safe work environment. These requirements are extensive and quite detailed and beyond the scope of this chapter, and the company should engage professional advice from time to time to ensure that such requirements are being met.

For example, the company may have to appoint a joint health and safety committee, as well as prepare and implement a workplace harassment policy and workplace violence policy.[23] It may also have to register with its provincial workers compensation and insurance authority and pay the applicable premiums.[24] Furthermore, it will have to ensure that its ongoing dealings with employees conform to the requirements of human rights legislation,[25] as well as privacy legislation.[26]

While the advantages to the company of having employment contracts, confidentiality agreements and intellectual property agreements with each of its employees have been discussed above, the company can also derive significant benefits from preparing a comprehensive employee manual which contains various policies and procedures aimed at complying with these statutes and regulations governing the workplace. Such a manual can assist company managers when dealing with employees on a day-to-day basis, and also serve to limit the liabilities the company may face for failure to comply.

The manual may address many topics. Benefits, holidays, overtime pay, leaves of absence and sick leave, work-related travel, workplace harassment and violence, ethical code of conduct, performance reviews, discipline, human rights, even computer use, may all be covered in the manual.

Although some of these topics are easier to address than others, devising the company's policy over the use of its computers and the Internet by employees can be more challenging than first thought, especially when the employees' expectations of personal privacy are taken into consideration. But the company should certainly attempt to maintain the security of its computer network and ensure the network is not being compromised or used for illegal or improper purposes, including the exchange of harassing or discriminatory messages. In so doing, the company may decide that the computer use policy should specifically state that the entire computer system is company property, that its use by employees will be monitored, and that employees should not expect any personal privacy when using it.

Protecting Intellectual Property

Whether the company is just starting up or is at a later stage in its lifecycle, it will likely have to deal at some time with its development or acquisition of intellectual property and with the various issues surrounding the protection of intellectual property.

In some cases, perhaps in the company's earliest stages, its owners or managers might be inspired by the possibility of creating a particular product or service which will be unique in the marketplace, or at least significantly different from other products or services. This uniqueness or significant difference, however, may not last long once the product or service is first released or distributed, since it may well be duplicated by others. Its competitive advantage may then be lost.

Protecting and maintaining that competitive advantage often depends on how well the company is able to protect and maintain the intellectual property underlying the product or service.

This chapter attempts to describe the most common forms of intellectual property, together with the means generally available to protect them. It will look at patents, copyright, trademarks and industrial designs, each protected by special legislation, as well as trade secrets which are generally protected under the common law. Less common forms of intellectual property, such as plant breeders' rights,[1] integrated circuit topographies,[2] and personality rights,[3] will not be discussed.

This chapter will also attempt to generally describe some of the challenges the company may face when asserting its intellectual property ownership. Determining the extent of its actual ownership often proves to be its biggest challenge.

DETERMINING OWNERSHIP

Whenever considering whether to acquire or develop intellectual property, the company must seriously consider who owns or will own it. But the ownership of intellectual property is not always easy to determine. Attempting to establish a trail of all the people who may have been involved in its creation can be a frustrating task. More than one author may have contributed to a literary work, or more than one inventor may have contributed to an invention. A thorough analysis may have to be done.

As discussed in the *Dealing with Employees* chapter, former employers of the company's employees may have rights to certain intellectual property which the company, perhaps mistakenly, believes has been solely "created" by the employees after they joined the company. The employees, for example, may have previously assigned their intellectual property rights in software which has now been integrated by them into new or enhanced software which they have developed for the company.

In addition to determining the possible rights of former employers in intellectual property created by the company's employees, there may be a need to determine the rights of any academic institutions, experimental laboratories or other organizations which may have provided research and development information leading to the company's inventions and products. A similar concern arises in connection with the rights of any government departments or agencies which may have provided grants or other financial assistance to the company or to any of the company's employees to support the company's research and development efforts.

There may also be a number of outside contractors and consultants who have assisted the company in the past and who may be tempted to claim an interest in a company product once it is successfully marketed. It is not unusual for outsiders to allege that a company product was conceived or developed jointly with them, and that their contribution deserves to be compensated.

Even where the company has obtained a license to use the intellectual property of another person, the license may not be broad enough to permit the use intended by the company. Or the license may specifically prohibit the company from using the intellectual property for certain purposes, or place extremely onerous conditions upon the company which must be satisfied to permit the use intended.

The need for the company to consider all of these possible claims against its intellectual property should not be taken lightly. While fending off allegations of patent, trademark or copyright infringement can be time-consuming and expensive, any "cloud" on its intellectual property ownership can have even more serious implications for the company by frustrating its attempts to obtain external financing. If a bank or other financier is relying upon the company's intellectual property as security for a proposed debt financing, the financing may be postponed or cancelled if an intellectual property "audit" reveals imperfect ownership or pending claims of infringement.

MAINTAINING OWNERSHIP

The company should endeavour to maintain "clean" ownership of its intellectual property. In addition to making inquiries into the ownership history of the intellectual property it acquires or develops, it should also take some of the steps identified in the rest of this chapter as a means of securing and protecting the intellectual property it thinks it owns.

Obtaining intellectual property assignments and waivers of moral rights from employees and outside contractors is usually regarded as an essential practice, as described in the previous chapter. If outright ownership of specific intellectual property from an outside contractor cannot be obtained, the company should attempt to obtain an exclusive license of it instead.

Sometimes there will be circumstances where an outside contractor insists on retaining ownership of the intellectual property it is paid to develop for the company. For example, some software developers use their own core intellectual property when developing "new" software for their customers, and are prepared to grant to their customers only non-exclusive licenses for use of the new software.

If the company and its outside contractor are unable to initially agree on who should own the intellectual property being developed, they should keep negotiating and resist the temptation to hold the intellectual property jointly. A joint arrangement can create practical difficulties, since a joint owner may not license the intellectual property without the consent of the other joint owner. Furthermore, the registration and enforcement of jointly owned intellectual property rights can become complicated if the parties cannot agree on where to apply for registration or whether to initiate infringement proceedings.

TRADE SECRETS AND CONFIDENTIAL INFORMATION

A trade secret is ordinarily information which derives its value from not being generally known or not being readily available to others, and which is subjected to certain efforts to retain its secrecy. For many companies, their trade secrets will often be comprised of their ideas, designs, processes, methods of business operation, financial matters, pricing policies, marketing plans, employee compensation, customer arrangements, and much more.

In order to realize the full economic potential of its trade secrets, it is usually necessary for the company to disclose at least some of its trade secrets to others. But while disclosure to certain outside contractors, customers, professional advisers, bankers and other financiers may be required, the value of the trade secrets disclosed can be preserved by taking steps to restrict their subsequent dissemination and use.

While trade secrets are often described as intellectual property, only some trade secrets qualify for intellectual property protection afforded by statute, as is the case with patents. The protection of trade secrets arises under the common law duty of confidence,[4] which is why they are usually described instead as confidential information.[5] The duty of confidence arises when a person receiving confidential information is notified that it is confidential or agrees that it is confidential.

Because the company may have difficulty proving that notice of confidentiality was given to another person, it is always preferable for the company to have a written confidentiality or non-disclosure agreement in place with that person before releasing any confidential information to her. In general, a confidentiality agreement confines the use of the disclosed information to specified circumstances or purposes, and prohibits any further disclosure of the information except to specified persons where the confidentiality is similarly preserved.

When entering into a confidentiality agreement with an outside party, the company should ensure that the agreement contains a number of essential terms. For example, a comprehensive definition of what is regarded as confidential information and what is not confidential information should be set out. Information which is already in the public domain, or becomes known to the receiving party through other sources, or has been independently developed by the receiving party, is usually exempted.

Furthermore, the extent of the permission granted to use the confidential information should be specified in the agreement, such as the particular purpose for the disclosure, so that the information is not to be used by the recipient for any other purpose nor disclosed to any other party. While further disclosure is usually permissible to employees and certain outside advisers such as lawyers and accountants who have a need to know the information in order to provide their advice, disclosure to any advisers should be permitted only if satisfactory confidentiality arrangements are in place with them, and any confidential information disclosed to them should be marked as being confidential.

A further exception for disclosure to others is generally made for disclosure required under court order or pursuant to applicable statutory or regulatory authority. However, some confidentiality agreements provide that if the recipient is required to disclose confidential information to third parties, the party originally disclosing the information to the recipient must first be given notice of the requirement. That party then has the right to review and approve, often within a very short time frame, the contents of any statement that is to be released or filed by the recipient with the applicable authority.

The company should also ensure that the confidentiality agreement provides it will not be held responsible for any loss incurred by the receiving party in the event that the disclosed information turns out to be incomplete or inaccurate. Such a duty of care during negotiations is not ordinarily imposed upon negotiating parties under common law.[6] However, in addition to its right to sue for damages in the event that the receiving party breaches the agreement, the company should also be given the right to apply to the courts for an injunction. Many confidentiality agreements state that breach will cause irreparable harm to the innocent party which cannot be adequately compensated by damages alone, and that injunctive relief should be permitted.

A specific statement should also be added in the confidentiality agreement that the company is and will remain the owner of the information being disclosed, and that no property rights in the disclosed information are being granted by the company to the receiving party. And it should also provide that the disclosed information is to be returned to the company when the purpose for the original disclosure has been accomplished, or alternatively, provide for the destruction by the receiving party of all unreturned confidential information remaining in her possession, along with the delivery to the company of a certificate attesting to such destruction.

Despite the foregoing comments about the essential terms which should be included by the company in its confidentiality agreements with outsiders, the company should not rely only upon such agreements as the primary means for protecting its confidential information. As useful as the agreements are, a comprehensive information protection program should be implemented by the company, if for no reason other than to prove that its sensitive information is indeed confidential.

The company should therefore undertake a number of specific additional tasks as part of a program to protect its confidential information. As a minimum, it should identify and mark as confidential all of its confidential documents, control and document all access to such documents by its employees, implement a proper document destruction policy, and restrict access to its premises by visitors. Marketing materials, executive speeches and other public disclosures should be reviewed to avoid the inclusion of confidential information, and employee seminars on dealing with confidential documents should be conducted from time to time.

Although obtaining confidentiality agreements with outside parties should be an essential practice, some parties may refuse to sign them. Many venture capital firms, for example, refuse to sign them simply on the grounds that they receive so many business plans to look at which are all so similar, that they can't keep them all straight. In those cases, the company may have to carefully consider the reputation of the outside party and make sure to mark as confidential every document sent or delivered to that party. Furthermore, it may be prudent for the company to have a phased disclosure schedule, under which the most sensitive information is provided to the other party only when considerable trust between them has been built up and a transaction between them appears imminent. If the other party has close business dealings with a competitor of the company, the company may have to be quite selective of the confidential information it is prepared to disclose.

PATENTS

Unlike confidential information and trade secrets which derive much of their value from being kept secret, patents provide value to trade secrets which are disclosed to the public. In order to encourage the disclosure of confidential information for the benefit of the public, while maintaining an incentive for inventors to invent, the Canadian patent system provides inventors with an exclusive right to make, use or sell their invention. This "monopoly" provided by a patent lasts for 20 years from the date the patent application is filed,[7] after which period the invention may be used by anyone. However, the inventor's exclusive right is not enforceable until the patent is granted, which may occur two to four years after the application.

The inventor, or an assignee of the inventor, may apply for a patent, and the person first filing an application in respect of the invention will be entitled to receive a patent for the invention if the invention is "patentable". In order to be patentable, the invention must be novel as well as useful,[8] and not be obvious to any person skilled in the art or science to which the invention relates.[9] It may also be a new combination of old, well-known elements, if the combined elements produce a result which is more than the sum of the results produced by the elements individually. It must not have been disclosed to the public before the application, although public disclosure within a one-year grace period of the application is permitted.[10]

If the company acquires an invention, perhaps by way of an assignment contained in an employment contract with the inventor, it should consider the advantages of obtaining patent protection for the invention. Obtaining a patent will protect the company's right to manufacture and sell the invention as a core product, will inhibit any attempts by competitors to duplicate it, will allow for potential alternative revenue through licensing it to others, will provide protection against possible infringement claims, and will increase the ability of the company to secure additional financing.

Since the patenting process is expensive and time-consuming, seeking a patent for every invention held by the company may not be warranted. Furthermore, there are different ways the company may decide to use or expand upon the patents granted to it. For example, it may prefer to rely upon only a few patents to protect its core technology and not seek to obtain patent protection for any improvement or modifications to it. This approach may save time and money, but may enable its competitors to patent the improvements for themselves and then seek to license the improvements to the company.

Alternatively, despite the high cost, the company may choose to apply for as many patents as possible within a given product area in an effort to deter any competitors from operating in that area. Or, the company may initially seek patents only for its core technology and then branch out as the technology evolves into related fields, deciding at that time whether additional patent protection is warranted.

Although the company may decide to file a patent application quickly to secure a priority date and obtain a patent as soon as possible despite the cost involved, it may prefer to delay any filing and protect the invention instead as confidential information, as described above, to give it more time to assess the potential commercial viability of the invention in the marketplace. This latter approach runs the risk that a competitor might independently come up with the invention and file a patent application first.

A further approach the company may take is the "partial" patent application, which is a less expensive, interim procedure involving the filing of only a general description of the invention without the detailed claims and other formalities ordinarily required. A filing date is thereby obtained which can later be used as a priority date, provided that a complete application is filed no more than 12 months later. A partial application, however, runs the risk that innovations developed after the partial filing which are not contained in the general description will not benefit from the early priority date.

The process for obtaining a Canadian patent begins with the filing of a patent application in the Canadian Patent Office, which is part of the Canadian Intellectual Property Office. The application must describe the invention, explain how to put the invention into practice, and include any claims that define the limit of the monopoly sought. The application is then reviewed in the Patent Office by a patent examiner who will attempt to determine whether a patent should be issued. The application will be compared with other products and processes known to the Patent Office, resulting in possible amendments to the application so that it more accurately reflects the inventive aspects of the invention.

Since the exclusive rights under a Canadian patent are available only in Canada, the company may wish to consider applying for patent protection in other countries which represent a significant market for the company. Since it is often difficult for a company to decide where else it ought to apply, it may choose to file a patent application under the Patent Cooperation Treaty, or PCT. Under the PCT, a national of one of the member countries may file an international application designating those member countries in which it seeks patent protection, and such a filing will have the same effect as if a separate national patent filing had been made in each country designated.[11]

COPYRIGHT

Just as patents provide inventors with protection for their inventions, copyright provides authors with protection for their original literary, dramatic, musical and artistic works. This protection applies to separate and independent rights to produce, reproduce or perform the work, or any substantial portion of it, anywhere in Canada.[12] Copyright is therefore a "bundle" of rights, and the author is the first owner.[13]

To use a technology example, patent protection may be available for certain types of computer hardware,[14] but copyright protection of literary works extends to computer software.[15] Since copyright does not protect an idea but only the expression of that idea, the intended function of a software program to perform a specific task may not be protected by copyright, but the source code and user interface of the program will be. Furthermore, a software program can take on and survive in many different formats, including related software products, films and music, all subject to copyright protection.

Copyright arises upon the creation of the work and lasts for 50 years after the year of the death of the author.[16] Unlike a patent, no filing or registration is required to create copyright. Since copyright is automatic, few owners choose to register their rights. But while registration is not necessary to gain copyright protection, there can be certain advantages to registration in the Canadian Copyright Office. In the event of a dispute over ownership or use of copyright, a certificate of registration provides "rebuttable" evidence that the work is protected by copyright and the person registered is the owner of the copyright.[17]

In light of this procedural advantage in possible copyright litigation, the company may consider registering its copyright interests. But the company should remain aware that registration is not conclusive of ownership and is not regarded as complete copyright protection. Entries on the copyright register do not indicate whether the owner is claiming all or part ownership in the work, or whether ownership has reverted to the author by reason of a contract, or whether ownership has been assigned since registration, or whether there has been more than one version of the work.

However, the company should "mark" its copyrightable works, whether they be marketing brochures, product manuals, customers lists, or websites. While there is no requirement to mark or otherwise provide a copyright notice in Canada on any works to obtain copyright, it is still considered a prudent practice to insert the symbol "©" or word "copyright" followed by the year of first publication and the name of the copyright owner.[18] This notice creates a presumption of ownership, not unlike registration.

If the company is considering the purchase of another party's works, a search of the Canadian Copyright Office records is a good starting point when investigating the seller's ownership of the works being sold. The company should also attempt to obtain from the seller a warranty that the seller has absolute "right, title and interest" in those works. Any assignment or grant of copyright by the seller to the company must be in writing.

As mentioned in the *Dealing with Employees* chapter, when an author creates a work in the course of her employment, it is her employer who owns copyright,[19] but when the author is an independent contractor, the contractor retains ownership in the absence of a written assignment of copyright. The company should therefore obtain such an assignment from its independent contractors, as well as a waiver of moral rights from both employees and contractors, as also mentioned in that chapter.

TRADEMARKS

A trademark is a mark that it used to distinguish the wares or services which are "manufactured, sold, leased, hired or performed" by the owner of the trademark from the wares or services of others.[20] It can take many different forms, from a single word or phrase, to a label or picture, or the shape of a product or its packaging, or even its colour or "get up".[21]

If the company uses a trademark to distinguish its wares or services, it should consider the need to protect it. While a trademark does not have to be registered, since an unregistered trademark can be enforced by means of a "passing-off" action against an infringer,[22] there are advantages to the company through registration if its trademark is "registrable".

When applying to register its trademark with the Canadian Trademarks Office, the company should have used or made known the trademark in Canada, or should at least intend to use the trademark in Canada and does in fact use it after its application is allowed but before registration.[23] In order to be registrable, the trademark cannot be merely the name or surname of an individual, and cannot be merely descriptive (or deceptively misdescriptive) of the character, quality, or place of origin of the related wares or services. It also cannot be confusing with another registered trademark.[24]

If the company succeeds in registering its trademark, the company will then have the right to exclusive use of the trademark throughout Canada for 15 years for the wares or services for which it is registered, and will have a further right to renew the trademark for successive 15 year periods indefinitely.[25] This right to exclusive use across Canada provides a significant advantage to a registered trademark, in contrast to an unregistered trademark which may provide its owner with rights to use the mark in connection with certain wares or services only within a certain geographical area.

With a registered trademark, the company will be able to bring an action for infringement and/or passing-off against any person who sells, distributes or advertises wares or services with a confusingly similar trademark or trade-name. The legal remedies for infringement then available to the company will include an injunction, an accounting for profits, and the destruction of any infringing wares and materials.[26]

But registration of a trademark, as with registration of copyright, is not conclusive evidence of ownership. A registered trademark may be invalid because of third party rights which are unknown to the company, or because the rights are incapable of being owned by the company alone. For this reason, if the company attempts to acquire a registered trademark from another party, whether by way of an assignment or license, the assignor or licensor will likely refuse to provide the company with a warranty of absolute ownership of that trademark.

More significantly, the company can lose its registration if it ceases to use its trademark. If the company is requested at any time after three years from the date of the registration to furnish evidence that the trademark was in use in Canada at any time during the three years prior to such request, but fails to do so, and the absence of use has not been due to special circumstances, the registration of the trademark is liable to be expunged or amended accordingly.[27]

The company's concern over protecting its trademark becomes extremely important if it chooses to license the trademark to another party. From a commercial perspective, the company as licensor will want to ensure that the licensee will maintain standards of quality throughout the term of the license agreement, since the sale of inferior merchandise will tarnish the reputation and goodwill associated with the trademark and its value, and may impair the company's ability to license the trademark in the future.

From a trademark perspective, controlling the ongoing quality is essential to protect the trademark as being distinctive of the owner, so that the trademark represents a trusted source of the merchandise. When licensing its trademark, the company must have direct or indirect control over the character or quality of the licensee's wares or services.[28]

The quality control provisions in a trademark license agreement are typically quite lengthy, and contain a number of restrictions. For example, the licensee will not be allowed to modify the trade mark or materially change its products, and the owner will have the right to approve all of the licensee's promotional materials, receive samples of the licensee's products from time to time, and inspect the licensee's premises during regular business hours to ensure quality control. A notice will have to appear in all of the licensee's materials stating that the trademark is registered to the company and is used under license.[29]

Since unlicensed use of the trademark, whether by a former licensee or others, can affect the distinctiveness and even validity of the trademark, the company must be able to control how the trademark is used at all times, particularly after termination of the licensing agreement. Upon termination, the company must be able to prevent the licensee from continuing to advertise and distribute trademarked products, especially if the company wants to contract with another licensee, and may require the return or destruction of all materials displaying the trademark.

INDUSTRIAL DESIGN

Should the company wish to protect the shape, ornamentation or appearance of any its products, it may consider registering that appearance as an industrial design.[30] However, registration is not available for methods or principles of construction, or for how the product may be configured, but for how it looks.

Application for registration as an industrial design must occur within one year from when the design is first offered to the public.[31] The "first proprietor" of the design is entitled to apply, which in the case of a design made by an employee in the course of her company employment, is deemed to be the company.[32] In order for registration to take place, the design should be original and novel, and have aesthetic appeal.[33]

Upon registration in the Industrial Design Office, the company receives the exclusive right[34] to apply the industrial design to any article for the purpose of sale for a term of 10 years.[35] As with a patent registration, an industrial design registration allows the company to assert its rights against any person who may have independently created a similar design but who failed to register the design first. Registration, absent evidence to the contrary, is proof of the design, its originality, the name of the "proprietor", and the commencement and term of the registration, and is presumed to be valid if challenged in court.[36]

If any other person applies or imitates the design for the purpose of sale without the company's permission, registration allows the company to bring an action for damages against that person, and the company may be awarded an injunction, an accounting for profits, and the recovery of all infringing material.[37]

However, in order to recover damages, the company must have "marked" or placed an industrial design notice featuring a capital "D" in a circle and the name of the company on all or substantially all of the company's articles to which the design relates.[38]

Certain industrial designs may have functional aspects or elements which may qualify for patent protection, if such elements are new, commercially useful and inventive. They may also have elements, perhaps in the shape of a product or its packaging, which may be registered as "distinguishing guise" trademarks.[39] However, copyright protection is not available if the design is capable of being registered as an industrial design and the article is manufactured in over 50 copies anywhere in the world.[40]

Creditor Proofing

Most prudent owners and managers of a private company recognize the need to reduce risk and safeguard the company's assets from possible claims brought by other parties. While they may not specifically describe what they need as a creditor proofing plan, they know they need to protect the company's assets as well as their own assets.

Perhaps before the company was even incorporated, they may have been operating their business as a sole proprietorship, or as a partnership with someone else, and realized that incorporating the business was an essential component of their protection plan.

A business owner attempting to escape personal liability for the debts of his sole proprietorship or partnership usually transfers the proprietorship or partnership business assets to a new company. The company then gradually pays off those earlier debts for which the owner was personally liable while incurring new debts with lenders and suppliers. These new debts are the company's obligations, not the owner's.

If the owner does decide to operate the business through a company, the use of a single company is often as far as his business protection plan goes, supplemented only by property and general liability insurance, perhaps with business interruption insurance as well.

This chapter will attempt to look at some of the additional actions that owners and managers of a private company can take when implementing a more comprehensive creditor proofing plan. Since it will be addressing structures which are ordinarily used within Canada, offshore asset protection trusts will not be discussed.

Creditor proofing should be undertaken at a time when the company is able to meet its debts generally as they become due. If any asset transfers are made to a related corporation with the intent to hinder or defeat existing creditors, such transfers may be overturned. However, there is ordinarily nothing wrong with structuring the business operations to minimize liability before any concerns over possible insolvency arise. In other words, effective creditor proofing is designed to isolate the business and its assets from the future claims of future creditors, not from the current claims of current creditors.[1]

Many of the statutory restrictions outlined below apply when a transferor is insolvent, and many of the exemptions from such restrictions apply only when a transfer is made in the ordinary course of business. It is usually difficult to argue that transfers carried out when implementing a creditor proofing plan are part of the ordinary course of business.

Some of these statutory restrictions are in place to deter debtors from taking unusual and extraordinary steps to prevent an orderly distribution of their property to their creditors when they anticipate a bankruptcy on their horizon. These steps include transferring property in an attempt to place it beyond the reach of creditors, preferring one creditor over others, or declaring dividends prior to a bankruptcy in order to keep money away from creditors. This chapter will provide a brief overview of such statutory restrictions.

It's helpful to keep in mind who might try to attack a creditor proofing plan when attempting to set the plan up. While planners normally think of secured creditors, preferred creditors like landlords and taxing authorities, and ordinary trade creditors as being the most likely to attack such plans, potential attacks from employees and shareholders, and even from Crown prosecutors, shouldn't be disregarded. The possible application of the *Criminal Code*,[2] as hereinafter discussed, can certainly cause the planners to think carefully before proceeding.

COMPONENTS OF A CREDITOR PROOFING PLAN

Use of Multiple Corporations

As with an owner's own investment portfolio, the owner of more than one business shouldn't put all of his "eggs in one basket". He should diversify his risk, and use more than one corporation to carry on his separate businesses. Separately incorporating each business owned can make sense, so that if one business should fail, the others will not be endangered. A business which is a potential loser should be isolated from those businesses which are current winners by simply compartmentalizing the owner's overall business arrangements into separate corporations.

Operating many businesses through one entity may offer some tax or operational benefits, but these factors alone should not determine the structure. Asset protection may be far more important, particularly when a business is at an early stage and most vulnerable. Only when the businesses become more mature and more stable should tax, financing, creditor relations and operational factors be equal to liability protection as a planning objective.

However, it still should be kept in mind that transferring assets from one corporation to another can have negative tax consequences, although proper structuring can reduce or avoid such consequences.[3]

Multiple corporations can be held through one holding company, so that each operating company becomes a subsidiary. Parent company guarantees can then be substituted for the personal guarantees of the owner. Profits of each operating company can be distributed to the holding company as tax-free inter-corporate dividends[4] and protected from possible claims against the operating company. If any of the operating companies require working capital, the holding company can loan the funds back on a secured basis.

New or separate business divisions or projects can be set up in separate companies in order to insulate the other companies in the related group from risk. If one of the companies becomes financially troubled, it can be liquidated, sold off, or rehabilitated without jeopardizing the other healthy businesses. For example, real estate developers generally put each new project into a separate corporation, so that the failure of the new project won't put the developer's other properties and projects at risk.

Separating Ownership of Valuable Assets from the Operating Business

Valuable assets used by an operating business should be owned by another company and simply leased or licensed back to the operating company. This limits the access of business creditors to the fewest and least valuable assets possible. In most cases, an operating company should not own any more assets than are necessary to carry on the company's business activities. The operating company's assets should usually be restricted to its contracts, accounts receivable and inventory.

If the operating company runs into difficulty, the valuable assets owned by the other company will not be available to satisfy the claims of the operating company's creditors. The leases or licenses can simply terminate. Real estate is one asset that should be held outside of the operating company. Equipment, vehicles, furniture, fixtures, trademarks, trade names, copyrights and patents are also assets that should be held by entities separate from the operating company.

Investing in the Operating Business by Secured Loan
If investment in the operating company is made by way of secured loans instead of by way of straight equity, those making the secured loans, whether they be the owner, or friends or family of the owner, will have priority over the various unsecured creditors of the operating company. Whether or not those lending funds on a secured basis are also shareholders of the operating company, they will control what happens to the operating company. If they are friendly to the owner, they might realize on their security after a default and sell the business back to the owner. A related company might invest in the operating company, again by way of a secured loan.

Even if most of the business assets of the operating company already stand as security for existing indebtedness, perhaps as general security to a bank or other financial institution regarded as the "senior lender" of the business, the other investors who are secured creditors can still be next in line after the bank has been satisfied should the business fail. These investors often evidence their investment by way of a non-interest bearing note, secured by a registered general security agreement. If these investors don't take security, they will end up within the ranks of the unsecured creditors to the business who may get nothing upon an insolvency.

A financial institution which is not currently a lender to the operating company will usually require those creditors who are secured to postpone and subordinate their security in favour of the financial institution before it advances any funds to the operating company.

Providing Services to the Operating Business through Another Company
An affiliated company may provide consulting, information processing, administrative or other services to the company operating the business,

and the amounts which the affiliated company is owed for such services can be secured by the assets of the operating company.

Holding Valuable Lease Separate from Operating Business

If the operating business is carried on out of leased premises with a valuable location, it may be disadvantageous for the operating business to hold the lease. If the operating company holds the lease and then becomes bankrupt, the lease may end up being assigned or terminated.

It may be safer having another company lease the valuable location, and that company in turn sublet the premises to the operating company, possibly on a month-to-month basis. The other company therefore controls the lease, and can evict the failing operating company on default and re-sublet to a different, more solvent tenant, including a new business established to succeed the failing operating company at the same location under a new sublease.

Conversely, a separate or "shell" company with few assets might be used to execute a lease on behalf of an operating company. If the tenant company fails, the landlord has recourse only to the "shell" and not against the operating company. Alternatively, if the lease is held by the operating company, a related company may enter into an option with the landlord to lease the valuable premises should the operating company tenant become insolvent.

Keep Deposits and Loans Separate

Given that the financial institution where the operating company keeps its funds on deposit might try to offset such funds against any outstanding loans which the operating company may have with such institution, it's generally advisable for the operating company to borrow where it doesn't maintain a deposit account.

Stripping Equity

An operating company may engage in an ongoing effort to reduce the amount of its assets which might be vulnerable to potential creditor claims by simply converting them to cash and distributing the cash to its shareholders, which may be one of the related companies discussed above.

Selling or factoring accounts receivable, reducing inventory to the lowest level possible without jeopardizing sales, selling and then leasing back equipment, or selling intellectual property and licensing it back, are all techniques that can be used to generate cash to be dividended out by the operating company to thereby reduce the assets subject to possible attack from creditors in the future.

Dividing Ownership amongst Family Members

Creditors may be deterred from attempting to go after shares in any of the related companies if such shares don't represent a controlling interest. By selling additional shares to other family members of the owner, or other family controlled corporations, or family trusts, or even limited partnerships, ownership may become diluted enough to avoid creditor efforts to seize the shares. Spreading ownership of a corporation amongst family members so that no one family member owns more than 49 per cent may achieve the desired result.

However, just as with any transfers of personal assets by a business owner to members of his immediate family, transferring shares to family members still requires an owner to consider the stability of his marriage and his relationship with his children prior to the transfer. While transferring assets to family members may provide creditor protection, the owner may lose control of the assets as a result.[5] Use of a family trust to hold the assets may be a preferred alternative.

Furthermore, while mentioned in more detail below, bankruptcy and insolvency, fraudulent conveyance, and creditor preference legislation makes transfers to family members particularly suspect. While putting assets in a spouse's or adult child's name may be a popular form of creditor proofing, such transfers if at "undervalue" may be void if the transferor becomes insolvent within one year of the transfer, or within five years of the transfer if the transferor was insolvent at the time and intended to defraud, defeat or delay a creditor.[6]

Also, transfers to children may have adverse tax consequences for the owner, given the capital gains[7] and income attribution rules[8] which may apply.

COMMONLY USED STRUCTURES

Creditor proofing often involves the transfer of assets between related corporations using one of three methods in an effort to reduce or defer the amount of taxes which would otherwise be payable upon such transfers. Transfers may be effected by an operating company to a new parent company, or to a new subsidiary, or to a new sibling company. Such transfers are ordinarily accomplished by way of tax-free rollovers.[9] The consent of the bank or other financial services company currently providing credit to the operating company, whether on a secured or unsecured basis, will most likely be required in order to carry out any of these three methods.

Transfer of Assets to a Holding Company

The shareholders of the operating company transfer their shares in the operating company to a newly incorporated holding company on a tax-free basis.[10] The operating company then declares and pays a dividend in favour of the holding company,[11] and any of the dividend proceeds received by the holding company which are needed by the operating company are then loaned back to the operating company. Such a loan is secured by way of a general security agreement covering the operating company's personal property and possibly a mortgage covering its real property, although such security is usually subordinated and postponed to any security held by the operating company's principal banker.

This process can be repeated over time as additional profits earned by the operating company are paid out to the holding company as dividends and then lent back to the operating company when needed. However, while this method may serve to creditor proof the profits of the operating company, it doesn't creditor proof the real estate, equipment, intellectual property or other valuable assets which remain with the operating company.

Transfer of Assets to a Subsidiary

Since the above "dividend" method leaves valuable assets with the operating company which are potentially available to creditors, it has its limitations. As an alternative, the operating company incorporates a new subsidiary and transfers its inventory, accounts receivable and minor operating assets to the subsidiary on tax-free basis,[12] while retaining its real estate, intellectual property, major equipment and other valuable assets.

Which assets stay and which assets are to be transferred may depend upon the position of the operating company's principal banker, including whether some of the existing bank debt will be transferred to the new subsidiary and whether guaranties and other security will be given by both companies. Which contracts are to be transferred, particularly those with suppliers, customers and equipment lessors, may depend upon whether consents to such transfers are required and can be obtained.

The new subsidiary then acquires from the original operating company, at fair market rates, leases for the real estate and major equipment and licenses for the intellectual property which it needs in order to carry on its business. Funds needed by the new subsidiary for working capital are then loaned by the original operating company from time to time, with such loans being secured by a general security agreement covering the assets of the new subsidiary.

As a result, the new subsidiary continues the business of the original operating company and incurs any future liabilities relating to the business, thereby leaving the original operating company with assets unaffected by such liabilities. But like the previous method, this "subsidiary" method also has limitations. Both the retained assets and transferred assets remain potentially available to the creditors of the original operating company at the time of the transfer because the transferred assets are indirectly held by it through the subsidiary's shares which it owns.

In order to avoid the limitations of both methods, and to potentially isolate the transferred assets from both the existing and future creditors of the business, the following third method, sometimes referred to as the "butterfly" method, may be undertaken instead.

Transfer of Assets to a Sibling Company

The shareholders of the operating company transfer some of their shares in the operating company to a newly incorporated sibling company in exchange for common shares of the sibling company. The operating company then transfers its real estate, intellectual property, major equipment and other valuable assets to the sibling company in exchange for preference shares of the sibling company which are redeemable for the amount of the fair market value of the assets being transferred to the sibling company. The transfers of the operating company shares and assets to the sibling company are both made on a tax-free basis.[13]

The operating company then purchases for cancellation its shares held by the sibling company at a price equal to the redemption amount of the sibling company's preference shares held by the operating company, and the sibling company then redeems its preference shares held by the operating company.[14] The purchase and redemption are each paid for by way of a promissory note, and the promissory notes are then set off against each other. The operating company then carries on the business, leasing back from the sibling company any assets required for the business.

As with an asset transfer to a subsidiary, being able to complete these steps may depend upon the position of the operating company's principal banker. Since it now holds the valuable assets, the sibling company will likely be required to guarantee the credit facilities extended to the operating company.

LEGISLATIVE RESTRICTIONS

One of the main objectives of bankruptcy and insolvency legislation is that all ordinary unsecured creditors are to be treated equally. The general concept of equality among the ordinary unsecured creditors has been backed up by the provisions of federal[15] as well as provincial statutes.[16] These statutes provide a trustee in bankruptcy or the creditors of the debtor with various ways to challenge improper transactions and recover property which has been improperly disposed of by the debtor.

While the debtor is solvent and operating in the ordinary course of business, preferring one creditor over another is both common and acceptable because, at common law, a debtor is entitled to pay its creditors in whatever order it pleases. It is generally assumed that if a debtor is continuing in business, each of its creditors will be paid eventually over time, some just sooner than others.

But when the debtor is insolvent, it is assumed that the debtor will not be able to continue in business and, over time, pay all of its creditors. In such circumstances, these statutes impose a concept of equality to correct creditor preferences by providing the means to recover property which is transferred to one creditor in preference over another creditor.

Under federal bankruptcy legislation, in the event of a bankruptcy, particular transactions between the bankrupt and its creditors can be declared void as against the trustee in bankruptcy if it is determined that the transactions constitute a preference. A broad range of transactions can be challenged: a transfer of property, provision of services, the creation of a charge on property, every payment made, every obligation incurred, and any judicial proceeding taken or suffered, by the debtor. [17]

In order for a transaction to be challenged as a preference, the following requirements must be met: the debtor was insolvent at the time of the transaction; the debtor intended to give the creditor a preference; and the transaction took place within three months of the debtor's bankruptcy. If the transaction is with a party related to the debtor, such as a parent company or subsidiary, the three month period extends to twelve months. Even though these tests are met, the transaction is only presumed to be a preference. It may not be declared void, for example, if it can be proven that it was done in the ordinary course of business, or done to enable the debtor to remain in business.

Also under federal bankruptcy legislation, a transaction which takes place at "undervalue" may be declared void as against the trustee in bankruptcy, or any party to such a transaction can be ordered to pay the difference between the value received and the value given by the debtor, if such party dealt with the debtor at arm's length, if the transaction occurred within one year of the debtor's bankruptcy, and if the debtor was insolvent at the time of the transaction and intended to defraud, defeat or delay a creditor. The same consequences may be faced if the party to the transaction was not dealing at arm's length with the debtor, if the transaction occurred within five years of the debtor's bankruptcy, and the debtor was either insolvent at the time of the transaction or intended to defraud, defeat or delay a creditor.[18]

Furthermore, any payment of dividends, or any redemption or purchase of its shares, made by an insolvent corporation within one year of bankruptcy can be attacked by the trustee in bankruptcy. The Court can award judgment against any director for the amount of the dividend, redemption price or purchase price that hasn't been repaid to the corporation unless the director protested against the corporation taking such actions at the time. A shareholder receiving funds resulting from such actions can be similarly liable. There is no requirement for the trustee to prove any fraudulent intent.[19]

Under provincial fraudulent conveyance legislation, conveyances made by a debtor with the intent to defeat, hinder, delay or defraud creditors can be challenged and need not fall within the same time limitations as described above for transactions at "undervalue" which are attacked under the federal legislation. Although proof of the debtor's intent to defeat creditors is required,[20] proof that the debtor was insolvent at the time the property was conveyed is not required, nor is proof that creditors were actually defeated by the conveyance. Conveyances to parties for good consideration who take in good faith without notice or knowledge of an intent to defeat creditors are however exempt.[21]

Under provincial creditor preference legislation, conveyances made by a debtor with the intent to defeat, hinder, delay or prejudice creditors at the time the debtor was insolvent can be challenged. Unlike under provincial fraudulent conveyance legislation, challenges under this legislation require proof that the debtor was insolvent at the time the property was conveyed.[22] If a conveyance which gives a creditor a preference over other creditors is attacked within 60 days after being made, or if the debtor makes an assignment for the benefit of its creditors within 60 days after such a conveyance, the debtor's intention to defeat creditors will be presumed.[23] If these time limits are not met, the presumptions will not arise and the party attacking the conveyance will have to prove that the debtor intended to create an unjust preference. Conveyances made in good faith for fair value in the ordinary course of business are however exempt, including paying money to existing creditors or granting security for a present advance.[24]

Federal and provincial corporation law statutes contain similar prohibitions. A corporation is prohibited from purchasing its shares,[25] from redeeming its shares,[26] and from declaring a dividend,[27] where there are reasonable grounds for believing that (a) the corporation is unable to pay its liabilities as they become due, or would be unable to do so after the payment is made, or (b) the realizable value of the corporation's assets after the payment would be less than the aggregate amount of its liabilities and stated capital for all classes of shares (or for those classes ranking ahead of or equal to the class being redeemed, in the case of share redemption). Directors who authorize an improper dividend or improper share purchase or redemption are liable[28] to restore to the corporation any amount so distributed.

A creditor of a corporation may be able to apply to the Court for an "oppression remedy"[29] as a "complainant" where an act or omission of the corporation effects a result, or where the business of the corporation or powers of the directors are being carried out in a manner, that unfairly disregards the interests of the creditor, and the Court may make an order to rectify the matters complained of.

Certain actions taken when implementing a creditor proofing plan can run afoul of the *Criminal Code* whether or not taken during, or on the eve of, insolvency. Anyone who conveys property or conceals property with intent to defraud his creditors commits an indictable offence and is liable to imprisonment for two years, as is anyone who receives property from someone with intent to defraud his creditors.[30] Anyone who commits forgery or who knowingly uses a forged document as if it were genuine is guilty of either an indictable offence or an offence punishable on summary conviction.[31]

Any owners or managers, or their professional advisers, who work on the implementation of a creditor proofing plan should be aware that the *Criminal Code* provides that anyone is party to an offence who actually commits it, or aids or abets any person in its commission. It also provides that where two or more persons form an intention in common to carry out an unlawful purpose and to assist each other to that end, and one of them commits an offence, then each of them can be a party to that offence.[32]

THINGS TO AVOID

In the past, many attacks on creditor proofing plans in non-bankruptcy situations have been made under provincial fraudulent conveyance legislation and have often relied upon the traditional "badges of fraud" to create a presumption of intent on the part of a grantor of property to defraud. These badges of fraud have been expanded over time and include certain actions which should be considered and hopefully avoided by those setting up a creditor proofing plan for an operating company, especially if the company's financial position is taking a bad turn. While these badges of fraud are of assistance in determining whether an intent to defraud exists, they are not conclusive evidence of fraud. More importantly, if none of the badges is present, a conveyance is unlikely to be successfully attacked.[33]

The badges of fraud include a transferor of property continuing to show ownership of, or retaining some interest in, the property after its purported transfer. They also include the absence of any change in possession of the property, or the existence of a trust over the property, after its purported transfer. The inadequacy of the consideration paid, the payment of the consideration by way of cash instead of cheque, and the absence of any documentation relating to the transfer, have also been regarded as badges of fraud.

In practice, avoiding these badges of fraud when setting up a creditor proofing plan often means creating evidence that each corporation in the plan is engaged in business as a legitimate legal entity, separate and apart from each of the other corporations and their owners, and that each transfer of property amongst them is documented as if it were an arm's length transfer.

Creditors may try to claim that the corporation receiving the property or the property transfer itself is nothing more than a sham. The onus is on the creditors to prove this, but they may have a tougher time in proving this if the related corporations avoid the following pitfalls:

Commingling of Assets
Each corporation should be operated as a distinct entity, and the cash and other assets of one corporation should be clearly segregated from those of each other. A failing business must appear to the creditors as a separate entity, unconnected to other healthy businesses.

Sharing of bank accounts, or commingling of cash, inventory or other assets, or utilizing one payroll account, by related corporations may result in creditors attempting to pierce the "corporate veil" and argue that a failing business and a healthy business are being carried on by the same corporation.

Failing to Identify the Business as a Separate Corporation
While there are advantages from a marketing perspective to represent a number of related corporations through the use of a common trade name, all dealings with third parties should clearly identify which corporation is involved.

All signage, letterhead, marketing materials, invoices, checks, e-mail and all other means of communicating with third parties should use the correct corporate name and not simply a trade name. All contracts should set out the corporate name and clearly be signed by an officer of that corporation in his corporate capacity. All required business licenses should be issued in the correct corporate name. A separate telephone number or telephone listing, and separate business and e-mail address, help to distance one related corporation from another.

Interlocking Boards and Management
Multiple corporations should be managed autonomously, each with separate and not identical or interlocking boards of directors. If convenience requires that board meetings of each related corporation be held at the same place and on the same day, they should be held consecutively, not

concurrently. Officers of related corporations should occupy different positions.

Failing to Maintain Separate Records and Record Inter-corporate Transfers

All transfers of assets, particularly inventory, between corporations should be recorded, and each corporation should maintain not just separate accounting records, but also corporate minute books which record separately the director and shareholder meetings of each corporation.

Transferring Assets for only Nominal Consideration

All transfers of assets between corporations should be for good consideration which is preferably set at the aggregate fair market value of the assets being transferred. Obtaining current appraisals of the assets from reliable, independent third parties, or a least referring to commercially available valuation databases, in an effort to establish a reasonable range of fair market values can be helpful in defending against an attack on the transfers.

EXAMPLE OF A CREDITOR PROOFING STRUCTURE

There are numerous reported court decisions which describe different creditor proofing structures and the various ways of attacking them. Some of the structures featured in the decisions are quite creative, while others are quite complicated. Of the many decisions which could be selected to illustrate the structures discussed above, the decision of the Ontario Court of Appeal in *Downtown Eatery (1993) v. Ontario*[34] provides a good example of just how far a private company owner or manager will go in order to achieve creditor proofing.

The *Downtown Eatery* decision looked at one creditor proofing structure in attempting to determine the extent to which an unsatisfied judgment for damages for wrongful dismissal rendered against one company could be collected from other related companies. In short, the Court of Appeal recognized that a business does not have to operate through a single company and that there is nothing unlawful or suspicious about choosing a complex structure, provided that the complexity doesn't defeat the rights of wrongfully dismissed employees.

The structure chosen by the two individual defendants in the case who controlled the various defendant companies was indeed complex. In order to carry on a nightclub business in downtown Toronto, one company was used to own the nightclub's premises, which were leased to another company which owned the nightclub's trademark and held the necessary liquor and entertainment licenses. A further company owned the nightclub's chattels and equipment and was a licensee of the trademark. And still a further company, Best Beaver Management Inc., paid the nightclub's employees. All of these companies were owned by two holding companies, which were in turn owned by Grad and Grosman, the two individual defendants.

Joseph Alouche, a former manager of the nightclub, obtained a judgment for damages for wrongful dismissal against Best Beaver Management Inc. which had previously been paying him but which had failed to satisfy the judgment. In fact, that company had ceased to carry on business and its assets were distributed to other companies related to the nightclub before the judgment was even rendered. When a small amount of cash, allegedly belonging to the company which owned the nightclub's chattels and equipment, was seized by sheriffs executing on the Alouche judgment, that company claimed against Alouche. Alouche then counterclaimed against all of the related companies, along with Grad and Grosman, to recover his unsatisfied judgment.

At trial, Alouche argued the "common employer doctrine" and oppression, as well as fraudulent conveyance, but lost on all three grounds. On appeal, he argued and won on the first two. The Court of Appeal held that the asset distribution to related companies was oppressive conduct on the part of Grad and Grosman, and that the related companies were collectively Alouche's employer, accountable for his wrongful dismissal.

The appeal decision is useful as a reminder of the types of conduct that can give rise to an oppression remedy, as well as being noteworthy in its discussion of the common employer doctrine and the liability to employees which companies within a related group may face.

In dealing with the common employer doctrine, the Court of Appeal cites the following passage from another decision[35] which it regarded as being particularly persuasive:

The old-fashioned notion that no man can serve two masters fails to recognize the realities of modern-day business, accounting and tax considerations. There is nothing sinister or irregular about the apparently complex intercorporate relationship existing between Cyril and Dover. It is, in fact, a perfectly normal arrangement frequently encountered in the business world in one form or another. Similar arrangements may result from corporate take-overs, from tax planning considerations, or, from other legitimate business motives too numerous to catalogue. As long as there exists a sufficient degree of relationship between the different legal entities who apparently compete for the role of employer, there is no reason in law or in equity why they ought not all to be regarded as one for the purpose of determining liability for obligations toward those employees who, in effect, have served all without regard for any precise notion of to whom they were bound in contract.

The Court of Appeal adds this caution to owners and managers planning such a "perfectly normal" and "frequently encountered" arrangement:

However, although an employer is entitled to establish complex corporate structures and relationships, the law should be vigilant to ensure that permissible complexity in corporate arrangements does not work an injustice in the realm of employment law. At the end of the day, Alouche's situation is a simple, common and important one - he is a man who had a job, with a salary, benefits and duties. He was fired - wrongfully. His employer must meet its legal responsibility to compensate him for its unlawful conduct. The definition of 'employer' in this simple and common scenario should be one that recognizes the complexity of modern corporate structures, but does not permit that complexity to defeat the legitimate entitlements of wrongfully dismissed employees.

In dealing with the oppression remedy, the Court of Appeal adds this further caution:

It was the reasonable expectation of Alouche that Grad and Grosman, in terminating the operations of Best Beaver and leaving it without assets to respond to a possible judgment, should have retained a reserve to meet the very contingency that resulted. In failing to do so, the benefit to Grad and Grosman, as the shareholders and sole controlling owners of this small, closely held company, is clear. By diverting the accumulated profits of Best Beaver to other companies that they owned, they were able to insulate these funds from being available to satisfy Alouche's judgment. For the foregoing reasons, it is our opinion that Alouche has demonstrated his entitlement to an oppression remedy against Grad and Grosman.

PROCEED WITH CAUTION

While the *Downtown Eatery* decision may confirm that there is nothing inherently sinister or irregular about carrying on a business through a number of related companies, the legislative restrictions outlined above certainly require those attempting to set up a creditor proofing plan to act long before the business is insolvent or on the eve of insolvency. Ensuring that each of the companies participating in the plan is established for valid business purposes, and that each of the asset transfers between them is made at fair market value, will help to defend against an attack.

Implementing a plan when the business is in financial difficulty, or undertaking a transfer which defeats, hinders or delays creditors, can encourage a successful attack being made. Oppressive conduct on the part of the directors of any of the participating companies in the plan can further encourage successful attacks.

Yet even in the absence of such circumstances, cases like *Downtown Eatery* make it difficult for owners or managers to have complete confidence that their transfer of assets between related companies will be 100 per cent creditor proof.

Leasing Commercial Property

Despite the rise of electronic commerce and virtual offices, there continues to be a need for a physical "bricks and mortar" presence for many
businesses, and the owners and managers of a private company will likely
consider entering into a commercial lease at some time if the company
isn't already occupying commercial space.

Although some private companies satisfy their real estate requirements
though outright purchase, many others decide to lease. Even those with
sufficient cash to complete a purchase may still prefer the flexibility
leasing provides. Leasing can also permit occupancy of certain kinds of
premises which are not available for purchase. Retail space in shopping
centres and office space in high rise buildings are usually occupied on a
leased basis.

But even though commercial leases are commonplace in the business
world, and are probably more frequently encountered by private company owners and managers than the other forms of business agreements
which are described elsewhere in this book, they should nonetheless be
carefully reviewed and considered before being signed and returned to
the landlord. They are ordinarily quite lengthy and complex, and given
that they are prepared by the landlord, contain many provisions that are
designed to protect the landlord.

While the owners and managers of a private company may have personal experience in renting residential premises, and may have come to
appreciate the rigorous statutory protection afforded tenants under provincial residential tenancy legislation, they may have to adjust their expectations regarding tenant rights when the company becomes a commercial tenant.[1]

This chapter will attempt to discuss some of the main issues which
need to be addressed by a private company intending to become a tenant

of commercial property. While written generally to cover those situations when the company is dealing directly as a potential tenant with the land-lord under an original lease, much of this chapter also applies to those situations when the company is assuming an existing lease from the current tenant.

OFFER TO LEASE

Although this chapter addresses a number of clauses ordinarily found in a commercial lease, a potential tenant should be aware that the leasing process often entails the prior signing of an offer to lease which contains the principal commercial terms of a more comprehensive lease which is intended to follow.

Since an offer to lease is signed, and often countersigned or "signed back" with numerous amendments, well before the final lease is executed and delivered, the tenant should be careful to ensure that the offer does not incorporate other terms which will form part of the final lease.

An offer to lease, once the signed-back amendments are agreed upon, becomes a legally binding agreement, even though the final lease when eventually signed is intended to replace it. But since the final lease is often prepared and signed after, sometimes long after, the tenant has moved into the leased premises, the offer to lease governs the tenancy in the meantime.

If the offer to lease requires the tenant to execute a certain form of lease, as is commonly the case, the tenant will effectively be deprived of the opportunity to negotiate further improvements or other changes to the lease.

GROSS LEASE VS. NET LEASE

The lease presented to the company by the landlord will typically follow one of two models, either the "gross" lease or the "net" lease. The main difference between the two relates to how each allocates responsibility for operating costs relating to the leased premises such as taxes, mainte-nance, repairs and insurance, often referred to as "TMI" or "additional rent".

Under a gross lease, the TMI is generally paid by the landlord and then recovered from the tenant by way of the tenant's monthly rent. The landlord effectively estimates the TMI which will be payable over the entire term of the lease and then builds into the monthly rent a prorated amount of the estimated TMI. Consequently, if the actual TMI is more than the estimate, the landlord pays for the difference, but if the actual TMI is less than the estimate, the landlord keeps the difference.

One variation of the gross lease involves certain costs being bench-marked at a certain level, so that any excess of such costs incurred above the benchmark have to be paid by the tenant as additional rent. Sometimes the benchmark is also increased to reflect inflation, often using the Consumer Price Index published by Statistics Canada.

Under a net lease, the tenant's monthly payment of "minimum" or "basic" rent does not include, or is "net" of, taxes, maintenance and repairs, and insurance, giving rise to the expression "triple net lease". The net lease is designed to eliminate the landlord's risk of a shortfall between the actual and estimated TMI as occurs with the gross lease. The TMI under the net lease is usually estimated by the landlord at the start of each lease year and paid by the tenant in monthly installments, subject to being adjusted at the end of the lease year when the actual TMI has been determined. Consequently, the tenant bears the risk of any increase in TMI actually incurred, whether due to inflation or otherwise, although any decrease in TMI will benefit the tenant.

From the tenant's perspective, a gross lease may appear to motivate a landlord to hold back on performing necessary maintenance and repairs, or carrying out desirable improvements. On the other hand, a gross lease affords the tenant some certainty when budgeting for her occupancy costs during the remainder of the term of the lease.

If the tenant is negotiating a net lease, the lease should require the landlord to reconcile the estimated and actual operating costs and calculate the appropriate rental adjustment within a relatively short period after the end of the relevant lease year. The lease should also be very specific on which expenditures incurred by the landlord will be treated as operating costs which may be allocated to the tenant. Since there is generally no clear distinction between a capital expense, ordinarily for the account of the landlord, and a repair and maintenance expense, the net lease should explicitly state in its definition of operating costs what costs are included and what costs are excluded.

PERCENTAGE RENT

For leases covering retail space in a shopping centre or mall, there is commonly required "percentage rent" from the tenant in addition to basic rent and TMI. Percentage rent is a specified percentage of the tenant's gross revenues, often between three per cent and 10 per cent, and usually entails monthly calculations and payments by the tenant, subject to an annual adjustment.

If a tenant has no sales and therefore owes no percentage rent for a particular month, the tenant must still pay basic rent and TMI for that month. The landlord consequently enjoys the benefits of a successful tenant. Because the percentage rent is based upon the tenant's gross revenues and not profits, a tenant undertaking significant promotional efforts resulting in greater sales but lower profits ends up paying more percentage rent.

Even if the tenant fails to generate sufficient sales to trigger an obligation to pay percentage rent, the tenant must still incur the costs of fulfilling the obligations ordinarily required under a lease providing for percentage rent to maintain proper sales records and regularly report her sales to the landlord.

Some leases with percentage rent contain a "radius clause" which calculates the tenant's gross revenues as including her revenues from any additional or expansion stores within a certain radius of the tenant's leased premises under the lease. The radius clause is intended to prohibit a tenant from competing with herself and reducing the gross revenue from the premises covered under the lease by expanding the geographical area from which the landlord can collect percentage rent. Yet the radius clause acts as a deterrent against the tenant from attempting to grow her business by establishing or acquiring other locations.

ASSIGNMENT AND SUBLETTING

It is essential for a tenant in a commercial lease to be able to transfer her lease, particularly if she decides to sell her business or undergo a corporate reorganization. The assignment and subletting clause found in most commercial leases permits a tenant to assign or sublease only with the landlord's prior written consent.

The main difference between an assignment of the lease by the tenant and a sublease is that an assignment involves the transfer by the tenant of her rights and obligations under the lease to a third party, whereas a sublease involves the tenant allowing a third party to occupy the leased premises without altering the obligations between the landlord and the tenant.

The need for the tenant to obtain the landlord's consent in either case should be qualified in the lease so that the consent is not unreasonably withheld or delayed.[2] Furthermore, the landlord's consent should not be required if the lease is to be transferred to an affiliate or other party related to the tenant.

Furthermore, the tenant should ensure that provisions elsewhere in the lease do not render the tenant's opportunity to transfer the lease difficult to implement. For example, the restrictions on the permitted business use of the leased premises can be so narrow that very few third parties would be able to take over the tenant's space. If the lease requires that the premises be used solely for a particular type of business carried on under a particular trade name, and may not be used for any other business or purpose, the premises may not be usable by anyone else.

The assignment and sublease clause in some commercial leases contains a "recapture" feature which allows the landlord to unilaterally terminate the lease when it receives a tenant's request for consent to assign or sublease. The landlord's exercise of her recapture option may be advantageous to the tenant, but not always. If the tenant wants to vacate the premises when it asks for consent and the landlord then exercises her recapture option, the tenant will be released from all further liability under the lease. However, if the tenant wants to sell her business as a going concern when it asks for consent, the landlord's exercise of the recapture option can effectively frustrate the tenant's sale efforts if the leased location is integral to the value and marketability of the business.

Even if the landlord consents to an assignment of the lease, the original tenant is usually required to remain liable to the landlord for any defaults caused by the new tenant under the lease unless the lease requires the landlord to release the original tenant upon an assignment. Only when the new tenant is significantly more creditworthy than the original tenant will the landlord be inclined to release the original tenant when consenting to the assignment.

OPTION TO RENEW AND RIGHT TO EXTEND

Most tenants insist upon having either an option to renew the lease or a right to extend the term of the lease. The difference between a renewal and an extension is, technically, based upon what happens at the end of the original term of the lease.

A lease that is renewed for an additional term terminates for an instant when the original term ends, so that the renewal effectively creates a new lease. This momentary termination causes any clauses which are "personal" to the tenant, such as a right to purchase the property, or a guarantee, or a right of first refusal to lease other premises, to lapse and fail to flow through to the renewal term, even if the renewal is on the same terms and conditions as the original lease, unless those personal rights are specifically made part of the renewal option.

For this reason, a tenant should not simply assume that all of her rights applicable to the original term will apply to the renewal term. She should also insist that all of her personal rights are expressly stated in the renewal clause.

A lease that is extended, however, automatically carries forward all those personal clauses existing in the original term to the extended term.

But whether negotiating an option to renew or a right to extend, a tenant must ensure that such rights come with sufficient certainty. For example, merely agreeing to a renewal or extension at a "rent to be negotiated" results in a clause which it too ambiguous to be enforceable. It is preferable to insert a clause providing for the future rent to be based upon some objective, third party standard, such as fair market rentals for comparable premises located within a certain radius as established by a certain valuator, or as determined by binding arbitration if the parties cannot otherwise agree on the rent.

Given the importance an option to renew or a right to extend may have to a tenant, particularly if suitable, alternative space becomes unavailable and when moving and other business relocation costs are considered, the tenant should be careful when approving the notice provisions in the lease covering the exercise of the renewal option or extension right. For example, if notice to exercise is to be given by the tenant to the landlord not fewer than six months before the expiry of the original term of the lease, the lease might require the landlord to give the tenant a prior notice of the renewal or extension deadline in order to reduce the likelihood of the tenant losing her rights due to an oversight.

Many renewal and extension clauses are conditional upon the tenant never having been in default under the lease. Some of these clauses contain other conditions, such as the tenant completing certain renovations to the premises before the lease may be renewed or extended. If these clauses are subject to a no-default condition, any assignee of the lease hoping to exercise the option to renew or right to extend must ensure that the original tenant was not in default under the lease at any time before the lease was assigned.

OPTION TO PURCHASE AND RIGHT OF REFUSAL

An option to purchase the property governed by the lease can prove to be quite beneficial to the tenant, depending upon the purchase price set out in the lease and the market value of the property prevailing at the time when the tenant wishes to exercise her option. The need for certainty in the drafting of options to purchase is just as important as the drafting of options to renew. Establishing the purchase price and prescribing the purchase process must be objectively and specifically laid out.

In contrast to an option to purchase which allows the tenant to purchase the property at the discretion of the tenant and represents a registerable interest in land, a right of first refusal is not an interest in land but merely a contractual right enjoyed by the tenant to purchase the property on the same terms as a third party offer for the property which the landlord is prepared to accept. Because it depends upon the landlord first receiving an acceptable offer for the property, often required to come from an arm's length third party and made in good faith, it is not as valuable to the tenant as an option to purchase.

As an alternative to a right of first refusal, the tenant might request that a right of first offer be inserted into the lease. Unlike a right of first refusal which requires that the landlord first receive an offer from a third party, a right of first offer requires the landlord, if it wishes to sell the property, to invite the tenant to submit an offer within a certain period of time. If the landlord and tenant cannot agree upon the terms of sale, again within a certain period of time, the landlord then has the right to sell to a third party.

Therefore, while the purchase price for the property is determined by a third party in the case of a right of first refusal, the purchase price is determined by the landlord in the case of a right of first offer.

For a tenant considering the expansion of her business in the future, rights of first refusal or first offer may also be requested by the tenant in connection with the leasing of other space from the landlord, either adjacent to her existing space or elsewhere within the same building or mall. A preferred rental rate for the additional space might also be set out.

EXCLUSIVITY AND OTHER RESTRICTIONS

For a tenant leasing retail space in a shopping centre or mall, an "exclusivity" clause from the landlord may afford the tenant a significant advantage. Such a clause is designed to provide the tenant with an exclusive right to be the only retailer, or one of a restricted number of retailers, of particular products or services within the shopping centre or mall. Without the benefit of an exclusivity clause, a tenant may be faced with a direct competitor leasing premises right next door.

But an exclusivity clause can be either too broad or too narrow in its description of what constitutes restricted competition to achieve the tenant's desired result. For example, the vendor of Vietnamese food would be better protected if the clause gave exclusivity for Asian food, not just Vietnamese food, in order to preclude Chinese and Thai food vendors that serve a similar market to occupy adjacent premises.

Some restrictive clauses are designed not to provide exclusivity but to prohibit the leasing of adjacent premises to others who may be inappropriate neighbours. For example, a religious book store may not want a liquor store or "adult" entertainment store nearby, or an outlet offering vegetarian food may not want a butcher shop next door.

While these kinds of restrictive clauses are usually confined to retail commercial leasing, they may be found in other types of commercial leases. The landlord of an office tower may be prevented from changing the name of the tower so as to avoid the possibility of one tenant's name being used when competitors of that tenant occupy space within the same tower. For example, an accounting firm tenant would not want the name of her building changed to the name of another accounting firm.

SUBORDINATION AND ATTORNMENT

As mentioned above, the tenant may need to protect herself from the actions not only of the landlord but also of any mortgagee of the leased property. Should the landlord default under a mortgage on the property, the mortgagee may foreclose or otherwise take possession, and if the mortgagee has "priority" over the tenant, such as when the mortgage is registered against the property before the tenant enters into the lease, the mortgagee may be able to evict the tenant, even though the tenant is not in default under the lease.

The tenant should be alert to the possible insertion in the lease of what is called a "subordination" clause which makes the lease subordinate to any mortgage on the leased property regardless of the order of registration or other rule governing priorities. Such a clause ensures that any mortgagee foreclosing on the landlord will have the necessary priority to evict the tenant.

The tenant should also be aware of any "attornment" clause appearing in the lease. An attornment clause is related to a subordination clause and forces the tenant to recognize the mortgagee as the "proper" landlord, not the landlord owner that has defaulted.

Since it is generally difficult for a tenant to negotiate the removal of the subordination and attornment clauses from the lease, especially since the mortgagee has likely required that they appear in the landlord's standard form of lease as a condition of mortgage financing, the tenant should instead attempt to obtain a non-disturbance agreement. Such an agreement is made between the tenant and the mortgagee and causes the tenant to attorn to the mortgagee should the mortgagee foreclose so long as the mortgagee agrees not to disturb the tenant if the tenant otherwise complies with the lease. Consequently, the tenant can continue to be a tenant under the same terms and conditions as the original lease except that, upon foreclosure, it pays directly to the mortgagee the rents and other amounts due under the lease.

By insisting that the landlord obtain a non-disturbance agreement in favour of the tenant from the mortgagee before entering into the lease, the tenant will continue to enjoy any option to renew or right of first refusal contained in the lease which might otherwise terminate upon the mortgage foreclosure.

LEASEHOLD IMPROVEMENTS

Most commercial leases specify that everything the tenant installs in the leased premises, with the exception of the tenant's own trade fixtures and merchandise, is a "leasehold improvement" which becomes the landlord's property once affixed to the premises, without requiring any payment by the landlord.

The tenant should attempt to negotiate a revision to such a clause so that any such improvement does not become the landlord's property until the end of the lease in order to enable the tenant to maintain control of the improvement and deduct applicable depreciation for accounting and tax purposes for the duration of the term.

Furthermore, the tenant should try to reduce those items which come within the definition of leasehold improvements under the lease and to expand upon those items which come within the definition of trade fixtures.

INSURANCE

Except for leases covering stand-alone industrial buildings, a commercial lease will generally impose an obligation upon the landlord to obtain and maintain insurance on the leased building, although the tenants of the building will indirectly pay for such insurance through their proportionate share of TMI. Each tenant, however, will usually be required to arrange for liability and property insurance in connection with her own leased premises, including coverage for her leasehold improvements.

Requiring a landlord with multiple tenants to obtain casualty insurance on the entire building results in the landlord effectively becoming the insurance administrator for all of the tenants, by not only collecting the premiums but also in paying out the proceeds of an insured loss. But consequently, the insurer will ordinarily recognize only the landlord as the insured when paying out on a claim, and may attempt to seek restitution from any party other than the landlord to recover some of the amount paid.

For example, should the leased building be damaged by a fire caused by a tenant, the insurer will likely be subrogated under the insurance policy on the building to the rights of the landlord and become entitled to sue the tenant for the entire loss even though the tenant had been indirectly paying her share of the premiums under the policy.

Given this risk, while arguably remote, any tenant entering into a commercial lease with such standard insurance provisions should attempt to obtain waivers of subrogation and releases from the insurers involved.

Given that the insurance requirements imposed upon tenants in some commercial leases are often difficult to meet, the tenant should determine with her insurance agent if the prescribed coverage is actually available and, more importantly, affordable before the tenant signs the lease.

ENVIRONMENTAL INDEMNITY

A commercial lease will often contain an environmental indemnity clause under which the tenant is responsible for the clean-up or remediation of any contamination of the leased premises which occurs during the term of the lease.

Such clauses are quite broadly drafted, and the tenant should attempt to restrict her liability under any such clause in the lease to contamination proven to be actually caused by the tenant and which is the subject of a government remediation order.

Furthermore, the tenant should also try to limit her clean-up liability to any such contamination which is discovered during the term or just a short period of time thereafter, in an effort to minimize her residual liabilities once the lease has expired.

CO-TENANCY

When entering into a commercial lease for retail space in a shopping centre or mall, a tenant should request what is commonly referred to as a co-tenancy clause. Such a clause allows the tenant to get a reduction in rent from the landlord in the event that a key tenant or a certain number of tenants leave the mall.

Co-tenants are typically the anchor tenants in a mall. They are a big draw for customer traffic that spills over to other stores in the mall, and are often one of the major reasons a tenant chooses to locate in that mall. A co-tenancy clause provides the tenant with some form of protection by reducing the tenant's rent to compensate for the loss of traffic.

In addition to receiving a reduction in rent, the tenant may also try to include in the co-tenancy clause a right to terminate the lease upon the exit of an anchor tenant.

RELOCATION

Most commercial leases for space in a shopping centre or mall, and many office leases, contain a clause allowing the landlord to relocate the tenant to other premises within the mall or building. Relocation clauses are ordinarily designed to facilitate the renovation plans of the landlord for the benefit of all the tenants, and to avoid the possibility of just one tenant preventing the renovation from being carried out. They also afford the landlord some flexibility to rearrange space in order to satisfy the requirements of larger tenants.

Unlike demolition or sale clauses, discussed below, that usually involve the landlord's termination of the lease and acquiring vacant possession of the leased premises, relocation clauses generally reflect the landlord's desire to keep the lease in force while increasing the density or making better use of the existing mall or building.

While there are many variations of the type of relocation clause which may appear in a commercial lease, they are always drafted for the advantage of the landlord, and the tenant needs to carefully assess the potential impact of a notice from the landlord to relocate at any time during the term of the lease.

Although the tenant's main concern will likely be the amount of money the landlord will have to pay the tenant as compensation for being forced to move, the tenant will also have to consider the size and suitability of the alternative premises that may be offered, as well as the applicable rent for such premises. The alternative premises should be comparable to the original premises in not only size but also in proximity to an anchor tenant, frontage, visibility and pedestrian flow, if for retail space, or in view and height, if for office space. The design of fixtures and improvements existing in the alternative space may be a concern as well.

While some relocation clauses provide that the landlord may relocate the tenant to alternative premises at the landlord's expense, such an obligation to absorb the tenant's relocation costs may be qualified by an obligation of the tenant to remain in possession of the alternative premises for a period beyond the term of the original lease. After all, if there is only a short amount of time remaining on the original lease, and if the landlord is going to refit new premises for the tenant, the landlord will want some assurance that the tenant will be paying rent for a longer period.

Other relocation clauses limit the amount of money a landlord will pay the tenant upon relocation. Compensation may be restricted to the amount of undepreciated or unamortized cost of the leasehold improvements in the leased premises paid for by the tenant. Under this type of clause, the tenant runs the risk that she will have to pay for her move as well as the improvements to the new premises. In such circumstances, the tenant should argue for the right to extend the term of her lease.

Occasionally, a commercial lease may allow the landlord to simply terminate the lease with a certain amount of prior notice, although the landlord will likely be required to pay some compensation which may be roughly equal to the tenant's undepreciated cost of leasehold improvements.

Whatever the form of relocation clause presented by the landlord to the tenant in the lease, the tenant should attempt to expand the scope of compensation payable by the landlord and require the landlord to provide suitable alternative space. Providing new space may effectively create a separate lease for this space and may invite negotiation over a number of issues, such as the length of the term, rent, and payment for improvements.

However, any negotiations over the lease for the alternative premises should not permit the landlord to force prevailing commercial leasing terms upon the tenant. Instead of allowing the landlord to re-write the lease to reflect market conditions at the time of the relocation, the tenant should argue that her rent for the alternative premises should be the lower of prevailing market rent and the rent payable under the original lease.

Since a relocation clause has the potential for abuse by the landlord, the tenant should insist that the clause may be exercised only when the landlord is attempting in good faith to expand or redevelop the shopping centre or office building, or is required to meet the demands of a major tenant. The tenant should also receive some assurance that she will not be forced to move just to accommodate some other similarly sized tenant.

The tenant should also try to obtain a commitment that she will be permitted to stay in her existing premises until the alternative premises are suitable for occupancy. If not, there should be some abatement of the rent during the occupation of any temporary premises. Furthermore, the tenant should attempt to restrict any forced relocation in order to ensure that she will not have to move during her busiest season.

The tenant should also argue for a right to terminate the lease in the event that the alternative space proposed by the landlord is not acceptable to the tenant. The tenant should then be entitled to receive payment for the undepreciated or unamortized portion of any improvements made to her existing premises.

DEMOLITION OR SALE

Unlike the proposed redevelopment of a shopping centre or office building which involves the continuity of existing leases (although the tenants may be relocated), proposed demolition usually involves lease termination. The sale of a mall or building may also involve the termination of leases where the buyer has made vacant possession a condition of closing the sale, even though many sales include existing leases and tenants because the buyer wants to continue receiving the rents after the sale is completed.

The demolition clause in a commercial lease may also include the provisions of a sale clause, or the sale of the shopping centre or office building may be addressed in a separate clause. Either way, the landlord is usually given the right to terminate the lease, and the tenant should exercise caution before simply agreeing to the form of clause presented by the landlord.

The tenant should attempt to place some restriction on when the landlord may terminate the lease. For example, if the tenant has one or more options to extend the term of the lease, the landlord's right to terminate might be exercisable only after the initial term has expired.

The landlord's right to terminate upon a proposed demolition is ordinarily triggered when something less than a complete demolition is to occur. Demolition is often defined to include a substantial renovation, perhaps involving 50 per cent or more of the rentable space in the mall or building where the tenant's premises are located, even though the tenant's space is not directly affected. To ensure that the landlord is acting in good faith and is not pretending to undergo a substantial renovation in order to terminate the tenant's lease, the tenant might insist that building permits, professionally prepared plans, or other objective evidence of the proposed project be produced before termination can be effective.

A demolition clause should contain a lengthy advance notice period to give the tenant sufficient time to find new space and relocate. It should also afford the tenant adequate compensation for the remaining value of the tenant's leasehold improvements, and require the landlord to provide the tenant with financial assistance for locating and moving to new premises, including brokerage commissions and the cost of new leasehold improvements.

A sale clause should give the tenant the same kind of protection as is found in a demolition clause. To ensure that the landlord acts in good faith when terminating the lease because of a sale, the tenant should require some evidence that an agreement of purchase and sale covering the mall or building has been signed by a third party purchaser unrelated to the landlord. However, such a requirement for a binding purchase agreement may lead to a relatively short notice period for the termination of the lease, depending upon the closing date set for the sale in the agreement. If the clause provides for the landlord's reimbursement of the tenant's costs in relocating, the notice period for termination could be even shorter.

While a sale may not lead to the termination of the lease because the buyer wishes to maintain the leasehold income stream generated by the mall or building, lease termination and vacant possession are often desired by a buyer in certain circumstances. For example, if a building has only one tenant, the buyer may want to acquire the building for her own occupation as well as an investment.

Or, if a retail mall has a number of underperforming tenants, and the buyer believes the mall will be more attractive to shoppers and other businesses if those tenants left and the mall goes "upmarket", the buyer will insist upon vacant possession as a condition of closing. As a means of deterring a landlord from terminating the lease in such circumstances, the tenant might try to include in the sale clause that termination is conditional upon the landlord terminating all of the other tenants, or a specific percentage of them, so that the landlord will have less opportunity to discriminate among her tenants when exercising her termination right.

REMOVAL AND RESTORATION

Although a tenant may be more concerned about issues arising at the beginning of the lease term than at the end when reviewing and negotiating the provisions of the lease, she should consider what her obligations will be when the lease eventually terminates.

Although a tenant's improvements which are affixed to the leased premises generally remain upon lease termination as the landlord's property, in contrast to the tenant's "trade fixtures" which can leave with the tenant, the lease may provide differently. The removal and restoration provisions of the lease may require the tenant to take out everything that the tenant built or installed on the premises.

In some commercial leases, the removal and restoration clause may be broad enough to require the tenant to remove not only her own equipment and improvements from the premises but also any equipment and improvements installed by a previous tenant or by the landlord for a previous tenant. Such a clause can effectively force the tenant to gut the premises and restore them to the landlord's current base building standards.

For example, in the case of premises used to operate a restaurant, cumbersome kitchen equipment, extensive wood paneling and specialty lighting systems might have to be removed. Or in the case of office premises, individual offices and board rooms constructed by the tenant might have to be destroyed in order for the leased space to be turned into a hallow cavern to be completely reconfigured by the next tenant. Returning the leased premises to the landlord in such stripped-down form can entail considerable expense for the departing tenant.

In an effort to avoid this possible expense on lease termination, the tenant should try to negotiate for an option to remove her fixtures and agree only to leave the premises in a clean condition. An option will allow the tenant to decide when the time comes whether to remove only the equipment which is easy to remove and re-use at her new premises. At least the major costs of any restoration on lease termination can then be shifted to the landlord.

DUE DILIGENCE

Although a due diligence investigation is usually conducted by a purchaser in connection with property that is about to be acquired, it is not commonly conducted by a tenant in connection with property that is about to be leased. Yet when a private company is considering whether it should lease a particular property, it should undertake a certain amount of due diligence before signing the lease.

The amount of due diligence required will vary greatly depending upon the nature of the lease and the extent of the obligations assumed under it by the tenant. For example, a lease for only a small area in an office tower will necessitate a different due diligence review than a single tenant lease of an industrial facility.

However, the following investigations are ordinarily carried out as part of lease due diligence.

Title Search

Before signing a commercial lease, particularly for a longer term and a larger space, a tenant should consider performing a title search of the property covered by the lease. A title search will enable the tenant to confirm that the landlord is the owner of the leased premises. If the lease is being signed not by the owner but by a property manager or leasing agent of the owner, the owner's consent to the lease, or confirmation of the authority of the manager or agent to act for the owner, should be obtained.

A title search will confirm that there are no restrictions on the title which might adversely affect the tenant's business. For example, a prior registration on title indicating an existing tenant's exclusive use may conflict with the incoming tenant's proposed use. An incoming tenant should request from the landlord a list of outstanding exclusive uses which the landlord has granted.

The tenant will also be able to identify any mortgagee who might attempt to take possession of the property in the event of a default by the landlord under a mortgage and who should be approached for a "non-disturbance agreement", as described above, before the tenant signs the lease.

The landlord's financial situation and her inability to honour her obligations under the lease may be revealed through a title search which indicates construction liens or arrears in realty taxes.

Zoning Compliance

Any tenant entering into a commercial lease should address the possible risk that municipal zoning by-laws may limit the kind of business that may be operated by the tenant out of the leased premises and render the tenant's business "illegal". The leasing of an industrial facility might also be affected by zoning by-laws that restrict access, emissions and noise. Furthermore, there may be restrictions on the number of signs that may be located on the property, as well as the size, location and type of sign that is permitted.

If the zoning by-laws change after the tenant takes possession of the premises, the tenant may be permitted to carry on her "legal non-conforming use", although what distinguishes an illegal use from a non-conforming use is not always clear, thereby exposing the tenant to potential by-law enforcement efforts.

Consequently, the tenant should attempt to obtain a representation from the landlord in the lease regarding the zoning applicable to the leased premises, although such a representation is not likely to be given, as well as conduct her own investigation of the zoning with the municipal authorities to satisfy herself that her intended use of the premises will comply. While the tenant may take some comfort from the fact that her use will be the same as the use of a previous tenant or other existing tenants in the same location, and therefore avoid the cost and time required for a zoning search, a tenant leasing space in a newly constructed building should confirm zoning compliance.

While the tenant may be able to achieve a minor variance of a by-law or a re-zoning order by applying to the local land use committee in order to ensure zoning compliance and avoid being forced to go out of business, it's ordinarily better for the tenant to confirm zoning compliance before signing the lease and moving in.

Condition of the Premises

The current condition of the premises at the start of the lease term may be of particular concern if the tenant is required under the lease to accept the premises "as is" or will assume the costs of repairs and maintenance either directly, as with a single tenant industrial facility, or through her share of operating expenses in the case of a multi-tenant building or mall. The tenant should attempt to find out what major repairs are necessary and how much they will cost before she signs the lease.

A cautious tenant will obtain an independent building inspection report covering the condition of the building's roof and its heating, plumbing and drainage systems, and an environmental report addressing possible contamination on the building site and the existence of asbestos, PCBs and lead, before leasing a single tenant facility. The costs of any required repair and remediation should be assumed by the landlord.

In addition to determining the need for repairs, the tenant may have to pay special attention to the suitability of the premises for the tenant's particular business. For example, the heating, ventilation and air-conditioning system must be adequate to support the tenant's business, especially if the tenant intends to operate a restaurant in an office tower and smoke and food odours have to be properly vented outside the building. If the building's HVAC system has to be turned on after regular office hours to accommodate the tenant's restaurant, the tenant may find herself paying the HVAC costs of the entire building incurred during that time.

Acquiring a Franchise

Many individuals think of acquiring a franchise because they want to own and operate a business but don't have the experience of starting one on their own. Acquiring a franchise lets them rely on the knowledge and experience of an established franchisor capable of providing the advice and support they need. A franchise is essentially a license to operate the franchisor's business system according to the franchisor's standards.

A franchisor's support may come in many forms. Franchisors often provide the use of a business name, methods of business operations, accounting systems, trademarks and marketing plans, along with inventory, equipment and other business related goods and services. By acquiring a franchise, an individual gets the benefits of "one-stop" shopping without having to separately source all of the things needed to get a business going.

In return, a franchisor can derive significant benefits in offering franchises. Franchising often allows the franchisor to increase his market share and broaden his customer base at relatively low cost. After all, it's the franchisee who generally pays an initial fee and ongoing royalties to the franchisor, and it's the franchisee's money which is used to organize and operate the individual franchise, even though the franchisor maintains control over how the franchise business is being run.

In short, a franchisor is selling, and a franchisee is buying, the use of a recognizable trademark and brand and the know-how associated with the franchisor's business system, along with the benefit of lower costs flowing from the purchasing power of the franchisor's extended buying group.

Any individual wanting a franchise may well decide to incorporate a new company to acquire the franchise and to operate the franchise business. The advantages of limited personal liability and more flexible tax planning afforded through the use of a corporate vehicle to carry on a business will generally apply, even though he may be required to personally guarantee some of the company's obligations to the franchisor.

Once he is an owner and manager of his new company, some of the chapters of this book may be immediately relevant to him, whereas other chapters may be more helpful over time, depending upon how successful his franchise business becomes.

But unlike acquiring other types of businesses, acquiring a franchise entails a number of issues which are quite specific to franchises, at least in those provinces which have special franchise legislation.[1]

This chapter will attempt to address many of these franchise specific issues. It generally deals with the acquisition of a franchise by a franchisee directly from the franchisor, although it also briefly discusses the acquisition of an existing franchise business from its current owner.

Acquiring a franchise is a document intensive process. In addition to having to review a lengthy disclosure document, required in those provinces with franchise legislation, a prospective franchisee will also have to review a franchise agreement and financial statements, and likely a sublease for commercial premises, a trademark license agreement protecting the franchisor's trademark, a general security agreement covering the franchisee's assets, a confidentiality agreement, a personal guarantee, and perhaps a construction and development agreement.

PRELIMINARY QUESTIONS

Any prospective franchisee will usually have to ask a number of preliminary questions before heading too far along the path to actually acquiring a franchise. Since his commitment to operate the franchisor's business system according to the franchisor's standards may last for anywhere between five and twenty years, he needs to exercise a certain amount of caution.

The amount of money he will be paying over the years for the rights to operate the franchise is often significant. In addition to the initial franchise fee for these rights, plus ongoing royalties usually linked to the gross sales of the franchised business, there is often a requirement for the franchisee to make regular contributions to a national advertising fund so that the franchisor can advertise his brand in higher cost broadcast and print media.

When all of the other costs associated with operating the franchise business are taken into account, including the expenses for inventory, equipment and rent, acquiring a franchise usually represents the single largest business investment an individual will ever make in his life. Furthermore, if the franchisee is to construct and develop the business premises himself at his own cost or, instead, buys the constructed premises on a "turnkey" basis from the franchisor, there are considerable additional costs he will be facing.

Many of the basic questions which should be asked by a prospective franchisee at the outset relate to the potential costs and liabilities which he will be incurring, the various parties with whom he will be dealing, and the numerous restrictions he will be under.

For example, his initial questions might include whether he will be personally liable for the obligations of the franchise business, as he (and possibly his spouse) may be required to provide a guarantee, and whether the guarantee can be limited to a fixed amount.

He should also be asking whether the business will be leasing premises directly from a landlord or subleasing from the franchisor. As between the franchisor and franchisee, who will control the lease for the franchised location, and who will arrange for the construction and development of the franchised location? If the franchisor is developing the location himself, assuming he will receive certain cash inducements from the landlord for signing the head lease, will the franchisee share in these inducements? What happens if the franchisor is developing the location but the location isn't open in a timely manner?

Other questions might relate to the ongoing supply of goods and services to the franchisee. What portion of rebates from suppliers will the franchisor direct back to the franchisee? What assurance is given that the products for sale by the franchisor can be bought by the franchisee at competitive prices? Will the advertising fund mainly be spent on advertisements in media far away from the franchised location where it may not help the franchisee get new customers?

A prospective franchisee may need to "ask around" about whether his proposed franchise terms really reflect the "going rate". Is his initial franchise fee too high for the industry, or his royalty percentage outside the normal range for the industry?

As part of his asking around, a prospective franchisee will want to determine early on how other franchisees are doing, whether they are making a decent living and whether they are getting along with the franchisor. Ideally a prospective franchisee will obtain a list of all franchisees in the system and talk to as many of them as possible, inquiring if they are satisfied with their franchise experience so far, what they would like to change in their franchise agreement if they could, and whether they would buy the franchise again knowing what they currently know.

More specifically, a prospective franchisee might ask former or current franchisees whether they experienced any unexpected costs and had to make any unexpected investments when operating their respective franchise, or whether they had difficulty meeting any sales targets or quotas, or whether they always earned a profit.

They might also be asked whether the franchisor's training and support during the franchise start-up were adequate, whether any inventory, equipment, supplies or services required to operate the franchise were generally provided by the franchisor in satisfactory condition and on time, whether the franchisor attempted to promptly rectify any problems that arose, and whether there was a suitable process in place for resolving any disagreements with the franchisor. It's certainly helpful to know if there is any litigation between any of the franchisees and the franchisor.

Of the many preliminary questions to be asked by a prospective franchisee, some of them have a decidedly legal aspect.

For example, a prospective franchisee will have to determine just how protected is his "protected" territory, and whether his "exclusive" territory is really exclusive. What will be the term of his franchise agreement, and what rights of renewal will he have? How easy will it be for him to resell the franchised business? What is the extent of the franchisor's discretion or right of approval on a resale or renewal? Will the franchisor have a right to buy the franchised business himself?

Since one of the main benefits in acquiring a franchise is the right to use the franchisor's trademark, a prospective franchisee should attempt to determine early on whether the franchisor actually owns or controls the trademark. The status of the franchisor's trademark should be confirmed, and preferably a certificate of registration[2] obtained.

It's important for a prospective franchisee to determine whether the franchisor will be fully complying with the disclosure requirements imposed by law, particularly in those provinces with franchise legislation as discussed below. Some U.S. based franchisors provide disclosure in Canada based upon U.S. franchise laws and practice, and often fail to adequately "Canadianize" their franchise agreements and other documentation. Sometimes their documentation fails to distinguish between U.S. and Canadian dollars, or fails to include certain Canadian terms such as GST or PST.

LEGISLATIVE OVERVIEW

The rights and relationships of franchisors and franchisees are governed in certain provinces by specific franchise legislation.[3] While these provincial statutes are similar, there are differences, and the owners and managers of a private company intending to acquire a franchise should consult the franchise law applicable in their particular province. The comments in this chapter are based upon Ontario's franchise statute, the *Arthur Wishart Act (Franchise Disclosure), 2000* (the "Act").

Since Ontario and the other provinces with specific franchise legislation have not established special purpose agencies to enforce the legislation, franchisees must make their own informed investment decisions about whether to acquire a franchise and cannot expect the government to review and approve franchisors and franchise documentation. It is up to the franchisors and franchisees themselves to pursue their own remedies under the legislation, often by way of court action.

It is sometimes difficult to determine when the Act applies, given that the definition of "franchise" is so broad that it captures business relationships which the parties may not have considered to be franchises. What the parties may regard as a "distributorship" may well be governed by the Act as a franchise.

If a franchisor grants a franchisee the right to sell or distribute goods or services associated with the franchisor's trademark or trade name, and exercises significant control or provides significant assistance in connection with the franchisee's business operations, and if the franchisee pays the franchisor when operating the business, their relationship will be governed by the Act as a franchise.[4]

This "business method" definition of a franchise is how most people view a franchise although the payment requirement may be met not just by up-front payments such as initial franchise fees or ongoing payments such as royalties for trademark use but instead by any payment made to the franchisor (or an associated party) in the course of operating the business, such as amounts paid to purchase inventory or for premises rent.[5]

If a business relationship falls within the franchise definition set out in the Act, it will be governed by the Act regardless of any attempt to "contract out" of its requirements. Any waiver or release by a franchisee of his rights under the Act, or of any obligation imposed by the Act on a franchisor or associated party, is deemed to be void.[6]

The Act is generally designed for the protection of franchisees and attempts to address the power imbalance which usually exists between franchisors and franchisees. The franchisor invariably has much more information about the franchise system than a prospective franchisee. Yet the franchisee, at least at the start, has relatively more at stake when acquiring a franchise. While the franchisor's risk may be spread out over a number of locations, the franchisee's risk is ordinarily concentrated on just one. Often a franchisee's net worth, as well as ongoing livelihood, depends largely upon the success of the franchise. As mentioned above, the franchise is likely to be the franchisee's largest, if not only, investment.

Duty of Disclosure
The main obligation imposed under the Act is the franchisor's duty to disclose to a prospective franchisee all the information necessary to allow the franchisee to make a properly informed decision about whether to acquire the franchise being offered.[7]

Such disclosure is to be made by way of a disclosure document to be provided by the franchisor to the prospective franchisee not fewer than 14 days before the franchisee signs any agreement relating to the franchise or pays any amounts to the franchisor or associated party, whichever occurs earlier.[8]

Therefore the signing by the prospective franchisee of even a preliminary document such as a confidentiality agreement or letter of intent, or the payment by the franchisee of a deposit, should not take place unless the franchisee has had at least two weeks to consider the disclosure document.

The disclosure document must set out all material facts[9] relating to the franchise and contain a number of items required by the Act, including relevant financial statements and any franchise and other agreements to be signed by the franchisee.[10] Not only historical information about the franchise should be provided but also the assumptions behind any projected revenue and profit numbers.

Information which is specifically required to be disclosed includes all deposits, fees and other costs, a description of any exclusive territory, any obligations to purchase from certain suppliers, the conditions of termination, renewal and franchise transfer, any policy on volume rebates, any training and assistance programs, a description of the franchisor's mediation process if one is used, the need to contribute to advertising funds, and a list of current and former franchisees.

The disclosure document must also be one document delivered at one time.[11] Piecemeal disclosure by the franchisor over time is not permitted, and all of the agreements, statements, certificates and other required information must be contained together and delivered as one document. The document must include a certificate signed by at least two persons who are officers or directors of the franchisor certifying that the document contains no untrue information and includes every material fact. These signatories are personally liable for any misrepresentations found in the document.[12]

However, the franchisor is obliged to notify a prospective franchisee of any material change that has occurred in the information provided as soon as it is practical and before an agreement is signed or payment is made.[13]

Duty of Fair Dealing

In contrast to the franchisor's duty of disclosure, which is ordinarily performed before the franchisee starts to operate the franchise, both parties have a duty of fair dealing to each other which lasts throughout their franchise relationship.[14]

This duty of fair dealing applies to the enforcement as well as performance of the franchise agreement, and imposes a duty on the parties to act in good faith and in accordance with reasonable commercial standards. It is one way of addressing the power imbalance between the franchisor and franchisee mentioned above.[15]

Right to Associate

A franchisee is given under the Act a right to associate with other franchisees and to join an organization of franchisees.[16] The franchisor is not allowed to interfere with this right or to penalize the franchisee in any way for attempting to exercise this right.

Therefore, any provision in the franchise agreement which prohibits or restricts the franchisee's rights to associate with other franchisees is unenforceable.

Consequences of Non-compliance

The consequences to a franchisor for failing to comply with the Act are relatively severe.

If the franchisor fails to provide the disclosure document within the time required or if the disclosure document fails to contain the information required by the Act, the franchisee may rescind the agreement without penalty no later than 60 days after receiving the disclosure document.[17]

If the franchisor never provides a disclosure document, the franchisee may rescind the franchise agreement without penalty no later than two years after entering into the agreement.[18]

These rights of rescission following the franchisor's failure to make proper or timely disclosure allow the franchisee to simply walk away from the franchise while being put back into the same position the franchisee occupied before the franchise agreement was entered into. However, the franchisee must first deliver a rescission notice to the franchisor within the applicable 60 day or two year limitation period, depending upon whether the franchisor's disclosure was deficient or late, or was not given at all.

Restoring the position of the franchisee upon rescission requires the franchisor within 60 days to refund to the franchisee any money he received other than money paid for inventory, supplies or equipment. Any inventory remaining with the franchisee, along with any supplies and equipment purchased under the franchise agreement, have to be repurchased by the franchisor at the same price originally paid by the franchisee. More significantly, the franchisee has to be compensated for any additional losses incurred in acquiring, setting up and operating the franchise once the foregoing payments are subtracted.[19]

This obligation to compensate for losses includes all operating losses incurred by the franchisee up to the date of rescission, and therefore could cover the franchisee's first two years of business if the franchisor failed to provide the required disclosure statement.

In addition to these rights of rescission, a franchisee may also bring an action for damages against the franchisor for breach of the Act's requirements.

While an action by a franchisee for damages may arise in connection with a breach of the franchisor's duty of fair dealing (although such a duty is also owed by the franchisee to the franchisor), it may also arise in connection with a breach of the franchisor's duty to disclose.

If a franchisee suffers a loss because of a misrepresentation, whether contained in the disclosure document or a statement of material change, or arising out of the franchisor's failure to comply with the Act's disclosure requirements, the franchisee may bring an action for damages against not only the franchisor but also the franchisor's agent, broker, associate and any person who has signed the disclosure statement or statement of material change.[20] The misrepresentation need not be intentional. The franchisee is deemed to have relied upon the document or statement regardless of whether the inaccuracy or omission was inadvertent or malicious.[21]

FRANCHISE AGREEMENTS

When reviewing the various terms and conditions of a franchise agreement before signing it, a prospective franchisee has to keep in mind that the agreement will likely be a "one sided" document which favours the franchisor despite the above described protection afforded under the Act. There may be little negotiation over the form of the agreement, which the franchisor will maintain is a "standard" document to be used by all of his franchisees. The agreement is prepared by the franchisor and is unlikely to contain many provisions that are designed to directly benefit the franchisee. A prospective franchisee has to be as concerned about those terms which may be omitted as those terms which may appear.

If the franchisor is prepared to make certain concessions to the franchisee, such negotiated concessions will likely be reflected in a separate amending agreement, not in the franchise agreement itself, so that the franchisor can more easily monitor those franchisees with non-standard arrangements and ensure that the special terms are included in the franchisee's disclosure document.

This part of the chapter attempts to discuss many of the key terms and issues which often arise under a franchise agreement. While some of these terms and issues apply to most types of contract, others are unique to the franchise relationship.

One of the main challenges facing a prospective franchisee when considering the implications of a franchise agreement is to anticipate the specific business and legal issues that might appear sometime in the future but which are not addressed in the franchise agreement under review. Although the need to anticipate change is relevant in the preparation of most contracts, it is increased in the context of franchise agreements since many such agreements last a lot longer than most contracts. Some franchise agreements are 10 or 20 years or more in duration, and while it is not possible when originally drafting the agreement to anticipate every change that may occur, both franchisor and franchisee often recognize that the agreement has to be flexible enough to respond to changes to the franchise system that may have to be made over time.

In giving themselves some degree of flexibility, some franchisors use their operations manual and policy statements as a way of revising their standards for the franchise system to accommodate any changes that may become necessary after the franchise agreement has been signed. This is accomplished by incorporating the operations manual by reference into the franchise agreement and by generally distributing manual updates and revised policies throughout the term of the franchise agreement, as described in greater detail below.

But this challenge of anticipating change in the agreement is coupled with the challenge of providing an accurate, clear and concise disclosure document under the Act which necessarily includes the franchise agreement and all of the other related documents that are to be signed by the prospective franchisee. Consequently, the agreement has to be drafted accurately, clearly and concisely, while providing for changes over the life of the agreement and avoiding any conflicts or inconsistencies with the disclosure document.

While many franchisors may wish to provide their prospective franchisees with franchise agreements in "plain" language bearing as little "legalese" as possible, hoping their agreements will serve as marketing tools for the franchise system, few franchisors succeed in providing user-friendly documents. Because franchisors have an overriding need to be legally protected from their franchisees while complying with the disclosure requirements of the Act, most franchise agreements comprehensively set out the rights, obligations and remedies of the franchisor and franchisee, and of the guarantors if any. The sale, transfer and termination of the franchise, the payment obligations of the franchisee, the manner in which the franchisee is required to operate the franchise business, and how the value of the franchise brand, trademarks, trade secrets and confidential and proprietary information will be protected, are all covered in the franchise agreement.

The key terms and issues involving many franchise agreements are discussed below.

Parties to the Franchise Agreement

Since a franchisee may be either an individual or a corporation, or in some cases a partnership, many prospective franchisees prefer to incorporate a company, if they are not already incorporated, for the purposes of signing the franchise agreement. In the absence of personal guarantees, if a corporate franchisee enters into the agreement, the individual shareholders of that corporation will not be personally responsible for the debts and obligations of the corporation.

But many franchisors require an individual to enter into the franchise agreement in his personal capacity, either in lieu of or in addition to a corporate franchisee. When the franchise agreement is executed by an individual, some franchisors may permit an assignment of the agreement to a corporation controlled by the individual, although the individual will then be required to personally guarantee the obligations of the corporate franchisee. Furthermore, many franchisors require that all of the principal shareholders of a corporate franchisee guarantee the obligations of the franchisee, thereby imposing personal liability on the individual shareholders for fulfilling those obligations.

Providing a guarantee not only makes the individual guarantor personally responsible for the payment of fees and other amounts owing under the franchise agreement, but also subjects the individual to the same noncompetition restrictions and confidentiality obligations which are imposed on the corporate franchisee.

Grant of Licence and Reservation of Rights

An essential term in any franchise agreement is the grant of a licence by the franchisor to the franchisee to operate a business selling products or services in association with the franchisor's know-how and trademarks in accordance with the franchisor's standards, methods and specifications. This licence is ordinarily limited in both time and territory, and may be exclusive, non-exclusive, or exclusive within a specified territory. While the franchise agreement will itemize all of the rights that are granted to the franchisee, it will also itemize all of the rights that are specifically reserved or "carved out" for the franchisor.

If the licence granted is non-exclusive, the franchisee has no assurance that the franchisor will not directly or indirectly compete with the franchisee, either through his own corporate outlets or through other franchisees. If, however, the licence granted is exclusive, the franchisor agrees not to compete with the franchisee within a defined territory, by refraining from either operating the same business or by granting a competing franchise within that territory.

Yet even if the franchisor has granted an exclusive licence, the franchisor will typically reserve to himself certain itemized rights, such as the right to operate or license others to operate a competing business using different trademarks, or to use different distribution channels. It's not unusual for a franchisor to reserve the right to sell his products and services through certain direct channels, including toll-free telephone and the Internet, or at alternative locations, such as kiosks, grocery and convenience stores, even movie theatres.

Term and Renewal

The term of the franchise agreement specifies how long the franchisee will be authorized to use the franchisor's system and trademarks to carry on business. The length of the initial term, whether it be 5, 10 or 20 years, will depend upon the nature of the franchised business, the practice generally prevailing within the industry, and the size of the initial investment the franchisee is required to make.

The franchisee may be offered a right of renewal for a further period of time, which may or may not be for the same period as the initial term. Typically certain conditions must be satisfied in order for the franchisee to exercise his right of renewal.

For example, should the franchisee wish to renew the franchise agreement beyond the initial term, he may be required to have substantially complied with all of the provisions of the franchise agreement and all of the other agreements between the franchisee and the franchisor during the initial term. He may also be required to have fully paid all amounts owing to the franchisor prior to renewal, including the required renewal fee, as well as all amounts owing to suppliers and other creditors.

Renewal is often subject to the franchisee's execution of the franchisor's then current form of franchise agreement and all other agreements and documents customarily used by the franchisor when granting franchises. The franchisee is ordinarily required to give notice to the franchisor prior to the expiry of the current term of his intention to renew the franchise agreement.

It is a common renewal condition that the franchisee has secured the right to remain in possession of his current premises, or other premises acceptable to the franchisor, throughout the renewal term.

Renewal may also be conditional upon the franchisee having made all reasonable capital expenditures required by the franchisor to upgrade his equipment, systems or software, or to renovate or redecorate the franchisee's premises so that they reflect the current image of the franchised business. This requirement is intended to ensure that long-time franchisees do not fall behind newer franchises when judged in terms of appearance and quality, and allows the franchisor to maintain consistency across all franchises regardless of how long a particular franchisee may have been part of the franchise system. This perceived need for continual upgrading can cause a franchisor to insist on shorter initial and renewal terms. Consequently, it may be common for the franchise agreement to contain an initial term of 5 years with an option to renew for a further 5 year period, in contrast to simply one single 10 year term.

Territory

The grant of the right to carry on the franchised business is usually limited to a defined territory. The size of the territory will vary depending on the nature of the business, being narrowly limited in some cases to the franchisee's actual premises or parts of a shopping mall, or enlarged in other cases to cover an entire city or even a province. A larger territory may be granted in the case of a service-based franchise which does not operate at a specific physical location.

If the franchisee is granted an exclusive right to carry on the franchised business within a defined territory, making the territory "protected", the franchisor will likely attempt to impose on the franchisee certain minimum performance standards, including base sales targets. These standards will allow the franchisor to assess whether the franchisee is adequately serving the needs of all the customers within the territory. The franchisee's failure to meet or exceed the minimum performance standards may allow the franchisor to reduce the scope of the protected territory, or perhaps even revoke the franchisee's exclusive rights altogether.

In the event that the franchisor decides that the protected territory can support another franchise, the agreement may grant the franchisee a right of first refusal to acquire the additional franchise. Provided the franchisee has complied with all of his obligations under the franchise agreement and satisfies the franchisor's capability criteria for operating multiple franchises, the franchisor is then required to offer the new location to the existing franchisee in the protected territory. If the franchisee does not exercise his right of first refusal, the new franchise may then be offered by the franchisor to a third party and the franchisee's protected territory re-described accordingly.

The franchisee may also be granted a right of first refusal in connection with a new franchise opportunity being made available by the franchisor outside the franchisee's protected territory. Ordinarily such a right would arise only if the new location is in proximity to the franchisee's current location.

Site Selection and Development
The franchisor will ordinarily want to control the location of the franchised business along with its overall appearance, particularly if it carries on as a retail store-front operation. The site's location and appearance has to be consistent with the image and branding that the franchisor generally conveys to the marketplace.

However, it is sometimes left to negotiation to determine whether the franchisor or the franchisee should initiate the site selection process. If the franchisee is responsible for selecting the site, the franchisor usually retains the right to either approve or reject the franchisee's choice of location.

When the franchisor has the right to select the site on behalf of the franchisee, he often has the additional right to either construct the premises to be used for the franchised business or insist that the franchisee use only building plans, contractors and construction materials which are approved by the franchisor. Therefore the franchisor will participate to some extent in the construction process.

The franchise agreement usually identifies which party will be entering into the lease for the location selected. The franchisor may enter into the lease itself and then sublease the site to the franchisee, or the franchisee may enter into the lease directly provided that the lease affords sufficient protection to the franchisor, its trademarks and the franchise system. Either way, the franchisor will typically be involved in the negotiation of the lease for the franchise location with the landlord.

If negotiating the lease on behalf of the franchisee, the franchisor will attempt to remove any provision of the lease that might prevent the franchisee from operating the franchised business at the leased location in accordance with the franchise agreement. If the franchisor enters into the lease, he will want to be able to sublet the leased premises without first obtaining the consent of the landlord, particularly if the franchise is terminated and another franchisee is selected to replace the terminated franchisee at the leased site.

However, despite the degree of control which the franchisor may wish to exercise over the franchise site, the franchise agreement will likely stipulate that all matters relating to the site selection and development process are exclusively the franchisee's sole responsibility, regardless of any assistance which the franchisor may have provided, and that neither the franchisor nor any other party associated with the franchisor is in any way liable for such matters.

Specifically, the franchise agreement may provide that the franchisee is responsible for reviewing documents, negotiating the lease, selecting developers and contractors, obtaining financing, complying with local regulation, and retaining architectural and engineering services to prepare surveys and site plans, all in accordance with the franchisor's requirements. Placing responsibility for these matters on the franchisee instead of the franchisor under the agreement is intended to encourage the franchisee's "buy-in" to the start-up process and reduce the potential for franchisee complaints.

The franchisor's desire to avoid any liability for these matters may be reflected in certain provisions. The franchise agreement will often state that the franchisor has made no representation regarding the costs of development and construction of the site, or the date on which the franchise will be open for business. It will also state that the franchisor's consent to any plans submitted by the franchisee, or the franchisor's submission of any plans and rendering of any assistance, are solely for the purpose of determining compliance with the franchise system standards, and that the franchisee is to be held solely responsible for constructing and operating his franchise in compliance with all applicable requirements.

Fees

As mentioned above, a franchise agreement usually prescribes more than one kind of payment to be made by the franchisee. There is a one-time initial franchise fee, an ongoing royalty fee, and often an ongoing advertising fee.

The initial franchise fee represents the fee payable for the franchisee's right to operate the franchised business using the franchisor's system and trademarks. It is separate from any training charges, construction or development expenses, or any other costs associated with opening the franchised business.

The initial fee is normally due upon execution of the franchise agreement and is non-refundable. However, some franchisors may refund the initial fee, perhaps when a franchisee has failed to demonstrate the qualities which the franchisor deems a successful franchise operator must have, or when a franchisee fails to complete the initial franchise training program. In those circumstances, the franchisor may have reserved the right to terminate the franchise agreement, and upon such termination, may refund the initial franchise fee less any administrative, accounting, training and legal expenses reasonably incurred by the franchisor. If a deposit was previously required in order to process a prospective franchisee's application, the amount of the deposit is normally deducted from the initial franchise fee.

The amount of the initial franchise fee varies considerably among franchise systems. Smaller, home-based franchisees are commonly required to pay an initial franchise fee which is relatively low when compared to the initial fee required by well-known and long established franchise systems, particularly in the hotel and restaurant industry.

Most franchise systems require franchisees to pay an ongoing periodic royalty fee. This fee ordinarily serves as the main source of a franchisor's revenues from franchisees, often payable on a weekly or monthly basis and calculated as a percentage of "gross sales". Of all the definitions found in a franchise agreement, the definition of gross sales deserves special attention from a prospective franchisee to ensure that the definition excludes certain items which are beyond the franchisee's control.

For example, while gross sales may be defined to include all sales and other income of the franchisee relating to the franchised business regardless of source, including all proceeds from any business interruption insurance, the definition should exclude all refunds and discounts made to customers, all taxes which are collected and remitted by the franchisee to any governmental body, and the value of all coupons or allowances authorized by the franchisor which are credited by the franchisee towards the purchase price of any item or service offered by the franchisee.

In addition to the obligation to pay an initial franchise fee and ongoing royalty fees, franchisees are often required to pay an ongoing advertising fee, sometimes described as a marketing fund fee, which is usually calculated as a percentage of gross sales though lower than the royalty fee.

An advertising or marketing fund is designed to take advantage of the benefits of standardized advertising and promotion of the franchise system on a national or regional basis, although it is commonly associated with more established franchise systems. The franchisor normally decides how the fund will be directed and administered, and selects the mix of print, broadcast and online media, and forms of promotion such as discounts or coupons, to be used.

In reviewing the franchise agreement's provisions which deal with the advertising fund, a prospective franchise should try to determine if the advertising fund will be accounted for separately from the franchisor's other funds. Specifically, will the franchisor's overhead costs incurred in administering the fund be allocated and paid out of the fund, will the franchisor's corporate outlets contribute to the fund, and will the ongoing expenditures of the fund be disclosed to the franchisee? Furthermore, will the franchisee have to spend a minimum amount on local advertising, or will the franchisee be constrained in his ability to advertise and promote his business in particular media and marketing channels?

Financial Reporting

The franchise agreement imposes certain record keeping and reporting obligations on the franchisee.

The franchisee is ordinarily required to maintain complete and accurate records of his gross sales and submit periodic reports containing his financial statements to the franchisor. The financial statements will likely have to be prepared by independent accountants approved by the franchisor, although they may not necessarily have to be audited. Copies of the franchisee's income, sales and goods and services tax returns may have to be submitted to the franchisor as well.

To ensure consistency of reporting within the overall franchise system, and to ensure that royalty and advertising fees have been calculated accurately, the franchisor will generally insist that the franchisee use the franchisor's approved accounting, record keeping, reporting and computer systems.

Furthermore, the franchisor will usually reserve the right to audit all of the franchisee's records, books of account and tax returns. While the expense of such an audit will typically be paid by the franchisor, the franchisee may have to pay for the audit if the audit reveals that the franchisee has remitted to the franchisor less than a specified percentage of the ongoing fees it should have remitted.

Trademark Protection

Since strong trademarks are essential to the continuing success of any franchise system, the franchise agreement contains numerous provisions which are intended to protect the franchisor's trademarks and minimize the risks of the franchisor losing the goodwill connected to his trademarks and franchise system.

The definition of "trademarks" in the franchise agreement is usually quite broad in order to allow the franchisor to add or remove any trademarks throughout the term of the agreement. The definition will include not only the trademarks, logos and trade names that are specifically listed in the agreement but also any others subsequently used by the franchise system which may be set out in the franchisor's operations manual. Depending upon the nature of the franchise system, the definition may be broad enough to cover the use of certain distinctive trade dress such as colour schemes, uniforms, and building décor.

The trademark provisions of the franchise agreement reflect the statutory requirement that the franchisor must authorize and control the franchisee's use of the franchisor's trademarks if such use by the franchisee is to be deemed use of the trademarks by the franchisor.[22] Control of the trademarks is often exercised by the franchisor providing the franchisee with guidelines for the proper use of the trademarks, implementing a compliance program to monitor the franchisee's use of the trademarks, and frequently inspecting the goods or services displaying the trademarks.

The following specific provisions designed to protect the trademarks are likely to appear in the franchise agreement.

The franchisee is required to publicly acknowledge that the trademarks are exclusively owned or licensed by the franchisor, perhaps by posting a sign at the franchise location or indicating on the franchisee's letterhead and promotional materials to that effect. Ordinarily the agreement will set out quite detailed limitations on the franchisee's usage of the trademarks in association with the franchisee's stationary, contracts, invoices, signs, product catalogues, order forms, websites and advertising.

The franchisee also agrees that he will not impair or contest the ownership of the trademarks, that his rights to their use are limited to the operation of the franchised business, and that such usage will be in compliance with the franchise agreement and all applicable law. The franchisee then agrees that all goodwill generated by such usage is for the benefit of the franchisor, and that upon the termination of the franchise agreement, the franchisee will not identify himself as a franchisee or former franchisee of the franchisor.

The franchisee is normally required to notify the franchisor of any infringement of the trademarks and to undertake whatever steps are necessary to protect the franchisor's rights to them, although the franchisor will retain complete control over the registration or abandonment of the trademarks, or the prosecution of any infringement.

The franchisee generally agrees that he will maintain the confidentiality of all trade secrets and confidential information belonging to the franchisor, and that he will implement various procedures to ensure his employees, contractors and agents maintain such confidentiality.

While the franchisee is often prohibited in the agreement from registering a domain name which is similar to the franchisor's trademarks or trade names, the franchisee may be permitted to develop his own website, or his own "franchisee pages" accessible through the franchisor's main website, for the purpose of promoting a more local presence to his customer base and providing community interest content.

Approved Suppliers and Volume Rebates

In order to keep the franchise system intact and ensure that uniform standards, methods and specifications will be followed by all franchisees, the franchise agreement typically requires the franchisee to offer for sale only those products and services, and use and install only such inventory, equipment, signs, furnishings and other items, that are authorized in writing by the franchisor. The agreement often requires the franchisee to purchase all such items from the franchisor, or an affiliate of the franchisor, or a franchisor-approved supplier.

This uniformity may allow the franchisee to take advantage of the franchise system's volume purchasing because the franchisor often realizes a profit or receives rebates, discounts or other allowances as a consequence of bulk purchasing by all franchisees and corporate outlets. The franchise agreement may give the franchisee the right to participate on the same basis as other franchisees in any group purchasing programs for products and services which the franchisor may use, even though any profits and allowances from such programs may be retained by the franchisor. If such profits and allowances need not be shared with the franchisee, the existence of such profits or allowances should at least be disclosed under the agreement to the franchisee.

Should the franchisee want to obtain products or services from suppliers other than those pre-approved by the franchisor, the franchise agreement should set out an approval process. Often the franchisee will be required to provide samples or submit to testing in order to obtain the franchisor's approval before sourcing from outside of the franchise system.

Security

The franchise agreement often allows the franchisor to take a security interest over the franchisee's assets, particularly when the franchisor or an affiliate of the franchisor is the main supplier of products and services to the franchisee. The security is given for the payment and performance by the franchisee of his obligations not only under the franchise agreement but also under other arrangements with suppliers to the franchisee.

Included in the franchise agreement will often be a requirement for the franchisee to execute a general security agreement, guarantee, and other supporting security documentation as may be requested by the franchisor or such suppliers. The franchise agreement and security documentation will usually contain reciprocal "cross-default" clauses, which stipulate that a default or breach under one agreement is deemed to be a default or breach under the other agreements.

Because the security interest will likely be registered under the personal property security system of each province in which the franchisee is carrying on business, it will affect the franchisee's ability to obtain financing from other sources, including institutional lenders that generally require security for any credit facilities they may provide. As discussed in greater detail in the *Debt Financing and Commitment Letters* chapter, a postponement and subordination arrangement may have to be worked out between the franchisor, lenders and other suppliers in order to accommodate the franchisee's financing needs.

Operations Manual and System Modification

As mentioned above, many franchise agreements incorporate the franchisor's operations manual into the franchise agreement so that the manual is deemed to form a part of the franchise agreement itself. The operations manual is usually designed to consolidate and update all of the franchisor's standards, procedures and policies that are necessary to enable the franchisee to operate the franchised business in a manner consistent with the franchise system.

Because the franchise relationship evolves over the often lengthy duration of the franchise agreement, the definition of the "operations manual" in the agreement is usually quite flexible in order to permit changes to the system. The definition typically includes not only the form of the manual that it delivered to the franchisee at the start of the franchise but also any later amendments, both additions and deletions. Furthermore, the definition may include various bulletins, directives, instructions and other types of communication which may be distributed by the franchisor to the franchisee throughout the term of the agreement. The flexibility of this definition is reinforced by a specific right of the franchisor in the agreement to amend or replace the manual, and to supplement it with additional information communicated from time to time.

To protect the confidentiality of the manual, .the franchise agreement ordinarily requires the franchisee to keep the contents of the manual confidential and stipulates that the manual is being loaned to the franchisee, rather than given or sold, so that upon termination of the agreement, the franchisee is obligated to return all copies of the manual in his possession to the franchisor.

The franchisee is normally required under the franchise agreement to operate the franchised business strictly in accordance with the manual. Failure to meet the standards set out in the manual on a regular basis will constitute an event of default by the franchisee and thereby permit termination of the agreement by the franchisor. The agreement may provide, however, that the franchisee's failure to comply with a particular material standard may be sufficient alone to constitute default and justify termination.

Since incorporating the franchisor's operating manual into the agreement allows the franchisor to unilaterally amend the agreement from time to time, the franchisee should ensure that the agreement requires the franchisor to contribute to the franchisee's costs of implementing any changes requested, including reimbursement of his out-of-pocket expenses. The agreement typically requires the franchisor to pay all costs necessitated by a change to the franchisor's trademarks or trade names.

Training and Operating Assistance

Since the integrity and success of the franchise system may depend upon the training and operating assistance that is offered by the franchisor to the franchisee, the franchise agreement usually requires the franchisee to attend initial training sessions to prepare the franchisee for the challenges of opening and operating the franchise. The agreement may provide that all staff training at the franchisee level be conducted subject to the franchisor's oversight and control, and may even provide that the franchisee and his staff must successfully complete the necessary training before the franchisee is formally accepted into the franchise system.

After the initial training, the franchisor will likely offer ongoing operating assistance to the franchisee. This assistance may cover purchasing, advertising, staffing, bookkeeping and other general business advice, along with "refresher" courses periodically to bring the franchisee's staff up-to-date on new developments and procedures within the franchise system.

The franchise agreement may reserve a right to the franchisor to require the franchisee to undergo additional training if deemed under-performing, and to require the franchisee to train all of his employees in a manner consistent with the franchisor's standards. The agreement should identify which party is required to bear the initial and ongoing training costs of the franchisee, although the franchisee is typically required to assume the cost of travel to and from the training sites and is often required to train his own employees at his own expense.

Insurance

The franchise agreement usually requires the franchisee to purchase and maintain throughout the term of the agreement insurance coverage for such amounts as may be prescribed by the franchisor, although as an alternative, the franchisee may be required to contribute to a group insurance program which has been set up by the franchisor for purposes of the franchise system.

The agreement ordinarily requires that the franchisor be named as an additional insured party to those insurance policies taken out by the franchisee, and that proof of such policies be provided to the franchisor upon request. The types of insurance required will vary among franchise systems, but ordinarily coverage for general liability, property damage, personal injury, business interruption, and employee dishonesty will be prescribed in order to protect both the franchisee and franchisor.

Should the franchisee fail to maintain the required insurance, the agreement may permit the franchisor to purchase and maintain such insurance from an insurer chosen by the franchisor but at the sole expense of the franchisee.

Termination

Although the franchise agreement will automatically terminate at the end of the initial term, or at the end of the renewal term if the agreement has been renewed, it may also be terminated earlier by the franchisor upon the occurrence of certain events of default by the franchisee as set out in the agreement.

While some events of default may be corrected or "cured" by the franchisee, such as the failure to pay royalty fees or the failure to file certain reports, others may result in the immediate termination of the agreement, as may occur upon the bankruptcy or insolvency of the franchisee, or the abandonment of the franchise. Even though a default may be cured, the agreement will likely provide the franchisor with a further ground of termination when the franchisee has been given a certain number of notices of default within a certain period of time regardless of whether such defaults have been cured by the franchisee.

As mentioned above, the franchise agreement may give the franchisor a right to terminate early on in the initial term should the franchisee fail to demonstrate the qualities deemed necessary for the successful operation of the franchised business or should the franchisee fail to complete the initial training program to the satisfaction of the franchisor. If the agreement is terminated at this early stage, it should require the franchisor to refund the initial franchise fee less his reasonable administrative, accounting, training and legal costs.

If the agreement includes the "cross-default" provision discussed above, the franchisor may terminate all agreements between the franchisee and franchisor or his affiliate should there occur an event of a default by the franchisee under any one agreement. Such a provision, for example, can cause a failure by the franchisee to pay rent owing under the sublease to be a default under the franchise agreement, thereby permitting the franchisor to terminate both the sublease and the franchise agreement.

A number of post-termination obligations of the franchisee are usually prescribed in the agreement.

In addition to the franchisee's post-termination obligations of confidentiality and non-competition which are described in more detail below, and the obligations to pay to the franchisor and his affiliates all amounts owing under the franchise agreement or any other agreement between the franchisee and the franchisor or his affiliate, the franchisee will be required upon termination to cease operation of the franchised business and refrain from holding himself out to the public as a present or former franchisee of the franchisor. He will also have to stop using the franchisor's trademarks and trade names, as well as the confidential methods and procedures associated with the franchisor's system.

The franchisee will also be required upon termination to carry out a number of specific administrative actions. For example, the franchisee will have to return to the franchisor all copies of the operations manual, notify the telephone company and listing agencies of the termination of the franchisee's right to use the telephone numbers and directory listings of the franchised business, assign to the franchisor such telephone numbers and directory listings along with any e-mail addresses and domain names which use the franchisor's trademarks and trade names, and cancel any trade or business name registrations which contain any part of the trademarks or trade names.

The franchise agreement will likely also contain a post-termination provision which allows the franchisor to enter the franchisee's premises and remove not only any property of the franchisor but also any property of the franchisee which displays the franchisor's trademarks or any feature associated with the franchisor's system.

While the franchise agreement does not typically specify any post-termination obligations of the franchisor, it will often set out certain post-termination rights. The franchisor may be given an option to purchase some or all of the assets used by the franchisee in the operation of the franchised business, which may include the franchisee's leasehold improvements, inventory, furniture, and equipment. The "exercise price" of the option for the various assets may be determined in accordance with a specific formula. For example, the purchase price payable by the franchisor for the franchisee's inventory may be the lower of the inventory's cost or net realizable value, less a re-stocking charge of 25 per cent of such purchase price.

Transfer and Assignment

Although there are generally no restrictions on the franchisor's ability to assign the franchise agreement, the franchisee's assignment of the agreement usually requires the prior written consent of the franchisor, which is not likely to be given unless certain conditions are met. Because the franchisor's decision to initially grant the franchise was probably based upon the franchisee's personal qualifications to operate the business, the franchisor may be reluctant to allow the franchisee to transfer the franchise to some other party.

The transfer provisions of the agreement and the need for the franchisor's consent will usually be triggered by a proposed sale of the franchised business by the franchisee, either as a sale of the franchise assets or as a sale of the shares of the franchisee corporation.

Before giving his consent, the franchisor, for example, may require that the proposed assignee has completed all necessary training, that the existing franchisee is in full compliance with all of his obligations under the franchise agreement and any related agreements and has executed a complete release of the franchisor, that a franchise transfer fee has been paid, that the assignee has entered into the franchisor's then current form of franchise agreement, and that reasonable capital expenditures required by the franchisor to modernize the franchised business have or will be made. These conditions are similar to the ordinary conditions for renewal of the agreement.

The franchise agreement may also provide the franchisor with a right of first refusal when the franchisee has received an offer from an outside party to purchase the franchise. The agreement may require the franchisee to present every third party offer he receives to the franchisor, and the franchisor then has a specified period of time within which to decide whether or not he wants to purchase the franchise on the same terms and conditions as set out in the third party offer. The agreement ordinarily states that if the franchisor decides not to purchase the franchise, the proposed assignee remains subject to the same approval process for all transfers and that the transfer remains subject to the franchisor's prior written consent.

Non-competition

As part of his overall efforts to protect and maintain the franchise system, the franchisor typically requires that the franchisee and the franchisee's shareholders, directors and officers refrain from competing against the franchise business during the term of the franchise agreement and for a certain period of time thereafter. The franchise agreement usually contains a very broad proscription against operating any business which is "similar to or competitive with" the franchise business.

As will be described in greater detail in the discussion of negative covenants in the *Shareholder Agreements* chapter, this wording may be too broad in scope and may be held by a court as a "restraint of trade" and thereby unenforceable. The franchisee should attempt to negotiate as narrow a non-competition clause as possible. Although a non-competition clause will be enforced if it is reasonably necessary to protect a legitimate interest of the franchisor and is also reasonable from a public interest perspective, the franchisee should try to reduce the geographic scope of the restricted territory, the number of years during which the restriction applies, and the extent of business activity being restricted.

The franchisee should also attempt to have the non-competition clause cease to apply if the franchise is terminated by the franchisor. A court may be more inclined to enforce a non-competition clause following a voluntary sale of a franchised business by a franchisee than following the termination of the agreement by the franchisor on a without cause basis.

Furthermore, a court may be less inclined to enforce a non-competition clause that prohibits the departing franchisee from operating outside of the franchisee's former territory, rather than a clause that prohibits the franchisee from competing within that territory. A non-competition clause covering an area where the franchisor has no franchisees in operation is more likely to be held unenforceable.

Alternative Dispute Resolution
The franchise agreement normally contains provisions setting out alternative dispute resolution procedures such as mediation and arbitration. As will be discussed in greater detail in the *Dispute Resolution and Shareholder Remedies* chapter, each party to the agreement may be required to use these alternative procedures before seeking recourse against the other party in court.

Or, the franchisee and franchisor may be required to resolve all their disputes through arbitration if mediation fails. This approach often provides that the result of the arbitration is final and binding and that neither party has the right to appeal the decision of the arbitrator. Under this approach, the franchise agreement should stipulate which arbitration rules are to be followed, how the arbitrator is to be selected, and where the arbitration is to take place. The parties should be in a position to select an arbitrator who is familiar with the unique aspects of franchising and has experience with franchise disputes.

While the franchise agreement is likely to endorse the use of mediation and arbitration, it is not common for the agreement to impose mandatory and binding arbitration, given that the franchisor will generally prefer to maintain his right to seek injunctive relief in the courts to enforce the franchisee's various covenants upon termination of the franchise agreement.

While a mandatory arbitration provision in the agreement may serve to avoid or delay litigation and the public disclosure of a pending franchisee claim, it may nonetheless ultimately be held unenforceable by a court if it prevents the exercise of any of the statutory rights given to franchisees under the Act.

BUYING AN EXISTING FRANCHISE

While most of this chapter has dealt with the acquisition of a new franchise by a franchisee directly from the franchisor, there may be circumstances when an individual, or a company that he owns and manages, has
an opportunity to acquire an existing franchise business directly from the
franchisee, the current owner.

The sale of a franchise business by the franchisee and the need for the
franchisor's consent were mentioned above in the description of the
transfer and assignment provisions ordinarily found in franchise agreements. In giving his consent, the franchisor may be quite involved in the
sale, or not at all.

The franchisor may want to influence the purchase price being negotiated between the selling franchisee and buyer as a means of maintaining
the market price for franchises generally within its system, or as a way of
ensuring that the buyer doesn't pay too much since an over-valued franchise often results in a failing franchisee. However, the franchisor may
prefer to play quite a passive role in the sale to avoid having to provide
to the buyer the disclosure document required under the Act. As long as
the grant of a franchise "is not effected by or through the franchisor", a
disclosure document need not be provided by the franchisor.[23]

But in the absence of receiving a disclosure document prepared and
delivered by the franchisor, the buyer will still want to receive adequate
disclosure about the franchise business, just as any buyer should want to
learn about any business he's interested in buying. And he will have to
consider all of the other issues which relate generally to the purchase of
any business apart from obtaining adequate disclosure.

A comprehensive review of these other issues is beyond the scope of
this chapter but may be found in the relevant chapters of the author's
Business Transactions Guide.[24] The purchase of the franchise business
will likely follow what is referred to in that guide as the "deal continuum"
and involve the preparation of a letter of intent, the carrying out of various
due diligence investigations, the negotiation and preparation of a purchase and sale agreement, and the eventual closing of the purchase transaction.

While the remainder of this chapter will not address the deal continuum as it applies to the purchase and sale of an existing franchise, it will
briefly describe the types of due diligence investigations which should
be undertaken by the buyer in relation to the seller's franchise business.

While not a substitute for a disclosure statement from the franchisor, the buyer's due diligence investigations of the franchise business should reveal much the same information.

Specifically, the buyer will want to review the financial statements, franchise agreement, lease and sublease, and any other documentation relevant to the franchise business that would otherwise be contained in a disclosure document provided by the franchisor, and carry out the various searches and other investigations described below.

However, as with any business purchase, one of the issues to be addressed early on is whether the assets of the franchise business should be purchased or whether the shares of the company that operates the franchise business should be purchased. Buyers generally prefer to acquire a company by buying its assets, not shares.

In a share sale, the buyer acquires the company as a whole, with all of its liabilities as well as its assets, including those liabilities which may be unknown at the time of closing. In an asset sale, the buyer acquires only those assets, and assumes only those liabilities, of the company which are identified in the purchase agreement. Avoiding the obligation to take on undisclosed or hidden liabilities, and the potential risks such liabilities might entail, is often the main reason why a buyer will insist that the purchase be structured as an asset sale. A failing business will usually be sold by way of assets, not shares.

Avoiding the risk of unknown liabilities is not the only reason a buyer might have for preferring an asset sale. There are certain tax advantages to a buyer in an asset sale as well, especially when the assets being purchased have a fair market value in excess of the tax cost of such assets recorded on the company's books. The purchase price may be allocated by buyer and seller amongst the various purchased assets to provide the buyer with a higher cost base for such assets, thereby enabling the buyer to claim after closing larger capital cost allowances and eligible capital expenditures on such assets.[25]

How the purchase transaction is structured affects the investigations which the buyer should be conducting, but there are a number of investigations which should be carried out regardless of whether the transaction is an asset sale or share sale.

One of the first things to be determined is the status of the company which operates the franchise business. Its correct corporate name and continuing existence can be confirmed by searching applicable government records. If its shares are to be sold, there is a need to inquire about any shareholder agreements amongst its shareholders or any outstanding options or rights of first refusal to acquire its shares which may prevent the sale from taking place. The buyer has to confirm that all of the parties who have an interest in the franchise business which the buyer wants to buy are participating in the deal.

Many of the investigations to be undertaken relate to the ownership of the assets of the franchise business.

For example, if the business owns any real property, it's important to confirm the registered owner of the property and the absence of any charges or encumbrances outstanding against or affecting the property. If there are outstanding charges, the amounts owing, the duration of the charges and the other applicable terms and conditions need to be determined. If there are restrictions affecting the property, how they might affect the operation of the franchise later on has to be considered.

Any leases of real property used in the franchise business need to be investigated. As mentioned earlier in this chapter, the franchisor often holds the head lease and then subleases the premises to the franchisee. Accordingly, both the sublease and the head lease should be reviewed. It will also be necessary to determine if the sale of the franchise business involves an assignment of the lease or the entering into of a new lease between the buyer and the franchisor. Furthermore, if the landlord has mortgaged the property, it's important to determine if the mortgage holder can force the buyer of the franchise business out of the premises in which the business is carried on because of the landlord's default under the mortgage.

The buyer should obtain a list of all machinery, equipment, vehicles and other tangible personal property, both owned and leased, which are used to carry on the franchise business. The terms of all leases or similar documents relating to such assets used in the business will need to be reviewed. Similarly, a list of all security interests, liens and encumbrances that affect the assets of the business should be prepared in order to confirm the amounts that remain to be paid or confirm that the assets can be sold, either because they are not under lease or because they are not encumbered by a lien.

In addition to the foregoing investigations of the assets used in the franchise business, the buyer will want to conduct various searches to confirm that the seller has been in compliance with governmental rules and regulations that may regulate the way the franchise business may be conducted.

Since buying any business, including a franchise business, entails the consideration of numerous other issues, many of which cannot be adequately addressed through the kinds of searches mentioned above, it's important for the buyer of an existing franchise business to recognize that the amount of time and money available determines the extent of the due diligence undertaken. For those risks which cannot be adequately investigated, the buyer may still be able to cover off any remaining exposure in the legal documentation which will be used to complete the purchase transaction.

Business Succession and Estate Freezes

As the owner of a private company approaches retirement age, she may begin to question whether her ownership will need to be transferred. Perhaps long before she even reaches such an age, she may consider whether the members of her own family ought to succeed her as owners of the company. Or she may consider transferring her ownership instead to certain company employees, or to other shareholders of the company, or even to outside parties.

Transfers to each of these groups can involve quite different business issues. For the owner who has done little succession planning, retirement from the company may not be easily achieved. The numerous issues related to business succession can seem overwhelming to the owner, who is certainly tempted to deal with them at a later time. The day-to-day problems of the company always seem to be more important and demand immediate attention.

But dealing with business succession needn't evoke anxiety although it may take more time and require more thought and soul-searching than the owner might expect. Some of the questions aren't easily answered. How much is the company worth? How can the ownership of the company be transferred on a tax efficient basis? How can the owner's risk be reduced or eliminated in the transfer? Should the owner stay involved afterwards with the company?

This chapter initially discusses how the owner may create and start to implement a business succession plan. It then looks at how the owner may carry out the plan if the plan contemplates ownership of the company being transferred to her family, including the use of estate freezes and family trusts.

Even though this chapter assumes that the owner intends to transfer ownership of the company to her family, and focuses on the process to be followed to achieve that end, the owner should nonetheless keep in mind that her main goal should be to ensure the survival of the company as a going concern, and that she should engage in some management succession planning to leave the company in "good hands". She will likely be mindful of the adage "shirtsleeves to shirtsleeves in three generations" and the challenges of keeping a family business within the family. Various studies have concluded that only 30 per cent of family businesses successfully carry on from the first generation to the second, and only a third of those succeed in making it to the third generation.[1] The likelihood of the business being carried on by the owner's grandchildren is only one in 10.

And since she must consider her ability to pay any taxes which become due upon the transfer of her ownership along with her ability to afford a comfortable lifestyle and provide for her family if necessary afterwards, she should try to engage in some estate planning as well. Although this chapter is intended to assist the owner in transferring ownership of the company while she is still alive, she must nonetheless consider some of the issues which arise should she prefer to pass ownership to her family members upon her death through a will.

For example, if the owner has enough financial resources unrelated to the company, she may simply decide to leave her company shares to some or all of her children in her will and continue to hold on to her shares in the meantime upon her retirement while the company is operated by professional managers from outside the family. Waiting to transfer her shares to her children as an inheritance upon her death, however, will make her estate liable for any capital gains taxes then arising.[2]

PRELIMINARY QUESTIONS

Before contemplating any of the steps set out in this chapter, the owner has to ask herself a number of basic questions. Is she personally ready to retire? Is she prepared to disengage from the business, to finally let go? Does she have financial resources apart from the business? Will there be enough income from the business to pay her during her retirement? Will she be comfortably able to pay any taxes owing? Is she looking to the ownership transfer as the main source of her retirement income? If she retires, who will take over? If her successor requires that she stay on as a consultant to the business after the ownership transfer, will she agree? In essence, what goals should she set for herself?

The owner may not need to sell out. The company may have already established a retirement compensation arrangement or an individual pension plan for her, or undertaken to provide her with a substantial retiring allowance. Or she may have built up a sizeable registered retirement savings plan or non-registered investment portfolio, or acquired substantial holdings of income producing real estate. With sufficient financial assets, she may have more choices and be able to set different goals.

But the owner will still have to seriously question the goals she has set. Not all of the goals can co-exist harmoniously, and in order to reconcile the conflicts which appear among them, she may be faced with some awkward choices. Some goals will have to be sacrificed when setting priorities.

For example, she may wish that all of the employees of the company continue to be employed by her successor at the same compensation and with the same benefits as they were provided by the owner. Or that each member of her family receives an equivalent share of the company, or an equivalent amount of money following the sale of the company. Or that she will pay the minimum amount of tax. Or that her successor will provide uninterrupted service to all of the customers she worked so hard to please over the years. Or that she will be able to walk away from the company without any residual risks or liabilities. Only an extremely optimistic owner would consider all of these goals to be achievable at the same time.

ASSEMBLING THE TEAM

Only in the rarest of circumstance will an owner be prepared to embark on this process alone. Even when attempting to set her goals and determine priorities, she will generally want someone to bounce ideas off, preferably someone who is impartial and not timid about offering unpopular or contrary views. That person may be a long-time professional adviser; perhaps a stockbroker, lawyer, or accountant, who has become quite familiar over the years with the owner's personal and business interests, yet has remained independent and objective throughout.

But while such a person may play a key role in facilitating the various decisions which the owner has to make during the process, there is nonetheless a broader group of advisers which the owner will need to assemble in order to properly deal with all of the various issues that will arise. Many of those issues can be quite technical and become overwhelming to an owner struggling to resolve them. The owner will need some help in interpreting and simplifying them. Although this chapter may attempt to identify some of those issues, it cannot replace the insight and experience which such additional advisers will apply when considering the owner's particular circumstances.

The members of such an advisory team will vary from one business succession to another, but the team will usually consist of a lawyer, accountant, valuator and tax adviser. Of the different advisory roles required to be performed, some may be performed by the same individual depending upon the skills and experience each may possess when joining the team.

CREATING A BUSINESS SUCCESSION PLAN

The owner's initial objective should be the creation of a written business succession plan. While the plan needs to address how ownership of the business is to be transferred, it may also address how management of the business is to be transferred, particularly in connection with ownership transfers to family members. It essentially takes into consideration not only the needs of the owner and her family but also the needs of the business. It may cover a variety of issues affecting the company's survival, such as any skills gap in leadership, and provide a long-range business plan.

The plan should reflect the input which the owner has received from her team of advisers, and may also take into account the views expressed not only by the members of her own family but also by any senior managers of the business who are outside her family.

Although the owner may prefer that the plan remain her own private and confidential creation, sharing her plan with others may reinforce the financial and managerial stability of the business and foster harmony among its various stakeholders. The company's employees, suppliers, bankers and customers may be reassured by the existence of a succession plan and remain confident that their own interests will be protected despite the owner's retirement from the business.

For those business succession plans which attempt to address management succession as well as ownership succession, the owner and her team will look at how major business decisions will be made, and at how family members, business managers, and other shareholders if any, will relate to each other while the owner continues to be involved in the business as well as after the owner retires from active management or ceases to have an ownership stake. Many plans also provide for certain contingencies, such as the disability, marriage, divorce or death of the owner before the full succession has been completed, and include a certain amount of legal, tax and insurance planning.

In preparing the plan, the owner and her team first embark on gathering as much of the relevant information as possible, including obtaining through confidential interviews the views of family members, senior employees and possibly the representatives of major suppliers and the company's bank,. It is at this stage that the ability and motivations of potential successors as managers and owners can be explored, along with the financial rewards expected or deserved by family members, the existence of any conflicts among them, the desire of the owner for continuing control, and the owner's need for financial security. Eliciting the views of family members at this stage helps to support the planning process going forward and increases the likelihood that the family will accept the succession plan when it is eventually finalized.

While the owner and her team may then wish to share the results of their initial interviews and information gathering with the owner's family members, they must be careful not to divulge any confidential information obtained from one family member to the others, nor engage in debating or negotiating the various alternatives which the family feel should be taken into consideration in devising the plan.

These preliminary efforts usually lead to more detailed planning sessions. The planning sessions attempt to generate a number of alternative actions and analyze the merits and likelihood of transferring ownership to the owner's family as well as possibly transferring ownership to the company's employees or other shareholders, or to outside parties.

If transferring ownership to family members is being considered, how and when the shares are to be transferred, and whether they will be given away or sold, or whether they will be the subject of an estate freeze as described below, are likely to be examined in the planning sessions.

Since management succession issues take on greater significance in the context of ownership transfers to family, the team at this stage may spend a lot of time deliberating over the next "leader" of the company. That leader may or may not be a family member, and some thought may be given to selecting an "outsider" to serve as an interim leader until a family member is deemed to be suitable. The owner may even prepare a formal job description for her management successor as a way of identifying which skills and experience the successor will need.

If a particular individual is favoured as a management successor but is lacking in some of the skills and experience deemed necessary, the team may consider what additional training may be desirable for the successor in order to fill in the gaps. Perhaps an advisory board consisting of experienced outsiders may be established to provide support to the successor in those areas where gaps exist.

In addition to identifying the potential leader when ownership is expected to remain within the family, the planning sessions will likely address a number of other specific issues relating to management succession and corporate governance. For example, what roles, if any, will be played by the owner after ownership is transferred, what management duties will be assumed by family members, and what involvement in the company will family members have if they are not active in management? Should non–active family members be entitled to attend meetings of the directors or shareholders of the company, or to own shares in the company, or to receive some form of compensation from the company?

Treating all family members equally under the succession plan may prove to be a challenge for the owner and her team at this stage. Perhaps the most that can be achieved is the fair treatment of each family member. Those children who are not chosen to be a successor owner or who are not part of management may nonetheless become entitled to receive non-company assets or income in the spirit of "equalization". This solution may depend upon the extent of the owner's outside investments, or upon the diversity of the company's asset base which may allow for certain assets to be transferred to another company which may, in turn, be owned by the non–active family members.

After the detailed planning sessions have concluded, the owner and her team can prepare the written plan which identifies the various actions to be taken and sets out an appropriate timetable. The written plan will specify when ownership is to be transferred, whether to be transferred on a particular date or phased-in over time. Perhaps the ownership transfer will take place upon the satisfaction of certain conditions or the occurrence of certain events. If the plan addresses the transfer of management, it will state when the owner is to retire and assign various operational responsibilities to specific individuals, and may specify who might sit on the company's board of directors or advisory board. The plan will also address how particular contingencies are to be handled, such as specifying the need for certain insurance policies covering the possible death and permanent disability of the owner and the successor managers.

IMPLEMENTING THE BUSINESS SUCCESSION PLAN

Once the business succession plan has been written, the owner and her team will attempt to initiate the various actions proposed in accordance with the plan's timetable.

These might include preparing wills, trust documents, and shareholder agreements, arranging for insurance coverage, reallocating the owner's outside investments, enrolling a family member in a graduate business program, obtaining a valuation of the company, transferring existing company shares, creating new classes of shares, transferring company assets to a new corporation, disposing of an unprofitable company division or surplus company assets, or perhaps even retaining a business broker.

Implementing the plan might also require further communication with the same stakeholders who were consulted during the plan's creation. Meeting again with the company's employees, suppliers and customers, as well as the ownerscommand.'s family, may be necessary to facilitate the various actions proposed and reduce the likelihood of any resistance to them.

While each succession plan has its own particular timetable, with some plans covering many years and others stretching over only a few months, it's important for the owner and her team to monitor not only the ongoing implementation of the plan but also the continuing appropriateness of the various actions proposed by the plan.

In some cases, the company's financial performance may fall below expectations and may not justify or support certain actions. For example, the redemption or repurchase of shares or payment of dividends may not be sensible, and may even be illegal if the company is unable to satisfy certain statutory solvency tests.[3] The cash required by the company to perform these actions may be put to much better use elsewhere.

In other cases, the people may have changed. For example, the death, disability or divorce of a key family member may cause the owner to reconsider the plan and the various roles in the company she intended her family to play. Or the owner may have changed her mind about her own retirement and the extent of her continuing participation in either the management or ownership of the company.

Continually reviewing the succession plan's implementation can result in changes to the company's operations, to the plan itself, or to both. The longer the timelines prescribed for carrying out the plan, the greater the chances that the plan will need to be revised.

The rest of this chapter is essentially about implementing many of the actions often found in a written business succession plan that calls for the owner's company shares to be transferred to members of her family while she is still alive.

GIFT OF SHARES

Instead of deciding that the transfer of her shares should be delayed until after her death, the owner may be in the financial position to simply give all of her company shares to her children while she is still living and then pay the capital gains taxes owing.[4] Such taxes may arise because she is deemed upon the gift to have disposed of her shares at their fair market value and to have received such value in return.

Depending upon the company's valuation, and the amount of her lifetime capital gains exemption still available to her which applies to the sale of shares of a qualified small business corporation, or QSBC,[5] it is possible that no such taxes will become payable, in which case an outright gift of her shares may then make sense.

However, if the shares are worth considerably more than the owner's available exemption, the excess gain will be taxable. One-half of the excess gain will be included in her income and taxed at her applicable marginal rate. In such circumstances, giving the shares away to her children should be avoided.

While the owner may believe that the fair market value of her shares is less than the amount available to her under her lifetime capital gains exemption, there is nonetheless the possibility that the Canada Revenue Agency might determine a higher fair market value for her shares and assess capital gains tax accordingly on the gift. Since gifts of private company shares to family members are likely to be more closely examined than transfers to arm's length parties in the Agency's assessment of tax payable, the owner may face unexpected taxes after the gifts have taken place

SALE OF SHARES

Giving away her shares will not be an option for the owner who requires additional capital in order to retire successfully. While she may not necessarily need the capital provided by the sale of the company, she may need the income such capital might produce. It may therefore be possible for her children to acquire her shares without paying her what an outside buyer might pay so long as they agree to pay her what she would have made as investment income if she had sold the company to an outside buyer and invested the sale proceeds.

However, as with a gift of her shares, any sale of her shares to her family will be deemed to be made at fair market value, regardless of the amount the owner may receive. She will therefore be required to pay capital gains tax on the difference between the cost of her shares and the fair market value she is deemed to have received, subject to a reduction for the amount of her lifetime capital gains exemption still available to her. Unfortunately the children buying her shares for less than fair market value are only allowed to treat as their tax cost for the shares the amount they actually paid.[6]

Selling her shares to some of her children for cash, assuming they already have it or can borrow it, has the advantage of providing the owner with the funds she might need for retirement or might need to give to her other children who will remain unconnected with the business. With a cash sale, any capital gain arising will be included by the owner in her income for the year of the sale, less the amount of her available lifetime capital gains exemption.

Providing instead for payment of the purchase price to be deferred may not give the owner immediate access to funds which she needs, but may be the only way her children can afford to buy her out. If payment of the sale price includes a promissory note payable to the owner which permits installments to be made over time, the owner may be able to claim a reserve for the unpaid sale proceeds which requires that only a portion of the gain be taxed in the year of sale. Claiming a reserve ordinarily permits the applicable capital gain to be spread out over a period of five years, although in the case of a sale to a child, the owner may be able to claim a reserve covering 10 years.[7]

ESTATE FREEZE

If the owner has decided to transfer ownership of her shares to her family, she may attempt to make the transfer by way of an "estate freeze" and thereby reduce the taxes that she might otherwise pay if she made an outright gift or transfer,[8] or which her estate might pay upon the deemed disposition of the shares upon her death.[9]

An estate freeze is particularly useful when the owner doesn't need cash proceeds from a sale of her shares. It allows her children to acquire equity in the company for a nominal investment. It also permits the splitting with her adult children of any future earnings of the company and any gains realized on a subsequent sale of the company's shares. Any future increase in the value of the company's shares accrues to the benefit of the owner's family. When used as a tool in estate planning, a freeze may save enough in taxes owing upon the death of the owner to mean the difference between having to sell the company's assets to satisfy the tax liability and being able to keep the company operating as usual.

The freeze essentially limits the tax liability that arises on death by fixing the owner's shares at their value when the freeze is implemented. It defers a portion of the tax that would otherwise have been payable on the owner's death since the tax on future growth in the value of the shares isn't payable until her children dispose of their shares.

When an estate freeze is put into place, the owner usually exchanges her common shares with the company for redeemable preferred shares. Her children, or a family trust for their benefit as described below, then subscribe for common shares for nominal value. The owner's interest in the company is fixed at the redemption value of her preferred shares, and the children then get the benefit of any future increase in the value of the common shares. The redemption value of the preferred shares is usually fixed at the fair market value of the common shares being exchanged in order to avoid a benefit being conferred on the children by the owner.[10]

In addition to providing both the company and the owner with the right to redeem the preferred shares, such shares often provide preferential dividend rights, requiring that any dividends on the preferred shares be paid before any dividends on the common shares. The dividends on the preferred shares, often set at a particular percentage of the redemption amount, may be either discretionary, as deemed desirable by the company's directors, or mandatory. The preference shares usually have priority over the common shares in any return of capital upon the company's liquidation, and may have voting rights to allow the owner to maintain voting control as discussed below.

Ordinarily the capital gain or loss incurred upon the exchange of her common shares for preferred shares can be deferred, since the cost of the preferred shares is deemed to be the same as the adjusted cost base of her common shares. The owner's gain on the common shares will effectively be taxed when the preferred shares are eventually disposed.

However, the freeze can be implemented in a slightly different way which allows the owner to elect that the share exchange takes place for more than the adjusted cost base of her common shares so that she can create a capital gain and crystallize her lifetime capital gains exemption.[11]

If the owner will not have an immediate need for the proceeds resulting from her redemption of the preferred shares to fund her retirement, she may be able to defer the tax that would otherwise be owing upon the share redemption by transferring her preferred shares to a new holding corporation which she might create. The share transfer could be made with no immediate tax consequences so long as she receives shares from the holding corporation,[12] and the proceeds resulting from any subsequent redemption of the preferred shares by the company would result in the holding corporation receiving a tax-free deemed dividend from the company. These proceeds could then be invested by the holding corporation, which would pay the applicable corporate tax on any investment income. Should the owner need additional funds later on, the holding corporation could pay dividends at that time to her, and she would then be liable to pay tax on the dividends she receives.

Another use of a holding corporation in carrying out an estate freeze might also be considered by the owner. Instead of exchanging her common shares for preferred shares in the company, the owner might set up a new holding corporation and transfer her company shares to the holding corporation in return for preferred shares of the holding corporation. Her children are issued in turn common shares of the holding corporation.[13] However, such an approach may not be as tax-effective if the holding corporation cannot meet the tests of a QSBC when the children are given the opportunity to sell their shares and are then unable to use their own lifetime capital gains exemption.

It should be kept in mind that the lifetime capital gains exemption can be multiplied among a family holding shares of a QSBC should each family member be able to use her respective exemption in the disposition of QSBC shares. Adding more individual family members as shareholders therefore increases the number of available exemptions. This is just another reason for implementing an estate freeze even though the owner may wish to eventually sell the company to an outside party, particularly when she feels the company may substantially increase in value. The freeze then becomes merely an interim step to multiply the number of capital gains exemptions available upon an outside sale rather than the means used by the owner for a final ownership transfer to her children.

RETAINING CONTROL

The preferred shares received by the owner on a freeze are often voting shares which give the owner the ability to continue to control the company, at least until a certain percentage of her preferred shares are redeemed by the company. Alternatively, the owner may be issued a separate class of voting special shares in addition to being issued the preferred shares. This separate voting class of shares can allow the owner to maintain control of the company even after her preferred shares have been redeemed.

The owner's control may be reinforced by a shareholder agreement which affords her the right to appoint a majority of the company's directors or to veto certain company decisions, such as the declaration of dividends or issuance of shares.

The shareholder agreement can also be used to impose various restrictions upon the children who have acquired company shares under the freeze. While such restrictions may appear to be undesirable when planning for a sale to a third party, they may be necessary to ensure that the company is in "good hands" when continuing under family ownership. The agreement might therefore provide for rights of first refusal and various buy-sell rights, including call rights which might give those children who are actively involved in the company a right to buy the shares of those children who aren't.

A more comprehensive description of these rights and restrictions can be found in the chapter *Shareholder Agreements*.

ENSURING LIQUIDITY

When receiving the preferred shares under a freeze, the owner is often concerned that the redemption value will not be enough to retire on. In order to provide the owner with funds if and when necessary, the owner and the company often enter into an agreement requiring the company to repurchase or redeem the owner's preferred shares over time in accordance with a series of prescribed dates or milestones. The amounts received by the owner under this redemption schedule will usually be taxed as deemed dividends.[14]

The owner might also receive funds by way of actual dividends, since the preferred shares issued to the owner often provide for a discretionary dividend which permits the directors to pay dividends to the owner sufficient for her needs before paying dividends to the children or the family trust on the common shares.

Either way, whether through share redemptions or dividends, the owner may not be able to receive adequate funds quickly enough for retirement purposes. The business may simply not be capable of generating sufficient funds for the redemption of her shares or payment of dividends. For this reason, an estate freeze may not be appropriate for the owner who has an immediate need to realize upon the value she has built up in the company. In some instances, the owner may have left it too late to establish an estate freeze which will be able to satisfy her financial objectives.

However, in setting up an estate freeze, the owner will at least learn how much her interest in the company is worth and how much tax will likely be payable on her death when her interest is deemed to be disposed. She can then address how the tax might be paid by her estate, hopefully without requiring a sale of the company or a significant portion of its assets.

Implementing an estate freeze often involves the purchase of life insurance which can help in satisfying the tax liabilities arising on the owner's death. The insurance proceeds can be used to pay the taxes owing on the accrued gains on the owner's preferred shares which are deemed to be disposed upon her death. Insurance proceeds can also be used to fund the company's redemption of the owner's preferred shares and thereby avoid the possibility of having to sell some of the company's assets to generate sufficient monies for the redemption. The surviving spouse of the owner may also receive insurance proceeds as a replacement for the distributions from the company previously received by the owner.

FAMILY TRUSTS

Despite the tax-savings which may result from the implementation of an estate freeze, the freeze may actually prove to be an obstacle to carrying out the business succession which the owner might prefer later on. Since many freezes treat all of the owner's children equally, and provide each of them with a similar number of common shares of the company, the child who may eventually turn out to be the most logical and capable successor may be forced to negotiate with the other siblings to buy their shares.

The owner, if still living, might then try to encourage the others to sell out, or at least come to some "first amongst equals" solution for the overall benefit of the company, using the argument that a single successor can minimize the conflicts that tend to arise when there are multiple leaders. The others may simply refuse to do so, especially when selling their shares to the chosen successor might trigger a capital gains tax liability which was intended to be deferred when the freeze was set up.

One way to avoid this situation from arising is through the owner's use of a family trust with discretionary distribution powers to hold the common shares instead of providing for the children to hold the shares directly. While the owner would still exchange her common shares for preferred or "freeze" shares of the company, the common or "growth" shares would be issued to the family trust. The trustees of the trust would then be given the power to distribute the trust property, such as the shares, when and to whom they feel appropriate. They are thereby allowed to benefit a beneficiary disproportionately, or perhaps exclude a beneficiary altogether. They are also allowed to distribute income earned by the trust to any one or more of the beneficiaries in their discretion.

The family trust in these circumstances is an "inter vivos" trust, created while the owner is still alive to hold company shares and other property for the benefit of her family. It is different from a "testamentary" trust, which may be created under the owner's will as a means of ultimately transferring her shares and other property to her family members after her death.

Unlike a corporation, a trust is not a separate legal entity but is instead a legal relationship or obligation involving a trustee who holds and deals with property for the benefit of the beneficiaries. The person who creates the trust is usually referred to as the "settlor". The trustee's main obligation is to carry out the instructions of the settlor as contained in the terms of the trust.

Certain features of trusts make them quite useful in the succession planning context. Their separation of legal and beneficial ownership of the trust property, their ability to provide for a number of successive beneficial interests spanning a considerable period of time, and the discretion they can offer the trustees when dealing with the trust property, including how and when the beneficiaries may actually receive a benefit, can help the owner accomplish her overall business succession objectives. Trusts can be used to provide the owner's children with the enjoyment of property without the powers of management or control.

Even though a trust may not be a separate legal entity, it is nonetheless treated as an individual for tax purposes.[15] It is therefore subject to tax on the taxable income it earns from property or a business, although it can flow such income to its beneficiaries so that the beneficiaries, not the trust, pay the tax owing on any "flowed through" amounts.[16] The trust is allowed a deduction for the amounts paid to the beneficiaries when calculating its income for tax purposes.[17]

Although commonly used in estate freezes, when a family trust acquires new common shares of the company after the owner has exchanged her own common shares for preferred shares, a family trust can also be used to acquire all of the owner's common shares directly from her. As described above in connection with the gift or sale of her shares to her children, a family trust acquiring her shares will be deemed to have acquired the shares at their fair market value, and the owner will be deemed to have disposed of the shares at their fair market value.[18]

If the value of her shares is less than the amount still available to her under her lifetime capital gains exemption, she may consider an outright transfer of her shares to a family trust rather than creating an estate freeze. However, she should not be the sole trustee of the family trust in order to avoid the possible attribution back to her of any capital gains or income earned by the trust in connection with the shares.[19] Often the trustees of a family trust include the owner, her chosen successor and a third party familiar with the family's affairs.

Although a trust established as a family trust involving the owner's children may be more commonly used by an owner for business succession, she may also consider using a trust established for the benefit of her spouse. The owner may elect to transfer her shares to a qualifying spousal trust at her adjusted cost base on a tax-deferred rollover basis,[20] or elect not to claim the rollover so that the transfer will take place at fair market value.[21] In order for a spousal trust to qualify for rollover treatment, the spouse must be entitled to receive all of the income of the trust that arises before his death, and during the spouse's lifetime, no other person may receive any of the income or capital of the trust.

Even though an inter vivos trust may be established by the owner to hold her shares and possibly her other property for the benefit of her family members, the trust cannot hold the property for an indefinite period as a way of deferring the taxation of capital gains. A trust is deemed to have disposed and then reacquired its capital property every 21 years for proceeds equal to its fair market value.[22] Consequently trust property which has appreciated in value is often distributed to the beneficiaries on a tax-deferred basis[23] before the 21-year period has expired, assuming the trust deed or other instrument creating the trust allows for such a distribution to take place.

Whether the family trust acquires the owner's common shares directly from her or acquires new common shares of the company upon an estate freeze, the trust can still be used to ensure that the ownership of the company ends up in the hands of the beneficiary who deserves to control and ultimately own the company. With just one beneficiary as the intended successor, the shares can be distributed to that beneficiary on a tax-free basis and no capital gains will be realized until the beneficiary eventually disposes of the shares. The beneficiary acquires the shares at the adjusted cost base of the trust.[24] Even though the trust is deemed to dispose of its assets after 21 years, the trustees are given considerable time before being required to select which beneficiaries ought to acquire the shares.

If the owner wishes for each of her children to be involved in the company, a family trust can still be used to multiply the number of lifetime capital gains exemptions used among the family. Each child receiving the company's shares from the trust can shelter the proceeds eventually received upon the sale of such shares from capital gains tax up to the amount available under the child's own lifetime exemption.

A family trust with discretionary distribution powers can also be used for income-splitting purposes. The trustees might distribute dividends to the children on a discretionary basis so that income can be made available to the children without giving them control of the company.

Furthermore, a family trust might be used to provide some measure of creditor proofing. A trust holding the common shares may protect the shares from being attacked by the children's creditors.

A family trust can also be used to avoid the consequences of children predeceasing the owner. If the owner's common shares, or the new common shares created upon a freeze, are transferred directly to a particular child, and that child then dies, the shares will be dealt with under the child's will and could end up being transferred to someone the owner might regard as an unsuitable successor. Having the shares held instead by a family trust enables the trustees to decide who should receive the shares, as the shares are governed by the trust agreement which can reflect the owner's wishes in the event of a child's death, and not the deceased child's will.

If the parents are included as additional beneficiaries of the family trust, an estate freeze which uses a family trust can effectively be "reversed" if the children turn out to be unsuitable successors or if an irreconcilable intra-family dispute appears to threaten the viability of the company. The trustees might then exercise their discretion to distribute the company's common or "growth" shares to the parents who would then consider other alternatives in dealing with them. Reversing a freeze in favour of the owner may also be appropriate in the event that the value of the company has appreciated considerably after the freeze was created and the redemption value of the owner's preferred or "freeze" shares is inadequate to meet her needs in retirement.

If the owner and her spouse are the only trustees of the family trust, they will clearly have a conflict of interest in exercising their discretion to distribute trust assets to themselves as beneficiaries. Even though the deed establishing the trust may permit such distributions to be made despite the conflict, the children may nonetheless bring legal proceedings to overturn them. It is therefore preferable for the trust to have a third trustee, thereby allowing the parents to abstain from voting on any distributions in their favour.

DIFFERENT VS. EQUAL TREATMENT OF CHILDREN

In setting up an estate freeze or family trust, the owner may have to decide which of her children should benefit from the growth of the company's business. She may wish to favour those children who are active in the company over those who are not. This favouritism can be accomplished by different means.

If an estate freeze is established by issuing new company shares directly to the owner's children, different classes of shares may be issued to different children. For example, those children less involved or less capable in managing the company might receive shares with rights to dividends but not rights to vote except in the event that the company is to be sold to an outside party.

However, deciding how much of the company's profits should be paid to the non-active children as dividends on their shares can be a challenge, especially if the owner wishes that all children be compensated as equally as possible. While the non-active children may be looking to the company for generous dividend income, the active children may prefer to reinvest the profits in the company to finance further growth. Giving the non-active children a preference over the active children to a specified annual dividend can create considerable dissension amongst the family, since the active children may feel they are working very hard and making personal sacrifices in order to pay their non-active siblings first.

If new company shares are to be issued to a family trust when a freeze is established, the owner will have to determine which of her children should be the beneficiaries of the trust in order to eventually receive the "growth" shares created under the freeze. Those who are not involved in the company could be excluded as beneficiaries. Often a family trust supporting a freeze will name as beneficiaries not only the chosen successor but also the successor's children and spouse, although a spouse who is separated from the successor is usually excluded as a beneficiary.

Although all of the owner's children may initially be made beneficiaries of the family trust created to support an estate freeze, the trust may continue to include as a beneficiary only the chosen successor after a particular period of time. While having the non-involved children as beneficiaries allows them to share in the proceeds of a company sale occurring in the short term after the freeze is set up, dropping them as beneficiaries later on provides the successor, who is likely to still be involved in the business, with the benefits of increasing the company's sale value.[25]

Equalizing how her children are treated may be accomplished by the owner through other means. Assets of the company which are not integral to the company's business operations such as real estate can be transferred to another corporation owned by those children not chosen as the company's successor. Even if each child is willing and qualified to be a successor, equalization may still be possible if the company's assets and operations can be divided up amongst separate corporations, each owned by a different child, or alternatively divided up amongst separate divisions of the company, each managed by a different child.

If the owner provides for just one child to become the successor of the business, and if the size and diversity of her other holdings are sufficient, she may also be able to equalize the entitlements of all of her children when she dies. Since the preferred shares which she receives when the freeze is created might be transferred to the successor under her will, the will might then contain what is called a "hotchpot" clause, which specifically excludes the successor from additional benefits under the owner's estate.

ARM'S LENGTH TREATMENT

While an estate freeze may be used as part of an owner's plan to transfer ownership of the company to the members of her family, she may decide instead to deal with her chosen successors as if they were unrelated to her and follow the procedures ordinarily followed when shares are transferred to outside parties.

While such procedures may not provide the same tax advantages and generally entail the use of a negotiated purchase and sale agreement and due diligence investigations, such an "arm's length" approach may be appropriate in certain family situations. The owner may feel that a freeze might be difficult to implement because of certain rivalries and distrust among her children, and that her best form of exit might be to simply sell to the child who is the highest bidder.

Furthermore, implementing an estate freeze may not provide her with enough to retire on, or at least not enough when she wants to retire. Her wishes for an early exit may make her too late for a freeze. Even though the redemption value of the preferred shares she would receive on a freeze is usually equal to the fair market value of her common shares in the company, the company may not be in a position to redeem the shares for quite a while. She may wish to obtain something more right away. Treating her children as outside parties may yield a purchase price, payable to her immediately, well in excess of the redemption amount she would eventually receive under a freeze.

FAMILY LAW CONSIDERATIONS

Any decisions which the owner may make regarding the transfer of her company shares to her family members may have to take into account the impact of applicable provincial family law.[26]

In short, if her chosen successor is married, the owner should be aware that her successor's spouse may have certain rights relating to the value of those shares after the transfer in the event that the successor and her spouse separate. Any appreciation in the value of the shares once transferred to the successor may end up being subject to equal division between the spouses.

However, while shares sold to her successor may be subject to such division, shares which she gives to her successor may not. The value of certain types of property is not subject to division between spouses, such as property acquired by gift or inheritance after the date of marriage and income earned from such property.[27]

Upon separation, an equalization payment is ordinarily required to be made by the spouse with the greater value of assets to the spouse with the lesser value. Such a payment attempts to ensure that the value of assets accumulated by the spouses during their marriage is evenly divided between them regardless of which spouse owns the assets when the marriage breaks down. The equalization process allows the spouses to effectively share the increase in the value of their assets during their marriage.

However, the process also creates the possibility of a married successor being required to sell the company shares acquired from the owner in order to satisfy an equalization obligation, thereby frustrating the owner's original intentions for ownership succession.

Transferring the owner's company shares to an existing family trust which includes the successor as a beneficiary will not take the value of the shares outside of the equalization calculation if the successor was already a beneficiary at the time she was married. The successor's beneficial interest in the trust, even a discretionary trust, is still property to be included in the calculation, although determining its value may be a challenge.

Protecting the company shares from an equalization obligation is often accomplished by means of a marriage contract which excludes a spouse's shares from the equalization calculation. While many married couples have marriage contracts, many don't. Those who do cannot always depend upon such contracts being fully enforceable by the courts, since enforceability often depends upon complete financial disclosure being made at the time the contracts were entered into. Furthermore, because the personal circumstances of the spouses may become quite different, variation of a marriage contract after separation is often justified.

For the chosen successor, a marriage contract may not be an option, particularly if the successor is already married or is disinclined to exchange personal financial information. However, the company shares can still be protected in the absence of a marriage contract if they are given directly to the successor after the successor becomes married. Alternatively, they might be transferred to a family trust created after the successor is married, since a beneficial interest in the trust acquired by the successor as a gift after the date of marriage will be excluded from an equalization calculation.

This need for the share transfer to be a gift to the successor after marriage rather than a purchase by the successor after marriage in order to achieve an exclusion from an equalization calculation has implications for the standard estate freeze. Ordinarily the owner's children, as described above, subscribe for newly issued common or "growth" shares of the company for only nominal consideration, often just $1 a share. But their subscription is effectively a purchase, not a gift, taking their common shares outside of the definition of property excluded from the equalization calculation.

Consequently, to avoid potential family law concerns, an estate freeze might be established differently, with the owner exchanging her common shares in the company for new preferred shares as well as new common shares, so that the new common shares might then be given to her children. This gift might also provide that any income thereafter earned from the shares would also be exempt from the property used to determine a married child's equalization payments.

Valuation

In order to carry out some of the actions described in this book, the owners and managers of a private company may have to determine the company's fair market value.

Whether they intend to implement a business succession plan and an estate freeze, or establish an employee stock purchase or option plan, or raise equity from outside investors, or purchase company shares held by a deceased or terminated employee under a shareholder agreement, or honour the appraisal rights[1] of a company shareholder who dissents to a significant change proposed by the company, they should retain a valuator to analyze the company and determine its fair market value using accepted valuation principles and methods. The valuator may also recommend various actions the owners and managers might take to increase the company's value.

While there is no one, absolute definition of the term "fair market value" when used to describe what a particular business might be worth, it is often taken to mean the price that a buyer would reasonably be expected to pay, and a seller would reasonably be expected to accept, if the business were for sale on the open market for a reasonable period of time, and assuming that both buyer and seller had all the pertinent facts and that neither was under any compulsion to act.[2]

Determining the company's fair market value may be mandatory in certain circumstances. If a share transfer to family members is intended, fair market value is often required to be used as the value for tax purposes regardless of any other values selected by the family for the transfer.[3] If a transfer to other shareholders is intended, an existing shareholder agreement may require that the transfer be made at fair market value. Even if a transfer to an outside party is intended, a valuator's determination of fair market value may appear to be necessary to allow the owner to more objectively assess the adequacy of any offers to purchase which he may receive.

And objectivity is often what's needed in the circumstances. While an owner or manager may well have a value in mind for the company which he firmly believes is an accurate reflection of what the company is worth, his assessment is likely based upon the company's past and present, and may be too wrapped up in sentiment, nostalgia and perhaps ego to provide an accurate reflection of the company's fair market value.

A valuator, however, focuses on the company's potential for the future, and attempts to determine the value of the company as if it's no longer in the owner's hands. A valuator assesses the company's transferable value and establishes what the company might be worth to another owner. To accomplish this, the valuator looks at how dependent the business is upon the current owner. A business which is heavily dependent upon the personality or specific skills of the owner is more difficult to sell.

But the valuator looks at a number of other things as well. The extent of customer concentration, the diversity of suppliers, the experience and skills of the management team apart from the owner, the effectiveness of the company's governance and reporting systems, and the severity of any specific industry or company risk factors are all analyzed by the valuator. The company's valuation can be negatively affected by its reliance on just a few customers or a few key employees, or by outstanding litigation or contentious labour relations.

Valuations will vary by the amount of independent review and analysis undertaken, and the amount of backup and verification required. A comprehensive valuation report will look at industry and economic factors and not just at the business itself. Some valuators have expertise in particular industries and types of businesses. A valuator may need to retain other specialists, such as equipment and real estate appraisers or compensation consultants, to assist in valuing certain assets or liabilities.

Yet valuation still comes down to working with numbers, and the valuator will attempt to arrive at some forecast of the company's future revenues and earnings, even though a considerable level of discretion may have to be exercised. The process is more art than science.

Since there is no open market to determine the value of the company's shares as exists for the shares of publicly traded companies, the valuator will normally use hypothetical or notional methods to arrive at a value for the shares while exercising a degree of professional judgment. The valuator's notional methods will be applied using certain assumptions and conditions that may not exist in an open market context. In the event that more than one valuator is retained, different valuators can arrive at widely differing valuations.

Often the financial statements of the company which are provided to the valuator will have to be adjusted by the valuator to more properly reflect the real value of the company to an independent, outside party. Discretionary expenses, non-recurring or extraordinary amounts, non-arm's length transactions and other dealings with related parties may all give rise to a need to adjust the company's earnings in order to arrive at an appropriate valuation.

Arriving at one value that can be used for all purposes is not an easy exercise, particularly in the case of a company which is owned and operated by just one or more family members. Such a company often poses specific valuation challenges, especially when the compensation paid to family members and the company's holding of personal use assets are considered.

NORMALIZING ADJUSTMENTS

The compensation paid to family members who are managing the company, often achieved by a mix of salary, bonuses and dividends, may be well in excess of what would be the market value of the services they provide. The total compensation paid to the owner and his family may be allocated in such a way among various family members that the deduction from the company's income is maximized and the total personal taxes paid are minimized.[4] To arrive at an accurate valuation for the company, it may be necessary to estimate the market salary that would have to be paid when hiring replacements for the owner and any other family members actively involved in the company.

Many expenses of a personal nature may have been charged through the company, including entertainment, travel and vehicle expenses. These expenses, or at least the non-business portion of them, may have to be added back into the income of the company in order to arrive at a proper valuation.

Other expenses may have been charged for services provided by related parties, such as rent or management fees, which may need to be adjusted to reflect more appropriate arm's length values. If the company has been financed by interest-free loans from family members, it may be necessary to assume more conventional financing from outside sources and add in expenses for interest at prevailing rates.

A similar approach may apply to many assets of the company which are of a personal nature, including artwork, furniture, equipment, vehicles and personal residences. If they are not needed for the operations of the company, they may have to be excluded from the company's valuation. Also to be excluded may be other assets which are held for investment rather than operational purposes, including real estate holdings, loans to family members and subsidiaries engaged in unrelated businesses.

These various adjustments for above-market compensation, personal expenses, non-essential assets, and related party services and loans, are sometimes referred to as "normalizing" adjustments. Although normalizing adjustments may be commonplace in the valuation of most businesses in order to eliminate expenses and assets which are not essential to ongoing operations or which entail payments to non-arm's length parties, the need for these adjustments tends to be greater in the context of family businesses in order to give the owners a realistic assessment of what an outside party might be prepared to pay.

VALUATION METHODS

There is no one method which a valuator will always use to determine a company's valuation. Assuming the business is viable and the company is intended to continue as a going concern and not be liquidated, the valuator may choose from a number of commonly used methods, one or more of which may be used in the particular circumstances.

The valuator may deem the "capitalized earnings" approach to be the most appropriate, and proceed to estimate the future after-tax income derived from the company's operations, which is then multiplied by a capitalization rate after being normalized as discussed above to arrive at the fair market value for the company. Or the valuator may use a "discounted cash flow" approach and discount the projected cash flows from operations for a number of years to arrive at the present value of those cash flows which will be received by the company in the future.

Or the valuator may calculate "adjusted book value" by adjusting the net book value of the assets and liabilities of the business to their respective fair market value. This method may be used when the earnings or cash flows of the business are not considered to reflect the fair market values of the underlying net assets.

While earnings based methods include non-cash amounts such as depreciation and amortization, cash flow based methods are concerned with the cash that will be spent or taken in by a company. Because valuators are trying to measure the economic benefit which shareholders will actually receive from a company, which usually comes by way of cash distributions, they may be more inclined to apply cash flow based methods unless future earnings and future cash flows for the company are expected to be roughly similar. Such similarity may occur in companies which are not capital intensive and have little depreciation expense.

Where cash flow based methods are applied to arrive at a company's value, the valuator may focus on the company's "discretionary" cash flows, which are determined net of capital expenditures, working capital requirements, and income taxes,[5] and on the rate of return or discount rate to be used. This rate reflects the time value of money as well as the opportunities and risks relating to the company's business and industry.

Whichever valuation method is used, the resulting valuation may then be supported by using a conventional "rule of thumb" multiple, or by comparing it with valuations for similar companies appearing in publicly available financial information. However, the use of these open market multiples can give rise to a misleading result, since the details of the various transactions which influence the multiples may not be readily apparent. The impact of the particular terms of the transactions on the prices paid, the respective negotiating strengths of the parties involved, and the extent of post-transaction "synergies" available to the buyers, are all relevant and should be known if used to support the company's "unique" valuation.

The valuation ultimately arrived at is more likely to be expressed within a range of values, and not as a specific number. But regardless of the method used in valuation, the valuator may not be able to reflect the synergies or influence on value which a particular buyer may have. This concern is discussed below in connection with the purchase price that may be paid.

If the valuation is being conducted to facilitate a transfer of ownership to the company's other shareholders, the valuator may be required to follow the methodology prescribed in a shareholder agreement if one exists. However, such agreements often lack the degree of guidance which a valuator needs, and sometimes contain inconsistent instructions which the valuator finds difficult to reconcile, particularly in connection with goodwill and the various possible discounts and premiums described below.

GOODWILL

In addition to making the normalizing adjustments, the valuator may wish to take into account certain other factors. The valuator may attempt to attribute some value to the "goodwill" of the business, which is an intangible asset representing the value of the business over and above its "net identifiable assets". The net identifiable assets include the tangible operating assets, which are required to carry on the business, along with its identifiable intangible assets, such as patents, trade names and copyrights, all net of liabilities.

Goodwill is essentially the aggregate of the company's non-identifiable or non-specific intangible assets. It may be a result of the particular product, service, location or other commercial feature of the business, or a result of the personal contacts, reputation, and efforts of key people in the company.

The valuator has to decide how much of the goodwill is commercial and how much is personal, since ordinarily only commercial goodwill is transferable when the company's ownership changes and has value as a result. The goodwill should be enduring, giving rise to earnings from future operations.

Although some goodwill may appear to be attributable to certain individuals while employed by the company, their goodwill may have no value if their roles can be performed by others if they should leave the company. However, in recognizing that some new owners, particularly family members or long-standing employees, are more likely than others to maintain or take advantage of an individual's goodwill, the price to be paid for goodwill may depend to some extent upon who is intended to be the new owner. Individual goodwill may be transferred, or at least protected, through the use of customer introductions, non-competition agreements, and consulting agreements.

VARIOUS DISCOUNTS AND PREMIUMS

In determining the company's fair market value, the valuator may want to consider the impact of any income taxes, professional fees and various additional costs which may be incurred by the company in implementing the changes giving rise to the need for a valuation and reduce the value accordingly. Yet other discounts may be warranted, especially when the company has more than one shareholder.

If the company is controlled by one individual, the valuator may deem a "key person discount" to be appropriate. This discount is the reduction in value resulting from the actual or potential loss of a key person in the business.

If the company has any shareholders holding 50 per cent or less of the company's voting shares, the valuator may attach a "minority discount" to their shares. The application of a minority discount can be complicated and involve a number of factors. It is intended to reflect a minority share-holder's inability to influence key company decisions and the value of his investment, including the payment of dividends and the approval of share transfers, often owing to the absence of a board seat.

The size of a particular minority holding can become important when viewed in relation to other holdings. A shareholder with a 20 per cent interest in a company with only one other shareholder is in a different position from a shareholder with 20 per cent of a company with four other shareholders each holding 20 per cent.

A minority discount can also be affected by the existence of a share-holder agreement affording buy-sell rights or a board seat to a minority shareholder, or by the existence of a number of related shareholders who are likely to act or vote the same way.

However, the size of a particular minority holding can be significant enough to result not in a discount but in a premium. Since a vote of two-thirds of all shareholders can be required for fundamental corporate changes,[6] a minority shareholder holding more than a third of the votes that may be cast at a shareholder meeting may enjoy a premium for "blocking power."

A premium often reflected in valuations is a "control premium", which is afforded to the shareholder who is able to exercise control over the company. Control is normally achieved by holding shares with the right to cast a majority of votes at a shareholder meeting, and flows from the right to elect a majority on the company's board of directors. A control premium is the additional amount an investor would pay over the pro-rated value of a non-controlling interest to achieve a controlling interest.

In the event that the company has more than one class of shares, the fair market value determined by the valuator for the entire company using one or more of the valuation methods described above must then be allocated amongst the various share classes. This value allocation is often based upon the terms and conditions of each particular class. For example, if there is outstanding a class of preference shares which has a priority over the other classes to be paid out first upon the liquidation of the company, the allocation of the company's fair market value should take into account this priority in ranking.

LIMITATIONS OF VALUATION METHODS

Despite the importance of obtaining a valuation as described above, the owners and managers of the company should nevertheless be aware that the valuation obtained may be quite different from the price that may be paid for the company in an open market transaction. Whatever fair market value may be determined by the valuator as the company's value, the price which the company or a current shareholder may receive from a prospective buyer of the company's shares may well be higher or lower.

In accordance with the above definition of fair market value, the notional valuation methods applied by the valuator generally attempt to arrive at the highest cash price available in an open and unrestricted market between informed and prudent parties who are acting at arm's length under no compulsion to act.

Yet these assumptions and conditions seldom exist in the open market context.

For example, having an open market from which no potential buyer is excluded and in which all potential buyers have the motivation and resources to act rarely occurs in an actual business sale. Having a market free from any statutory or contractual restrictions on a sale seldom applies to private companies which are usually subject to share transfer constraints in their articles of incorporation or shareholder agreements.

Assuming that the parties are well informed about the company and have all the facts that are relevant to determining its value is questionable, regardless of the amount of due diligence which has been undertaken. In an open market transaction, a buyer may not be fully informed about the company's financial position, business prospects or competitive pressures. Even assuming that the buyer is acting prudently can be a flawed approach, since due diligence investigations are often prioritized and either shortened or sacrificed in practice because of time and cost considerations.

An assumption that the parties are under no compulsion to undertake a transaction often fails to reflect reality. In open market deals, sellers may be forced to sell because their business is failing, or because their health is failing, or both.

Two other assumptions inherent in the definition of fair market value deserve particular attention.

First is the assumption that the value will be the highest price, since without exposing the business for sale, the highest price can't be ascertained with any certainty due to the possible existence of special interest buyers who are willing to pay for expected post-acquisition benefits or synergies. Without open market negotiations, it is difficult to quantify with any accuracy how much a buyer would be prepared to pay for such synergies.

Second is the assumption that the value will be expressed in terms of cash. Transactions in the open market are frequently completed with just a portion of the purchase price being paid in cash, with the balance payable in shares of the buyer, under a promissory note, or under an "earn-out" formula requiring the company's earnings to exceed a prescribed threshold.

The questionable validly of each of these two assumptions in the open market context is discussed in greater detail below.

INFLUENCE OF BUYER SYNERGIES ON PRICE

While the definition of fair market value mentioned above means the highest price generally available in a marketplace consisting of all potential buyers, there may be a special buyer who will enjoy certain synergistic or strategic benefits in buying the company which are unavailable to other potential buyers. Such benefits may arise, for example, if the buyer is a direct competitor of the company, or is perhaps an existing company customer.

These synergies essentially represent an incremental value over the company's "intrinsic" value consisting of its net identifiable assets and goodwill as described above. This incremental value is unique to each potential buyer, and may be based on additional revenues, cost savings or risk reduction that the buyer expects will result from combining the purchased business with its own existing operations.

The buyer will determine the amount of this incremental value representing its expected synergies and add some or all of it to the company's intrinsic value to arrive at a possible purchase price for the company.

However, the buyer will still have to adjust this incremental value by the costs to be incurred in realizing such synergies. These costs can include such things as severance payments, relocation expenses and restructuring costs. For those synergies expected in the form of incremental revenues, the buyer should consider the additional costs necessary to generate those revenues, such as additional personnel, new equipment and higher levels of required working capital. These expenditures are ordinarily made "up front" soon after the transaction has been completed in the hope that the synergies will materialize as planned.

In deciding how much of the expected synergies it wants to pay for, the buyer can take into account any potential shortfalls in the company's cash flows which may occur after the deal closes and thereby reduce the purchase price being offered. By fully paying for the expected synergies, the buyer may later feel he paid too much if the post-acquisition benefits fail to materialize.

In other words, even though a buyer may be prepared to pay extra for these benefits, how much extra is very difficult for the valuator to determine when applying standard valuation methods and is usually settled only during the purchase negotiations between the parties themselves.

INFLUENCE OF PAYMENT TERMS ON PRICE

In addition to the impact of buyer synergies on the determination of a purchase price for the company, the terms of payment represent another significant factor to be considered when explaining the likely difference between price and value.

While the above valuation methods applied by a valuator provide a possible "cash equivalent" price for the company, not all deals are completed in cash on closing. Some exceptions have already been suggested. Payment may be made by way of shares of the buyer, or under the seller's "take-back financing" which permits the buyer to pay a number of purchase price installments over time pursuant to a promissory note. Payment may also be made in accordance with an earn-out formula which requires the buyer to pay an additional amount only if the company exceeds certain financial targets after closing.

Furthermore, many buyers want to retain a portion of the purchase price as a "holdback" for a period of time after closing against which the buyer can offset any liabilities which were undisclosed at closing but which appear later on.

Each of these alternative forms of consideration which may be used to complete a transaction instead of paying the entire purchase price in cash on closing represent certain risks as well as rewards.

For the seller, the buyer's shares may drop in value after closing, or the buyer may default in paying some of the purchase price installments or the holdback to the seller when agreed upon, or the earnings of the company may plummet once the buyer takes over, thereby removing any chance of earn-out payments. The seller may require the purchase price to be increased to offset these risks.

The buyer, on the other hand, may regard these alternative forms of consideration as providing some extra protection to offset the overall risks of buying the company and as a way to avoid paying too much. After all, should the company's cash flows fail to generate a rate of return which exceeds the buyer's cost of capital when measured against the purchase price, the acquisition is likely to be regarded as a bad deal. Lower revenues or higher operating and financing costs than expected, or the inability to realize the synergies anticipated, can easily cause this to happen.

OTHER INFLUENCES ON PRICE

To understand the gap between the company's valuation and the price to be paid to acquire the company, the seller has to understand more than just the buyer's potential synergies and the various forms of consideration.

The seller will also have to keep in mind that a negotiated purchase price is generally influenced by a number of additional factors which are not reflected in the notional methods used by the valuator. These include the competitive bidding environment, the relative importance of the transaction to the parties and the availability of alternatives to it, the sense of urgency felt by the parties to complete the transaction, and their respective negotiating power and ability.

And, significantly, the other terms of the deal.

For example, various representations, warranties and indemnities from a seller, or non-competition agreements and employment contracts with the seller and the company's senior officers, can allocate some of the risk, as well as the rewards, of the transaction between the buyer and seller, and can greatly influence the amount of the purchase price to be paid.

The price may also be affected by whether the transaction is structured as the sale of assets or the sale of shares. Buyers usually prefer to buy the assets of a company in order to avoid hidden liabilities and for certain tax advantages, whereas sellers usually prefer to sell shares for their own tax benefit. However, the buyer may benefit from a purchase of shares if the seller is prepared to reduce the purchase price while allowing holdbacks or other protection mechanisms that reduce the risk of the buyer assuming hidden liabilities.

The particular type of business operated by the company can create specific valuation challenges and increase the likelihood that the eventual purchase price negotiated in the open market context will vary considerably from the valuation given.

For example, while many of the foregoing factors which influence price are generally applicable to all kinds of businesses, franchises, along with dealerships and distributorships, present certain difficult valuation problems. Because trademarks are usually involved, the scope of the trademark license granted to a franchisee and whether it is exclusive or non-exclusive must be considered. Furthermore, the risk of non-renewal of the franchise agreement, the restrictions on franchise transfer, and the franchisor's rights of approval of proposed transferees must be taken into account in determining value.

What can be more problematic in the valuation of a franchise is the impact of the franchisor's right of first refusal, described in the *Acquiring a Franchise* chapter, which can be a serious impediment to marketability. When a franchisor holds such a right, a potential buyer of the franchise from the franchisee will be concerned that the franchisor is always a potential bidder, and the franchisor is likely to know more about the available franchise than any other outside party. As a result, an outside buyer might have to spend a lot of time and money in order to come close to matching the franchisor's knowledge of the available franchise. Without that knowledge, the outside buyer may offer either too little and risk losing out to the franchisor, or too much and risk making a bad deal in acquiring the franchise.

In light of all of the many factors outlined above which can affect the price ultimately payable by a buyer for the company in the open market, the valuation initially obtained may serve only as a rough guide for the company or current shareholders in predicting how much will be eventually received for their shares should any of the changes necessitating the valuation take place.

Debt Financing and Commitment Letters

Once the company moves past its start-up stage, the owners and managers may need to look beyond their friends and family as sources of additional company financing. While some of the required financing from outside parties may come by way of equity investment, as will be discussed in a later chapter, other outside financing may be provided by way of loans from banks and other financial institutions.

Successfully tapping into these external debt financing sources often depends upon whether the company is actually ready and qualified to receive such financing. If the company has more pressing needs than money, such as better products or services, stronger management, or more customers, it will probably not receive the outside funds it wants. It may be faced with the prospect of requesting additional loans from its current shareholders for a while longer.

As mentioned in the *Introduction* chapter, the different stages of a company in its lifecycle will govern the different types of financing it will likely receive and the different funding sources it should approach. While the company may have passed through its start-up stage, it may still be unable to borrow from any outside parties, even though government sponsored agencies, and possibly wealthy individuals or "angel" investors, may provide sufficient equity financing in the meantime.

It may not be until the revenues and customers of the business have increased enough during the company's "growth" stage that the chartered banks, mezzanine lenders, leasing companies and other financial institutions will be prepared to provide debt financing to the company. These institutions usually look for a dependable revenue stream which will permit debt repayments, along with tangible liquid assets to secure the debt obligation, both of which are ordinarily lacking in early stage companies.

However, once involved with the company, these institutions may well stay involved with the company and continue to provide various financial services to it right through the "established" stage of its lifecycle when its business has matured and has earned a place in the market with loyal customers. These institutions will also be there during its "expansion" stage, should the business experience a new period of growth by expanding into new markets and distribution channels, or by adding new products or services.

Whichever stage the company may be in when a bank or other financial institution is inclined to provide it with a loan or credit facility, the discussions between them will be about not only the maximum principal amount to be borrowed, applicable interest rate and repayment terms, but also the need for any guarantees and other forms of security to be obtained and the extent of any restrictions on the company's business to be imposed.

COMMITMENT LETTERS GENERALLY

When these discussions get to a point at which the company, as a borrower, and the bank or other financial institution, as a lender, have agreed upon the principal business terms of their deal and wish to record those terms in written form, a preliminary transaction document usually described as a commitment letter will be prepared.

Often a borrower wants a commitment letter in order to show to others that it has obtained financing for a specific project or transaction, as might be the case when the borrower wishes to buy a business and the seller is skeptical that the borrower has sufficient funds available for payment of the purchase price.

Commitment letters come in various forms and can serve various purposes. While some are quite brief and simply provide a summary of the basic deal terms, others are much longer and set out many additional provisions which the parties have agreed upon. Regardless of their length, they are usually intended to be contractually binding upon the lender, though subject to many conditions which must be satisfied by the borrower before becoming legally enforceable. They are, after all, intended to evidence a "commitment" on the part of lender to provide credit.

In contrast to a legally binding commitment letter, a term sheet may be issued by a lender to a borrower which may contain many of the same provisions as a commitment letter but which is not legally binding. While term sheets can be quiet lengthy, they are often set out in point form or with "bullets", possibly containing more numbers than words, and are intended to be replaced by a more comprehensive loan or credit agreement. They generally stipulate the amount and purpose of the loan, interest rate options, and fees, and state that they are subject not only to satisfactory due diligence and documentation but also to approval from the lender's internal credit committee.

Although this chapter describes the provisions generally found in a lender's commitment letter, such provisions are often found in a lender's term sheet, and therefore most of the comments made in this chapter will apply equally to term sheets. However, it should be kept in mind that term sheets, unlike commitment letters, are not legally binding and are always intended to be followed by a comprehensive loan or credit agreement.

The form which a commitment letter follows will generally depend upon the nature of the loan being granted, and whether the commitment letter will eventually be superseded by a more definitive agreement. Unlike letters of intent for the purchase of a business which are usually intended to be superseded by a comprehensive purchase and sale agreement, a commitment letter is not always intended to be superseded by a comprehensive loan or credit agreement.

For those loans which are fully secured and for relatively smaller amounts, the lender may avoid the expense of preparing a comprehensive loan or credit agreement, an expense which is often absorbed by the borrower, and instead rely upon the provisions of the security documents.

For those loans which are unsecured and involve relatively larger amounts, however, the lender will likely be relying upon numerous representations, warranties and covenants of the borrower, and the commitment letter, though describing the basic terms of the deal, will refer to a separate, comprehensive loan or credit agreement to be executed by the parties before any funds are advanced.

Although a credit agreement ordinarily sets out the terms applicable to more than one type of loan or credit facility, this chapter and the next chapter in this book dealing with comprehensive credit and loan agreements will refer to such agreements as simply loan agreements.

This chapter will look at those commitment letters which serve as the full loan agreement between the parties as well as those commitment letters which serve as a preliminary document intended to be replaced by a comprehensive loan agreement.

When negotiating the principal business terms of the financing arrangement, the lender is likely aware of the borrower's financial resources and creditworthiness, especially if there has been a prior lending relationship, but may not be all that aware of the borrower's other existing obligations or recent changes to its business. While the lender will usually recognize the borrower's ability to shop around for alternative sources of financing, it will also usually recognize the need for further due diligence investigations of the borrower before the commitment letter may be issued.

Most commitment letters state that the borrower has been approved for a certain credit facility, while specifying the amount, type and purpose of the loan, the applicable interest rate and fees being charged, the representations, warranties and covenants being given, the security being taken, and the circumstances constituting events of default.

From the lender's perspective, it is important that the commitment letter includes all the terms and conditions which the lender wishes to rely upon if the letter is not to be replaced by a more comprehensive loan agreement. Since the lender will not be able to require that the mortgage or other security documents to be delivered upon closing contain terms which conflict with the commitment letter, the letter needs to be carefully prepared.

Basically stated, in the absence of a comprehensive loan agreement, the commitment letter is the operative contract between the borrower and lender entitling the borrower to expect that the lender will advance the monies agreed upon if the prescribed conditions are met. Only when the commitment letter reserves a discretion to the lender not to advance, whether on a unlimited basis or only in certain circumstances, can the lender be excused from its obligation to advance funds.

The rest of this chapter will look at some of the terms and conditions which a lender ordinarily inserts into a commitment letter. However, these terms and conditions will also be examined in greater detail in the *Credit and Loan Agreements* chapter.

CREDIT FACILITIES

Although there are many kinds of loan and credit facilities, which kind will be made available to a borrower by a lender will normally depend upon the borrower's purpose for the funds requested. Whether or not the borrower needs the funds to satisfy working capital requirements, to purchase specific assets or a business, or to refinance other existing obligations, will determine which facility is appropriate.

The two more common facilities offered are the operating or revolving facility, and the non-revolving term facility.

The operating facility is generally used to finance the borrower's on-going business operations, and funds are provided to the borrower up to a specified amount for a specified term, or until the lender demands repayment of the funds advanced. Often an operating facility will be provided on a yearly basis, to be renewed for the following year if the borrower's financial position has not deteriorated significantly.

During the term of the operating facility, only interest on the amounts advanced must be paid by the borrower, while any repayments of the principal by the borrower are generally optional. The borrower is entitled to obtain funds at any time, and usually repays and reborrows funds from time to time throughout the term.

The main security for an operating facility is ordinarily the borrower's more liquid and current assets, such as its accounts receivable and inventory, over which the lender will take a first charge. The amount that the borrower may borrow is typically calculated as a prescribed percentage of the value of the receivables and inventory, perhaps 85 per cent and 50 per cent respectively, which are usually described as the borrowing base. A detailed definition of the borrowing base citing its inclusions and many exclusions, as more fully described in the *Credit and Loan Agreements* chapter, may be contained in the commitment letter.

The non-revolving term facility, on the other hand, generally provides for the lender to advance funds to the borrower in specified amounts at specified times during a specified period. The funds are normally used by the borrower to finance purchases of real property, equipment or another business, or to refinance existing obligations. The lender will ordinarily obtain a first charge over all of the borrower's assets, including any assets purchased, as security for the advances made.

Under a term facility, the amounts advanced are due at the end of the term, known as the maturity date, although borrowers often make payments of principal throughout the term in addition to regular required interest payments. However, the borrower may be required to make principal payments in certain circumstances or upon certain events, perhaps when it has excess cash flow, or when it receives insurance proceeds or proceeds from the sale of a substantial asset.

Instead of being offered either a revolving or term facility, the borrower might simply be offered a swingline or overdraft facility with respect to its bank account in order to cover its day-to-day cash management requirements.

AVAILMENT

Many commitment letters provide for more than one type of availment or method for obtaining funds under a particular credit facility so that the borrower has some choice in getting the lowest cost funds at the time of borrowing. Which method is selected to draw funds will depend upon the interest option the borrower wants.

For example, should the borrower want a floating interest rate to apply to its advances, the commitment letter may provide for advances in Canadian dollars, U.S. dollars, or such other currencies as the borrower and lender may agree upon, with the applicable interest rate being at the Canadian prime rate, U.S. base rate, or some other published rate. An extra margin or specific percentage may be added to the applicable interest rate reflecting the creditworthiness of the borrower, with a higher margin being assigned to borrowers with lower creditworthiness.

The borrower may also be given the option to obtain funds at the London Interbank Offered Rate, or LIBOR, plus an agreed upon margin. This interest rate is the average of the rates which leading banks in the London interbank market quote for deposits in U.S. dollars and other major currencies for fixed short terms, usually up to one year. To make a LIBOR advance, the lender obtains deposits in the London market for the specified currency in the amount and for the number of days requested by the borrower, at a rate which is then charged plus the applicable margin to the borrower.

Funds may also be advanced to the borrower by means of bankers' acceptances, which are negotiable instruments issued by the borrower to pay a fixed amount on a certain date, and are "accepted" or guaranteed by the lender and either held by the lender until maturity or sold in the marketplace. The borrower ordinarily receives the face amount of the instrument, discounted by a certain percentage and less a "stamping" fee, although remains obligated to reimburse the lender for the face amount at maturity. The discount rate is equal to the rate which the lender would use for its own instruments for a similar amount and term, and which is generally lower than the interest rate ordinarily payable by the borrower. As with LIBOR advances, bankers' acceptances are usually for short, fixed terms which cannot be repaid prior to the end of the term.

A commitment letter may also permit the borrower to obtain credit through the issuance by the lender of a letter of credit in favour of a beneficiary, such as the seller of goods being purchased by the borrower. Under a letter of credit, the lender promises to pay the beneficiary a fixed sum of money upon the fulfillment of certain conditions, often the presentation of specific documents in the case of documentary credits. The borrower is thereby able to receive the purchased goods on deferred payment terms, reimbursing the bank for any amounts drawn by the beneficiary under the letter of credit, together with applicable fees.

REPRESENTATIONS AND WARRANTIES

Where a comprehensive loan agreement will be following the commitment letter, it would be unusual for the commitment letter to set out in any detail the representations and warranties which the lender is expecting the borrower to give unless the nature of the borrower's business requires that certain representations be identified early on to determine if the borrower will be unable to give them when the loan agreement is presented or when the deal is about to close. This may relate to a particular risk which the lender has identified at the outset.

However, if the commitment letter is to serve as the full loan agreement, it should contain all of the representations and warranties which the lender wishes to be given by the borrower since it may be too late to ask for them later once the commitment letter is signed.

The lender normally requests that the representations and warranties be unqualified so that it retains the discretion to terminate the deal and either refuse to advance the funds, or later demand repayment if funds are advanced. The representations and warranties imposed by the lender are continuing obligations of the borrower which must be true not only on the day when the commitment letter is signed but also on every day thereafter, giving the lender the ongoing right to enforce them.

The borrower, on the other hand, may wish to amend the proposed representations and warranties so that they exclude various actions or events which the borrower believes are unlikely to have the potential to adversely affect the borrower's financial position or its ability to perform its financial obligations. Even if the lender refuses to allow such exclusions, the borrower may still want to qualify the representations and warranties, either by restricting them to the actual knowledge of certain individuals representing the borrower, or by limiting them to only material matters, so that they may be given at all.

The extent of the representations and warranties contained in the commitment letter will depend upon the terms of the loan, the amounts involved, and any risks which may be specific to the borrower or the borrower's particular industry at the time.

Most commitment letters which serve as a full loan agreement will include representations and warranties confirming that the borrower is validly constituted and subsisting under applicable law, that it has the power to enter into the loan transaction and give security, and that the transaction will not put it in breach of any other contractual obligations. This last representation may be difficult to give if there are agreements in place between the borrower and another creditor which contain a "negative pledge" preventing the borrower from pledging its assets in favour of other parties, which would include the lender.

Other representations and warranties confirm that the borrower's financial statements are correct and complete, that it has complied with all applicable laws and other contractual commitments, that there are no proceedings or investigations against it, and that its property is free and clear of any charges or encumbrances unless specifically permitted, as described below. If the transaction relates to real property, there may be representations and warranties concerning applicable zoning or the existence of certain easements, along with the property's environmental condition.

COVENANTS

The covenants to be observed by the borrower, both positive and negative, will generally be included in a commitment letter, whether it serves as the full loan agreement or not. The positive covenants represent various actions or conditions which the borrower must carry out or maintain, and the negative covenants represent those actions and conditions which the borrower must retrain from taking or avoid.

The covenants are important to the lender, because by monitoring the borrower's compliance with the covenants, the lender is able to continually assess the risks associated with the loan. A borrower's failure to fully comply with the covenants provides an early warning that the borrower may fail to repay the loan when required, and may constitute an event of default permitting the lender to demand repayment of all amounts owed.

As with the representations and warranties discussed above, the extent of the covenants contained in the commitment letter will depend upon the nature of the loan, the amounts involved, and the other terms and conditions.

Commonly found covenants prescribe the financial ratios that must be maintained by the borrower, such as the borrower's debt to equity ratio, current ratio or interest coverage ratio. Defining these ratios is not always straightforward, as discussed in more detail in the next chapter. Other financial covenants are likely to impose upon the borrower a requirement to maintain a minimum amount of working capital and shareholder equity, and place restrictions upon the amount of dividends that may be declared or capital returned in any year, or limit the amount of annual capital expenditures.

Still other financial covenants may prohibit the borrower from incurring additional indebtedness, giving guarantees, or transferring or pledging its assets as security other than in the normal course of business, or paying compensation to its directors and officers in excess of a specified limit, or leasing equipment for more than a stipulated annual rent, or lending to or investing in other businesses more than a set amount, or amalgamating or merging with any other business.

The financial covenants are usually based upon financial projections provided by the borrower to the lender in support of the credit approval process. By monitoring the borrower's ongoing compliance with these covenants, the lender is effectively measuring the borrower's actual financial performance against the projections. It is therefore important for the borrower when negotiating these covenants for inclusion in the commitment letter, or in a full loan agreement, that the covenants allow for some variance from the projections, even by 20 per cent or more, in order to avoid their breach and a possible default.

While many borrowers may be in "technical" breach of one or more of these financial covenants at some time throughout the term of their loans, the lenders in practice seldom treat such breach as a default sufficient to justify the enforcement of the lenders' remedies. A lender will ordinarily weigh the extent and duration of the breach, the steps taken by the borrower to cure the breach, and the change, if any, of the risk associated with the loan.

There are many other kinds of covenants which may be imposed in a commitment letter, although their breach, as with the breach of the financial covenants, doesn't necessarily amount to a default and lead to the lender's enforcement of its default rights as discussed below.

For example, the commitment letter may contain covenants on the part of the borrower to keep its assets and business fully insured, to provide the lender with current audited financial statements and up-to-date reports on its accounts receivable and inventory, to give the lender access to inspect the borrower's premises, to comply with all environmental and other laws, and to advise the lender of any material litigation against the borrower or of any change in the borrower's business.

The borrower should avoid giving covenants over matters which are beyond its control, such as a requirement of the borrower to obtain the consent of a third party for the assignment of a particular contract or licence. Instead, such matters should be treated as conditions precedent to the advance of the loan as described below.

PERMITTED ENCUMBRANCES

Since the lender attempts to ensure that it has adequate security for the loan and other credit facilities being provided, the commitment letter ordinarily places restrictions on how the borrower may use its assets so long as the facilities remain in place. The covenants, along with the representations and warranties, contained in the commitment letter often require the borrower to keep its assets free and clear of the claims of parties other than the lender.

Even the conditions which must be satisfied before the lender will advance funds may be used for the same purpose. For example, it may be a condition that the borrower must obtain the discharge of all security interests over the borrower's assets which would rank ahead of the lender's security, or at least obtain an agreement with the other lenders holding such security interests to postpone and subordinate their interests to those of the lender.

The borrower, however, needs to be able to continue to operate its business without having to obtain the lender's consent just to carry out everyday transactions involving its assets. It will attempt to have the lender's restrictions loosened to some extent, perhaps by having certain thresholds prescribed which involve only material changes or additional costs, in order to give it as much flexibility to deal with its own assets as possible.

To find the appropriate balance between the concern of the lender that its security over the borrower's assets is not diminished, and the desire of the borrower for the freedom to manage its own assets, the parties may arrive at a list of "permitted encumbrances" which tries to achieve such balance. The list is often attached as a schedule to the commitment letter. References to the permitted encumbrances ordinarily appear as exceptions to the covenants, representations and warranties, and closing conditions.

There are wide variations among the lists of permitted encumbrances found in practice, depending upon the complexity and size of the borrower's business and its relative negotiating power with the lender. Most lists, however, exempt liens or security in favour of government authorities, or any minor title defects or security interests which do not impair the value or use of the borrower's assets.

Other lists may permit specific security interests over a specific asset or category of assets, perhaps including assets which the lender does not regard as its main form of security for the loan transaction. This may occur with respect to particular pieces of equipment or certain kinds of inventory. Some lists even permit a subsequent security interest in favour of a third party which secures a purchase money obligation and which charges only the asset then being acquired by the borrower but no other asset.

EVENTS OF DEFAULT

Those events which constitute a borrower's default and which permit a lender to act immediately to realize upon its security often comprise the most contentious issue between the borrower and lender when negotiating the commitment letter.

At the very least, the borrower will argue for lengthy grace periods to enable it to cure any breach before such breach is deemed to be an event of default. It will also argue that any breach must materially and adversely affect the lender before being an event of default. However, given the implications an event of default has for both parties, the commitment letter requiring a beach to be material before it can be a default should attempt to define materiality as objectively as possible, perhaps by using a specific dollar amount threshold.

If the lender is to provide more than one type of loan or credit facility, the borrower will normally argue for a provision in the commitment letter which states that each facility is separate and not tied to each other, so that a default under one should not be deemed to be a default under the others. The lender, however, is likely to take the view that when a default occurs under one facility, it will simply be a matter of time before the borrower defaults under the other facilities. The lender will probably insist upon the inclusion of such a "cross-default" provision in the commitment letter so that it can take what are effectively pre-emptive steps to reduce its risk and realize upon its security.

The events of default which the parties agree upon are often set out in a separate schedule which is attached to the commitment letter. Such a schedule ordinarily provides for default when the borrower fails to observe any covenant, including the obligation to pay any amounts owed, or when any of its representations and warranties are untrue, or a material change occurs in its financial condition, or any government licence or permit required for the operation of its business is revoked.

The schedule will also generally define as an event of default the bankruptcy, insolvency or winding-up of the borrower, any sale of a substantial portion of its assets, or the cessation of its business operations. A decision by the lender made in good faith that the borrower is not able to perform its covenants or that the security given is in jeopardy may also be included in the schedule as an event of default.

SECURITY

Since the lender's preparedness to provide credit facilities to a borrower and advance funds often depends upon the adequacy of the collateral pledged as security, some commitment letters describe in considerable detail the real and personal property to be given as security, if security is to be given at all. Others simply indicate the name of the security documents to be provided by the borrower on closing, requiring that such documents be in a form satisfactory to the lender and its counsel. This approach is usually taken when the lender is acquiring a security interest in all, or almost all, of the assets used by the borrower in carrying on its business.

Under either approach, the actual security documents to be provided by the borrower must contain a sufficient description of the collateral enabling it to be identified. An inadequate collateral description can result in the rights of the lender being subordinated to the rights of other creditors having claims to the collateral, including a trustee in bankruptcy, and being deprived of its rights to enforce its security upon an event of a default.

In addition to its right to permit security being given over certain assets as described above under *Permitted Encumbrances*, the borrower may also be given the right to deal with certain assets in the normal course even though they have been pledged as security to the lender. For example, the borrower may be able to deal on its own account with rent proceeds it receives from a tenant up to an event of default, even though the borrower has previously assigned such rents to the lender as security.

The commitment letter may require just one form of security document or many forms. It may stipulate that only a general security agreement or a real property mortgage needs to be executed and registered on or before closing. Or it may also require that a debenture, general assignment of accounts receivable, hypothecation of shares, assignment of rents and/ or leases, assignment of specific intellectual property, assignment of specific promissory notes, guarantees, and assignment of insurance policies be provided on closing as well. Where the lender is a chartered bank, an assignment of the borrower's inventory in favour of the lender under section 427 of the federal *Bank Act* may also be required.[1]

POSTPONEMENT

As mentioned above, the borrower may already be indebted to other creditors who have taken security over some or all of the borrower's assets, and the commitment letter may provide as a condition to closing that such security be discharged before funds may be advanced to the borrower under the commitment letter or the comprehensive loan agreement which supersedes it.   Requiring a discharge of such prior security, however, ordinarily requires repayment of the outstanding debt relating to that security. Such repayment may not be feasible or desirable from the borrower's perspective, especially if the outstanding debt is owed to shareholders or other parties related to the borrower, not to other financial institutions.

Furthermore, the existence of this outstanding debt and prior security may not even be discovered by the lender until after the commitment letter has been signed and the lender is completing its due diligence investigations, including its searches for registered security interests, in connection with the borrower. For this reason, the commitment letter normally includes a general requirement that the other creditors must postpone their rights to payment and subordinate their security in favour of the lender before new funds will be advanced by the lender.

This provision, in unqualified form, can threaten the closing of the deal, especially if the lender is unprepared to allow payments to continue to flow from the borrower to the existing creditors as in the past. The borrower should therefore attempt to address this issue at the outset by having the commitment letter specify which particular payments or distributions may continue to be made after the deal closes, in order to prevent a major shareholder or previous lender from objecting.

As a compromise, the commitment letter may state that such postponement is only required upon an event of default. Yet even with these qualifications to the requirement to obtain postponement from the other creditors, obtaining their postponement, often by way of a written priorities or inter-creditor agreement, can take considerable time to negotiate and complete, especially if the other lenders are large financial institutions, and thereby threaten the closing of the loan transaction.

CONDITIONS PRECEDENT

The conditions which must be satisfied by the borrower before the initial advance of funds can take place are generally set out in the commitment letter, though expanded upon in the loan agreement if a loan agreement is to be provided later.

Some of the basic conditions ordinarily include the absence of any event of default, the accuracy and completeness of all representations and warranties, the adequacy of insurance coverage, the receipt of a satisfactory environmental report, the delivery and registration of all requested security documents and discharges, the receipt of all requested postponements and other inter-creditor documents, the payment of all necessary fees, and the delivery of all documents needed to prove due authorization for the borrower to proceed with the credit transaction.

There is likely to be a similar, though shorter, list of conditions which must be satisfied by the borrower for each and every subsequent advance which may take place throughout the duration of the loan arrangements. Each representation and warranty made with respect to the initial advance must normally be repeated for subsequent advances.

ACQUISITION FINANCING

The foregoing provisions generally found in a commitment letter may be supplemented or varied somewhat when funds are required by the borrower to finance the purchase of a business. While many acquisitions are financed by shareholder loans, sale and leaseback transactions, subordinated or "mezzanine" debt or, most commonly, vendor "take-back" debt, the use of "senior" debt provided by a financial institution to the purchaser is often required to fill the financing gap created by these other financing sources.

The credit facilities provided for a business acquisition often include a term loan, which finances part of the purchase price, and a revolving loan, designed to provide ongoing working capital for the acquired business. The loans may be added on to an existing facility with an exiting borrower or may be provided to a new borrower, often a special purpose acquisition vehicle or "newco".

If the loans are being made to an existing borrower, the commitment letter will typically provide for an additional term loan, along with an increase in the existing operating line to cover the working capital requirements of both the existing and acquired businesses. The loan documents which are currently in place will probably continue to apply though they will need to be amended to reflect the additional facilities.

If the loans are being made to a newco, however, all new loan documentation will need to be negotiated and executed by the parties, and the structuring of the loan transaction will become more complicated and likely adopt the leveraged buy-out model. This model ordinarily requires the acquisition debt to reside with the entity generating the earnings from the acquired business so that the interest paid on the debt can be deducted from the earnings for tax purposes.

Consequently, if the business is to be acquired through the purchase of assets, the commitment letter will provide for newco to borrow the necessary funds and acquire the assets. If the business is to be acquired through the purchase of shares of the company operating the business, referred to as the "target" company, the commitment letter will provide for newco to borrow the funds and acquire the shares of the target company, and then amalgamate with the target company. The required amalgamation will then combine the acquisition debt taken on by newco with the assets and business of the target company in one continuing, amalgamated company.

Where the acquisition debt is being added on to an existing facility with an existing borrower to finance an asset purchase, the commitment letter will require the assets to be acquired by the borrower and thereby covered by the lender's security which is already in place. Although the lender will conduct its own searches for any liens on those assets, there will be little need, if any, to amend the existing security documents.

If the acquisition debt is being added to an existing facility to finance a share purchase, or is being made to a newco to purchase assets, the commitment letter will require that a new package of security documents be obtained from newco and the target company. The lender will then ordinarily request general security over all of newco's assets and, following amalgamation with the target, over all of the amalgamated company's assets. Since the lender usually attempts to register its security against the target company as well as against newco before the closing of the purchase transaction and the advance of funds, the seller often requests an undertaking from the lender to discharge such security if the financing or purchase transactions fail to close.

The lender may also request in the commitment letter further security by way of an assignment of the borrower's indemnity claims under the purchase agreement. Should the borrower default under its acquisition loan arrangements, the lender would then be in a position to step into the borrower's shoes and enforce the borrower's rights to indemnification from the seller, provided the purchase agreement does not prohibit its assignment.

Unlike a loan designed to finance a borrower's ongoing business operations which tends to focus on the loan agreement and applicable security documents, a loan to finance the purchase of a business needs to focus on the purchase agreement between the buyer and seller as well. The loan agreement should reflect, or at least not conflict with, the terms of the purchase agreement, and the basic components of the debt financing structure should be addressed when the purchase agreement is being negotiated.

This seldom occurs in practice, however, because the buyer invariably settles the terms of the purchase first, particularly the purchase price, before incurring the expense of negotiating and documenting the financing arrangements. Consequently the financing needed, or at least the senior debt needed, will be recorded only in a commitment letter or term sheet when the purchase agreement is signed by the buyer and seller. The loan agreement and security agreements will be negotiated between the signing of the purchase agreement and the closing of the purchase transaction.

The conditions precedent identified in a commitment letter and later reflected in the loan agreement for acquisition financing will contain not only the more standard conditions set out immediately above but also additional conditions relating to the purchase transaction and the business being acquired. For example, satisfaction of the final terms and conditions of the purchase agreement, receipt of all necessary consents from third parties to the purchase, the absence of any litigation or any material adverse changes involving the acquired business, and the satisfaction of any outstanding due diligence items, may all be added to the commitment letter as conditions precedent to funds being advanced.

Such a combined list of conditions makes the conditions in favour of the lender under the loan transaction broader than the conditions in favour of the borrower under the purchase transaction, and places a risk upon the borrower for the difference. For example, while the lender's commitment to fund is often conditional upon satisfactory due diligence results, the purchase agreement is unlikely to have a similar due diligence condition or "out" for the benefit of the borrower. This disparity in the two sets of conditions could leave the borrower, unable to satisfy the lender's condition, without financing and unable to close the purchase transaction, exposing it to possible litigation launched by the seller for breach of the purchase agreement. Ideally, from the borrower's perspective, the conditions in the commitment letter should be the same as the conditions in the purchase agreement.

To avoid this risk, the borrower may attempt to insert into the purchase agreement a condition that closing the purchase is subject to the borrower being able to complete its financing on satisfactory terms. The seller, however, is unlikely to accede to such a request, since it would effectively provide the borrower with a very broad right to walk away from the purchase transaction.

As a result, the borrower needs to assess which conditions in the commitment letter it has control over and represent a relatively small risk, and which conditions are beyond its control. For those beyond its control, which usually include approvals or reports from third parties regarding the purchased business, the borrower should insist that they be included as conditions in the purchase agreement which allow it to walk away if they fail to be satisfied.

A similar risk is faced by the borrower when negotiating the representations and warranties to be given to the lender in the commitment letter and eventually the loan agreement, which are likely to be broader than those received from the seller in the purchase agreement. Unlike in a conventional debt financing when the borrower is making representations about itself with presumably sufficient knowledge to do so, an acquisition financing requires the borrower to make representations about the business being acquired before it has acquired the business and gained such knowledge. While it may have learned certain things about the business in the course of its due diligence investigations, it will nonetheless be relying upon the seller's representations in the purchase agreement.

As with the need to harmonize the conditions in the purchase agreement with those in the loan agreement, the borrower should attempt to harmonize the representations as well. However, the borrower continues to run some risk by virtue of the different consequences flowing from the breach of representation in the two types of agreement regardless of whether the representations are harmonized or not. While the breach of a representation in the purchase agreement usually only allows the buyer to claim indemnification from the seller for any damages resulting from the breach, the breach of a representation in the loan agreement usually allows the lender to pursue a number of different remedies against the borrower, including the cessation of further advances, demanding repayment and enforcing its security.

Having an indemnity claim against the seller may then be cold comfort to the borrower whose acquisition loan has been called and assets taken over by the lender. Therefore, the borrower should attempt to resist making any representations about the acquired business to the lender in the commitment letter and eventually the loan agreement unless they are restricted to its own knowledge. Furthermore, the borrower should request that the breach of a representation to the lender about the acquired business should not comprise an event of default if a similar representation in the purchase agreement has been breached by the seller and indemnification from the seller has been claimed.

The challenges faced by the borrower in learning enough about the acquired business in order to give the representations and accept the conditions of closing in the commitment letter also apply to the financial covenants to be met after closing. While the covenants described above for conventional debt financing may be generally similar to those used in acquisition financing, they differ in at least one substantive respect. The covenants for acquisition financing relate to a large extent to the business or target company being acquired, whether they are add-on loans to existing borrowers or new loans to new borrowers.

These covenants often require a reduction in debt over time, not only by prescribing decreasing leverage ratios but also by providing for prepayment of the term loan facility out of the proceeds received from any asset sales, insurance recoveries or later financings.

If the seller is helping to partially finance the acquisition by agreeing to accept payment of the purchase price in installments after the purchase transaction closes, the commitment letter will likely require an intercreditor agreement between the seller and lender as a condition of the acquisition financing.

Under such an agreement, the seller often postpones all of its payments due under its "take back" financing in favour of all payments due to the lender, and subordinates any security it may have to the lender's security, although the seller is usually entitled to receive any required and scheduled payments of principal and interest in the absence of any default under the lender's acquisition debt. The inter-creditor agreement usually limits the seller's rights to enforce its take-back loan security on default, often by imposing a "standstill" period during which it may not exercise its remedies so as to give the lender time to take control of the realization process. It also usually prevents the seller from assigning its take-back debt and security to any other party.

Since an inter-creditor agreement between the seller and the lender on such terms deprives the seller of the rights and remedies it would normally have as a creditor, and reduces the borrower's incentive to comply with the terms of the take-back loan, the negotiation of the inter-creditor agreement can be difficult and lengthy and threaten the closing of the purchase transaction.

Credit and Loan Agreements

Even though the principal business terms of a loan and other credit facilities may have been settled between the company and the bank or other financial institution, and a commitment letter has been executed by them, there nonetheless are likely to remain a number of issues which need to be addressed in the various definitive agreements which expand upon and generally replace the commitment letter.

The owners and managers of the company need to be aware that these definitive agreements can create significant qualifications and exceptions to the more general provisions of the commitment letter. After all, the commitment letter may only confirm the main terms of the financing deal which the parties have agreed upon, leaving the details to be negotiated afterwards and more comprehensively recorded in the other agreements. As a result, the company's owners and managers must continue to be vigilant following the commitment letter to ensure that their original expectations of the deal will still be met once these additional agreements are put into place.

The main definitive agreement, often regarded as the master agreement which governs the other definitive agreements required to close the loan transaction, is the credit or loan agreement, unless the commitment letter is intended to serve as the full loan agreement between the parties. For the purposes of this chapter, the credit or loan agreement will be referred to as the loan agreement, the company will be referred to as the borrower, and the bank or other financial institution will be referred to as the lender.

If the loan agreement is intended to replace the commitment letter, it will usually repeat many of the terms found in the commitment letter but supplement them with more comprehensive terms and qualifications. It may also vary them to reflect the results of further negotiations between the parties, often initiated by the lender in response to the results of the lender's due diligence investigations of the borrower, if the commitment letter reserves a right to the lender to make such changes.

The extent of negotiations over the loan agreement and the respective bargaining power of the borrower and lender will depend upon a number of factors, including the historical relationship of the parties, the quality of the security being given by the borrower, the amount of due diligence conducted, the overall term of the loan agreement, and the borrower's creditworthiness.

Even though the lender may appear to be able to always get his own way, the negotiations do not necessarily favour the lender. The lender must balance his negotiating demands with his desire to make the loan and later obtain referrals from the borrower for other business. The borrower, on the other hand, has the ultimate recourse of refinancing with a new lender, although such refinancing will entail additional costs and likely prepayment penalties.

This chapter attempts to describe some of the more comprehensive provisions often found in the loan agreement which either expand upon or qualify the essential terms contained in the commitment letter. It also attempts to describe some of the actions that a borrower may take to delay or avoid the exercise of the lender's remedies provided under the loan agreement.

CALCULATION OF INTEREST

Although the commitment letter will set out the rate of interest applicable to each credit facility being provided by the lender, the loan agreement usually provides a number of rules for calculating the interest that will be payable by the borrower throughout the term of the agreement.

For example, the agreement ordinarily requires that interest be calculated on a nominal, not effective, basis. An effective rate of interest is the rate which a borrower actually pays when the borrower's payments over a year are aggregated, and is equal to the nominal rate only when interest is both calculated and payable annually. When interest is payable more frequently than once a year, the nominal rate will result in the borrower paying more in interest over a year. For example, if interest is set at a nominal 6 per cent per annum and payable monthly, the borrower pays interest of .5 per cent each month, which equals an effective annual rate of approximately 6.17 per cent.

Even though interest may be calculated and payable on a monthly basis, the agreement will still specify the applicable rate of interest on an annual basis. The expression of interest at an annual rate is required under the *Interest Act*, and the failure to give an annual rate in a loan agreement (except for a mortgage) can restrict the interest payable to a maximum of 5 per cent per annum.[1]

The loan agreement ordinarily states that interest shall be paid without allowance or deduction for deemed reinvestment. This provision is designed to override the deemed reinvestment principle, which gives the borrower the benefit of the time value of all interest payments made over the year when payments are made monthly but interest is expressed at an annual rate, and which would otherwise reduce the amount of interest paid by the borrower.

AVAILMENT RESTRICTIONS

As briefly described in the previous chapter, the amount of credit available to a borrower under a revolving facility will often be limited to specified percentages of the borrower's accounts receivable and inventory which constitute his "borrowing base". If the borrower carries on a seasonal business which experiences high fluctuations in receivables and inventory throughout the year, he may be faced with insufficient availment during his slow season.

Not all receivables and inventory qualify for inclusion in the borrowing base, and the loan agreement, and perhaps the commitment letter, will set out in detail the criteria to be applied when determining the borrowing base.

The lender will usually insist that receivables which have been outstanding for a certain period of time, perhaps 90 days after their invoice date, should be excluded on the basis that they are too stale to be regarded as collectible. The borrower, however, may resist such exclusion, arguing that the stale date selected by the lender is inappropriate given the particular nature of the borrower's industry and bad debt history, as well as the type of receivables concerned. For example, there may be receivables from a number of quite significant customers who have been given special payment terms of 120 days by the borrower, and these receivables should be included in the borrowing base despite the standard 90 day cutoff.

Foreign accounts receivable are ordinarily excluded by the lender, or have a much lower margin applied to them when calculating the borrowing base. If the borrower wishes to borrow against them or raise their value for margining purposes, he may consider obtaining accounts receivable insurance from insurers such as Export Development Canada and assigning the insurance benefits to the lender as a way of avoiding the lender's exclusion of such receivables. The lender, however, may also require that "lock-box" arrangements be implemented for the collection of foreign receivables.

If the borrower wants to have federal government receivables included in the borrowing base even though they are often excluded, he will likely be required under the loan agreement to carry out the requisite government notification and acknowledgement of such inclusion.[2]

Another exclusion usually imposed by the lender in the loan agreement relates to receivables which are subject to set-off claims or which are subject to a dispute, although the borrower should request that any such receivables are excluded only to the extent of the set-off claimed or amount disputed.

The lender may also attempt to reserve a right to exclude from the borrowing base any item at his discretion in response to ongoing changes to his own internal credit policies. While these policies are often intended to avoid the concentration of too many receivables with too few customers or in just one industry, the borrower should resist such a right because of the uncertainty it creates.

In restricting which inventory items may be included in his calculation of the borrowing base, the lender may want to exclude any inventory which is subject to an unpaid supplier's rights to reclaim such inventory.[3] Yet such an exclusion may not be appropriate for fast moving inventory which generates quick sales or for "just in time" inventory which is rapidly converted into manufactured goods.

Work in process is ordinarily excluded by lenders from the inventory comprising a borrower's borrowing base on the assumption that work in process, unlike raw materials and finished goods, is not readily saleable. Depending on the particular circumstances, the borrower may be able to convince the lender that the work in process can be quickly converted to finished products and therefore should not be excluded from the borrowing base.

The lender may also require a deduction from the borrowing base of any amounts which, if unpaid, might result in a charge on the borrower's assets ranking ahead of the lender, such as unpaid employee vacation pay or unremitted source deductions for income tax which constitute deemed trusts or statutory liens. However, the borrower should ensure that any payables which are deducted from the calculation of the borrowing base do, in fact, rank prior to a secured lender's position

In addition to restricting the borrower's availment rights by specifying a number of exclusions or deductions from the borrowing base, a lender may limit the borrower's rights to draw on funds in more than one currency.

For example, while the loan agreement will usually provide for credit to be extended to the borrower up to a specified maximum amount in Canadian dollars, it will likely require the conversion of all amounts advanced in other currencies into Canadian dollars pursuant to a prescribed formula in order to establish the total amount outstanding at any one time. Any amount exceeding the specified maximum must be repaid immediately. Such a provision requires the borrower to assume a currency exchange risk, since the credit maximum may be exceeded by reason only of fluctuations in exchange rates and not through any additional borrowing. To avoid such a result, the borrower might request that a slight cushion, perhaps 5 per cent, be inserted in the loan agreement so that the specified maximum may be exceeded by up to that amount to accommodate changes in exchange rates without requiring a repayment.

If LIBOR loans are made available, the loan agreement will usually restrict the borrower's rights to draw upon them in the event that the lender is unable to access LIBOR funds, at least at a rate which will allow the lender to profitably provide such funds to the borrower. In that event, the borrower is required to elect a different availment option, such as a U.S. dollar base rate loan, so long as the adverse LIBOR market conditions persist.

QUALIFICATIONS TO REPRESENTATIONS AND WARRANTIES

The borrower's representations and warranties which are normally requested by the lender may have to be qualified so that the borrower will be prepared or able to give them. Although the lender ordinarily wants a problem to be fixed by the borrower before funds are advanced, qualification can be achieved in a number of ways.

One way involves the borrower creating an exception from the representation for anything which might breach the representation, and setting out the exception in the agreement, or more commonly, in a schedule to the agreement. The lender can either agree to the exception as disclosed, or require that the breach be resolved before the loan is advanced.

A second way to qualify is to make the representation subject to the knowledge of the borrower, or of specific persons representing the borrower. Such qualification is often requested by the borrower in respect of representations over the absence of any threatened actions or events, such as litigation or labour strikes. The lender is generally reluctant to accept this means of qualification because of the difficulty in proving "knowledge", but may be inclined to do so if the borrower is required to make diligent inquiry about the matter represented in an effort to become knowledgeable about it.

The borrower may try to limit his knowledge about a particular matter to the contents of a report prepared by third party consultants. The lender is often inclined to reject such a limitation, especially in the case of reports on the environmental condition of the borrower's properties, because he shifts the risk of undisclosed deficiencies to the lender in the event the reports are incorrect or incomplete. The lender may have a similar concern with the borrower's request to restrict his knowledge to the contents of a report prepared by an insurance consultant to qualify his representation that he maintains adequate insurance over his properties.

A third way of qualification is to use a materiality threshold, so that the representation must only be about material matters, or its inaccuracy will have a material adverse effect upon the borrower. Such a qualification is often paired with a definition of materiality which deems any matter, such as a contract or lawsuit, to be material if it involves more than a specified dollar amount or percentage of the borrower's assets.

While the borrower's qualifications to the representations and warranties are not likely to be set out in much detail in the commitment letter unless it is intended to serve as the loan agreement between the parties, they will often appear in the loan agreement only after some negotiation.

Some representations and warranties are generally regarded as non-negotiable and fundamental to the lender / borrower relationship, such as those which relate to the existence, power and authority of the borrower, and will not be qualified.

Others may relate to matters over which the borrower has some control but is unable to ensure absolute compliance, such as the borrower's compliance with all applicable laws. A breach of this kind of representation and warranty is possible yet might be inadvertent with only minor consequences, suggesting that it ought to be qualified by a materiality threshold. Another example might be a representation and warranty that the borrower is not in breach of any agreement, which should be restricted to any material agreement, since the borrower is quite likely unaware of a number of breaches which are relatively insignificant.

Another type of representation and warranty which the borrower may wish to qualify but which the lender may insist remain without limitation involves matters which are beyond the borrower's control and which usually result from the action of a third party. Examples of this type might include the absence of litigation against the borrower, the enforceability of all of the borrower's contracts, the good standing of his customer relationships, the absence of environmental contamination on his properties, the validity of his various licences and permits, and so on. Such representations and warranties are often restricted to those matters which have only a "material adverse effect" upon the borrower's business, assets or financial condition.

Even if qualified to some extent, each representation and warranty usually has to be true and complete not only when the loan agreement is signed but also when each advance of funds under it takes place, and perhaps even upon the conversion or rollover of an outstanding advance to another form of credit. Therefore further qualification may be necessary to anticipate possibly changing circumstances. For example, a representation and warranty that there is no outstanding litigation against the borrower may have to be limited to the date the agreement is signed, which is then supported by a covenant of the borrower to provide the lender with ongoing reports of litigation so that the lender is aware of any changes prior to making a subsequent advance.

QUALIFICATIONS TO FINANCIAL COVENANTS

As breach of the borrower's financial covenants often represents the main cause of default under a loan agreement, the negotiation and drafting of the financial covenants can be a contentious exercise, particularly in the definition of the financial ratios referenced in the previous chapter. Since the ratios often appear as fractions, where a ratio of 5 to 2 is written as 5/2, there may well be considerable debate over which items should be included in the numerator and which items should be included in the denominator.

For example, when defining the debt to equity ratio or other leverage ratio which the borrower is expected to maintain, or not exceed, throughout the term of the agreement, it is not always clear what should comprise the "debt" in the numerator. The lender may argue that debt includes subordinated debt and shareholder loans, and perhaps preferred shares and even the borrower's obligations under hedging agreements. In establishing what should comprise "equity", the lender will attempt to exclude any assets which will have minimal value in liquidation, such as any goodwill reflected on the borrower's financial statements.

The application of an interest coverage ratio can pose a similar drafting challenge. Designed to measure the borrower's ability to meet his fixed financial obligations, the numerator is typically the borrower's operating cash flow, and the denominator is the borrower's fixed charges. In defining "operating cash flow", the borrower's EBITDA or earnings before interest, taxes, depreciation and amortization for the most recent four quarter period may be used, possibly adjusted to remove any one-time or extraordinary gains or losses. For the definition of the "fixed charges" appearing in the denominator, any interest on debt which is capitalized may be included, as well as any scheduled capital expenditures. The borrower may request that only scheduled principal payments, and not just any principal payments, be included as fixed charges so that the borrower may make voluntary principal payments without affecting the ratio.

The application of the financial covenants generally can have negative consequences to the borrower should the definitions provided in the loan agreement fail to take into account a possible acquisition or disposition by the borrower which may occur during the period used to determine compliance with the covenant. This failure can result in a mismatch between balance sheet items, such as debt which would include the amount of new debt taken on to fund an acquisition during the period, and income statement items, such as operating cash flow which would not give the borrower the benefit of all of the earnings of the acquired entity for the entire period. The borrower may argue that items such as operating cash flow or fixed charges for that period should be determined on a *pro forma* basis as if the acquisition or disposition occurred at the beginning of the period.

In order to have some flexibility in his deal making and avoid the need to continually request waivers from the lender, the borrower will often attempt to have the caps or ceilings on permitted dispositions and capital expenditures appearing in the loan agreement increased, and to have any restrictions against issuing or transferring shares removed as they apply to transfers among his subsidiaries or other affiliates. The borrower will also attempt, because of the standard covenant to maintain a minimum amount of equity, to have any restrictions on distributions amended to allow for the payment of dividends consistent with past practice or perhaps up to a certain percentage of net income.

To more easily monitor the borrower's compliance with the financial covenants, the lender will usually require that the loan agreement provide for the borrower to report on his compliance to the lender at the same time as he releases his quarterly financial statements.

PERMITTED ENCUMBRANCES
The loan agreement will usually prohibit the borrower, by way of what is often described as a "negative pledge", from placing any lien or charge upon the borrower's assets. However, as briefly mentioned in the previous chapter, an exception to this prohibition is given for any encumbrances which are specifically permitted by the lender.

While a commitment letter may set out a list of permitted encumbrances, especially when it is intended to serve as a loan agreement, a separate loan agreement often contains a more comprehensive list reflecting the detailed negotiations between the parties which may have occurred leading up to its execution. This comprehensive list may supplement the more generic list which often accompanies a commitment letter.

These additional encumbrances will usually address the kinds of liens, charges and security interests that are commonplace or required within the particular industry or business of the borrower.

For example, the borrower may ordinarily deal with suppliers which follow a practice of registering purchase money security interests against their customers, and the borrower should insist that such security interests be included as permitted encumbrances in order to maintain his regular sources of supply. A similar argument should be made by the borrower to include capital leases if the borrower ordinarily finances his equipment purchases though such leases. If the borrower intends to undertake a series of business acquisitions, he may request that any liens on the assets of the purchased businesses be permitted encumbrances.

For those borrowers in the construction industry who are regularly required to post performance bonds to participate in various projects, the security interests created under such bonds should be listed as permitted encumbrances in the loan agreement.

Where the borrower has succeeded in having a number of existing liens placed on the list of permitted encumbrances, he should also request that any subsequent liens resulting from the refinancing of the obligations creating the existing liens be added to the list. The lender may accede to such a request provided the subsequent liens do not increase the dollar amount secured or apply to additional collateral.

QUALIFICATIONS TO EVENTS OF DEFAULT

During the preparation and negotiation of the loan agreement, the parties may attempt to further define the events of default contained in the commitment letter, with the borrower suggesting various qualifications in an effort to reduce the likelihood of a default occurring.

The borrower will usually argue for lengthy grace periods to enable him to cure any breach before such breach is deemed to be an event of default. The lender will argue back that some breaches are more serious than others and do not deserve any grace period, and that other breaches cannot be cured at all.

There are many variations in the compromise that may be achieved. However, the parties often agree upon a few days grace, usually between one to five days, for the non-payment of interest or fees, but no grace period for the non-payment of principal. They may also agree generally that the borrower will have anywhere from 10 to 30 days to remedy any breach of covenant after being given notice of the breach by the lender. Alternatively, the grace period may start from the earlier of the date of the notice and the date on which the borrower becomes aware of the breach.

But a grace period is usually not allowed for breach of a representation and warranty in a "material respect" or for any breach of a financial covenant. Nor is a grace period usually given for bankruptcy or insolvency proceedings initiated by the borrower, although a short grace period may be given if such proceedings have been initiated by a third party since they may be without merit and the borrower should be given an opportunity to contest and have them stayed.

In addition to negotiating for longer and all-encompassing grace periods, the borrower may attempt to narrow down the application of any cross-default provision. Such a provision deems a default to have occurred under the loan agreement when and if the borrower defaults under some other obligation with a third party as well as under one of the other credit facilities provided by the lender to the borrower. The borrower should try to define such an obligation as a debt obligation over a certain materiality threshold and not some other form of contractual obligation, and try to exclude debts with affiliated companies.

Since an event of default under the loan agreement ordinarily includes a material adverse change in the business, operations or assets of the borrower, the borrower will usually try to avoid the potential for abuse which such a subjective and vague term invites by providing the lender with a more precise definition. At the very least, the borrower should insist that a material adverse change cannot be determined by the lender "in its sole and unfettered discretion", as some loan agreements provide. Furthermore, the borrower should try to confine the adverse change to the borrower's existing business and not to his "prospects" as an event of default.

Although a change in the ownership and control of the borrower may be an event of default under the loan agreement, the borrower may argue that such a provision is appropriate only when the lender is relying upon the borrower's parent company to enhance the credit and is assuming that the borrower will have access to the parent's funds. Such a provision may be removed by the lender if the borrower's shareholders are not expected to provide this kind of support in the absence of guarantees from them.

QUALIFICATIONS TO COST RECOVERY AND INDEMNIFICATION

The loan agreement typically affords the lender the right to be reimbursed for costs associated with making the loan, particularly unforeseen costs which might reduce or eliminate his expected financial return on the loan. The borrower is also required to indemnify the lender for all costs relating to the enforcement of the loan agreement and security documents, or to any default of the borrower, and to any proceedings brought by or against the lender because he has entered into the loan agreement.

Not only is there usually a general indemnity by the borrower to compensate the lender for these out-of-pocket costs but also a provision permitting the lender to pass along his increased costs to the borrower. Costs in providing the loan can increase in response to many factors, including additional taxes, increased capital requirements and regulatory changes.

The borrower, however, may attempt to qualify such a provision by allowing the lender to pass along his increased costs only if he is doing so to other borrowers in a comparable position. The borrower may also attempt to impose a time limit upon the lender in passing along such costs for reimbursement, together with a duty to make reasonable efforts to keep such increased costs to a minimum.

Another cost recovery provision usually inserted into the loan agreement by the lender relates to "grossing up" the borrower's payments to the lender by the amount of any taxes which are levied upon the lender on account of those payments so that the lender ends up with the full amount he expected to receive. The borrower, however, should ensure that the provision excludes certain taxes, such as taxes which apply to the lender's income generally and are not specific to the loan, and requires the lender to use reasonable efforts to minimize such taxes and apply for any credits which might serve to reduce them.

In addition to imposing a general indemnity in the loan agreement for his costs incurred in making the loan, the lender is likely to impose a specific indemnity upon the borrower for any liability under applicable environmental laws, especially if the borrower owns or occupies any real property. Because such laws impose liability on those having an interest in or who control contaminated property, regardless of when the contamination occurred, lenders have usually been concerned that they might attract liability for merely inspecting, advancing funds, and taking security on a borrower's real property, despite assurances from environmental regulators that such liability flows to lenders only when they possess such property or control the borrower's operations.

Faced with the inclusion of a specific environmental indemnity in the loan agreement, the borrower will usually attempt to restrict the application of the indemnity to contamination which occurred only when the borrower was in possession of the property. he will also attempt to limit the indemnity to liability only under applicable environmental statutes and not under any remediation guidelines and policies which have no legal effect.

RESTRICTIONS ON ASSIGNMENT

Since lenders generally wish to be able to assign their loans or bring in other lenders to share in the risks associated with a loan, the loan agreement usually gives the lender a right of assignment. The borrower may request that his consent to such assignment be mandatory, although such request is unlikely to be granted unless the borrower's consent cannot be unreasonably withheld. Even then, the lender will probably insist that assignment may take place without the consent of the borrower upon an event of default, in order to allow the lender to dispose of a bad loan.

The borrower may also attempt to limit such assignment to circumstances involving the acceleration of the loan and not simply upon an event of default. In addition, given that an assignee of the loan will have access to confidential financial information about the borrower, the borrower may request that certain lenders be listed in the loan agreement as ineligible assignees, particularly those lenders connected to the borrower's main competitors.

The assignment of the loan may entail additional costs and taxes for the lender which may be passed on to the borrower under the cost recovery provisions discussed above. Consequently, the borrower should attempt to qualify the lender's right to assign by adding in the loan agreement that the borrower will not be responsible for any additional costs and taxes attributable to an assignment by the lender.

REMEDIES ON DEFAULT

The loan agreement will usually provide more than one remedy which the lender may seek upon the default of the borrower.

The lender is often permitted to accelerate the liability of the borrower which is not then due, so that the borrower is required to repay all amounts advanced plus accrued interest and fees. The lender is also given the right to stop providing any further credit to the borrower, in addition to enforcing his rights to obtain payment of all amounts owed and realizing on the collateral given to secure payment of such amounts. The loan agreement usually provides that these remedies are cumulative and in addition to, not in substitution for, any other remedies the lender may have against the borrower.

Any remedy given to the lender is ordinarily optional, not mandatory, so that the lender will not be forced to call the loan when he is not prepared to do so, as may be the case when business conditions suggest a poor recovery.

Even though the loan agreement may give the lender the rights to accelerate the loan, demand full repayment, and realize on his security immediately upon an event of default, the lender is not permitted to exercise such rights without observing certain requirements imposed by law.[4] Generally speaking, the lender should give the borrower a reasonable time to pay after an event of default and acceleration but before realizing on the security. This requires the lender to give reasonable notice to the borrower before enforcing his rights. The borrower may not waive his right to receive such notice in the loan agreement or applicable security document.

As the borrower is usually required to provide ongoing financial information and reports of his compliance with the financial covenants in the loan agreement, the lender is likely to be aware of the early warning signs of a deterioration in the borrower's financial condition and will have initiated discussions with the borrower about possible corrective action well before the lender gives notice to enforce his remedies.

Even if the financial and compliance reports do not suggest possible deterioration, other changes may. The lender may become concerned if the owner of the borrower dies, or the borrower loses a major customer, or well-capitalized competitors of the borrower saturate the market, or currency exchange rates swing wildly, or any number of other events occur which may adversely affect the borrower's business.

In such circumstances, the past performance of the borrower's business may no longer appear relevant to the lender. The lender may become inclined to reassess the borrower's creditworthiness, determine whether the security behind the loan is sufficient and properly registered, and decide whether to continue to finance the business. He may then regard the loan as a "special loan", and insist various actions be taken.

For example, the lender may require that the terms of the loan agreement be amended to reduce the principal amount of the loan or impose stricter financial covenants. The lender may also request additional security in the form of collateral mortgages or personal guarantees. If the review of the borrower's existing security has revealed certain mistakes or deficiencies, the borrower may be asked to assist in the correction of these deficiencies.

As mentioned above, there are various options available to the lender when enforcing his security after a default. He can take possession of the secured property, appoint a private receiver, commence an action for payment and apply for a court order appointing a receiver, dispose of the secured property, or simply sue the borrower for the amount owed without seeking any other remedies.

Once the lender has decided to pursue any of these remedies, he will issue a demand for payment, assuming that an event of default has occurred. The demand will usually include a notice that default has occurred, along with a description of the default and the acceleration of the amount owing to the lender. The demand may then be followed by a notice of the lender's intention to enforce the security.[5]

Although it is unusual for a lender to enforce his remedies upon a single event of default, there may be circumstances when such action is justified. For example, a change in the ownership or control of the borrower may be perceived by the lender as sufficiently adverse as to warrant accelerating the loan, provided a change of control is included in the loan agreement as an event of default.

Which remedy is pursued by the lender will depend on the particular situation, including the marketability of the collateral, the capacity of the business to be carried on as a going concern by a receiver, and the amount of additional money the lender is prepared to spend in order to enforce its security.

There may be circumstances when the lender is better off by not enforcing his security or bringing an action to obtain a judgment. It's not unusual for a lender to simply walk away from a special loan because the borrower owes more to the Canada Revenue Agency for unremitted source deductions than the potential realizable value of the security held, or because nothing will be left over for the lender once amounts owed by the borrower to other prior secured creditors are paid first. Sometimes the professional fees and other costs related to taking possession of and selling the collateral are estimated to be higher than the amount to be obtained by selling the collateral, thereby dissuading the lender from taking any action.

BORROWER ACTIONS TO AVOID EXERCISE OF LENDER REMEDIES ON DEFAULT

When the borrower realizes that changing circumstances may cause his loan to become a special loan, he should consider taking certain actions well before the lender issues a formal demand for repayment.

Since his overriding goal may be to ensure that the lender continues to finance the borrower's business, the borrower should try to anticipate what the lender may require and then develop and present a plan that sets out a reasonable alternative to the lender calling the loan. Based on a business plan model indicating projected revenues and expenditures, the borrower's plan must be realistic, convey a clear message that the business is viable and profitable going forward, and inspire lender confidence in the borrower's management. It must also contain specific criteria for measuring the progress of the plan's implementation.

In addition to developing the plan, the borrower needs to consider whether a personal guarantee from the owner of the borrower if not already given, or a collateral mortgage on the owner's home, might be offered if the lender insists upon additional security in order to continue financing the business. Since the giving of a personal guarantee or offering personal assets as security for financing the business is similar to making an additional investment in the business, the owner has to ask whether the business is worth the extra investment and risk. After all, there is no "guarantee" from the lender that he will continue to provide financing for more than just the short term, regardless of the personal security taken from the owner.

The borrower also needs to consider whether retaining at his own expense an external consultant to provide assistance in restructuring the business would encourage the lender to support the business. The retention of a consultant sometimes provides "breathing space", allowing the borrower sufficient time to arrive at his own restructuring plan while the consultant's report is being prepared.

It is likely that the plan first presented to the lender will have to be amended to reflect various terms and conditions requested by the lender. However, if the lender respects the borrower's management and believes the amended plan might work, the lender may be prepared to co-operate with the borrower and give enough time to allow for the plan's implementation, assuming the lender's security will not erode in the meantime.

Even though the lender may be prepared to continue financing the borrower's business for a while longer, he may nonetheless decrease the amount of credit available. The borrower should therefore take another look at whether he has cut absolutely all the costs that may be cut from the business. He should also look at other alternatives, including his suppliers with a view to obtaining better payment terms. The suppliers may provide the borrower with more favourable terms as a way of keeping a customer.

Given that there are many different kinds of lenders in the financial services marketplace, the borrower may be able to find another lender that is quite prepared to take on the borrower as a new customer and refinance the current lender's position. For example, it is not unusual for an asset-based lender or "mezzanine" lender to become a borrower's main source of financing.

Given their potential personal liability for unpaid wages and vacation pay, and unremitted source deductions,[6] the directors of the borrower have to exercise ongoing diligence to ensure these obligations are kept current. If the lender is not prepared to provide funds sufficient to meet the borrower's payroll, the directors may have to consider closing the business to avoid the significant claims they could be facing personally.

If a specific default under the loan agreement has occurred, the borrower may try to obtain a waiver from the lender relating to that default. The lender may be prepared to give the waiver if he regards the default as immaterial. More likely, however, especially if the default is viewed by the lender as material, the lender will request a forbearance or standstill agreement in which the borrower acknowledges the amount of the outstanding loan and receipt of a demand for payment, and confirms the enforceability of any security and guarantees that are in place, in return for the lender agreeing not to proceed against the borrower at that time.

The forbearance agreement will also contain the terms and conditions under which the lender will continue to advance funds to the borrower, including even stricter events of default than are found in the loan agreement and a full release of the lender by the borrower preventing him from challenging any actions that may be taken by the lender.

If the borrower receives a demand for payment and notice of intention to enforce the security, he may attempt to delay the lender's enforcement rights by seeking a stay of proceedings against him[7] to provide time to negotiate with his creditors or to restructure his debt obligations. Should the lender believe that his rights will be adversely affected by a court awarding a stay of proceedings, particularly if the value of the collateral will materially dissipate over time, the lender may ask the court to impose certain controls upon the borrower or seek to lift the stay of proceedings to allow the lender to enforce his security.

If the borrower comes to the painful conclusion that the business has little hope of becoming profitable, it may be preferable for the borrower to work with the lender in arranging for an orderly liquidation of the business in an effort to reduce costs and minimize the exposure on any outstanding personal guarantees.

Security Agreements and Guarantees

The previous two chapters describe some of the issues which a company owner or manager should consider when arranging debt financing for the company and negotiating the provisions of a commitment letter and loan agreement. But their need to carefully examine the documentation presented to them is not confined to these two items.

While the commitment letter and loan agreement may reflect the fundamental terms governing the loan arrangements between the company as borrower and its lender, the security package intended to secure the loan and consisting of various security agreements and guarantees will have to be reviewed as well.

Sometimes these security documents appear in standard, relatively short printed forms which are used by the lender for most of its customers, and which are generally regarded as non-negotiable. Yet they nonetheless have significant business consequences for the borrower and give rise to a number of possibly contentious issues. This chapter will address some of these issues.

CONFLICTS WITH LOAN AGREEMENT

Attempting to ensure that the terms of the standardized security documents are consistent with the terms of the commitment letter and loan agreement is not always an easy task. Often these security documents will contain representations, warranties, and covenants as well as events of default.

These provisions create concerns about the ongoing monitoring of them, especially since security documents, as opposed to loan agreements, are seldom looked at after a financing closes except to ascertain the lender's enforcement rights when an event of default has occurred. Therefore any representations, warranties and covenants which they contain should be limited to the specific collateral charged and should not require ongoing monitoring.

These provisions also create potential conflicts with similar provisions in the loan agreement. Consequently, any redundant provisions should be removed from the security documents, particularly any events of default. There is usually no need for separate events of default to be set out in the security documents, which can create ambiguity and confusion when the lender attempts to enforce its rights. The events of default, and preferably any representations and warranties and most covenants, should be fully and exclusively contained in the loan agreement.

To prevent any inconsistencies or conflicts between the security documents and the loan agreement from jeopardizing the lender's enforcement or the borrower's rights to avoid such enforcement, the loan agreement might include what is called a "paramountcy clause". Such a clause effectively confirms that the loan agreement is the paramount document to be consulted when determining the relationship between the borrower and lender, and that the provisions of the loan agreement will override any inconsistent or conflicting provisions in the security documents, which are perhaps more likely to appear when the lender's standard printed forms are used

DESCRIBING THE OBLIGATIONS SECURED

Deciding how broadly or narrowly to describe the obligations being secured or guaranteed affects whether additional loans can later be made or a refinancing completed without having to significantly amend or replace the security documents. Because such amendment or replacement is almost always at the borrower's expense, the borrower will usually request that the security documents be able to accommodate as many foreseeable events as possible.

For example, the obligations secured should refer to the obligations under the loan agreement as it may be amended, restated or replaced from time to time. Furthermore, they should include future financings which the parties wish to be covered by the same collateral, or any other credit facilities or advances which the lender may provide to the borrower.

GUARANTEES

In an effort to enhance the credit of the borrower and improve upon the security taken for the loan, the lender often requires that a guarantee of the loan be obtained from a third party, which may or may not be secured in turn by the assets of that third party. If the borrower defaults on a guaranteed loan, the lender may then enforce its own remedies against the guarantor.

A guarantee essentially defines the guaranteed obligations and contains the promise of the guarantor to pay the guaranteed obligations. The lender usually insists that the guarantee be absolute and unconditional so that it does not have to first exhaust its recourse against the borrower before seeking payment from the guarantor.

The form of guarantee requested by the lender may cover all past, present and future indebtedness of the borrower without limitation, and will likely contain a waiver by the guarantor of all defences it may attempt to raise to avoid liability under the guarantee.

However, recourse under the guarantee may be limited to specific collateral which the guarantor has given to the lender to secure the guarantee, such as shares which may have been pledged to the lender. The guarantee may also be limited to a specific dollar amount.

In some circumstances, the guarantee may be the main reason the lender is prepared to grant a loan to the borrower, especially when the borrower's own assets appear to be inadequate to fully secure any amounts advanced. Sometimes the guarantee of the borrower's parent corporation, or personal guarantees from a few of the borrower's shareholders if it is a closely-held company, may be the only security which the lender requires in order for the loan arrangements to be completed.

POSTPONEMENT AND ASSIGNMENT

Although the borrower and lender may have already addressed the extent of creditor postponement applicable to their loan arrangements in the loan agreement and possibly in the commitment letter, the issue of postponement also arises in connection with the preparation of the security documents, particularly the guarantee.

As mentioned previously, postponement generally restricts the borrower's ability to pay one or more of its other creditors before paying the lender the amounts owed under the loan agreement. One creditor, in other words, is to be paid before another. Most standard forms of guarantee contain a postponement by the guarantor of all obligations owed by the borrower to the guarantor, together with an assignment of those obligations to the lender.

The guarantee thereby gives the lender control over the cash that would otherwise flow directly from the borrower to the guarantor, as well as additional security by way of the assignment from the guarantor. The guarantor, however, may be reluctant or unable to provide the assignment as part of the guarantee, especially if the assignment will place the guarantor in breach of any negative pledge contained in its own financing arrangements which prevent it from assigning its own assets as security.

The postponement can adversely affect the flow of funds between a parent and subsidiary or within a group of related companies if guarantees have been given by them to the lender. The ongoing servicing or repayment of inter-company loans would be restricted as a consequence. To permit such payments to be made, the borrower will often request that the postponement be effective only upon and during an event of default.

GENERAL SECURITY

The principal security document ordinarily requested by most lenders is a general security agreement which is intended to charge all of the assets of the borrower. When it is registered under the applicable provincial personal property security system,[1] it will create a valid security interest in most types of personal property, but not all. Ordinarily a lender will search for liens and take security in each province in which the borrower has a business location or tangible assets with more than nominal value.

A general security agreement normally creates a security interest in favour of the lender in all present and future personal property, assets and undertakings of the borrower. It typically refers to the various classes of collateral recognized by the applicable provincial personal property security statute, such as inventory, accounts, equipment, securities, intangibles, chattel paper and the proceeds of all such collateral. Although it is the most comprehensive form of security document, it does not ordinarily extend to real property.

Because the general security agreement often secures all present and future indebtedness and liabilities of the borrower to the lender, it can be left in place to secure a number of subsequent transactions without the need to prepare, execute and register further security documents.

SPECIFIC SECURITY

Even though the lender may request a general security agreement, there may be certain key assets of the borrower which the lender is specifically relying upon for security and which deserve special treatment.

If real property represents a significant portion of the borrower's overall assets, the lender is likely to request a mortgage of that property, and if it is leased to any third parties, perhaps also a specific assignment of the rents receivable from the tenants.

Alternatively, the lender may request a debenture which is a convenient way to obtain security over both real and personal property, since security can be evidenced in just one document instead of two or more, and can be registered in more than one province rather than using a separate mortgage in each province.

Occasionally a debenture is accompanied by a debenture pledge agreement which pledges the debenture to the lender as security for the amounts owed by the borrower under the loan agreement and often varies the rights and obligations expressed in the debenture to conform to the terms of the loan agreement. The pledge agreement is often used to simplify the practical effect of the debenture by reducing it to a demand security while leaving the comprehensive terms and conditions in the loan agreement to govern the parties.

As mentioned in the chapter on commitment letters, the lender may request a variety of other forms of specific security that might otherwise be caught by a general security agreement. These might include a general assignment of accounts receivable, share pledge, specific assignment of promissory notes or intellectual property, and possibly security under section 427 of the *Bank Act* if the lender is a bank. These forms of security will ordinarily be requested if the lender foresees the need to realize upon certain assets.

The borrower often attempts to resist the lender's use of overlapping or redundant security because of the additional costs involved in preparation and registration. For example, a general security agreement and demand debenture tend to contain the same security items, and a separate assignment of contracts or specific security over intellectual property is usually already covered in a general security agreement.

However, redundancy and unwarranted extra costs are not the main concerns which the borrower should have with the security documents requested by the lender. The borrower should probably be more concerned with over-collateralization which can restrict the borrower's ability to dispose of its assets or to offer its assets as collateral in future financings. The borrower should try to limit the collateral it gives to the lender to the value of the loan, and ensure that the collateral is identified as precisely as possible. It should also request that a partial release of the collateral be given upon a partial repayment of the loan.

SPECIAL TREATMENT OF CERTAIN ASSETS

The lender often requests additional security documents and follows additional steps in order to acquire an enforceable security interest against certain types of property. Similarly, the borrower often requests that certain amendments be made to the security documents to address particular problems that relate to certain types of property.

For example, the lender may wish to acquire security over the borrower's contracts, but many contracts contain a prohibition against assignment. By allowing all such contracts to be included in a general security agreement, the borrower may be breaching the non-assignment provisions they may contain.

To accommodate this concern, the borrower may insist that the general security agreement contain an exception or "carve-out" for any contracts that would be breached by creating a security interest in them. However, there are likely to be certain contracts which the lender wishes to take as security even though they may contain a prohibition against assignment. In this case, the lender may insist that the borrower obtain the consent of the counterparties to such contracts permitting such assignment.

Even if such consents are obtained, the assigned contracts may not provide much security to the lender if they can be terminated by the counterparty on the same events of default of the borrower which the lender relies upon to enforce its own security. It may therefore be necessary in such circumstances to modify the contract between the borrower and counterparty to avoid such termination and allow the lender to step into the shoes of the borrower under it.

For example, if the lender is financing a business franchise, the borrower's franchise agreement may be more important to the lender as security for the loan than the borrower's equipment or inventory. The lender may wish to receive a specific assignment of the franchise agreement from the borrower which has been negotiated with the franchisor and which gives the lender special rights. These rights might include the right of the lender to step into the franchisee's shoes upon default under the franchise agreement, in contrast to the franchisor's usual right to find a new franchisee unrestricted by the lender. The lender may want to be given notice of any defaults under the franchise agreement and be given the opportunity to cure such defaults to keep the franchise in good standing.

Another example of such an arrangement occurs when a lender wishes to take security over a borrower's leasehold interest and an agreement between the landlord, borrower and lender is entered into which varies the rights the landlord would otherwise have. This often occurs when the borrower's lease is for a particular location which is essential to its business or for a manufacturing facility containing expensive heavy equipment which is not easily moved.

In addition to contracts which pose potential problems for lenders when taking security, the borrower's intellectual property can create problems as well. Many lenders rely upon a general security agreement, which is sometimes supplemented by a specific intellectual property security agreement, to create charges over a borrower's intellectual property. These charges are then "perfected" under the applicable provincial personal property security system.

However, intellectual property is the subject of specific federal legislation[2] which permits third parties to record assignments and security agreements against the existing registrations as well as pending applications for trademarks, patents and copyrights. Because of this federal registration regime for intellectual property, some uncertainty exists for lenders registering their security against intellectual property only under the applicable provincial system. As a result, many lenders search and register under both federal and provincial regimes when taking security over a borrower's intellectual property, particularly when it represents a significant portion of the borrower's overall assets.

While most lenders will look to the borrower's accounts receivable as forming an important part of the security being given, accounts owed to the borrower by the federal government can pose another problem for the lender. Federal government receivables cannot be charged by the borrower in favour of the lender unless the government is notified of the security interest and acknowledges it.[3]

As compliance with such requirements may seem impractical, the lender may choose to rely upon other security when financing the borrower unless the government receivable represents a substantial part of the security sought by the lender. Yet the lender will still have a charge under the general security agreement on the monies paid to the borrower under the receivable if not a charge on the receivable itself. Some lenders, however, will either exclude federal government receivables from the calculation of the borrower's borrowing base or place a limit on the extent to which they may be included.

As with government receivables, government licences also represent a category of assets which can create problems for the lender when acquiring security. If a licence is subject to considerable governmental discretion, it may not constitute property which can be charged under applicable provincial personal property security legislation. Where the licence is transferable, or where its revocation or renewal is based upon fairly objective criteria, the lender may be able to rely upon the licence as valid security.

PRIORITY OF OTHER SECURITY

As described in the earlier chapters on commitment letters and loan agreements in connection with permitted encumbrances, the borrower will usually have a number of liens already registered against its property when negotiating for new credit facilities with the lender.

Some of these liens will be discharged either before closing or shortly thereafter. Others, however, will survive the closing and remain outstanding against specific assets of the borrower in priority to the security being given to the lender under the new facility. The existing creditors who provided the borrower with funds to purchase or otherwise acquire such assets are ordinarily not expected to subordinate their security to the security of the lender, and the borrower is ordinarily not expected to pay off such creditors, especially if the penalties for prepayment would be too onerous.

But the security of these existing creditors must contain a specific description of the collateral involved, which is seldom the case, in order to avoid the lender's requirement that they be paid off. All too often their security is described in very broad terms, such as simply "equipment". In such circumstances, the borrower will usually be requested to provide the lender with an "estoppel" or "acknowledgment" letter or some form of disclaimer in which the existing creditor confirms which assets are specifically subject to its security interest and assures the lender that it will not look to its prior security registration to protect or shelter any future security interests it may claim against the borrower.

For those liens of other creditors which will survive the closing but which are not intended to cover any specific assets, being more likely a general charge over the borrower's assets, the lender may require some form of priority agreement with them.

A priority agreement will ordinarily set out the relative ranking of the security of the lender and of the other existing creditors over the borrower's assets, along with the postponement of payment by the borrower to one or more of the existing creditors in favour of the lender. It will probably also set out the remedies which each of the creditors may exercise upon a default, often requiring that advance notice be given to the lender and the other creditors before exercising such rights and perhaps imposing some form of moratorium or standstill period during which such rights may not be exercised at all.

Equity Financing and Term Sheets

The previous three chapters in this book have discussed what happens when the owners and managers of a private company look beyond their friends and family as sources of additional company financing and seek outside financing provided by way of loans from banks and other financial institutions.

But if the company is not at a stage in its lifecycle when it has the revenues and assets making it eligible to receive debt financing, or if it has already raised money by way of loan but faces certain limits in its borrowing capacity or is close to breaching the financial covenants with its current lender, its owners and managers may have to consider raising equity by selling its shares to outside parties.

But convincing an outsider to invest in the company's shares is no easy task. Investing in equities is often regarded as riskier than other types of investing, with no guarantee that the shares purchased will increase in value or that the investor will ever find someone to buy his shares when he eventually wants to sell them. This is particularly the case for private company shares, in contrast to the shares of public companies which are listed on a stock exchange and traded freely among the public.

For this reason, equity investments in private companies are often made only by those investors with some connection to the company, such as the friends and family of the company's founders, or by those investors who have a special interest and knowledge, and risk-preparedness, for private company investing.

Once deciding to pursue an equity investment from an outsider, the company may try to approach one or more "angel" investors, individuals who are usually experienced business people with sufficient cash to invest in smaller private companies and who are motivated by the potential to earn significant returns as well as be involved with a new venture. Angels tend to invest in businesses with which they are already familiar and in geographical proximity to where they live. But finding such an individual who might consider investing in the company can be a time-consuming and very random process. The company may be more successful in approaching professional fund managers who invest other people's money.

Yet getting the attention of one of these professional investors is not easy either, especially when the criteria they set can be difficult for many businesses to meet. Chances are that a business will have to have, at a minimum, a highly marketable product or service, an achievable business plan, an experienced and capable management team, a network of sophisticated strategic partners, and preferably be placed among the top three in its market space.

Whenever the business satisfies these criteria and gets the attention of a professional investor willing to invest, the basic terms of the proposed investment are often set out in what's commonly called a "term sheet". The term sheet is intended to be replaced by a number of more comprehensive, definitive agreements, including a subscription or share purchase agreement and a shareholder agreement, along with amendments to the company's articles and by-laws, as the parties get closer to finalizing the investment. The term sheet may or may not be legally binding, although it may well be both, containing some items which are binding and many items which are not binding.

This chapter will attempt to review the basic terms generally set out in a term sheet governing an equity investment in a private company by a professional investor. Although the terms discussed may be appropriate for an equity investment by an angel, this chapter assumes that the investor will more likely be a venture capital or private equity firm, venture subsidiary of a larger corporation in a related business, or a merchant bank or other institutional investor.

However, this chapter will also attempt to discuss how these terms are viewed by the owners and managers of the company as well as by the professional investor, and will look at the variations of these terms which each may propose to the other during the negotiation of the term sheet.

This chapter will assume that the investment is being made by way of convertible preferred shares, although some of the terms discussed may be relevant to an investment made by way of common shares, or by debentures or other debt instruments convertible into common shares or accompanied by warrants to acquire common shares. It will also assume that there will be only one holder, to be called the "Investor", of the company's preferred shares despite the common practice of having more than one professional investor "co-invest" in a company at the same time.

This chapter will also consider a few of the terms which are requested by U.S. based investors, since such investors often co-invest with, and sometimes invest directly on their own without, participation by Canadian based investors. An initial public offering (an "IPO") by a Canadian company which allows an investor an "exit" from its investment may just as likely take place on an American stock exchange, such as the NASDAQ, as on a Canadian exchange.

OWNERS AND MANAGERS VS. INVESTOR

While the owners and managers and the Investor may want the company to grow and prosper, their interests aren't always aligned, and the Investor may look at issues with a shorter time frame in mind. Even though both may fear a loss on their investment in the company, the owners and managers may be just as fearful of losing control of the company. The Investor, on the other hand, may fear being stuck with a bad investment which it can't unload on someone else. Therefore, the Investor's desire for an exit from the company with a guaranteed rate of return on its investment often conflicts with the desire of the owners and managers to stay with the company indefinitely and personally identify with its continuing success.

Ordinarily the Investor will be prepared to give the owners and managers considerable latitude and autonomy in the running of the company so long as pre-approved budgets and business plans are being met. The term sheet, subscription or share purchase agreement, shareholder agreement and other documents covering the investment are often silent on how the company should be run on a day-to-day basis. Many of the provisions of these documents apply only on the occurrence of certain events or upon the satisfaction of certain conditions. However, because the Investor often views itself as supplying board representation, strategic planning, financial advice and industry contacts as well as capital, it generally retains a right to approve certain company decisions.

And because it is seeking to maximize its financial returns, the Investor will ensure that the term sheet and the later documents set out the rules for subsequent issuances and transfers of equity interests. It may request that the documents provide the Investor with "piggyback rights" or "co-sale rights" allowing it to participate in any equity sales by the owners and managers, and "drag- along" rights allowing it to force the owners and managers to participate in any sale of its own equity interest. It may also request that the documents provide priority downside protection against loss, allowing the Investor to manage and control its investment if the company appears unable to meet the business plan, and to enjoy certain exit rights through a sale of the company to a strategic buyer or upon an IPO.

In contrast to what the Investor generally wants to be contained in the term sheet and the other documents, the owners and managers of the company usually want to obtain funding as quickly as possible, minimize dilution of their own equity interests and ensure that they retain control over all of the key decision-making functions. They often want the documents to afford them some flexibility for tax and estate planning purposes, allowing their interests to be freely tradeable among family members, personal trusts and holding companies without the application of any mandatory prior approval or right of first refusal provisions.

In attempting to address many of these items in their negotiations over the term sheet, the Investor and the owners and managers may find it difficult to reconcile their conflicting objectives and approaches.

If the Investor wants to proceed cautiously before investing in the company, it will demand broad access for reviewing relevant documents and spend considerable time in carrying out its due diligence investigations of the company. It may also insist that the closing of its investment in the company be subject to numerous conditions which many require considerable time and money to be spent in satisfying them. This caution on the part of the Investor often conflicts with the desire of the owners and managers to get the money in as quickly as possible with a minimum amount of time being spent by the owners and managers in dealing with due diligence requests and a minimum amount of money being spent by the company in satisfying conditions.

If the Investor wants to ensure that its investment in the company is protected once made, the Investor may insist on the right to veto future capital raising proposals and on anti-dilution protection. The Investor may also insist that it has to be able to exercise some control over the company's operations. This desire for protection on the part of the Investor comes into conflict with the desires of the owners and managers to raise money whenever they feel it is necessary and from whomever they feel is a desirable investor. It also comes into conflict with the overall desire of the owners and managers to have complete freedom to manage the company in their own way.

However the various issues are resolved and reflected in the term sheet, and in the later definitive agreements, the Investor and the owners and managers must still operate on the basis that their arrangements represent a longer term commercial relationship, despite their conflicting interests. They are not engaging in merely an isolated transaction. Without the liquidity which an investment in a public company might provide, the Investor, perhaps begrudgingly, must acknowledge that it may be involved with the company for some time to come, well after the time when its desired exit opportunity was to arise, but didn't.

It is in this context that the terms described in the remainder of this chapter must be considered. When negotiating the term sheet, the Investor and the owners and managers should be aware that, much to their own surprise and possible disappointment, they may find themselves negotiating all over again the provision of additional funds to the company in a later, much needed "follow-on" round of financing because no other source of equity financing is then available to the company.

VALUATION

Although the owners and managers may be fairly confident that their valuation of the company, likely obtained with the help of an outside business valuator as discussed in the *Valuation* chapter, is the proper valuation of the company to be used when determining the price to be paid by the Investor for the company's shares, the Investor may well disagree.

Since many valuations are expressed within a range of probable values rather than as one specific number, there is usually sufficient room for negotiation between the Investor and the owners and managers to arrive at the valuation to be used for their deal. That valuation will likely become the "pre-money" valuation of the company, representing its value before the contribution of funds from the Investor. While the owners and managers may want as high a pre-money valuation as possible, its benefits can be lost if the term sheet contains a number of unfavourable or onerous conditions imposed by the Investor.

If the company is still in its early stages of growth when its lack of consistent revenues and tangible assets makes the use of ordinary valuation techniques questionable, the company's valuation may be based upon an estimate of the amount of money needed from the Investor to fund the company's operations until it reaches a certain critical milestone in its development. The company will then equate the amount needed with the percentage of ownership desired by the Investor for its investment, ordinarily between 30 and 40 per cent, which will lead to a valuation for 100 per cent of the company.

USE OF PROCEEDS AND FUNDING

The typical term sheet will ordinarily address at the outset the purpose for the Investor's funds, along with the timing and amount of each installment or "tranche" being contributed.

The Investor will probably require that the proceeds from its investment are to be used for the company's ongoing working capital requirements and any pre-approved capital expenditures, but are not to be used to pay any existing debts, particularly any monies owed to the owners and managers under any previously made loans or on account of past services rendered to the company.

The payment of each tranche may be triggered by the occurrence of a specified performance milestone, such as launching a new product or reaching a revenue goal. However, the achievement of a milestone may be delayed or frustrated through causes well beyond the company's control, and a certain amount of Investor discretion may be necessary in order to determine whether a particular milestone has indeed been achieved. Furthermore, a milestone may quickly lose its importance or value as a strategic goal for the company, but may nonetheless have to be pursued in order for the company to receive funding.

Therefore the owners and managers should be cautious when agreeing to milestone based funding for the company. A funding schedule based on fixed dates, not on milestones, allows the company to more easily prepare a financial plan and more accurately predict its cash flow requirements. If milestones are to be used, they should be measurable and meaningful.

DIVIDEND RIGHTS

Because the Investor expects to derive most of its financial return in the form of capital appreciation of its preferred shares, it may allow such shares to be dividend-free for a while so that the company's cash flow can be dedicated to funding future growth. However, the Investor may argue for a dividend to be made payable in the event of later stage or expansion financing when the company's projected cash flow is strong enough to provide the Investor with a current, as opposed to a deferred capital, return.

The Investor will most likely require the company to first pay dividends to the holders of the preferred shares before paying dividends to the holders of the common shares. This preference is designed to encourage the owners and managers holding only common shares to use the company's retained earnings for working capital purposes. This preference may apply to the payment of dividends in whatever amount may be declared by the company's board of directors. Alternatively, it may apply only to a fixed dollar amount, usually between 5 per cent to 10 per cent of the original purchase price of the preferred shares, before dividends can be paid on the company's common shares.

In addition to requesting a preference for dividends on the preferred shares, the Investor may request that dividends be "participating", so that the Investor is entitled to receive additional dividends rateably with the holders of the company's common shares once all of the preferences have been satisfied.

Depending upon how the company's financial future is regarded by the Investor, the Investor may also require the company's preferred shares to have cumulative as well as preferential and participating dividends, so that unpaid dividends accumulate from year-to-year, and that all cumulative dividends must first be paid to the holders of the preferred shares before dividends can be paid to the holders of the common shares.

The imposition of preferential, participating or cumulative dividend requirements isn't necessarily onerous on the company. These requirements place a burden on the company only when the owners and managers want to pay dividends to the holders of the common shares, and are prevented from doing so unless they also pay the holders of the preferred shares.

However, a heavy burden can be placed upon the company if the Investor demands mandatory cumulative dividends, requiring the company to accumulate and make periodic dividend payments on the preferred shares. Such a requirement may be imposed if the Investor believes its investment in the company carries considerable risk, even though the requirement may not be enforceable, depending upon the ability of the company to satisfy any prescribed solvency tests under corporate law.[1] In the absence of statutory prohibition, such a requirement may be justified if the Investor foresees little likelihood of an IPO or outside takeover of the company.

REDEMPTION RIGHTS

Although the preferred shares can be made redeemable by either the company, in calling the shares for repurchase, or by the Investor, in putting the shares to the company to receive cash back, it would be unusual if the company was allowed optional redemption. However, it is quite usual for the Investor to insist that the company redeem the preferred shares under certain conditions, if the Investor so elects. The redemption price is normally comprised of the original purchase price of the preferred shares, adjusted for any stock dividends, combinations or splits, plus all accrued and unpaid dividends, and, in many cases, a redemption premium.

Mandatory redemption of the preferred shares by the company on specified dates or upon specified events is not generally prescribed since it deprives the parties of the flexibility they may need to address the company's future capital needs. Mandatory redemption discourages other investors from participating in future rounds of company financing and can make it difficult for the company to obtain bank loans and trade credit.

Although the conditions under which a company may be required to redeem the preferred shares at the option of the Investor are far from standard, redemption is often permitted only after a sufficiently long period has elapsed, usually around five years. Payment upon such redemption is often required to be made in installments spread out over a number of months or even years. However, redemption may be accelerated in the event of a sale of a majority of the company's shares, or an IPO.

As an alternative to, or in addition to, prescribing redemption rights for the preferred shares, the Investor might be provided a "put" which gives the Investor the right, after a certain period of time if no other event permitting redemption has occurred, to sell its shares back to the company at a price equal to their fair market value as determined by an outside appraiser or upon application of a prescribed formula.

However, whether provided as "puts" or rights of redemption, these terms can be of limited practical value should the company be unable to pass the solvency tests prescribed under corporate law.[2]

LIQUIDATION PREFERENCE

Although the Investor may not succeed in obtaining early redemption rights, it will certainly argue that it is entitled to a preference in getting its investment back in the event that the company is liquidated, either upon insolvency or a sale of substantially all of the company's assets. After payment is made out of the liquidation proceeds to secured and unsecured creditors, payment must then be made to the Investor before any payment can be made to the company's common shareholders.

The amount of the payment to be made to the Investor is usually set at the original purchase price of the preferred shares, adjusted for any stock dividends, combinations or splits. The obligation to increase this amount to include any accrued but unpaid dividends, or, in the absence of cumulative dividends, a guaranteed return often between five per cent and 10 per cent of the original purchase price, can be the subject of intense negotiation.

In addition to receiving this preferential amount, the Investor may want to participate rateably in the distribution of the company's remaining proceeds of liquidation with the common shareholders. A frequent point of contention is whether the common shareholders should first receive back their own purchase price before the Investor then participates with the common shareholders in the remaining proceeds.

Another point of contention is whether the liquidation preference enjoyed by the Investor should be subordinated in any subsequent round of financing so that new investors will have a senior position on liquidation or at least rank equally with the Investor. This debate can be complicated if liquidation is defined in the term sheet or subsequent documents to include the acquisition of the company or its merger into another entity.

VOTING RIGHTS

The Investor is ordinarily granted the same number of votes as the votes carried by the common shares into which its preferred shares are convertible, generally on a one vote per share basis. However, in order for the Investor to carry out the special rights it might enjoy in electing directors and vetoing certain company decisions which are described in more detail below, the Investor may insist that certain actions require the approval of the preferred shareholders voting as a separate class.[3]

CONVERSION RIGHTS

There may not be much debate over when the preferred shares can be converted into common shares of the company, although the conversion rate can represent a contentious issue in the negotiations. Ordinarily the preferred shares are convertible into common shares at the option of the Investor at any time and are automatically converted into common shares on a mandatory basis in the event that the company makes an IPO or an offer is received to buy not less than a majority of its shares. Automatic conversion in the event of an IPO is seldom debated because the company is able to simplify its capital structure as a pre-requisite to the IPO, and the Investor is able to participate in it. Because the special voting rights and other terms of the preferred shares are often inconsistent with the terms, or absence of terms, of public market securities, the preferred shares are designed to simply disappear on an IPO through conversion.

There may be some debate, however, on the size of an IPO which triggers the conversion. The owners and managers and the Investor will generally try to establish a size sufficient to create an adequate "float" when the common shares trade publicly. Furthermore, as part of the conversion, the Investor may argue for payment of accrued but unpaid dividends, either in cash or shares, although accrued dividends are often waived. In the case of automatic conversion on a takeover offer, a minimum share price might also be required.

The conversion rate, along with the percentage ownership of the company which the Investor wants to acquire, depends on the pre-money valuation of the company and the dollar amount of the funds to be contributed by the Investor. The rate also depends on the projected value of the company, and the likelihood of the Investor receiving its required rate of return on invested capital in the event of a future sale of its shares in the company.

Determining the conversion rate can become quite complex, especially when later rounds of financing from other investors are anticipated and the percentage ownership of the Investor is diluted as a result. Generally speaking, the conversion rate of the preferred shares into the company's common shares is calculated by dividing the original purchase price of the preferred shares by a "conversion price" which is initially set at the original purchase price to achieve a 1-to-1 conversion of preferred shares into common shares.

ANTI-DILUTION PROTECTION

This conversion price is then automatically adjusted for any stock dividends, combinations or splits, in order that the preferred shares will convert into the number of common shares which will maintain the Investor's percentage of equity in the company. This provision is seldom debated.

What is usually debated is an adjustment to the conversion price should the company need to issue additional equity in subsequent rounds of financing at less than the original purchase price paid for the preferred shares by the Investor. The Investor will often insist that it be given the rights to obtain more common shares on conversion, without additional aggregate consideration, in the event that the company subsequently issues new common shares or equivalent securities at a price below the then current conversion price. The conversion price of the preferred shares is effectively decreased, resulting in more common shares per preferred share being issued upon conversion.

In requesting this anti-dilution protection, the Investor ordinarily argues that because there is no readily available, independent market price for the company's shares, it should be protected against having overpaid. Furthermore, the owners and managers holding common shares should have to pay through dilution if they don't succeed in increasing the value of the company by the next round of financing. From their point of view, however, any decrease in the value of the company could result from events beyond their control. In conceding to the inclusion of such anti-dilution protection, the company is arguably denied the flexibility it may need in a downturn to raise new financing at a lower price.

If anti-dilution protection is to be afforded to the Investor, the debate then shifts to whether a "weighted average" formula or "ratchet" formula should apply. The weighted average formula uses the discounted price and number of the new common shares sold in adjusting the conversion price of the preferred shares downwards. Under this formula, the sale by the company of a large number of common shares at a price slightly lower than the conversion price, and the sale of a small number of common shares at a much lower price, collectively result in a relatively small adjustment to the conversion price of the preferred shares. The ratchet formula, on the other hand, automatically decreases the conversion price of the preferred shares to the lowest price at which the new common shares have been issued, regardless of the number of new shares issued.

The owners and managers holding common shares generally want the weighted average formula to apply if discount stock is offered in the future, given the greater dilution of their shares if the ratchet formula is applied instead. To arrive at a formula, a hybrid of both the weighted average and the ratchet formulas may end up being used, such as applying the ratchet formula for the first two years of the Investor's investment and the weighted average formula thereafter in an effort to discourage the early issuance of discount stock. Alternatively, the ratchet formula might apply only if the discount stock is issued at a price below a specified threshold price.

Exceptions to these anti-dilution provisions may be requested by the owners and managers. The most common exception relates to the pool of shares, ranging somewhere between five per cent and 20 per cent of the outstanding fully-diluted shares of the company, which is set aside for issuance to key employees. The size of this pool may be adjusted from time to time to accommodate any future share issuances which have been approved by the Investor.

BOARD OF DIRECTORS

The general approach of the Investor, as mentioned above, is to leave the owners and managers free to operate the company on a day-to-day basis so long as the company is complying with its budgets and business plans and meeting any milestones that have been agreed upon. However, the Investor will usually insist that it be given the right to nominate one or more directors to the company's board, or at least be given the right to have a nominee attend board meetings as an observer.

Observers are usually entitled to receive notice of and to attend meetings of the board of directors, but are not entitled to vote. The Investor may prefer to limit the involvement of its nominees to observer status if the board already consists of nominees of other professional investors, or as a way of avoiding director liability or the policies of certain stock exchanges which place escrow requirements during an IPO on shareholders having board representation.

In addition to the Investor's nominees, the owners and managers holding common shares will also have the right to nominate a certain number of directors. The shareholder agreement will usually require the parties to vote in favour of the election of the prescribed nominees to the board of directors and to fill any vacancy on the board with the nominee of the party who was represented by a vacating director. The parties will also be required to remove any nominee director who contravenes or votes against the wishes of the party nominating him. A related provision, which is just as likely to be in the term sheet as well as the shareholder agreement, may limit the number of directors so that the right to nominate directors is equal to the right to control a specified portion of the board.

The Investor may request that the term sheet, and later the shareholder agreement, require audit and compensation committees of the board to be established, comprised solely of directors unrelated to the owners and managers, and that directors' and officers' liability insurance be put into place. The Investor will usually require board meetings to be held quarterly, if not more frequently, and will insist that the quorum requirements not allow such meetings to proceed in the absence of its nominee director.

To provide the Investor with the right to become more involved should the company's financial position deteriorate, the term sheet may contain "voting switch provisions". These provisions give the Investor the right to elect more directors, even a majority of the company's board, upon the occurrence of certain materially adverse events, such as the failure by the company to meet specified milestones or the breach by the company of a covenant in any of the definitive agreements. These provisions may even include the right to relieve any of the current owners and managers from their management duties upon relatively short notice without cause, but subject to an obligation to pay appropriate severance and to buy back any company shares the owners and managers may hold.

MANAGEMENT AND CONTROL

In addition to its right to elect directors, the Investor ordinarily wants to play some role, possibly by exercising veto rights, in important management matters. These matters generally include operating budgets, major capital expenditures, executive hiring and firing, compensation levels, equity and debt financings, material strategic alliances, larger acquisitions and sales, dividend payments, share redemptions, and other significant actions out of the ordinary course of the company's business.

The term sheet may specify that control over these particular matters be implemented by the Investor as a preferred shareholder voting on them as a separate class, or by establishing super-majority voting rules at the board level, or by simply requiring written approval of the Investor. The term sheet may also specify that the right to vote on such matters as a separate class be incorporated into the terms of the preferred shares and reflected in the company's articles or other charter documents, instead of being merely reflected in a shareholder agreement. However, depending upon the nature of such terms and the need of the parties for confidentiality, it may not be appropriate for the terms to be placed in the company's articles and thereby subject to possible public scrutiny.

EMPLOYEES

To ensure that the company's key management positions are filled by people with suitable skills and experience, the Investor may insist that the term sheet specifically name certain individuals recommended by the Investor to serve, for example, as the chief financial officer or chief marketing officer of the company. The Investor will usually require that all of the company's top managers enter into comprehensive employment agreements not only setting out their respective duties, compensation (including bonus entitlement and participation in stock purchase and option plans), and rights on termination, but also their assignment of intellectual property rights and their non-disclosure, non-competition and no "moonlighting" obligations. The maintenance of "key person" insurance for them will also be a requirement.

The treatment of options and shares held by the owners and managers is often subject to considerable debate during the negotiation of the term sheet. Ordinarily any rights to acquire discounted shares or options will be vested in the owners and managers over a three to five year period. Any shares acquired by them will usually be subject to transfer restrictions, as well as call rights in favour of the company and possibly the Investor upon the termination of employment, death or permanent disability of the owners and managers. The Investor will want to be assured that current management of the company will be motivated through appreciation in the value of the company's shares to stay and work, and will be discouraged from leaving by means of the call provisions.

INFORMATION RIGHTS

The term sheet will usually require the company to provide ongoing financial information to the Investor directly on a regular basis and not simply by way of its nominee director at board meetings. The information to be provided will include monthly or quarterly management financial statements and audited annual financial statements. Other information generally to be provided may include management budgets, forecasts and variance reports, along with research and development reports and certificates from the chief financial officer that all statutory deductions and other amounts for which directors may be personally liable have been appropriately withheld and remitted.

The Investor will usually be granted ongoing inspection and audit rights which permit it to visit and inspect the company's properties, examine the company's accounts and records, and discuss the company's affairs and finances with company officers. However, the owners and managers will likely try to qualify such rights by excluding the provision of any information which the company reasonably believes to be trade secrets or other confidential information unless the company is satisfied with the confidentiality arrangements made with the inspecting parties.

PRE-EMPTIVE RIGHTS

In order to maintain its percentage of equity ownership in the company, the Investor will usually insist that it be given a right of first refusal on the purchase of any shares, and any securities exchangeable or convertible into shares, including rights, options and warrants, which may be offered by the company in the future. This right, commonly called a "pre-emptive right", normally entitles the Investor to receive notice of the offering and to subscribe for a portion of the offering that is equal to its existing percentage of the company's outstanding equity under the same terms offered to other investors.

This right may also entitle the Investor to purchase shares not purchased by other shareholders under their own rights of first refusal. If fewer than all of the holders having such rights elect to participate, or if they participate for less than their full entitlement, the term sheet may provide for the re-allotment of the unsubscribed portion among those already taking up their full entitlement. The available shares are simply pro-rated among the buying shareholders in proportion to their pre-existing shareholdings.

The owners and managers will often request that the term sheet provide for reciprocal pre-emptive rights, if an existing shareholder agreement for the company doesn't already provide such rights, along with a number of exemptions. These requested exemptions from pre-emptive rights may cover shares issued to employees, officers, directors and consultants pursuant to incentive compensation arrangements, or to shares issued upon conversion of other company securities or in connection with stock dividends or stock splits, or to shares issued to commercial lenders and equipment lessors in the ordinary course of business. Shares issued pursuant to the company's acquisition of another entity may also be exempted, although the Investor may wish to restrict such exemption to only certain specified acquisitions.

RIGHTS OF FIRST REFUSAL

The term sheet will usually provide for the Investor to be given a right of first refusal on the transfer of any company shares proposed by any other shareholders in the future. In contrast to pre-emptive rights which are intended to maintain its percentage of equity ownership in the company, rights of first refusal are intended to increase its equity ownership in the company in the event that any of the other shareholders decides to sell. As with pre-emptive rights, rights of first refusal often apply to any shares, or securities exchangeable or convertible into shares, including rights, options or warrants, and not just to the preferred shares or other shares of the same class as are already held by the Investor.

The owners and managers will often request reciprocal rights of first refusal, if an existing shareholder agreement for the company doesn't already provide such rights. They will also request a number of exemptions. Exemptions are ordinarily given for transfers to a registered retirement savings plan or other trust of which the shareholder is the beneficial owner, or to a shareholder's spouse, or to a shareholder's personal holding company provided that the shareholders of the holding company agree not to transfer their shares in the holding company unless they concurrently transfer the shares of the company to another exempt party.

In the case of corporate shareholders, exemptions from rights of first refusal may be available to cover transfers to affiliates. In the case of the Investor, exempt transfers may include transfers to other funds or corporations managed by the Investor, and possibly include distributions of shares to the investors of such other funds or corporations.

During the preparation of the term sheet, a debate often occurs over which events specifically trigger the right of first refusal. Some term sheets require that a "bona fide offer" must be received by the selling shareholder from a third party before notice is to be given to the other shareholders of their purchase rights. Obviously this requirement deters potential third party purchasers from incurring the time and expense involved in preparing a serious offer which may be ignored if any one of the other current shareholders elects to exercise its purchase rights.

As an alternative, the term sheet may provide what is commonly called a "right of first offer", which permits the selling shareholder to simply give notice to the other shareholders of its intention to sell at an acceptable price. This alternative, however, may encourage the selling shareholder to specify an inflated price with the expectation that the other shareholders will elect to purchase at the inflated price rather than risk a third party becoming a shareholder.

PIGGYBACK RIGHTS

As a way of achieving liquidity of its investment as well as denying the owners and managers holding company shares an exit from the company before the Investor is able to exit, the Investor may insist upon "piggyback" rights. These provisions generally allow the Investor, and usually any other significant shareholders, to participate in a shareholder's proposed sale of company shares. Ordinarily only a sale resulting in a change of control of the company, or a sale by the owners and managers of all or a substantial portion of their holdings of company shares, will trigger piggyback rights.

In contrast to piggyback rights which allow other shareholders to have included all of their shares in a third party purchase offer, the term sheet may provide for "co-sale" rights instead. Co-sale rights require the inclusion of only such portion of their shares which, when added to the portion held by the owners and managers, equals the number of shares which the third party wishes to purchase. The number of shares that the owners and managers can sell is effectively reduced and replaced by the number of shares that the other shareholders, including the Investor, elect to sell to the third party. In the event that the third party wishes to purchase all of the company's outstanding shares, the difference between piggyback rights and co-sale rights disappears in practice.

DRAG-ALONG RIGHTS

The Investor will often request it be given "drag-along" rights enabling it to force the owners and managers to participate in a sale of company shares by the Investor to a third party. Such rights increase the marketability of the Investor's shares since a third party purchaser may be more likely to want all of the shares of the company rather than have to deal with other company shareholders after the purchase. The owners and managers often counter with a request that the drag-along provisions also require the Investor to participate in a sale by the owners and managers.

REGISTRATION RIGHTS

If the Investor is U.S.-based or believes the company is likely to become eligible to list on NASDAQ or other American exchanges, it will request "registration rights". These rights allow the Investor to "demand" that the company qualify the Investor's shares in the company for public distribution, and thereby dictate the timing of a public offering. They also provide the Investor with piggyback rights under which its shares are included in any "primary registration", when the company files a registration statement to permit the sale of its shares from treasury, or in any "secondary registration", when the company files a registration statement to permit other shareholders to sell.

These rights are intended to give the Investor liquidity on an IPO when the perceived return from maintaining an ongoing investment in the company is below the Investor's threshold return requirements. The Investor is then able to liquidate its investment in the company and reinvest its funds elsewhere in the hope of earning a greater return.

Demand registration rights entitle the Investor to require the company to register the company's shares after a certain period of time, usually three to five years, with the U.S. Securities and Exchange Commission by filing a registration statement. The number of demands is usually negotiated, with the owners and managers insisting that one is enough and the Investor arguing for two or more. Granting demand registration rights can place a significant burden on the company given the time and cost involved if those rights are exercised. All expenses incurred in demand registrations are normally paid by the company. In practice, exercising the demand doesn't necessarily mean that a public offering will happen. Since the company's management has to go on the "road show" and make convincing presentations to the fund managers and brokers who will be buying the company's shares, management can usually resist the demand to register if business conditions are not favourable.

Piggyback registration rights obligate the company to use its best efforts to include the Investor's shares in any public registrations the company intends to make. However, such rights are always subject to the underwriter's discretion to exclude the Investor's shares from the offering. Such rights are also usually excluded from any offering of shares in the context of a corporate acquisition or employee stock option or purchase plan.

LOSS OF RIGHTS

If the owners and managers have significant bargaining power, they may successfully argue that the Investor should lose certain rights if the Investor declines to invest additional funds when required later on or if the Investor's equity holdings in the company fall below a specified percentage. The owners and managers often argue that this possible loss of rights by the Investor is a trade-off for the possible gain of rights by the Investor to elect more directors through the voting switch provisions mentioned above upon the occurrence of a material adverse event.

For example, the owners and managers may insist that the Investor lose its anti-dilution protection, and perhaps its liquidation preference and right to nominate directors, if it fails to make a pro rata investment in any future company financing. Such a "pay-to-play" provision encourages future investment and assistance by the Investor in helping the company to grow. A pay-to-play provision generally forces the Investor failing to participate in a future financing to convert its preferred shares into common shares or into a series of preferred shares lacking price-based anti-dilution protection, or to simply waive any anti-dilution adjustments it might otherwise be entitled to as a preferred shareholder.

In an effort to reduce the extent of the Investor's potential veto, especially if exercisable by way of mandatory written approval of various prescribed matters, the owners and managers may insist that the veto should disappear once the Investor's equity ownership in the company is reduced below a certain percentage. They may also insist that the information rights granted to the Investor should disappear as well if the Investor's equity ownership is correspondingly reduced.

REPRESENTATIONS AND WARRANTIES

Most of the representations and warranties to be given by the company, and possibly by the owners and managers, are most likely to be contained in the subscription or share purchase agreement. However, the term sheet may describe the representations and warranties to be given in fairly general language.

The term sheet often requires representations from the company about its good standing and its capital structure, the proper approval of the proposed financing, the ownership of its assets, and the extent of its contracts and financial obligations. It will also require company representations about the absence of litigation or probable claims against the company, the company's compliance with applicable laws, and anything else which may influence the Investor in making an informed decision about whether or not to invest in the company.

In support of the representations made by the company concerning its capital structure and the proper approval of the proposed financing, including the issuance of the preferred shares in conformity with applicable laws, the term sheet may require delivery of an opinion from the company's legal counsel at closing on such items.

The owners and managers usually explore during the negotiation of the term sheet the preparedness of the Investor to permit these representations of the company to be restricted to only "material" items, or to the "actual knowledge" of only specified owners or managers. Furthermore, they are likely to insist upon representations from the Investor about the proper approval of its investment, its qualification to purchase the company's shares under applicable laws, and the sufficiency of the access it has had to assess company information and ask all questions in order to allow it to make an informed investment decision.

PERSONAL LIABILITY

One of the more contentious issues usually arising during the negotiation of the term sheet is the extent to which any of the owners or managers should be personally liable to the Investor for any breach of the company's representations or covenants in any of the definitive agreements. The owners and managers are ordinarily prepared to accept personal liability only under the shareholder agreement as well as under any employment agreements and additional non-competition and confidentiality agreements which they may sign in their personal capacities.

However, few owners or managers are prepared to be jointly and severally liable with the company under any indemnity given in the subscription or share purchase agreement to cover any losses the Investor may suffer as a result of the company's breach of the representations or covenants contained in it. Despite the Investor's argument that some of the risk of unknown company liabilities should be placed under an indemnity upon the owners and managers who are in a better position to know or at least find out, the owners and managers already bear, and will continue to bear, such risk by holding company shares.

Given that the issuance of company shares to the Investor does not result in the owners or managers receiving funds personally from the Investor, as they might if they were selling their own shares directly, most owners and managers are able to argue convincingly that they receive no reward for taking on the extra risk of a personal indemnity for the company's potential breach. Should their refusal to provide such an indemnity cause the Investor to deny funds, the owners and managers may offer, as an alternative, personal indemnities for which they are only separately or severally liable to the extent of their respective proportionate holdings of company shares, collectively capped at the amount of the Investor's investment.

DUE DILIGENCE PERIOD

The term sheet will ordinarily set out the rights and obligations of the parties, sometimes on a legally binding basis, covering the time after its signing when the Investor undertakes due diligence investigations of the company. Completion of the investment will usually be stated in the term sheet, and possibly again in the subscription or share purchase agreement, as being dependent upon the Investor's satisfaction with the results of the investigations. During such investigations, legal counsel will work together in preparing the definitive agreements which attempt to reflect the provisions of the term sheet. Negotiations often continue during this period, especially when the investigations reveal information which causes the Investor to request amendments to any of the provisions in the term sheet.

Rights of access during normal business hours to the company's various properties to review its accounts and records, interview certain employees and inspect the business being carried on are generally given in the term sheet to the Investor by the owners and managers, subject to a duty to maintain confidentiality. The Investor may also be given a right of introduction to the company's customers, suppliers and consultants, all with a view to verifying the company's financial statements and projections of performance, as well as the representations to be made in the subscription or share purchase agreement.

LOCK-UP

Often the Investor will insist that the company agree to be bound by a "lock-up" or "no-shop" provision during which the company will not discuss its funding needs with any other parties. The lock-up provision, often a legally binding term in the term sheet which is repeated in the subscription or share purchase agreement, is intended to encourage the parties to focus on completing the transaction and not be distracted by other possible deals. Despite the potential recovery of its own expenses whether the transaction is completed or not, as discussed below, the Investor has to consider its "opportunity cost" when working on a deal. Because the Investor invests a lot of time in carrying out due diligence and in negotiating the documents, it wants to ensure that the company and the owners and managers won't be soliciting other professional investors at the same time and increasing the likelihood of the company switching to one of them.

The lock-up is often stated to be in effect until the closing of the transaction, or until a date by which the transaction is reasonably expected to close, whichever is earlier. However, as discussed below, there may well be more than one closing, and the Investor may argue that the lock-up should subsist until the final closing. Since the amount of time which the Investor ordinarily spends in financing the company is relatively greater up to the date of the initial closing, and relatively less when approaching subsequent closings (despite unexpected time required for ongoing monitoring and crisis management), the owners and managers often succeed in having any lock-up restricted to the period prior to the initial closing. However, the Investor is nonetheless protected thereafter through the veto rights it usually may exercise over future share issuances and significant company borrowing.

TIME OF CLOSING

The term sheet may specify that the closing of the transaction may take place immediately upon the execution of the definitive agreements, or within a certain time after their execution. The length of time after the execution of the definitive agreements which is required in order to close may depend upon whether the Investor will need more time to complete additional due diligence instead of relying upon the representations made by the company in the subscription or share purchase agreement. It may also depend upon the perceived difficulty in obtaining any internal approvals from the parties themselves or any consents required from third parties.

Closing is usually dependent upon board of director or investment committee approval in the case of the Investor, and on board of director as well as shareholder approval in the case of the company. The owners and managers, on the other hand, may resist such a delay in closing, depending upon their assessment of the company's financial needs. The company may simply not have sufficient cash reserves to continue operating between the time the definitive agreements are executed and a subsequent closing date.

If the Investor prefers that monies be contributed in installments or tranches over time upon completion of certain milestones, it may request an initial closing, at which all of the definitive agreements are executed and delivered and an initial payment made in exchange for a certificate for a certain portion of the overall number of preferred shares being purchased. The Investor may then request one or more subsequent closings to take place within a certain period of time following applicable milestones, at which the balance of the purchase price will be paid in exchange for additional share certificates, and other documents will be delivered which update any information given in a previous closing which has become stale or misleading.

The Investor is likely to want the subsequent closings to remain subject to its discretion, whether the applicable milestones have been met or not. As mentioned earlier in this chapter, the owners and managers will normally attempt to avoid having milestone dependent closings, and will certainly resist any request to make a closing subject to the discretion of the Investor. They want and need certainty for the company's funding schedules.

EXPENSES

While the term sheet may allow the funds contributed by the Investor to be used for the company's ongoing working capital requirements, the Investor may resist allowing payment of the company's transaction costs out of the proceeds.

However, the Investor will likely request the company to pay the reasonable legal expenses incurred by the Investor in negotiating and drafting all of the documents and in conducting due diligence, whether the transaction closes or not. While the owners and managers are usually unable to refuse this request, they may succeed at having the amount of reimbursable expenses capped at a specific dollar amount.

The Investor may also request the company to provide a cash retainer to the lawyers acting for the Investor, although the owners and managers may be able to negotiate this requirement away. The legal fees charged by the Investor's lawyers are generally deducted from the investment proceeds before being paid over to the company.

Subscription Agreements

Once the basic terms covering the Investor's equity investment in the company have been set out in a term sheet as described in the previous chapter, and the Investor's due diligence investigations of the company are well under way, if not substantially completed, the parties may begin the negotiation and preparation of a legally binding subscription agreement governing the transaction.

Although a shareholder agreement, discussed in a later chapter, along with other definitive agreements and various amendments to the company's articles and by-laws will ordinarily be required to accompany the subscription agreement in converting the provisions of the term sheet into legally binding form, the subscription agreement is generally regarded as the master agreement documenting the Investor's equity investment. While it may be called a share purchase agreement or purchase and sale agreement instead, this chapter will refer to the main agreement between the Investor and the company covering the issuance and purchase of company shares as a subscription agreement.

Unless the due diligence investigations have revealed such serious problems with the company as to cause the Investor to avoid proceeding with the transaction, the Investor's legal counsel may be instructed to prepare a first draft of the agreement.

This first draft may deviate from the principal business terms reflected in the term sheet. If certain problems were discovered during the due diligence process, they may be solved by imposing special conditions in the draft agreement which need to be satisfied before the deal can close. Or the draft may simply introduce either a reduction in the subscription price or a provision for deferred or escrowed payments.

One of the reasons for the agreement's considerable size by comparison with the term sheet is the presence of numerous representations and warranties which the company makes in respect of its business as well as the indemnification of the Investor by the company in the event that the representations turn out to be false.

The representations and warranties attempt to address all aspects of the company's business and the ability of the company to issue the shares to the Investor free and clear from the claims of others. They cover all of the items which the Investor may have attempted to investigate during the due diligence period, plus many more, and serve as a contractual "backstop" to the due diligence by providing the Investor with recourse against the company for any problems which weren't discovered during the Investor's investigations.

The representations and warranties covered in the draft agreement address potential undisclosed or undiscovered problems which might arise after closing and adversely affect the value of the Investor's company shares. The agreement will usually represent the absolute ownership of the assets used in the business and the absence of any undisclosed mortgages or liens on such assets, the proper operating condition of the equipment, the saleability of the inventory, the collectability of the receivables, the compliance with all applicable laws, the adequacy of all insurance, and the absence of any environmental contamination or intellectual property infringement. It will also contain representations regarding the disclosure of all material contracts, the payment of all taxes, the completeness of all financial statements, and the absence of any lawsuits.

As a means of permitting the Investor to recover from the company for any losses and expenses which the Investor may incur in the event that any of the representations turn out to be false after the deal closes, the draft agreement will ordinarily include certain indemnification provisions which prescribe the process under which the Investor may make a claim against the company for a false representation.

These indemnification provisions are usually the only way the Investor can seek recourse against the company after the deal closes, and are often limited or "capped" at the amount of the subscription price paid. However, if a percentage of the subscription price is to be paid over time after closing in installments, the Investor may be able to reduce such installments by the amount it claims as an indemnity. If there are to be multiple closings instead, each representing a separate installment or tranche with separate closing conditions, the Investor will more likely abstain from the subsequent closings whether or not its indemnification claim is settled.

Alternatively, the draft agreement may provide for a certain percentage of the purchase price to be deposited on closing with a third party, such as a trust company or perhaps one of the law firms acting on the deal, to be held in escrow and applied to any indemnity claims made by the Investor within a prescribed period of time. Often the representations, and the indemnification and escrow provisions supporting them, will be enforceable for a period of two years after the deal closes.

Although the term sheet will usually specify certain conditions which must be satisfied before the deal can be closed, the draft agreement may contain a number of additional conditions, depending upon the results of the due diligence investigations and any changes to the terms of the deal arising out of the ongoing deal negotiations.

The approval of a specific regulatory body, the preparation of updated financial statements, the completion of an environmental audit, the consent of a certain creditor or landlord, the extension of a major supply agreement, the commitment of a major financial institution, the hiring of key employees, and the approval of the Investor's board of directors, are all examples of closing conditions that may be inserted into the draft agreement.

The remainder of this chapter addresses some of the more contentious terms of the subscription agreement. Because these terms will become legally enforceable upon execution of the agreement, they form the basis for not only the liability of the parties up to closing but also their residual liability for the deal after closing. However, those issues which have already been discussed in the previous chapter will not be repeated here even though they are just as applicable to subscription agreements.

SUBSCRIPTION PRICE

There are a number of different ways the subscription price can be paid, and a number of different means used to secure its payment if spread out over a number of installments.

Even if a deposit is not provided for in the term sheet, the agreement may still add a requirement for a deposit to be paid on signing which is to be held in an interest-bearing bank account, perhaps in the name of the company's lawyer. The agreement will usually state that the deposit is either to be applied on closing to the subscription price owing, or is to be forfeited by the Investor should the Investor fail to close.

The payments on closing may include one amount to an escrow agent, to be held pursuant to a separate escrow agreement entered into between the parties and the escrow agent, and for another amount to the company. Further amounts payable to the company may be made in later installments under a promissory note.

While the placing in escrow of a certain portion of the subscription price may be requested by a Investor to provide a dedicated fund against which claims for indemnification may generally be made, some of the subscription price might also be placed in escrow to be used to satisfy a liability which is not quantifiable at the closing date, such as the amount needed to remediate polluted real estate.

In the event that a promissory note is given by an Investor to evidence the balance it owes to the company on account of the subscription price, the payments under the note may be secured by a charge over the Investor's assets pursuant to a general security agreement, or the company may request a guarantee from the Investor's controlling shareholder.

Because the company is generally not permitted to issue shares until the subscription price has been fully paid in money or the equivalent in property or past services,[1] and a promissory note is deemed not to be property for the payment of shares,[2] an Investor cannot receive its full share allotment until all of its installments of the subscription price have been paid.

Consequently, as an alternative to providing for one closing with subsequent installment payments, the agreement may provide for multiple closings, each of which requires the issuance by the company of a certain percentage of the allotted shares in exchange for payment by the Investor of the same percentage of the overall subscription price in cash. Usually only the first closing will require the production of numerous definitive agreements and other documentation, leaving the subsequent closings to require only updated information where necessary.

However, each subsequent closing may be dependent upon the satisfaction of quite separate and different conditions if the transaction is based on the achievement by the company of specific milestones, as mentioned in the previous chapter, with additional amounts of the subscription price being payable only when a particular milestone is achieved.

REPRESENTATIONS AND WARRANTIES

The company's representations and warranties set out in the agreement constitute a comprehensive description of the company and its business. They usually appear in most subscription agreements under the heading of "representations and warranties", reflecting a technical distinction between the two terms. Representations are statements of past or existing facts, whereas warranties are promises that existing or future facts are or will be true. For convenience, the remainder of this chapter will refer to them as simply representations.

The company's representations have three main purposes. First, they disclose to the Investor important information about the company and its business. The representations, and the exceptions to them which may be expressed in either the representations themselves or in schedules to the agreement, should provide the Investor with enough detailed information about the company to motivate the Investor to complete the deal and justify the subscription price the Investor has agreed to pay. Second, they provide a means of escape from the deal, since the Investor's obligation to complete the deal is usually subject to a condition in the agreement that the representations are true and accurate at the time of closing. Third, they allocate some or all of the risk in relation to a particular matter or liability between the Investor and the company. An Investor discovering a breach of a representation after closing will normally have a right to be indemnified for that breach by the company.

The extent of the company's representations will depend upon the relative bargaining strengths of the parties. If two or more potential investors are competing to invest in the company, the balance of power may shift to the company. If the company is motivated by the desire to sell its shares quickly, perhaps because of pressure from its banker or uncertainty over future profitability of its business, and the Investor is aware of that motivation, the Investor may have the power to insist on more extensive representations.

Who the Investor is will also influence the extent of the company's representations. Some Investors may not want or require the same level of disclosure about the business as others. If an Investor is already quite familiar with the business, it may be willing to accept fewer or more heavily qualified representations.

Representations are generally qualified three ways: the agreement may set out specific exceptions to them, or limit them to the knowledge of the company, or limit them by reference to materiality.

Qualifying a representation by specific exceptions can be accomplished in the schedules to the agreement or in the text of the representation itself. The Investor will ordinarily insist that any exceptions should be quite specific and avoid general or vague wording. The company may seek a right in the agreement to update the various disclosure schedules during the interim period between signing and closing and thereby shift the risk associated with any changes during such period to the Investor.

The Investor will also want the agreement to state that the company's representations are not qualified or affected by the Investor's due diligence. Such a provision ensures that the company will not escape liability, even if the Investor discovers certain facts during the due diligence process that would make a representation incorrect, subject of course to the applicable limitation periods. The company should try to negotiate the removal of such a provision on the basis that it would be unfair for the Investor to withhold knowledge of a breach of a representation in order to claim against the company after the closing.

The company may also qualify a representation by limiting it to those facts of which the company is aware. A qualification based upon knowledge attempts to limit the company's risk and shifts to the Investor the burden of proving that the company knew of the breach of representation. However, the Investor is likely to resist such a qualification when the company or the company's advisors are in a position to confirm the truth of the representation. Even when the company does not know and is not in a position to discover the facts, the Investor may still take the position that all of the risk relating to things unknown should be borne by the company.

The company may also qualify a representation by making it subject to a materiality threshold. For example, a representation regarding the records of the business may be qualified by stating that they are complete and accurate records of all "material" matters relating to the business. Sometimes a subscription agreement will define materiality by using a monetary threshold. A company may represent, for example, the completeness of a list of all material contracts of the business, with "material" being defined as representing at least $100,000 worth of goods or services.

However, if the indemnification provisions of the agreement, as discussed below, give the Investor a right to indemnity for breaches of representations only if the Investor's damages exceed a specified threshold or "floor" level, the Investor may resist any qualifications based on materiality. Such qualifications, when combined with a floor for indemnities, will permit the company to avoid liability for non-material breaches even though such breaches in the aggregate exceed the floor amount.

The specific representations discussed below often deserve particular attention from the company and possible qualification.

Financial Statements

Since a review of the financial statements is an essential part of the Investor's due diligence investigation of the company and its business, the Investor will usually require a representation that the annual financial statements are "complete and accurate". The company, however, may well object to giving such a representation because it goes beyond the kind of assurance ordinarily given by the accountants who prepared the statements.

The company may also object to a representation in the agreement that any interim financial statements are presented fairly in accordance with generally accepted accounting principles, or GAAP, or international financial reporting standards, or IFRS, because these statements do not include year-end adjustments or notes. If the financial statements are not audited but merely prepared on a "notice to reader" basis which would not entail a GAAP or IFRS analysis or review being undertaken by the accountants involved, such a representation should be restricted to the company's knowledge or possibly not given at all.

Dividends and Distributions

A draft subscription agreement may contain a representation that cash or other assets have not been removed from the company by way of dividends or share redemptions since the date of the latest annual financial statements which were given to the Investor to review. If the company insists that it should be allowed to distribute cash prior to closing in order repay any outstanding shareholder loans or remove all or part of the company's retained earnings, this representation will need to be qualified accordingly.

Compliance with Laws

A representation will usually be included in the draft agreement that the business has complied with all laws, both current and historical. The company may attempt to change this representation so that it refers only to compliance since a certain date, arguing that non-compliance before then has long been irrelevant. The company may also try to restrict this representation to only material violations.

Furthermore, the company may prefer to make any required disclosure of actual or potential violations outside of the agreement or the schedules as these documents may become available to third parties or regulatory authorities.

Accounts Receivable

There will often be a representation in the draft agreement that the accounts receivable are collectable, subject to a reasonable allowance consistent with past practice for doubtful accounts. Sometimes an Investor will want this representation to state that the accounts receivable will be fully collected, subject to a reserve, by a certain date.

The company should be aware that a representation that the receivables are collectable, as opposed to a representation that they are legitimate or bona fide, can operate as a subscription price "adjustment".

Customers and Suppliers

The draft agreement may contain a representation that all of the major customers and suppliers of the business have been listed on a schedule and that all arrangements with them are in good standing. It may also include a statement that the relationships with them will continue in the same manner after closing as before. Given the difficulty of making this kind of prediction, the company should attempt to qualify this representation by reference to the company's knowledge.

Leased Premises

Often a draft agreement will include comprehensive representations about leased as well as owned real estate. The company may resist giving such representations about any leased premises, arguing that it's unreasonable to expect the company occupying only a portion of a building as a tenant to have complete knowledge about such things as whether the building complies with zoning setbacks or whether there are any structural defects in the building. However, such an argument may not be very convincing if the company is a long-term tenant of all or substantially all of a building.

As a compromise, the parties may agree to separately identify those buildings with substantial leases as "major leased premises". The company may then agree to provide unqualified representations with respect to those premises, if the Investor then agrees to accept representations regarding all of the other leased premises which would be restricted to the company's knowledge.

Environmental Matters

Representations that the company is not responsible for any clean-up or corrective action under any environmental laws and that none of the owned or leased real estate has ever contained any hazardous substances are usually contained in the draft subscription agreement. The company should try to qualify these broad representations by restricting them to facts which the company knows about. Given the potential costs associated with environmental remediation, the Investor will likely resist any attempted qualification of these representations.

To remove such an impasse between them, the parties may retain an independent investigator to conduct an environmental assessment of the real estate used in the business and then allocate their respective liabilities based upon the remedial efforts recommended in the assessment report. As mentioned above, a holdback from payment of the subscription price to cover estimated remediation costs may also be used to resolve this issue.

Representations of the Investor

If the draft agreement sets out any representations by the Investor, they will be much less extensive than those given by the company. If they are given, they are likely to be similar to those given by the company, but generally confined to just the status, power and authority of the Investor to enter into the deal.

However, if a significant part of the subscription price is not to be paid at closing, the company may quite legitimately be entitled to expect additional representations regarding the Investor's financial capability and overall creditworthiness. If the company is to receive certain assets of the Investor in full or partial satisfaction of the subscription price, the company may reasonably expect to receive more comprehensive representations from the Investor about those assets which would closely parallel those given by the company in respect of its own assets.

To ensure that the company is able sell its shares by relying upon one of the exemptions to the prospectus and registration requirements under provincial securities legislation,[3] the company may insist that the agreement contain a representation that the Investor falls within one of the categories of purchaser prescribed by such exemptions.[4] Although this book has assumed that the company enjoys exemption as a "private issuer"[5] as stated in the first chapter, the representation requested from the Investor may address other possible exemptions.

For example, instead of the private issuer exemption, the company may wish to rely upon the "accredited investor" exemption,[6] which allows it to raise any amount of equity financing from any person coming within the definition of an accredited investor. This definition includes banks, securities dealers and high net worth individuals, as well as larger limited partnerships, trusts and corporations which are likely to include the outside professional investor wishing to acquire the company's shares.[7] A representation that the Investor is an accredited investor within the definition would then be inserted into the subscription agreement.

COVENANTS

A draft subscription agreement will ordinarily set out a number of specific covenants or agreements by the parties to take or refrain from taking various actions, primarily during the interim period between signing the agreement and the closing.

Compliance by each of the parties with their respective covenants is usually a condition of closing, although as with any condition, may be waived by the party in whose favour the covenant was made. Alternatively, the failure to satisfy a condition usually allows the innocent party to terminate the agreement and refuse to close the deal. The failure of a party to comply with its covenants may also give rise to a liability to indemnify the innocent party, as discussed later in this chapter.

The standard covenants discussed immediately below often require qualification by the company.

Prohibited Actions

A covenant is often found in the draft agreement prohibiting the company from taking certain actions which could adversely affect the value of the business. It is intended to generally maintain the state of the business without any changes in its assets and liabilities or general operations. These prohibited actions might include major capital expenditures, mortgaging real estate, signing joint venture or partnership agreements, entering into long-term leases, and selling material assets.

As well as wanting to exclude from such prohibitions any actions which are taken in the ordinary course of the business, the company may want to specifically permit the payment of dividends and repayment of shareholder loans during the interim period, at least in a manner consistent with past practices. The company may also want to ensure that any obligations the business may owe to parties related to the company can be fully performed without running afoul of the prohibitions.

Regulatory and Contractual Consents

Another covenant likely to be included in the draft agreement is the requirement imposed upon the company to obtain all consents from any regulatory authorities under applicable laws or third parties under existing contracts which may be needed for the deal to close. The company should ensure that this obligation is qualified, not absolute, perhaps by requiring only the use of "reasonable commercial efforts" to obtain the consents involved.

If the company fails to obtain a required consent, and the consent is a condition of closing, the Investor may be able to terminate the agreement and not complete the deal. However, with the company's obligation qualified and provided that the company has used reasonable commercial efforts to obtain the consent though unsuccessful, the Investor will at least have no claim against the company for breach of contract.

Instead of allowing the company to use only reasonable commercial efforts to obtain a required consent, the Investor may insist that the company use "best efforts". Since both terms invite debate over their respective meanings, the company should insist that the agreement provide a definition of whichever term is to be used. While the definition may require the company to use available internal resources, it should not require the company to incur any additional expenditure of funds or acquire external resources.

To avoid possible disputes over which consents may actually be needed to close the deal, or at least to prevent the company's inability to obtain a trivial consent being used by the Investor as a means of getting out of the deal, the company might insist that all of the required consents be specifically listed in the agreement or on a schedule.

Access to Information

Although the Investor's rights of access to the business for due diligence purposes may have already been provided for in the term sheet, the draft agreement may attempt to expand upon those rights, particularly if the preliminary investigations conducted by the Investor have raised the need for more comprehensive disclosure. While the Investor may insist upon the right to continue due diligence up to closing, the company should attempt to have such investigations terminate by a certain date before then.

The company will have to carefully consider whether the Investor should be permitted to contact any regulatory authorities regarding the compliance of the business with applicable laws. Not only may such inquiries prove to be disruptive to the business, they may also jeopardize the ongoing relations with such authorities, especially if the deal fails to close, as well as result in the loss of confidentiality of the deal. A similar concern applies to any approaches being made by the Investor to employees, customers and suppliers.

The Investor should be required to inform the company of all breaches or potential breaches of the agreement as soon as they are discovered in order to give the company an opportunity to cure them and avoid having the Investor either terminate the agreement, or closing the deal and then seeking indemnity for damages.

SURVIVAL OF COVENANTS AND REPRESENTATIONS

How long the covenants and representations will be enforceable or "survive" after closing is usually prescribed in the draft agreement. Determining survival periods is essentially the allocation of risk between the parties and assigning the length of time a particular risk should be borne by a party. The parties attempt to negotiate the "limitation period" which will apply to their deal in an effort to override any limitation period which might otherwise be imposed upon them by applicable limitation statutes.[8]

While the Investor may prefer to have indefinite recourse to the company for any breaches of the company's covenants and representations, the company will demand certainty over when its liabilities will end.

Often the parties will agree that any representations with respect to fundamental matters, such as corporate existence and authority, as well as the ownership of assets, survive indefinitely. Representations regarding tax matters will survive until the expiry of any assessment and possible appeal period. The survival period for the covenants and most other representations typically falls within a range of six months to two years. The parties often compromise at 18 months on the basis that most problems with the business are discovered by the completion of the next audit after closing.

CONDITIONS OF CLOSING

The draft agreement will itemize a number of conditions which have to be met for the deal to close. If a particular condition is not, the party for whose benefit it was given will be able to terminate the agreement and walk away from the deal unless the party's right to enforce compliance with that condition has already been waived.

The accuracy of the representations and compliance with the covenants set out in the agreement generally constitute important conditions. Often key representations or covenants will be reinforced by specific corresponding conditions which mirror or supplement their language.

The company may want to be aware of the implications of certain conditions discussed immediately below.

No Material Adverse Change

The draft agreement may contain a condition for the benefit of the Investor that there has not occurred a "material adverse change" in the business by the time of closing. The Investor may attempt to add that such change will be determined in the Investor's sole discretion or opinion, but such attempts should be resisted by the company.

Although it may be difficult for the parties to arrive at a mutually satisfactory definition of material adverse change, the company should at least ensure that the Investor is required to act in a commercially reasonable manner and does not have unfettered discretion.

No Adverse Law or Actions to Restrain

A condition that no law has been passed or legal action taken which adversely affects the business is usually included in the draft agreement. The company may want to narrow this condition so that it does not apply to laws or legal actions which existed at the time the Investor entered into the agreement but only to those which came into effect afterwards.

The company should not allow "threatened" litigation to be included in such a condition. Such litigation could be frivolous, without merit, or even orchestrated by the Investor as an excuse to get out of the deal. Furthermore, the company should oppose any effort by the Investor to expand this condition to include any laws which may merely be "proposed" by the time of closing.

Third Party Consents

A condition will usually be found in the agreement requiring the delivery at closing of all consents from third parties which are necessary or material to the business. These consents will at least include all required regulatory and contractual consents. As mentioned in the above section on *Covenants*, it is preferable for the company to have these consents reduced to a list set out in the agreement or in a schedule so that the Investor cannot back out of the deal just because a trivial consent is not obtained.

The company should be particularly wary if the condition includes any third party consents which apply only to the Investor and which are completely beyond the influence or control of the company. For example, the Investor may want to make closing of the deal conditional upon some other financing being made available to the Investor or upon the consent of one of its lenders being received. Such a condition can easily be abused by an Investor intent on escaping from a deal.

Certain Agreements

In order for the deal to close, the Investor may insist that certain individuals agree to provide consulting services or serve the business as employees for a specified period of time after the deal closes. The agreement may include as a closing condition the delivery of executed consulting or employment contracts with these individuals in a form acceptable to the Investor.

However, it is not unusual for a deal to be delayed, or even terminated, because the individuals involved would not sign the contracts presented to them by the Investor. In executing the subscription agreement without having first settled the terms of these consulting and employment contracts, both the Investor and the company are running the risk that these contracts will not be signed and the deal will be terminated.

To avoid such a possibility, the terms of the contracts should be settled with these individuals and attached to the agreement as a schedule before the agreement is executed by the Investor and the company. By leaving the negotiation and settlement of these contracts until after the subscription agreement is executed, the individuals concerned may become extremely difficult or self-interested and use a pending closing as extra leverage to obtain considerably more favourable terms.

The same concern applies to any non-competition or non-solicitation contracts with individuals who the Investor feels could diminish the value of the business after closing should they go to work for a competitor or solicit customers or employees of the business. The terms of these contracts should also be settled and attached to the subscription agreement before the agreement is executed.

Satisfactory Due Diligence Results
Although often appearing in term sheets, it is important for the company to strongly resist the appearance in the subscription agreement of any condition which allows the Investor to terminate the agreement and refuse to close if the results of the due diligence investigations prove to be unsatisfactory. The company usually wants certainty as early as possible that the Investor is not going to find an excuse to walk from the deal. However, even in the absence of such a due diligence "out", the Investor may still terminate the agreement and decline to close if it discovers facts about the business which would constitute breaches of representations or covenants which are not remedied by the company prior to closing.

Conditions for the Benefit of the Company
Apart from a condition relating to the accuracy of any representations and the performance of any covenants given by the Investor, the draft agreement is unlikely to contain any conditions in favour of the company.

However, the company may consider the need to include as conditions the release of any personal guarantees which may have been given to support any borrowing, leases or other obligations of the business which are to be repaid with the proceeds of the equity financing. Perhaps the repayment of a shareholder loan should be included as a condition.

The company may even require as a condition of closing the delivery of a legal opinion from the Investor's lawyers regarding the good standing of the Investor and the legal enforceability of the Investor's post-closing obligations, particularly those relating to indemnities and any subscription price holdbacks.

INDEMNIFICATION

The indemnification provisions may be among the most intensely negotiated provisions in a draft subscription agreement. While the Investor wants some protection for the company's representations and covenants, the company wants to avoid any residual liability to the Investor once the deal closes. These provisions usually require the company to indemnify and fully reimburse the Investor for all losses and damages the Investor might suffer as a result of the breach of any of the company's representations and covenants. The Investor, however, may be required to indemnify the company for any breaches of the Investor's representations and covenants.

Depending upon the relative bargaining power and level of sophistication of each of the parties, the negotiations can produce a wide variety of outcomes. The company may reluctantly have to agree to an open-ended indemnity if the business is failing and only one party appears to be interested in investing. More frequently, however, the parties will want to place a maximum on their respective total potential liabilities under the agreement, and may agree to a fixed limit for certain classes of liability.

Since the protection provided by an indemnity is dependent upon the creditworthiness of the party giving it, the other party may demand some collateral to support it. The Investor may request that personal guarantees or substantial holdbacks from the subscription price be included in the agreement. Similarly, if the company is concerned about the possibility of non-payment of any deferred portions of the subscription price, the Investor may be asked to give security for those continuing obligations.

If the parties have agreed upon the use of escrow amounts or hold-backs, the Investor may insist that the indemnification provisions in the agreement allow the Investor to set-off against these amounts any indemnity claims, and that any promissory notes and escrow agreement to be delivered at the closing should mirror such rights of set-off. The company should attempt to limit the Investor's set-off rights to those situations where all disputes over any claim have been definitively resolved.

Indemnification by the Company

Depending upon the nature of the business and the results of the due diligence investigations, the Investor may insist that the agreement contain specific indemnities from the company for specific risk categories. These categories might include unknowable environmental risks, probable changes in the laws affecting the business, the outcome of a disclosed lawsuit, or the loss of a major customer of the business.

Negotiating the terms of a specific environmental indemnification can be a difficult process because the degree of risk is usually unknown, any environmental problem can be hugely disruptive and expensive to the business, and claims can be made by government agencies or third parties which are not bound by the agreement. Furthermore, unlike most other types of liabilities which tend to decrease over time, environmental liabilities tend not to.

If required to provide the Investor with specific indemnification for environmental risks, the company should at least retain control over the handling of environmental claims and over any clean-up efforts. As a way of better quantifying the liability, the seller might avoid giving a separate environmental indemnification and deal with environmental risks by way of a subscription price reduction or an increase in any escrow amount or holdback.

Indemnification by the Investor

The first draft of a subscription agreement will frequently exclude any indemnification by the Investor of the company. If the Investor has no material representations or covenants which survive the closing of the deal, this exclusion may be acceptable to the company. However, a company with some bargaining power should always insist upon inclusion of such a provision in the agreement, especially if payment of any portion of the subscription price is deferred or the Investor has any significant obligations to be performed after closing.

Maximum and Minimum Amounts

The parties may decide that the agreement should include both a minimum or "floor", and a maximum or "ceiling", for indemnification. The floor operates like a deductible in an insurance policy so as to avoid any claims or disputes involving only minor amounts. The Investor may try to recover all damages, not just damages in excess of the floor amount, once the floor is reached. The parties may end up having different floors for different types of liabilities.

The company will often try to have a ceiling of not more than the total amount of the subscription price, arguing that the potential "burden" or indemnity claim that may be suffered should not exceed the "benefit" or subscription price received. Although the Investor may accept such an argument, certain claims, such as those for tax or environmental matters, may be permitted without a ceiling, or separate ceilings may be established for different heads of liability.

The agreement may provide that neither floors nor ceilings shall limit claims for breaches of representations which were known, or for covenants which were willfully ignored, by the indemnifying party.

Limitation on Remedies

The company should ensure that the indemnification provisions clearly indicate that the indemnity rights of the parties represent their exclusive remedies in connection with the deal. While the Investor may want to avoid such exclusiveness to preserve possible remedies outside of the agreement relating to breach of contract, fraud and certain statutory rights, the benefits of the indemnity ceiling to the company may be lost if the Investor is able to seek other legal recourse.

Closing the Deal

Once the loan agreement for a company debt financing or the subscription agreement for a company equity financing has been signed and the due diligence investigations have been completed, the owners and managers of the company will then turn their attention to ensuring that the agreement's various covenants will be fully performed and conditions satisfied. They will, in other words, enter the closing stage of the deal.

Yet getting the deal closed often proves to be more difficult than they might expect. While the closing conditions and list of deliverable documents set out in the agreement may provide some guidance on what has to be done, closing itself is seldom straightforward. The company under either type of agreement may encounter a number of challenges before actually "seeing the money".

This chapter will attempt to provide some understanding not only of the process leading up to the actual closing but also of the possible delays and obstacles which are likely to arise. The most frustrating of these invariably involves the need to obtain the consent of numerous third parties. Financial institutions, landlords and trade creditors represent just some of the third parties whose consents may not be easily or quickly obtained.

However, this chapter will not attempt to address the delays and obstacles which may be specific to a particular deal even though they can be extremely expensive and time-consuming to resolve. In this category belong outstanding lawsuits and regulatory proceedings, polluted land, damage or destruction of significant assets, labour disruptions, and any material changes to the business which unexpectedly occur just before closing.

Some delays and obstacles which seem to affect many debt and equity financings can be avoided or at least mitigated if they are addressed by the company earlier on, preferably well before the anticipated closing date. Viewed almost as pre-emptive actions by the company to increase the likelihood that a lender or equity investor will close the deal, they will be addressed first in this chapter. They might be regarded as simply putting the company into closing condition.

PUTTING THE COMPANY IN CLOSING CONDITION

Some problems can significantly delay, or even prevent, a debt or equity financing from closing unless they are fixed. For example, an equity financing may be postponed if it turns out that the company's main product lacks patent protection, or that the company's key employees are free to work for a competitor if they leave the company. A debt financing may be delayed if the company is carrying large amounts of obsolete inventory or uncollectable receivables.

In addition to fixing these more glaring problems, getting the company into closing condition also means confirming that the company's many relationships with its employees, customers and suppliers are well-documented, and its various records and government filings are up-to-date. Such actions should be regarded not just as good "housekeeping" but as a way of giving an investor or lender a better understanding of any risks arising from the company's past and some certainty in determining the profitability of the company in the future.

Some of the actions which the company's owners and managers might wish to specifically take in an effort to put the company into closing condition include the following.

Limiting or Removing Liabilities

It may be necessary for all of the company's liabilities to be reviewed in anticipation of an investor's or lender's resistance to them and to determine whether such liabilities can be either limited or entirely removed.

Some of these liabilities may relate to the company's current financing arrangements. An investor or lender may regard them as an unnecessary or imprudent burden, perhaps, if the current financing has been provided by a party associated with the company. If the company is likely to be asked by the investor or lender to pay off all amounts owing under such arrangements and to obtain a discharge of any security which may have been given, the company should inquire of the bank or other financing party in advance if there are any obstacles to accomplishing this.

The company may have to determine the existence of any guarantees which it may have given to support the financial obligations of other parties, including those related to the owners, and to make an effort to either have such company guarantees terminated or limited to a specific dollar amount.

Some company liabilities are not readily limited or removed. A lawsuit against the company for a material amount may not be easy to settle and its continuing defence may be perceived by an investor or lender as a huge drain on company resources with a very uncertain outcome. A material contract with a relatively long term may not be capable of amendment or early termination without the payment of considerable penalties.

Upgrading or Replacing Assets

In addition to conducting various sales and promotions in order to reduce excess inventory and to strengthening collection efforts to shorten the length of time the company's receivables are outstanding, the company may have to consider whether the condition of the company's physical assets might be a deterrent to an investor or lender in closing a financing. On-site inspections should encourage, not dissuade, the investor or lender in continuing with the deal.

In order for the company's facilities to show well on inspection, the owners and managers may decide to repair or replace malfunctioning or outdated machinery, equipment and vehicles, upgrade the company's computer software and hardware, and possibly renovate and refurnish its offices.

As an investor and possibly a lender are unlikely to want to finance company assets which are held primarily for the personal benefit of the owners or their respective families and are not required in the operations of the company's business, the company should attempt to identify any vehicles, recreational equipment, executive apartments, artwork, furniture and any other company assets held for only personal use and consider selling them or transferring them to a separate corporation.

Correcting or Updating Records and Filings

The holding of annual company meetings or signing of annual resolutions electing directors, appointing officers and approving financial statements may have generally been overlooked by the owners and managers as a minor administrative inconvenience. Annual and other periodic government filings the company is required to make, and the renewal of any licences or permits necessary to carry on the company's business, may also have been ignored. But since an investor or lender will want to be comfortable that the company has been properly administered before financing it, the company should have its minute books and corporate records reviewed to ensure that everything is up-to-date.

Given the possibility that the company was incorporated some time ago and may not have been properly organized at that time, the review of the company's minute book ideally should go back to the date of incorporation, particularly with a view to confirming that all outstanding shares have been properly issued and that the share register correctly records all share issuances and transfers in the meantime. Such an exercise will invariably be undertaken by the lawyers for an investor when carrying out due diligence investigations of the company. Hopefully any discrepancies which the company may discover in its review can be rectified right away in order to avoid the financing being postponed or terminated because the investor came across such discrepancies before closing.

It is not unusual for a closing to be delayed because the signature of a former shareholder is missing on a previous share transfer, or an unexpired option to purchase company shares has not been terminated.

Reviewing Employee Relationships
Since an investor and perhaps a lender may be quite concerned that the company's employees may leave the company to work elsewhere after the financing is completed, the owners and manager should attempt to address this possible concern early on in the deal process.

As described in the *Dealing with Employees* chapter, one place to start is the use of employment contracts with all of the company's employees which specify the causes of termination and appropriate notice periods, require that all trade secrets and other company information be kept confidential, provide for an assignment to the company of the employee's intellectual property acquired while employed, and restrict the rights of the employee to solicit other company employees or to provide services to the company's customers after leaving. It may be necessary to pay current employees a bonus, provide some additional benefit or give them a promotion as consideration for their signing of such a contract. New employees should be required to sign such a contract as a condition of their employment.

Ensuring that key employees will stay around with the company after the financing takes place may have already been accomplished by providing such employees various benefits such as group insurance and registered retirement savings plans, or by creating profit sharing, stock option, stock purchase, or phantom stock plans.

Reviewing Supplier Relationships

Having supply contracts with suppliers, especially when alternative suppliers are scarce or non-existent, can be essential to putting the company in closing condition. However, supply contracts which make the company deal exclusively with a supplier for particular products or services can deter the closing of a financing transaction.

The owners and managers should attempt to insert into such exclusive arrangements the right of the company to terminate them on relatively short notice, in the event that substitute products or services become available at a better price.

Reviewing Landlord Relationships

An investor and possibly a lender may be concerned that if the company operates out of leased premises, the applicable lease has too little time remaining under it or is capable of being easily terminated by the landlord. To ensure that the lease will not become a deterrent to a financing, the owners and managers should review the provisions of the lease to ascertain what rights of renewal or extension exist and what events might permit early termination.

If the lease contains a "change of control" provision, requiring the landlord to consent to any sale of the majority of the company's shares, the company may be facing the possibility that its new investors on an equity financing may not be acceptable to the landlord, and thereby put the lease in jeopardy, unless the company is able to get its landlord to amend or waive this provision.

Reviewing Customer Relationships

Having written customer contracts, particularly those of a longer term or which can be terminated only after a lengthy notice period, can be necessary to increase the chances that a financing will happen. An investor or lender will then be given some assurance that company revenues will persist once the deal is completed, as well as some understanding of the warranties and other obligations the company will be required to perform afterwards.

The company may also attempt to remove any restrictions in any customer contracts which prevent their assignment by the company, since it may be necessary to assign them to a lender as additional security for a loan.

Protecting Intellectual Property

If the company's value to an investor or its security to a lender depends heavily upon the brand names which the company uses in the marketplace, the owners and managers should attempt to obtain registered trademark protection for such names if they haven't already done so, as mentioned in the *Protecting Intellectual Property* chapter. Applying for patent protection should be considered for any inventions which the company has made or funded which an investor or lender may consider are integral to the company's product line or operations.

The company should ensure that all agreements with outside consultants contain their assignment of any intellectual property rights they may have acquired while providing services to the company, including all copyrights in any works they may author for the company, as well as their agreement to keep company information confidential.

Amending Shareholder Agreements

If there is a shareholder agreement in place, the owners and managers should review it in order to determine the extent to which an issuance of new shares to an investor, or a borrowing from a lender, might be restricted. For example, it might provide "pre-emptive rights", requiring the company to first offer any new shares to the company's other shareholders, usually on a pro-rata basis to their existing holdings, before offering them to an outside investor.

Or the shareholder agreement may give a certain percentage of the existing company shareholders a right to veto a proposed debt financing which exceeds a certain monetary threshold.

Shareholder agreements are discussed in much greater detail in the next chapter.

CLOSING AGENDA

Well before the expected closing date of a debt or equity financing, a draft closing agenda is usually prepared and circulated which identifies the various actions which must be taken and numerous documents which must be drafted in order for the deal to close. The lawyer for the investor in a share transaction, or the lawyer for the lender in a loan transaction, generally prepares the first draft of the agenda.

The agenda will ordinarily set out at a minimum the actions and documents itemized as closing conditions in the transaction agreement. It may bear some resemblance to the checklist which may have been provided to the company earlier on in the due diligence stage of the transaction. It will likely assign to the parties and their respective teams of advisors responsibility for various items needed for closing. The description of each document on the agenda will identify who drafts it, who has to sign and deliver it, and how many copies of it will be required on closing.

Many closing agendas also include items which are to be completed before or after closing so that the agenda will serve as a comprehensive checklist of everything to be done in connection with the transaction. For example, the "pre-closing" section might include the filing of articles of amendment to create a new class of preferred shares for the company which are to be issued to the investor, and the "post-closing" section might list notices of changes in company directors which need to be filed with appropriate government authorities.

Some closing agendas may be separated into two or more distinct parts, with separate closings for each part, if the transaction actually combines two or more transactions which may or may not be conditional on each other. Such separation may occur, for example, when an equity financing is immediately followed by a debt financing.

Whatever particular form the closing agenda may take, it will likely form the basis for the index or table of contents to appear in the transaction or closing book which will contain all of the documents delivered at the closing and which will be provided to the parties by their legal counsel after the deal closes.

DISCHARGING MORTGAGES AND LIENS

Almost always in a debt financing, and often in an equity financing, the owners and managers will likely have to deal with many of the parties who have financed the company over the years and who may still have various mortgages, liens, security interests and other "encumbrances" against the company's assets. Depending upon the terms of the particular financing involved, the company may be required to ensure that most or all of its assets are free and clear of all such encumbrances at closing. The loan agreement, and possibly the subscription agreement, will contain a representation and warranty from the company to this effect.

Unless the transaction agreement or a schedule to it permits a specific encumbrance to remain outstanding after the deal closes, a discharge or release of that encumbrance will therefore have to be produced on or before closing. But obtaining such a discharge can involve a time-consuming and sometimes convoluted process, especially when the encumbrance is held by a large, decentralized institution. Not only is a considerable amount of lead-time often required to obtain the required discharges by closing, but requesting such discharges arouses suspicion that a transaction may be imminent and thereby threaten any confidentiality which the parties want to maintain.

The creditors to be approached for discharges may comprise a large and diversified group. They may include leasing companies which provided financing for the motor vehicles, machinery and equipment used in the business, banks which made operating loans, insurance companies which gave long-term mortgages, factoring companies which collected accounts receivable, and suppliers which granted favourable credit terms.

Some of these creditors to be approached may need a written termination of their respective agreements with the company, or payment in full of all amounts they may be owed, before they will be able to provide the required discharges. While repayment may not be a problem for the relatively small amount that may be owed, for example, under a lease for a photocopier, paying off a large bank loan will pose a significant hurdle to the company which needs the closing proceeds to do so.

This can create a classic "chicken or egg" problem, since the deal can't be closed without a discharge, but the discharge can't be obtained without the money payable on closing. A resolution of this problem is often achieved by the willingness of the lender or investor to close the deal by relying upon a written undertaking. For example, the company, or possibly its lawyer, would undertake to obtain the necessary discharge within a certain period of days or weeks after closing.

Instead of obtaining a discharge from a third party to remove an encumbrance in a debt financing, the company may be able to work out a compromise with the lender by having the lender agree to exclude those assets with the third party encumbrance from the security given by the company for the loan transaction. Alternatively, written confirmation from the third party that its encumbrance does not cover the assets being given as security to the lender may be acceptable proof that the assets are free and clear. Often called an "estoppel" or "acknowledgment" letter, such confirmation is generally used to provide assurance that an outstanding encumbrance applies only to assets which are being excluded from the financing deal.

As another alternative to obtaining a discharge from a third party to remove an encumbrance, the lender and third party may enter into a postponement and subordination agreement, or an inter-creditor agreement, under which the third party generally postpones any right to claim payment from the company and subordinates its security in the encumbered asset to the lender in the event of a default by the company under the loan agreement between the company and the lender.

ASSIGNING CONTRACTS AND OBTAINING CONSENTS

Many closings are delayed because of a failure to obtain the consents necessary to assign specific contracts.

Since many contracts contain a clause which prohibits their assignment and transfer by one party without the written consent of the other party, the company in a loan transaction may have difficulty in receiving counterparty consent for the assignment of a particular contract required by the lender as security for the loan.

A related problem can arise in an equity transaction if the company's contracts can be terminated should there be any change in the company's ownership. As with many leases as discussed above, some contracts contain a change of control provision requiring the counterparty to consent to any sale of the majority of the company's shares. If the company is facing the possibility that its new investors on an equity financing may not be acceptable to the counterparties on its contracts, it may have to approach those counterparties to amend or waive this provision.

In a loan transaction, a counterparty may be reluctant to give consent to an assignment of a particular contract for the purposes of security if it is concerned that the lender or the lender's receiver or agent will end up performing under the contract, especially if performance might eventually fall to a competitor of the counterparty.

OBTAINING GOVERNMENT APPROVALS

Of those third parties which may have to be approached when attempting to satisfy the closing requirements identified on the closing agenda, certain government agencies may appear to require more time than other parties to produce a particular document.

Because the issuance of additional shares to an investor on an equity financing will alter the company's share ownership, the owners and managers may need to obtain new government licenses, permits, consents or other similar documents. While some of these documents may necessitate a comprehensive investigation of the parties by the government agency involved, other documents may simply require the written confirmation of information recorded in a government database.

It is often difficult to predict how long it will take to obtain a required government approval. While some approvals may be discretionary so that their receipt cannot be presumed, other approvals can be expected in the ordinary course. If a government approval is expected within a reasonable period of time, the parties may decide to close the deal in escrow while receipt of the approval is pending.

ORGANIZING THE CLOSING

Once the actions identified on the closing agenda have been taken and the terms of the necessary documents have been settled, the signing and exchanging of the final form of the documents and delivery or transfer of the proceeds can take place at the closing of the deal.

While some deals may be closed with the parties meeting at a common location "face-to-face", other deals may be closed remotely with the parties participating from a number of separate locations, and may even be closed through a "virtual deal room" on the Internet.

The more traditional face-to-face closing involves the parties to the transaction sitting around a large boardroom table and signing the various documents identified in the closing agenda one after another, following which certified cheques or bank drafts are delivered, the parties shake hands, and their lawyers then divide up the signed documents for eventual inclusion in the closing or transaction books. The boardroom may be exclusively used for the transaction over a number of days to allow for last minute negotiations and document amendments, and perhaps accommodate a "pre-closing" during which legal counsel for the parties finalize all of the documentation and oversee the execution of a number of documents in advance of the designated closing date.

Instead of meeting face-to-face to close the transaction, the parties may sign the documents in separate locations at their own offices, and then copies of those document pages bearing their signatures are either faxed to the others, or scanned and converted into electronic format and sent to the others by way of e-mail attachment. Funds are delivered by wire transfer or direct deposit, not by certified cheque or bank draft. While these remote closings may be more convenient to the signing parties and easier to schedule than face-to-face closings, they nonetheless entail some risk that the signature pages being transmitted may be mistakenly switched or relate to earlier draft documents, or even worse, bear fraudulent signatures.

As a further alternative, the closing may take place in a virtual deal room, which may be an extension of the secure website which the parties may have used for document reviews during the due diligence stage of the transaction. The documents identified in the closing agenda are made available for review, revision, and eventually, execution, and the completed signature pages can be uploaded to close the deal.

Whether the closing is face-to-face, remote or carried out in a virtual deal room, the parties conduct themselves on the basis that unless otherwise agreed, all documents and funds are to be held in escrow. The escrow is not terminated and the closing is not made final until all of the parties have agreed that the documents are in satisfactory form, and that all acts to be performed at the closing have been properly performed, including the completion of any searches and registration of any transfers of title or security interests.

Although the funds required for closing may have already been wired by bank transfer or delivered by certified cheque to a party's lawyer before the signed documents have been exchanged, they will continue to be held and not released until everything else has been done to terminate the escrow.

Even though the escrow may be terminated, and the deal regarded as closed, there will probably be a number of post–closing items which will need to be dealt with, as described above. The documents resulting from these post-closing items are often included in the transaction books which are prepared and distributed after the closing. The transaction books, however, are as likely to appear in electronic form as paper form.

Shareholder Agreements

Previous chapters of this book have briefly referred to the role played by a shareholder agreement in setting out certain rights and responsibilities of the company's shareholders and in providing for the ongoing governance of the company's business. Starting up the company, dealing with employees, implementing a business succession plan, and obtaining equity financing can all involve the preparation or amendment of a shareholder agreement.

There are a number of different circumstances in which a shareholder agreement can become quite useful to the parties involved.

If there is one shareholder holding a majority of the company's shares, the minority shareholders may want to ensure that they have a minimum number of seats on the board of directors so that they will have access to inside information and be able to participate in important decisions in the same way as the majority shareholder.

If the company shareholders represent a number of different and possibly conflicting interests, such as venture capitalists, employees and founding owners, the agreement may provide certain voting mechanisms for protecting their separate interests while reinforcing the different roles they play in ensuring the continuing success of the company's business.

If the business does not permit the company to consistently obtain financing from conventional outside sources, it may be necessary to use the agreement to prescribe how additional capital is to be obtained from the shareholders themselves.

If all of the company's shares are held by just one individual, and she has decided that members of her own family should hold shares in the company, either by direct gift or sale from her of her own shares, or by way of an estate freeze, a shareholder agreement might be used to provide her with continuing control of the company even though the others have acquired voting power through the shares issued to them. The agreement may give her the right to appoint a majority of the company's directors or to veto certain company decisions, such as the declaration of dividends or issuance of shares. It may also give her the right to receive sufficient funds to retire on by requiring the other shareholders or the company to purchase or redeem her shares over time in accordance with a series of prescribed dates or milestones.

A shareholder agreement can also be used to impose various restrictions upon the children who have acquired company shares under an estate freeze. To ensure that the company stays in "good hands" by remaining under family ownership, the agreement might provide for rights of first refusal and various buy-sell rights which are described below, including call rights which might give those children who are actively involved in the company a right to buy the shares of those children who aren't. It might require instead that a child's shares are to be sold to the company if the child ceases to work for the company on a full-time basis.

If the company's employees become shareholders, perhaps pursuant to an employee stock purchase or option plan, a shareholder agreement can be used to address what happens to their shares in the event that they cease to be employees, or they die or become disabled. They may be required, for example, to sell their shares back to the company, or alternatively, sell to the other shareholders at a specified price.

The employees may also be restricted in the agreement from having any rights to veto a major transaction or otherwise block any company action. In the event that the majority shareholder receives an offer to purchase all of her shares from an outside party, the agreement may allow that shareholder to "drag along" the shares of the employees when selling to the outsider, as discussed below.

If the majority shareholder has chosen to sell her shares to an outside party but is able to accomplish such a sale only in a series of installments or tranches which leave her holding a portion of her company shares pending final payment from the purchaser, a shareholder agreement may be used in such circumstances to govern her rights as a continuing shareholder in the meantime. Being reduced to a minority shareholder, she may still want to ensure that she has a seat on the company's board of directors in order to have access to inside information and be able to participate in important decisions in the same way as the purchaser.

Regardless of the many different circumstances in which a shareholder agreement may be useful, it is usually put into place because the shareholders anticipate problems which might arise in the future. They generally use a shareholder agreement to implement certain practices to deter such problems from arising at all. Some of these problems relate to control and management, others relate to financing and conflicts of interest, while others relate to the possible abuse of power by the majority shareholder.

The remainder of this chapter attempts to describe some of the provisions commonly found in shareholder agreements which are used to address such problems.

Some of these provisions have already been described in the *Equity Financing and Term Sheets* chapter, since most equity investments in a private company are conditional upon the delivery of a new or amended shareholder agreement which reflects the term sheet. However, they have been repeated in this chapter in order to provide the reader with a more comprehensive, stand-alone summary of the provisions often found in a shareholder agreement.

While the shareholders of private companies are most commonly individuals, they may well be corporations, partnerships or trusts, such as venture capital firms and institutional investors, and therefore some of the comments appearing below may relate more to these kinds of shareholder than to individuals.

Furthermore, while some shareholders such as the companyscommand.'s founder, members of her family or long serving employees may expect their shareholding to continue for some time, other shareholders, particularly financial investors, may view their holding only on a short-term basis as a means of achieving a certain financial return. Consequently, a number of the agreement provisions outlined below address the possible short-term goals of a shareholder who may prefer an early exit from the company.

But at the outset, a brief explanation of "unanimous shareholder agreements" may be helpful.

UNANIMOUS SHAREHOLDER AGREEMENTS

A unanimous shareholder agreement is an agreement among all of the company's shareholders, both voting and non-voting, which restricts the powers of the directors. It is specifically authorized by the CBCA[1] and is often used to allow a private company to operate much like a partnership but with limited liability. The shareholders can be empowered to run the company in the same way as partners run a partnership.

To qualify as a unanimous shareholder agreement, it must to some extent restrict the powers of the directors to manage, or supervise the management of, the business and affairs of the company. It thereby effectively transfers to the shareholders some or all of the rights, duties and liabilities of the directors. Although agreements to fetter the discretion of company directors have traditionally not been permitted under common law,[2] the CBCA allows the shareholders to take away that discretion by means of a unanimous shareholder agreement.

In the absence of a unanimous shareholder agreement, the ability of shareholders to control a private company is generally limited in practice to their power to elect and dismiss directors. It is the directors who have the fundamental power and duty[3] to manage the company unless restricted by a unanimous shareholder agreement.

Sometimes viewed as a hybrid concept[4] under corporate law, a unanimous shareholder agreement is part contractual and part constitutional in nature. It must be a written agreement among all of the shareholders of the company, or among all of the shareholders and other parties.[5] As a contract, it governs the personal rights of the shareholders. As a component of the company's constitution, it governs the overall management of the company, including the issuing of shares, passing of by-laws, and appointment of officers. It can also set higher standards than those required under the CBCA, such as the number of votes of directors or shareholders needed to approve any action.[6]

If a unanimous shareholder agreement is in place for a private company, any person acquiring the company's shares is deemed to be a party to it. If certificates are issued for the company's shares and do not conspicuously note or refer to the agreement, the agreement may be ineffective against a transferee who has no actual knowledge of it.[7]

A declaration by the only shareholder of a company which restricts the powers of the company's directors to manage is deemed to be a unanimous shareholder agreement.[8] Such a declaration is often used by foreign corporations wishing to maintain managerial control over their wholly-owned Canadian subsidiaries.

While a shareholder who is a party to a unanimous shareholder agreement acquires some or all of the rights, powers, duties and liabilities of the directors, including any defences available to the directors, the directors are relieved of their rights, powers, duties and liabilities to the same extent.[9] However, while the directors may be relieved of their liabilities under the CBCA, including their obligation[10] for 6 months wages remaining unpaid to the company's employees, such relief may not extend to all liabilities, including those imposed on directors by provincial legislation (even though it is unlikely a court will make a director liable for a company's conduct over which she has no control).

This rest of his chapter discusses some of the rights, powers and duties otherwise performed by directors which are often assumed by shareholders pursuant to a unanimous shareholder agreement. It also discusses some of the restrictions which are often imposed upon shareholders and some of the rules for governance and financing of the company's business which are normally found in such an agreement. Also discussed are the provisions of the agreement relating to the issuance of company shares and the transfer of company shares.

All of these provisions in the agreement which represent something other than restrictions on the directors' powers can sometimes cause confusion over whether the agreement actually qualifies as a unanimous shareholder agreement. But so long as the agreement is signed by all of the company's shareholders and restricts the powers of the directors to some extent, its inclusion of other items such as the rights of shareholders to acquire each other's shares or their obligations to finance company operations does not disqualify the agreement as a unanimous shareholder agreement.

BOARD AND MANAGEMENT REPRESENTATION

The shareholders may be quite prepared to leave the directors and officers free to operate the company on a day-to-day basis so long as the company is complying with its budgets and business plans and meeting any specific objectives or milestones that have been agreed upon. However, a shareholder may be given the right to nominate one or more directors to the company's board, or at least be given the right to have a nominee attend board meetings as an observer.

Observers are usually entitled to receive notice of and to attend meetings of the board of directors, but are not entitled to vote. Shareholders comprised of venture capital and private equity firms often prefer to limit the involvement of their nominees to observer status if the board already consists of nominees of other professional investors, or as a way of avoiding director liability or the policies of certain stock exchanges which place escrow requirements during an initial public offering on shareholders having board representation.

Although the right to appoint observers to the board may be appropriate in certain circumstances, most minority shareholders try to assert greater control over the management of the company by insisting upon guaranteed board representation. The shareholder agreement may provide that each shareholder, or related group of shareholders, has the right to nominate a number of directors which is roughly proportional to their shareholdings. This may allow a group with similar interests, perhaps a group of individual employees or financial investors, to have their respective representatives appointed to the board. The agreement may also provide that when the percentage shareholdings of the group changes, their right to board representation correspondingly changes.

The agreement will usually require that all of the shareholders vote in favour of the election of the prescribed nominees to the board of directors and to fill any vacancy on the board with the nominee of the shareholder who was represented by a vacating director. The shareholders will also be required to remove any nominee director who contravenes or votes against the wishes of the shareholder nominating her. A related provision may limit the number of directors so that the right to nominate directors is equal to the right to control a specified portion of the board.

The agreement may require that audit and compensation committees of the board be established, comprised solely of directors unrelated to a majority shareholder or current management, and that directors' and officers' liability insurance be put into place. It may also require that board meetings be held quarterly, if not more frequently, and that the board's quorum rules not allow such meetings to proceed in the absence of certain nominee directors.

To ensure that the company's key management positions are filled by people with suitable skills and experience, the shareholder agreement may specifically name certain individuals to serve, for example, as the chief financial officer or chief marketing officer of the company.

The agreement may even require that all of the company's top managers enter into comprehensive employment agreements not only setting out their respective duties, compensation (including bonus entitlement and participation in stock purchase and option plans), and rights on termination, but also their assignment of intellectual property rights and their non-disclosure, non-competition and no "moonlighting" obligations. The need to maintain "key person" insurance for them may also be stipulated.

To provide a shareholder with the right to become more involved with the company should the company's financial position deteriorate, the agreement may contain "voting switch" provisions. These provisions give the shareholder the right to elect more directors, even a majority of the company's board, upon the occurrence of certain materially adverse events, such as the failure by the company to meet certain objectives or milestones specified in the agreement or the breach by the company of any covenant in the agreement. Sometimes these provisions even include the right of the shareholder to relieve any of the managers from their management duties upon relatively short notice without cause, but subject to an obligation to pay appropriate severance and to buy back any company shares which the managers may hold.

For those companies with just two shareholders having equal or almost equal holdings, the prescribed number of their respective representatives on the board will likely be equal, leaving open the possibility of a deadlocked board on the more contentious issues. Repeated tie votes may result in the company being unable to take necessary action on a number of important matters, much like a partnership with feuding partners being unable to function.

One solution to breaking these possible tie votes is providing in the agreement for a right of the company's chairman to have a second or casting vote on the matter creating the tie. If such a right is included, the parties may insist that the agreement also include a rotation of the chairman position between the two shareholders at certain intervals, since the shareholder with the right to appoint the chairman effectively controls the board.

Each of these rights to appoint board and management representatives must be considered in the context of the company's overall governance and its need for directors and officers who have the skills and experience to properly manage the company's business.

A nominee director or officer still owes a fiduciary duty[11] to the company, not to any particular shareholder. Regardless of being appointed by that shareholder pursuant to a shareholder agreement, the director or officer may not subordinate the interests of the company while preferring the interests of the nominating shareholder. Individuals who are appointed to key company positions because of their loyalty to their nominating shareholder may soon be unable to reconcile the conflicts between the interests of the company and the interests of the shareholder nominating them.

INFORMATION RIGHTS

A shareholder may be entitled under a shareholder agreement to receive ongoing financial information directly from the company on a regular basis and not simply by way of her nominee director at board meetings, if she is entitled to nominate a director at all. The information to be provided usually includes monthly or quarterly management financial statements and audited annual financial statements. Other information generally to be provided includes management budgets, forecasts and variance reports, along with research and development reports and certificates from the chief financial officer that all statutory deductions have been appropriately withheld and remitted.

The shareholder may also be granted ongoing inspection and audit rights which permit her to visit and inspect the company's properties, examine the company's accounts and records, and discuss the company's affairs and finances with company officers. The company may, however, qualify such rights by excluding the provision of any information which it reasonably believes to be trade secrets or other confidential information unless it is satisfied with the confidentiality arrangements made with the inspecting parties.

MAJOR DECISIONS

Most shareholder agreements impose higher approval thresholds for major decisions. While some agreements simply require a higher than normal percentage for director approval, most agreements require the approval of the shareholders, and often specify a percentage well above a simple majority. It is not uncommon for an agreement to require the approval of three-quarters or four-fifths of the shareholders in order for a major decision to proceed. This need for shareholder approval is an example of the kinds of restrictions on director powers which unanimous shareholder agreements contain.

A list of the various company actions which comprise major decisions is often lengthy and is usually attached as a schedule to the agreement.

While it sets out a number of actions which can result in an increase in the company's liabilities or a dilution of the current shareholders' percentage interests, many of these actions are qualified or limited by certain exceptions when taken in the normal course of the company's business or which entail only minor or immaterial liabilities. The list is intended to include any action with the potential to have a material adverse effect on the company or its business.

The list ordinarily includes any changes to the company's articles or by-laws, the issuance of additional shares or securities convertible into shares (other than under an employee share ownership plan or option plan, or as may be required to obtain working capital financing), the redemption or repurchase of company shares, and the payment of any dividends.

Also included are any amalgamation agreement, any asset or share purchase agreement, any partnership or joint venture agreement, and any loan, guarantee or security agreement between the company and any other party. However, borrowing for working capital purposes, whether on a secured or unsecured basis, is generally a permitted exception.

Any proposal or assignment made by the company under applicable insolvency legislation, any attempt to dissolve or liquidate the company, and any prepayment by the company of any shareholder loans, are other actions likely to appear on the list.

Although the list may stay the same for some time, the percentage approval thresholds may have to change to reflect changes in the percentage holdings of the various shareholders. A current shareholder may not be prepared to invest more money in the company when the other shareholders decline to do so unless the approval thresholds are lowered. The agreement may specify that a lower threshold will apply in the event that the holdings of any shareholder rise above a prescribed percentage. For example, a three-quarters threshold might be reduced to two-thirds when a shareholder ends up with two-thirds of the outstanding shares.

USE OF PROFITS

Shareholders may have different expectations on how and when they will realize a return on their investment in the company. Some may be looking to dividends, while others may be anticipating a large increase in the value of their investment which they will receive when they eventually sell their shares. Some may have a more immediate, short-term view,

whereas others, often called "patient capital", may be investing for a
longer term.

Since the shareholders are unlikely to have a common view over how
often and how much the company should pay them as dividends, the
agreement may set out a desired dividend policy for the company to
follow when profits permit. The agreement may specify the percentage
of the company's earnings, over the amounts needed for operating purposes and required capital expenditures, which is to be distributed to the
shareholders as dividends.

Instead of providing guidance for the payment of dividends, the agreement may require that the company's profits first be used to expand the
company's operations, or pay down outstanding bank indebtedness, redeem company shares or repay shareholder loans.

BANK FINANCING AND GUARANTEES

Just as the shareholders may have different preferences for the use of the
company's profits, they may also have different preferences for how the
company raises funds to satisfy its ongoing capital requirements. Some
companies have more financing alternatives than others. Those with consistent earnings and substantial assets may be able to choose from a number of sources. Early stage companies usually cannot secure debt financing and may have to resort to equity capital to fund their growth.

For those companies able to raise money from outside sources, the
shareholders may want the agreement to stipulate that the company
should first try to obtain new financing from the chartered banks or other
financial institutions before calling upon the shareholders for additional
funds.

To obtain such financing on reasonable terms, especially in the earlier
stages of the company's life cycle, it may be necessary for one or more of
the shareholders to personally guarantee the repayment of all amounts
the company may borrow.

The agreement usually addresses this requirement by stipulating that
the shareholders provide their personal guarantees to support any bank
borrowing so long as their guarantees are limited to a percentage of the
amount borrowed which is equal to their percentage shareholding in the
company. It may also require the shareholders to indemnify one another
if any shareholder becomes liable under her guarantee for more than her
percentage interest in the company.

PRE-EMPTIVE RIGHTS

The agreement may also address the company's need to raise equity capital by allowing for voluntary share subscriptions by the current shareholders while providing them with some protection against the dilution of their current percentage holdings. This may be accomplished by giving them pre-emptive rights.

These rights apply when the company intends to issue additional shares, which must first be offered to all of the shareholders in proportion to their current holdings at the same price and on the same terms. While pre-emptive rights provide the shareholders with some protection against dilution of their equity interest in the company, such rights may hinder the company's ability to raise additional capital and may not be appropriate in every circumstance.

Notice of the proposed share issuance is to be given by the company to the shareholders, who then have a certain amount of time in which to reply that they want to buy their portion of the offered shares. Each shareholder is usually then given the right to buy more or less than the portion they are offered. If any shareholder subscribes for less than she is entitled to, the balance of the shares she is offered then becomes available for possible issuance to those other shareholders who subscribed for more than the portion they were entitled to, ordinarily in proportion to their own percentage holdings in the company.

Some agreements may alternatively prevent shareholders from subscribing for more shares than they are offered in the first round. Any unsubscribed shares are to then be re-offered to all participating shareholders based upon their respective percentage holdings until there are no shares left for subscription, or until there are no shareholders left who are willing to subscribe for more shares. If the company has a large number of shareholders, this process of providing notice of each successive offer may be quite time consuming to follow.

The agreement usually provides exemptions from pre-emptive rights for shares issued to employees, officers, directors and consultants pursuant to incentive compensation arrangements, or for shares issued upon conversion of other company securities or in connection with stock dividends or stock splits. Exemptions may also be available for shares issued to commercial lenders and equipment lessors in the ordinary course of business, and shares issued as consideration for the company's acquisition of another business.

MANDATORY SHAREHOLDER FUNDING

In addition to providing for voluntary share subscriptions by the current shareholders through pre-emptive rights, the agreement may impose mandatory subscriptions upon the shareholders as well. The agreement may require the shareholders to invest in additional shares within a certain amount of time after a "capital call" is made upon them. As with pre-emptive rights, capital calls are usually made upon shareholders in proportion to their respective percentage holdings of company shares.

Instead of calling for additional equity investment, the company may require the shareholders to provide additional capital by way of shareholder loans. The shareholders may prefer to advance funds as loans rather than as equity because of the possibility of receiving some security from the company for such loans. Even if their loans are unsecured, they will still rank as creditors in any insolvency or bankruptcy of the company.

While the agreement will likely require them to postpone payment of their loans and subordinate their security in favour of any bank or other financial institution which has provided financing to the company, lending funds to the company may still be preferred over investing in additional equity.

Any decision to include mandatory funding in an agreement should not be made lightly. The relative financial resources of each shareholder need to be considered; especially when such resources could be significantly reduced by the time a call is made. It may be appropriate for capital calls to be made only with the approval of a very high percentage of shareholder votes.

If the agreement does include mandatory funding provisions, it will likely also include a provision specifying what happens if a shareholder is unable or unwilling to satisfy any capital call.

Ordinarily those shareholders who meet their capital calls are given the right to subscribe for the shares or make the loans that a defaulting shareholder was called for. Their exercise of such right in the case of an equity funding call will result in the dilution of the defaulting shareholder's percentage interest. They may also be given an option upon such default to acquire the defaulting shareholder's shares at less than fair market value, resulting in the further dilution or complete transfer of the defaulting shareholder's interest if the option is exercised. In the case of a debt funding call, their additional loans may be set at a higher rate of interest and given a preference to be paid in priority to the company's ordinary shareholder loans.

FIRST REFUSAL RIGHTS

A shareholder may be given a right of first refusal on the transfer of any company shares proposed by any other shareholders in the future. In contrast to pre-emptive rights which are intended to maintain a shareholder's percentage of equity ownership in the company, rights of first refusal are intended to increase her equity ownership in the company in the event that any of the other shareholders decides to sell. As with pre-emptive rights, rights of first refusal often apply to any shares, or securities exchangeable or convertible into shares, including rights, options or warrants, and not just to shares of the same class as are already held by the shareholder.

Exemptions from rights of first refusal are ordinarily given for transfers to a registered retirement savings plan or other trust of which the shareholder is the beneficial owner, or to a shareholder's spouse, or to a shareholder's personal holding corporation provided that the shareholders of the holding corporation agree not to transfer their shares in the holding corporation unless they concurrently transfer the shares of the company to another exempt party.

In the case of corporate shareholders, exemptions from rights of first refusal may be available to cover transfers to affiliates. In the case of shareholders who are investment managers, exempt transfers might include transfers to other funds or corporations which they manage.

The events which specifically trigger the right of first refusal often vary. Some shareholder agreements require that a "bona fide offer" must be received by the selling shareholder for all of her shares from a third party before notice is to be given to the other shareholders of their rights to purchase such shares. They are then entitled to purchase a percentage of the shares equal to their percentage ownership of the company, at the same price and on the same terms as the third party offer. If the other shareholders do not take up all of the shares, the selling shareholder may then sell all of her shares to the third party at the price and on the terms of the original offer. In order to prevent any disputes over the value of non-cash consideration, the agreement usually provides that the price in the original offer be paid in cash on closing. It also usually provides that upon closing, the third party purchaser must become a party to the agreement.

Obviously this requirement deters potential third party purchasers from incurring the time and expense involved in preparing a serious offer which may be ignored if any one of the other shareholders elects to exercise her purchase rights. It does, however, benefit the existing shareholders by letting them know the identity of their prospective fellow shareholder and effectively giving them a veto over her. Perhaps more significantly, it gives them some indication of the fair value of the shares being offered to them, assuming the third party is acting at arm's length with the selling shareholder.

As an alternative, the agreement may provide what is commonly called a "right of first offer", which permits the selling shareholder to simply give notice to the other shareholders of her intention to sell at a price and on such terms as she chooses. They are then entitled to purchase a percentage of her shares equal to their percentage ownership of the company, but if they don't, she may then sell her shares to a third party provided the price and terms are no more favourable than those originally offered to the other shareholders.

While this alternative helps the selling shareholder to set a minimum price which she can then use in subsequently negotiating with third parties, it may encourage the selling shareholder to specify an inflated price with the expectation that the other shareholders will elect to purchase at that price rather than risk a third party becoming a shareholder. Furthermore, if the other shareholders have decided not to purchase the offered shares, it affords them no opportunity to prevent the selling shareholder from selling to a third party who they might regard as an undesirable shareholder. This latter concern, however, may be addressed by incorporating into the agreement a list of prohibited third party purchasers, which might include any competitors of the company or of the current shareholders.

Deciding which of these two alternatives is preferable for inclusion in the shareholder agreement requires the shareholders to weigh their desire for the potential liquidity of their shares against their desire to control who may become a new shareholder.

Despite the inclusion of any first refusal rights, the agreement may contain a prohibition against any share transfers to third parties for a certain period of time. Sometimes referred to as a "standstill" provision, it can be used to keep all of the current shareholders working together to promote the success of the company's business, perhaps during the crucial start-up or growth stage of the company's life cycle.

Under most rights of first refusal, the selling shareholder is required to offer all, but not less than all, of her shares to the other shareholders. Furthermore, once the other shareholders have declined to buy all of her shares, the selling shareholder is usually required to close her sale to the third party within a certain period of time, failing which the first refusal process has to start all over again. Rights of first offer may permit a longer time period, since the third party negotiations may not start until after all of the current shareholders have declined. However, the longer the time period, the greater the chance that the offer price will cease to reflect the current value of the shares because of intervening material changes to the company's business.

PIGGYBACK RIGHTS

A shareholder may be entitled under the agreement to participate in another shareholder's proposed sale of company shares, usually when the sale results in a change of control of the company or involves a substantial percentage of outstanding shares. Intended to enhance the liquidity of minority shareholdings, many shareholder agreements allow a shareholder to "piggyback" on a third party offer made to a majority shareholder.

A piggyback provision often applies when a shareholder or group of shareholders with a majority of the company's shares has complied with the rights of first refusal requirements and proposes to sell to a third party. She may proceed to sell her shares to the third party so long as she has caused the third party to offer to purchase the shares of the other shareholders at the same price and on the same terms. The piggyback provision effectively provides minority shareholders who can't afford to exercise their rights of first refusal with a possible exit from the company should they wish to avoid dealing with a new majority shareholder in the future.

The agreement may provide "co-sale" rights instead. Unlike piggyback rights which allow minority shareholders to have all of their shares included in a third party purchase offer, co-sale rights provide for the inclusion of only such portion of their shares which, when added to the portion held by the majority shareholders, equals the number of shares which the third party wishes to purchase. The number of shares that the majority can sell is effectively reduced and replaced by the number of shares that the minority shareholders elect to sell to the third party. In the event that the third party wishes to purchase all of the company's outstanding shares, the difference between piggyback rights and co-sale rights disappears in practice.

While rights of first refusal generally prohibit third party offers from consisting of non-cash consideration, piggyback rights, and drag-along rights discussed below, often permit non-cash consideration to be part of third party offers.

DRAG-ALONG RIGHTS

A minority shareholder may also be required to participate in a sale of company shares by a majority shareholder. Her own shares may be "dragged along" as a way of increasing the marketability of the majority shareholder's shares since a third party purchaser may be more likely to want all of the shares of the company rather than have to deal with other company shareholders after the purchase. The drag-along provision is also viewed as a way to eliminate minority positions in a private company.

A drag-along provision is effectively the reverse of a piggyback provision. It provides that if a third party makes an offer to purchase all of the shares of the company, those shareholders holding a majority or perhaps higher percentage of the company's shares who wish to accept the offer may require the other shareholders to sell their shares to the third party at the same price and on the same terms, so long as the right of first refusal provisions have first been complied with.

This provision allows the majority shareholder to market 100% of the company's shares and obtain the maximum sale price from a purchaser prepared to pay a higher price for all of the shares than it would pay for just majority control.

TRANSFER RIGHTS UPON CERTAIN EVENTS

A shareholder may be able to require the other shareholders to buy her shares upon the occurrence of certain events. Alternatively, the shareholder may be required to sell her shares to the others upon the occurrence of the same events. The death of the shareholder, if the shareholder is an individual, is the event specified in most shareholder agreements as requiring a share transfer. Other events triggering such a requirement include the termination of a shareholder's employment with the company, whether voluntary or involuntary, the shareholder's disability, bankruptcy or insolvency, or a breach of a material provision of the agreement.

These requirements usually appear as a number of "puts" and "calls" in the agreement. A put, or option to sell, gives a shareholder a right, but not an obligation, to sell her shares either to the company or to other shareholders upon the prescribed events. As the opposite of a put, a call gives a shareholder or the company a right, but again not an obligation, to buy the shares of another shareholder.

However, instead of structuring the requirements as a series of puts and calls, some agreements provide for mandatory, not optional, purchases. This approach is often thought to be desirable in the event of death or disability of the shareholder since the shares will have a ready buyer.

Most agreements require a shareholder to sell her shares when a call is exercised after a prescribed event. Yet they often vary over which party may exercise the call and purchase her shares. Some agreements give call rights to the company, some give them to just a majority shareholder or group of shareholders, while others give them to all of the shareholders based upon their percentage holdings of company shares.

Although selecting the company as the buyer may appear to be the easiest approach to take, it may result in undesirable consequences, apart from considerations of whether the company will have the funds available to pay for the shares.

For example, a company redemption or repurchase may well have negative tax implications for the selling shareholder.[12] Also, the proportionate voting rights of the other shareholders and voting control could be altered upon the cancellation of that shareholder's shares. Furthermore, the redemption or repurchase could possibly cause the company to be in default under the negative covenants in its financing agreements, or perhaps be in contravention of the statutory solvency test for the redemption or purchase of its shares.

Under this solvency test, the directors of the company are prohibited from repurchasing the company's shares if there are reasonable grounds for believing the company is, or after payment for the shares will be, unable to pay its liabilities as they become due, or if the realizable value of the company's assets will then be less than the aggregate of its liabilities and stated capital of all classes. A similar prohibition applies to the redemption of the company's shares, although the realizable value of the company's assets must not be less than the aggregate of its liabilities and the amount it has to pay to the holders of other shares before or rateably with the holders of the shares being redeemed.[13]

In light of these possible consequences, the agreement may provide that if the company is unable to buy the shares, then another shareholder or group of shareholders shall buy the shares instead.

The treatment of an employee's shares upon termination of employment often depends upon how and why the termination takes place. If it is "for cause", the company is likely to be given a call option to purchase the employee's shares, whereas the employee is likely to be given a put option to sell her shares if she is terminated without cause. If the employee simply resigns, the company usually can call the employee's shares.

VALUATION OF TRANSFERRED SHARES

Even though the shareholders may be able to agree upon the various puts and calls to be exercised in respect of their shares, they may have some difficulty in deciding which method should be used to value their shares when these options are exercised. Since there is no readily available market for determining their value, the shareholder agreement must provide some valuation guidance. Whether a share purchase is mandatory or optional, the agreement usually specifies one of three ways to arrive at a purchase price for the shares being purchased.

One approach requires the shareholders to review and annually adjust an initially agreed upon value. The second approach entails the application of a particular formula. As described in greater detail in the *Valuation* chapter, there are different formulas to choose from. The agreement may select an asset-based method, such as net book value or appraised asset value. Or it may select an earnings based or cash flow based method, perhaps using discounted cash flow or a multiple of earnings. Or it may select a specific industry rule of thumb, such as a dollar value per existing customer.

The third approach involves the retention of a professional business valuator to determine the value of the shares to be sold. The agreement will often specify who the valuator should be and who should pay the valuator's fees. It may also provide some general rules for the valuator regarding which valuation methods should be used or avoided, and which assumptions and adjustments ought to be made. For example, it may stipulate that no control premium or minority discount is to be considered, but that the goodwill associated with a departing shareholder may be taken into account.

Each approach has its advantages and disadvantages. But while all three afford the parties a mechanism for valuation, they don't guarantee either certainty or fairness of result. The annual share value review usually stops after the second year. The formula approach tends to be easier and faster than the valuator approach, but may not be suitable for every company. For example, a decision to use book and not appraised asset values, or a multiple of recent earnings and not a discount of projected earnings, may appear misguided in hindsight and create resentment.

By taking the valuator approach, assuming that all the parties can agree upon a choice of valuator, the valuator chosen may turn out to be more expensive and take much longer to perform the valuation than the parties originally expected. Often the closing date prescribed in the agreement becomes unworkable because of delays in receiving the valuator's report. If the agreement names the company's auditor as the valuator, the auditor may have difficulty reconciling the conflicts between audit and valuation duties. It's usually preferable for an independent party to be named as valuator, and for any closing date to be a specified number of days following delivery of the valuation.

Sometimes the agreement will prescribe a different method for the valuation of shares which can be "called" in the event that the holder becomes insolvent or bankrupt in order to arrive at a value which is lower than the value which would apply upon the occurrence of the other events triggering a call under the agreement. Net book value or the original subscription price for the shares might be the method chosen in these circumstances so that a lower price will be paid by the company or other shareholders when exercising their rights to redeem or purchase the shares, since the holder is unlikely to personally benefit from the proceeds actually paid.

SHOTGUN RIGHTS

Another provision involving the transfer of shares between shareholders is the "shotgun", which has its own particular valuation mechanism. Some shareholder agreements, normally between just two shareholders, will contain a shotgun provision to provide a means of resolving a possible deadlock between the two shareholders.

A shotgun essentially permits one shareholder to set a price at which she is willing to either sell her shares to the other shareholder, or buy the shares of the other shareholder. Once the shareholder has given notice of the shotgun price, the other shareholder then has to decide which of the two alternatives to accept. Many shotguns require the other shareholder to decide within a relatively short time period, often fewer than 30 days, and her failure to do so requires her to sell her shares at the price set.

While some shotguns then require payment of the entire purchase price after another relatively short period, again often fewer than 30 days, some provide for payment in regular instalments over as long as three or five years. The tight time frames dictated by the agreement can certainly work to the disadvantage of the other shareholder, who may have great difficulty in arranging suitable financing within the permitted time should she wish to buy. Her ability to pay on time effectively determines whether she buys or sells.

For this reason, shotguns are often only used when there are just two equal shareholders with roughly comparable financial resources. Although shotguns impose an obvious deterrent on the offering shareholder against setting a price that is too high or too low, such deterrence breaks down when the other shareholder lacks financial strength. When that is the case, the attempt to give some certainty to the exit process by adding a shotgun clause is then made at the expense of fairness, because a low-ball price becomes inevitable. The financially stronger shareholder will simply take advantage of the other.

Consequently, shotguns may be inappropriate for many companies and shareholders. For earlier stage companies that need to keep their shareholders committed, as well as patient for a payback on whatever time and effort has been invested, shotguns are often exercisable only after a period of 2 years or more has elapsed.

For those companies with shotgun provisions in their shareholder agreements, such provisions are infrequently exercised. Since shareholders appear reluctant to risk the consequences in practice, shotguns may reflect mutual deterrence. They may actually motivate deadlocked shareholders to negotiate a resolution to a problem rather than pull the trigger.

In other words, the main benefit to having a shotgun in place is the threat of its use, not the use itself.

AUCTION RIGHTS

Although not commonly found in shareholder agreements, shareholders may be given the right to initiate an auction for the company's outstanding shares. The right to hold an auction is usually provided as additional to, and sometimes as an alternative to, some of the rights described in this chapter.

As an alternative to the rights of first refusal, an auction may be chosen by the shareholders as providing the means for the sale of one shareholder's shares to the other shareholders. The auction gives the other shareholders an opportunity to buy a shareholder's shares but does not ensure that they will pay no more than a third party will pay. The auction procedures may require that all of the interested bidders attend at a certain location at a specified time and that a named auctioneer will conduct the auction in accordance with the rules set out in the agreement, with the highest bidder winning.

An auction may also be used instead of the right to exercise a shotgun. The shareholders, especially if there are more than two, may have the right under a shareholder agreement to initiate an auction for the company's outstanding shares. In this case, the auction procedures may prescribe that each shareholder is to make a sealed bid to buy all of the shares of the company and the shareholder with the highest bid wins.

NEGATIVE COVENANTS

In addition to placing restrictions on the powers of the directors and on the type of business which the company may carry on, the agreement may impose restrictions on the shareholders themselves, particularly on their conduct which may not be in the best interests of the company.

Although the directors are under a statutory duty to act in the best interests of the company, as mentioned above under *Board and Management Representation*, the shareholders are not. If the shareholders collectively decide that certain contractual duties should be placed upon their fellow shareholders to make up for the absence of certain statutory duties, a shareholder agreement may also be used for such a purpose.

The agreement may set out various shareholder duties, or "positive covenants", to do certain things. Examples of such covenants appear elsewhere in this chapter, such as a shareholder's obligation to give notice to the other shareholders of her desire to sell her company shares to an outside party so that they may exercise their rights of first refusal.

But the agreement is just as likely to set out various duties, or "negative covenants", not to do certain things. Examples of these covenants also appear elsewhere in this chapter, including the companion covenant to the right of first refusal which prohibits a shareholder from transferring her shares to an outside party.

Three negative covenants which ordinarily appear in the agreement to address possible conflicts of interest between a shareholder and the company are the non-disclosure covenant, the non-solicitation covenant and the non-competition covenant.

Non-disclosure Covenant

A shareholder of a private company is usually required under the agreement not to disclose to anyone outside the company any confidential or proprietary company information, including any intellectual property, trade secrets, sales and market data, and any other confidential information relating to the company and its business. This covenant is a companion covenant to the information rights discussed above, and generally applies whether the shareholder continues or ceases to be a shareholder.

The agreement ordinarily provides certain exceptions to this restriction. It does not apply to information which is known to the public, or information which the shareholder knew before becoming a shareholder, or information which the shareholder received from outside parties.

Non-solicitation Covenant

The non-solicitation covenant generally prevents a shareholder from soliciting any employees of the company to become employees of the shareholder, or any customers of the company to become customers of the shareholder, so long as the shareholder remains a shareholder of the company and for a certain period of time afterwards. The survival or continuing enforceability of this covenant generally lasts for a period of between 6 months and 2 years after the shareholder disposes of her shares, but longer terms are not unusual.

This provision in usually worded to prohibit only the active solicitation or inducement of company employees or customers by a departing shareholder, and is not intended to cover those employees or customers who approach the shareholder on their own. However, it can lead to a dispute between the company and a departing shareholder who subsequently employs company employees or supplies company customers, since the shareholder's subtle encouragement of the employees and customers is often inferred from the particular circumstances. The shareholder's protest that the employees or customers came on their accord is not always credible.

Non-competition Covenant

In addition to preventing a shareholder from soliciting company employees or customers, the agreement may also try to prevent the shareholder from competing against the company or its affiliates, either directly or indirectly. A non-competition covenant is usually limited to a certain geographical territory or market, and to a certain length of time. It may last as long as a non-solicitation covenant but is sometimes for a slightly shorter period. It represents a much broader restriction than a non-solicitation covenant since a shareholder bound by the latter may continue to participate and invest in the same business as the company.

Its prohibition against both direct and indirect competition ordinarily covers a very broad range of activities. It applies to acting as an employee, officer, director, shareholder, consultant or agent for a competing business, regardless of whether such business is carried on through a partnership, joint venture, trust, other corporation, or even a governmental agency.

Furthermore, the covenant usually prevents the shareholder from lending to, investing in, or otherwise having a financial interest in any business which is the same or substantially similar to the business being carried on by the company or its affiliates. An exception is often made for any investment in publicly traded securities provided such investment represents not more than 5 per cent of the total securities outstanding of any particular issuer.

Enforcement of Negative Covenants

As monetary damages may not be easily or expeditiously proven before a court or even obtained through the enforcement of a court judgment for a breach of any of these three covenants, the agreement is likely to provide that the company may also ask a court to award an injunction to prevent any continuing breach of them.

Efforts to enforce a non-solicitation or non-competition covenant can face an additional challenge since most courts are reluctant to award a remedy for breach of either covenant if it covers too long a time period, or in the case of a non-competition covenant, too broad a geographical territory.[14]

The courts have traditionally viewed these two kinds of restrictive covenants as restraints of trade and have needed to be convinced that the covenants are reasonably necessary to protect the company's legitimate proprietary interest before enforcing them. However, customer lists, trade secrets, business connections with customers and goodwill are all legitimate interests worthy of the court's protection.

Often a non–solicitation covenant will be enforced by a court but not a non-competition covenant on the basis that the non-solicitation covenant is all that is necessary to protect a company's interest, provided that it has reasonable time restrictions.

However, should the company or another shareholder have either a right or obligation to redeem or purchase a shareholder's shares under the agreement as discussed above, there is a greater chance that the non-competition covenant will be enforced by the court, especially if the agreement prescribes the purchase price to be paid for the shares.

Unlike non-competition covenants contained in employment agreements which are seldom enforced, non-competition covenants in share purchase agreements are frequently enforced, due in some part to the equality of bargaining power which ordinarily exists between a purchaser and seller, but not between an employer and employee. Also, a sale of a business often involves a payment for goodwill whereas no similar payment is made to an employee upon leaving employment. Yet in order for the non-competition covenant to be enforceable, it must still contain reasonable territorial and time restrictions.

FAMILY LAW COVENANTS

As described earlier in the *Business Succession and Estate Freezes* chapter, the family laws applicable in many Canadian provinces generally provide a community of property regime which allows for the equalization of family property acquired by spouses during their marriage upon their marriage breakdown.[15] Consequently, a shareholder agreement may contain a provision dealing with the implications of such laws upon a shareholder.

Under these laws, a court might order that company shares owned by one spouse be transferred to the other spouse, or that one spouse pay to the other a part of the profits earned by the company. Such orders can lead to a number of undesirable consequences for the company and its shareholders. Control of the company might change, covenants in the company's credit agreements might be breached, and adverse tax effects might result. The provisions in the agreement dealing with board representation and the approval of major decisions may cease to be acceptable to certain shareholders.

Furthermore, such legal proceedings may threaten the confidentially of sensitive company information, since its financial statements and other records may have to be produced and various details of its business described in a court judgment.

To address some of these potential concerns, the agreement may provide that any shareholder has the right to acquire for a prescribed price the shares of another shareholder who is facing a family law claim for property equalization. This call right, however, has disadvantages for both parties, since it requires the buyer to come up with the purchase funds which may be difficult to find, and may place an untimely tax liability upon the seller. A court may also be unprepared to accept the prescribed price as the correct value of the shares and wish to undertake its own assessment, thereby again threatening the confidentiality of the company's business information.

A preferred alternative is for the agreement to require the shareholders to have in place separate marriage contracts with their respective spouses which exclude their shares from any property equalization and which prevent their spouse from looking to the company to satisfy any equalization payment owing. These marriage contracts would be required immediately from shareholders who are married, and upon any subsequent marriage or remarriage of a shareholder. Any proposed amendment to those contracts which conflicts with the provisions of the shareholder agreement would have to be approved by all of the shareholders.

Whichever approach is taken, the agreement will still include a provision requiring a shareholder to notify the company and all of the other shareholders if she becomes involved in equalization proceedings.

MISCELLANEOUS MATTERS

In addition to the foregoing items, a shareholder agreement may set out a number of other items which are more procedural in nature or which address the day-to-day operations of the company, whether or not they are also contained in the company's by-laws.

For example, the agreement may specify the company's bankers, lawyers and accountants, its financial year-end, and those persons who are authorized to make bank deposits and sign contracts and cheques. It may also include any special notice and voting rules for directors' meetings, and the process for preparing and approving operating and capital budgets and the company's business plan.

Since the circumstances facing the company or its shareholder are likely to change during the term of the agreement, the procedure for its amendment is usually set out. Unless there are just a few shareholders, requiring the consent of all of the shareholders to any amendment may not be practicable. Normally the consent of a relatively high percentage of shareholders, perhaps 80 per cent, is all that is required to effect an amendment binding upon all of the shareholders.

While the agreement may well have an indefinite term, it may stipulate instead that it is to remain in effect for only a fixed term. The termination of the agreement may occur upon a certain date, upon a certain event taking place and result being achieved, or perhaps in the absence of such event or result by a particular date. Upon termination, the agreement may provide for the company to be liquidated and dissolved, unless the agreement has been terminated to facilitate a public offering of the company's shares.

Shareholder Statutory Rights – Part I

Whether or not the company undertakes an equity financing or becomes a party to a shareholder agreement as described in previous chapters, the owners and managers of a private company still have to be aware of the rights available to the company's shareholders generally.

Even though the shareholders of the company may not have changed since shares were first issued when the company was starting up, there will likely come a time when the shareholders, either individually or collectively, want to exercise their rights. While they may enjoy various rights under a subscription agreement or shareholder agreement, or under the actual terms of the shares issued to them, or under the company's articles of incorporation and by-laws, or even under the common law, there are other rights which are given to them by statute.

These statutory rights, available under the CBCA to shareholders of private companies governed by the CBCA, are in addition to the buy-sell rights, redemption rights, veto rights and the numerous other contractual rights previously discussed in this book.

Sometimes shareholders of private companies can become confused about their statutory rights and have slightly enhanced expectations of what the company should do for them because of the expanded set of rights enjoyed by shareholders of "distributing" corporations.[1] For distributing corporations, first referenced in the *Introduction* chapter, the CBCA imposes additional requirements and provides their shareholders with additional rights. For example, the requirements for an audit committee and shareholder proxy solicitation, or the need to comply with take-over bid rules, which are imposed by the CBCA on distributing corporations do not apply to private companies.

Not all shareholders want to know the same things about the private company in which they have invested. Some shareholders just want to know about the company's financial performance, or whether their dividends are likely to remain constant or increase. Others just want to know how to sell their shares when the opportunity arises, or perhaps how to buy more shares if the company continues to prosper. Others may want to know how to get their ideas considered by management, while others may simply want to know what to do when things go badly wrong.

This chapter and the next will look at what rights private company shareholders are given by statute under the CBCA. While some of the previous chapters have discussed the additional rights which a shareholder may acquire by contract, later chapters will examine some of the governance practices followed by private companies to provide additional shareholder protection, as well as the basic duties which company directors are expected to perform and the impact of shareholder meetings on how a shareholder is able to exercise his rights.

However, a shareholder assumes certain burdens in order to enjoy the benefits flowing from these various rights. A private company shareholder should be an active participant in the company, not a passive investor, in order to fully derive such benefits. Some of the obligations which must be fulfilled and actions taken by shareholders so that their rights and expectations can be realized are discussed in this and later chapters.

A shareholder usually invests in a private company's shares with the hope of receiving some return on that investment. The return may come as dividends representing a portion of the company's profits, as well as upon the sale of the shares if they are sold for more than their purchase price.

While the shareholders may own the company's equity, they don't play an active role in the day-to-day operations of the company's business. They may elect the directors, consider the company's financial statements and approve certain actions which may fundamentally change the nature of the company or its business, but they have very little say in how the company is operated. That's the role of the board of directors.

But the shareholders generally expect that the board will ensure that the company is operated properly in order that their desired return on investment will happen eventually.

And they generally expect that they can't lose more than their invest-ment. After all, one of the main advantages of investing in a company is its "limited liability". Except in a few exceptional circumstances, share-holders are not liable for the debts and other obligations of the company and they put no more at risk than the amount they have paid for their shares.[2] Such circumstances include the improper decrease of capital, or upon the dissolution of the company and distribution of the company's remaining property for a period of two years thereafter, or under a unan-imous shareholder agreement. Even though the company may lose money or incur liabilities well in excess of its assets, the shareholders are not required to pay more than they have already invested. Such is not the case when someone invests as a partner in a general partnership.

While the foregoing few rights and expectations may appear to many shareholders of private companies to be the only rights and expectations they are entitled to as shareholders, they are entitled to a lot more as will be explained. Whether they are prepared to fully pursue all that they are entitled to becomes a more complicated question for them to answer. While the *Dispute Resolution and Shareholder Remedies* chapter sets out how shareholders might seek redress for their grievances, the cost, time and uncertainty of outcome associated with litigation may deter them from acting further.

However, since the shares of private companies are not readily mar-ketable, the option of "voting with their feet" and selling their shares which may be available to the shareholders of public companies is seldom available to private company shareholders.

As a general rule, individual shareholders of a private company all have the same basic statutory rights so long as they are all holders of shares of the same class. If the company has only one class of shares, the holders are equal in all respects and are entitled to vote at shareholder meetings, receive any dividends that are declared, and receive the remaining prop-erty of the company upon its dissolution.[3] However, so long as the com-pany is ongoing, shareholders don't have rights to any of the company's underlying assets.

One of the exceptions to this general rule relates to issuance of a series of shares within the same class. The articles of the company may authorize the issuance of one or more series which have different rights, restrictions and conditions from any other series within the same class, provided a series is not given a priority in the payment of dividends or return of capital over any other series of the same class that are outstanding. A series may be created by the directors in their discretion without specific approval by the shareholders if the articles permit the directors to do so.[4]

Another exception relates to the shareholder's contractual rights, ordinarily achieved through a shareholder agreement with the other shareholders, which may restrict or expand upon the shareholder's statutory rights.

The equality of the shareholders can also disappear when more than one class of shares is created by the company. The rights to vote, to dividends and to receive property upon dissolution need not be attached to just one class of shares, and a number of additional rights can apply to one class but not another.[5] These may include redemption rights, preferences to receive dividends or a return of capital, conversion rights, and a number of other rights which have been described in greater detail in earlier chapters.

This chapter discusses the various statutory rights which shareholders of a private company have, regardless of how many company shares they hold (with exceptions for the right to requisition a meeting or make a proposal, discussed below). They can exercise these rights on their own, without the need to act collectively with any other shareholders in an effort to make something happen. These rights are effectively individual rights, in contrast to the rights discussed in the next chapter which involve shareholders' collective rights which are exercised at a shareholder meeting.

Although some of the individual rights described in this chapter can only be exercised in connection with a shareholder meeting, or by way of a resolution signed by all of the shareholders in lieu of a meeting, they nonetheless represent a shareholder's individual action.

CORPORATE RECORDS

Right to Examine Corporate Records

Shareholders of a private company are entitled to examine certain corporate records during the usual business hours of the company.[6] These records consist of the company's articles of incorporation and by-laws, any unanimous shareholder agreement, all minutes of meetings and resolutions of the shareholders, copies of government filings identifying the company's directors, and the securities register.[7]

However, the shareholders do not have the right to examine the company's accounting records or those records containing the minutes of meetings and resolutions of the directors. One exception to this is the right of a shareholder during usual business hours to examine any disclosures of interest which a director or officer may have made to the company, whether such disclosures have been recorded in the minutes of director meetings or in separate documents.[8]

Right to Copies of Certain Corporate Records

The shareholders are entitled at no charge to take extracts from those records which they may examine.[9] Each shareholder may also request one copy of the articles, by-laws and unanimous shareholder agreement without charge.[10]

Right to Examine Shareholder List

A shareholder may examine the list of shareholders who are entitled to receive notice of a meeting during the company's usual business hours at its registered office and at the meeting of shareholders for which the list was prepared.[11]

Right to Receive Shareholder List

A shareholder may require the company to furnish a shareholder list[12] within 10 days upon payment by the shareholder of a reasonable fee and sending of an affidavit stating the intended uses of the list. The list, which must set out the name and address of each shareholder of the company and the number of shares and series held by each shareholder, may only be used to influence shareholder voting or make an offer to acquire securities of the company, or be used in connection with the affairs of the company.[13] The shareholder may also require that the list include the name and address of anyone who has an option to acquire the company's shares.[14]

DISSENT AND APPRAISAL

When a fundamental change is made to the articles of incorporation of a company, or if the company is to be amalgamated, or wishes to transfer substantially all of its assets, undertake a squeeze-out transaction or continue under another jurisdiction, a shareholder has a right to dissent from the proposed action and claim payment of the fair value of his shares.[15] The claim must relate to all of the shares held by the shareholder. These actions which give rise to a right to dissent are described in greater detail in the next chapter.

Often called a "dissent and appraisal remedy", it is intended to ensure that minority shareholders are treated fairly by majority shareholders when significant corporate changes are proposed.

In order to exercise this right, the shareholder must send the company a written objection to the resolution being proposed on or before the meeting at which the resolution will be considered. Within 20 days after learning that the resolution has been adopted or receiving a notice from the company to that effect, the dissenting shareholder must then send to the company a written demand for payment of the fair value of the shareholder's shares, followed by the certificates for those shares not more than 30 days later.

The dissenting shareholder is entitled to receive within 7 days of sending the written demand for payment a written offer from the company to pay an amount considered by the directors to be fair value for the shares, along with a statement as to how the fair value was determined. Every offer for shares of the same class or series must be on the same terms. The company must pay the shareholder within 10 days after the offer has been accepted.

The dissenting shareholder may not be paid if the company is unable to meet a statutory solvency test. If there are reasonable grounds for believing that the company will be unable to pay its liabilities as they become due, or the realizable value of the company's assets will be less than the aggregate value of its liabilities, the company is prohibited from paying for the shares.

FINANCIAL STATEMENTS

Right to Examine Financial Statements
The shareholder has the right to examine the consolidated financial statements of the company and its subsidiaries during the company's usual business hours and may make extracts free of charge.[16]

Right to Receive Financial Statements
The company is required to send to the shareholders not fewer than 21 days before each annual meeting, or before the signing of a resolution in

lieu of an annual meeting, the comparative financial statements for the company's latest completed financial year and for the immediately preceding financial year, together with the auditor's report, if any, unless the shareholder has declined to receive them.[17] These statements must also be placed before the shareholders at the meeting.

The statements must be prepared as prescribed by the CBCA regulations and in accordance with Canadian generally accepted accounting principles.[18] They should include at least a balance sheet, statement of retained earnings, income statement, and statement of changes in financial position.

RECEIPT OF COMPANY DIVIDENDS

As mentioned above, every shareholder is entitled to receive any dividend declared by the company if the company has only one class of shares.[19] However, there is no statutory requirement that a company must declare dividends out of its profits and, to the contrary, there is a statutory prohibition against declaring and paying dividends if the company is unable to meet a test for solvency.[20]

This test will not be met if the company isn't able to pay its liabilities as they become due, or if the realizable value of its assets will be less than the aggregate of its liabilities and the stated capital of its shares. Dividends may be paid by means of fully paid shares of the company or, if it meets this test, in money or property.[21]

Since the decision to declare and pay dividends is made by the company's board of directors in their discretion, a shareholder does not have a right to be paid a dividend unless the dividend has first been declared by the board. Even though the company has earned significant profits and a shareholder wishes that some or all of those profits be paid out as dividends, the directors may prefer to use the profits instead to purchase additional inventory and equipment and hire more staff in order to expand the company's business. They may also decide to retain the profits for future capital expenditures or as a reserve for possible losses. The first thing a board often considers when the company's operations are losing money is the reduction or cessation of regular dividends.

However, while a company's dividend policy is normally implemented by the board, the policy may be prescribed by the shareholders in a unanimous shareholder agreement. As discussed in the *Shareholder Agreements* chapter, the directors may be required to declare a certain percentage of annual profits as dividends each year, subject to the above solvency test.

A shareholder's right to receive dividends also depends upon the terms of the shares he holds as well as any additional terms in a unanimous shareholder agreement. His shares may entitle him to receive preferential, participating and cumulative dividends. Or he may not be entitled to receive any dividends at all, if dividends may be payable to the holders of another class of the company's shares.

RECEIPT OF COMPANY PROPERTY ON DISSOLUTION

If the company has only one class of shares, each shareholder is entitled to receive his share of the remaining property of the company upon its dissolution, as described above.[22] If there is more than one class, the shareholder may not be entitled to receive any property at all, depending upon the terms of his shares. His rights on dissolution will be determined by the preferences and other features of his shares.

While shareholders often receive nothing upon the liquidation and dissolution of a company because of payments made to the company's secured and unsecured creditors, the shareholders may be required to reimburse any unpaid creditors and others with valid claims against the company out of any dissolution proceeds which they may receive, provided such claims are brought within two years of the dissolution.[23]

SHARE CERTIFICATES

Right to Receive Share Certificate

Shareholders are entitled to receive at their option either a share certificate or a non-transferable written acknowledgment of their right to obtain such a share certificate from the company. The certificate must be signed by a director or officer of the company or its registrar, transfer agent or trustee, although the signature may be printed or otherwise mechanically reproduced.

Each share certificate should show on its face the name of the company issuing the shares, the name of the shareholder, the number, class and series (if applicable) of the shares represented by the certificate, and a statement that the company is incorporated under the CBCA.

Any restrictions on share transfer, any lien or charge on the shares by the company, and the existence of a unanimous shareholder agreement, should be noted conspicuously on the share certificate, failing which they will be ineffective against any transferee who is unaware of them.

If the company issues shares of more than one class or series, the rights, restrictions and conditions attached to each class or series shall appear on the certificate for such class or series, or there shall appear a statement that the company will provide the full text of them to the shareholder on request.

If fractional shares arise, perhaps upon a share consolidation or conversion, or an amalgamation of the company with another corporation, the shareholder may receive either fractional certificates or scrip certificates as a result. A scrip certificate entitles the holder to receive a share certificate for a full share by exchanging scrip certificates for fractions totaling a full share. The holder of a fractional certificate may vote and receive dividends only upon a share consolidation or unless the articles so permit, but the holder of a scrip certificate may not vote nor receive dividends.[24]

Right to Receive Replacement Share Certificate

If the shareholder's share certificate has been lost, destroyed or wrongfully taken, the shareholder is entitled to receive a new certificate in place of the original if the shareholder provides an indemnity bond and satisfies any other requirements reasonably imposed by the company.

If, however, the shares represented by the original certificate turn out to have been already transferred to a *bona fide* purchaser, the company may recover the replacement certificate from the shareholder as well as claim against him on the indemnity bond.[25]

SHAREHOLDER MEETINGS

Right to Require Auditor Attendance

Any shareholder, whether entitled to vote or not, may give written notice not fewer than 10 days before a shareholder meeting to the company's auditor or former auditor to attend the meeting. The auditor or former auditor must then attend the meeting at the company's expense and answer any questions relating to their duties as auditor.[26]

Right to Requisition Meeting

A shareholder, or group of shareholders, holding not less than five per cent of the company's issued voting shares may requisition the directors to call a meeting of shareholders for the purposes stated in the requisition. If the directors do not call a meeting within 21 days of receiving the requisition, any shareholder who signed the requisition may call the meeting.

The shareholders who requisitioned the meeting are entitled to be reimbursed for the expenses reasonably incurred by them in requisitioning, calling and holding the meeting unless the shareholders at the meeting resolve otherwise.[27] Since the majority shareholders have this right to reject any claims for reimbursement by the minority shareholders requisitioning the meeting, the minority shareholders face the risk that they may have to pay their own costs in calling the meeting.

Right to Solicit Proxies

Any person, including an existing shareholder, can solicit proxies from other shareholders to vote their shares at a meeting. So long as the solicitation is not made by or on behalf of the company's management, and so long as it is made to only fifteen or fewer shareholders, it can be made without the need to prepare and distribute what's called a "dissident proxy circular". Such a circular must be in a prescribed form, and involves considerable time and expense to prepare.[28]

Right to Submit Proposals

Although applicable in practice to more widely held companies, any voting shareholder has the right to submit to the company notice of any matter he would like to propose at an annual meeting of shareholders.[29] The shareholder is entitled to provide a statement in favour of the proposal which the company is required to include in the management proxy circular for the meeting if the company solicits proxies so long as the statement is not more than 500 words.

However, the company is not required to solicit proxies with the notice of meeting if it has just 50 or fewer shareholders entitled to vote.[30] Since a private company for the purposes of this book is defined to have not more than 50 shareholders, a proposal aimed at private company shareholders may not be distributed by the company in advance of the meeting.

Yet the shareholder is still entitled to discuss at any annual meeting any matter on which he would have been entitled to submit a proposal.

The company may request that a proposer show proof of being a shareholder, and refuse to include the proposal if the proposer holds less than one per cent of the company's total outstanding voting shares or holds shares worth less than $2,000, or has been a shareholder for fewer than six months.

The company may refuse to include the proposal for a number of additional reasons. For example, if the proposal is not submitted at least 90 days before the anniversary of the date of the company's notice of the last annual meeting. Or if its primary purpose clearly appears to be the enforcement of a personal claim or redress of a personal grievance against the company, or its directors, officers or security holders. Or if it does not relate to the company's business in any significant way, or is being abused to secure publicity. Or a similar proposal was previously submitted to the shareholders and received less than a prescribed minimum amount of support.

The proposal may include nominations for the election of directors at the meeting provided it is signed by the holders of not less than five per cent of the company's outstanding voting shares, although nominations may still be made at the meeting.

If a shareholder makes a proposal to amend the company's articles, the notice of meeting shall set out the proposed amendment and state that any dissenting shareholders shall be entitled to be paid the fair value of their shares in accordance with the dissent and appraisal rights discussed above.[31]

Right to Vote

Unless the company's articles otherwise provide, each share issued by the company entitles its holder to one vote at a shareholder meeting. If the shareholder is a corporation or association, its right to vote may be exercised by any individual authorized by a resolution of the directors or governing body of the corporation or association to vote. If two or more people hold shares jointly, one of them attending the meeting in the absence of the others may vote those shares, but if two or more of them are present, they shall vote their shares as one.[32]

A shareholder entitled to vote may appoint by means of proxy in writing a proxyholder to attend, vote and act at the meeting as the shareholder's nominee to the extent authorized under the proxy.[33] A proxy-holder need not be a shareholder. A proxy may be revoked by the shareholder after it is given at any time up to the holding of the meeting or any adjournment.

Although voting may take place by a show of hands unless the company's by-laws otherwise provide, any shareholder or proxyholder may demand that a ballot be taken, either before or after a vote by a show of hands.[34]

The rights of a shareholder to vote can be affected by an agreement he may have signed with other shareholders. Referred to as a "pooling agreement", such an agreement requires that the shares held by the parties be voted in a prescribed manner. It is often used to ensure that all of the shares they hold are voted the same way as a block to maximize their voting power, and can be effective for employee shareholders who want greater influence over company management.[35]

Shareholder Statutory Rights – Part II

In contrast to the various individual rights discussed in the previous chapter, there are a number of rights which shareholders can exercise collectively in order to accomplish certain things. Ordinarily these rights are exercised at a meeting of company shareholders or by way of a written resolution circulated among all of the shareholders for their signature.

However, any shareholder alone may be able to authorize a particular action through her exercise of these collective rights if she holds a sufficient number of shares to cast either a majority or two-thirds of the votes at a shareholder meeting, depending upon the particular matter.

As with the shareholders' individual rights, these collective rights as a general rule are basically shared by all of the shareholders of a private company so long as they are all holders of shares of the same class. However, the holders of different classes may not all have the same collective rights, especially the holders of non-voting shares.

Shareholders generally exercise their collective rights by way of an "ordinary resolution" which entails a simple majority of the votes cast by the shareholders at a meeting on any particular matter. It may also be reflected in a written resolution signed by all of the shareholders who may vote on that matter without holding a meeting.[1] For those companies with only a few shareholders, shareholder approval will usually be obtained by way of a written resolution circulated among the shareholders to avoid the costs and delays normally incurred in sending out notices and holding a shareholder meeting.

However, many of the rights described in this chapter are to be exercised by a "special resolution" of the shareholders, which is a resolution passed by a majority of not less than two-thirds of the votes cast by the shareholders or which is signed by all of the shareholders entitled to vote on the resolution.[2]

Some of the rights to be exercised by special resolution are accompanied by the rights of the holders of a particular class or series to vote separately as a class or series, thereby leading to more than one vote being taken. For example, to amend the articles or approve the transfer of substantially all of the company's assets, approval from each class or series must be given by a special resolution.[3]

AMALGAMATION

If the company proposes to be amalgamated with another corporation, the amalgamation agreement is to be submitted for approval at a meeting of the company's shareholders. Each share, whether voting or non-voting, carries a right to vote in respect of an amalgamation agreement.

The agreement is adopted when it is approved by a special resolution of the company's shareholders. The holders of each class or series of shares are entitled to vote on the agreement as a separate class or series if the agreement provides for amended articles which would give rise to such separate class rights as discussed immediately below under *Amending Articles*.[4]

This right of the shareholders to approve an amalgamation does not apply when the company is being amalgamated with its subsidiary or parent corporation, or with another related subsidiary. Such amalgamations, often referred to as "short form" amalgamations, only require the approval of the directors of the corporations involved.[5]

Since shareholders have dissent and appraisal rights in connection with amalgamations as mentioned in the previous chapter, the special resolution may allow the directors to abandon the amalgamation if difficulties arise from the exercise of such rights.

The company may amalgamate only with another CBCA corporation, although that corporation may have been incorporated under the laws of another jurisdiction and then continued under the CBCA, as described below, just before the amalgamation. An amalgamation of two CBCA corporations does not create a new corporation but rather brings them together as one corporation just as two rivers meet and continue as one river.[6] This is different from the American notion of amalgamation or merger which involves the transfer of assets from a merging corporation into a surviving corporation and then the disappearance of the merging corporation.

Under the CBCA, an amalgamation is a specific procedure involving the consolidation of two or more corporations into one. It is not the same as the sale of assets from one corporation to another, or an exchange of shares among corporations. Upon an amalgamation, the property and liabilities of each amalgamating corporation continue to be the property and liabilities of the amalgamated corporation, including any civil or criminal proceedings or judgments which may be prosecuted or enforced against the amalgamated corporation.[7]

The amalgamation agreement which the company's shareholders are requested to approve by special resolution must set out a number of things.[8] It must describe the provisions required to be included in articles of incorporation, such as the corporate name, registered office, share classes, restrictions on share transfer, and the number of directors, along with the names and addresses of those proposed to be directors of the amalgamated corporation. It must specify how shares of the amalgamating companies are to be converted into shares of the amalgamated company.

In addition, the amalgamation agreement must set out what the shareholders are to receive in cash if their shares are not being converted into shares of the amalgamated corporation. It must also state whether the by-laws of the amalgamated corporation will be the same as the by-laws of one of the amalgamating corporations, and if not, it must contain a copy of the proposed by-laws. It must also provide details of any arrangements necessary to complete the amalgamation and provide for the subsequent management and operation of the amalgamated corporation.

In approving the amalgamation agreement, the shareholders should be particularly concerned about the assets and liabilities of the other amalgamating corporation, and whether their shareholding in the amalgamated corporation will be subject to greater risk once the amalgamation takes place, despite the operational synergies which may result. The shareholders should also be concerned that the valuation of each of the amalgamating corporations is reasonably accurate and that the share-exchange ratios provided in the agreement are fair and equitable.

After the amalgamation agreement has been approved by the shareholders of the amalgamating corporations, articles of amalgamation are filed with the Director under the CBCA who must be satisfied that certain facts exist to allow the amalgamation to proceed. Unlike the Director's concern for both creditors and shareholders under a continuance, discussed below, the Director's concern is for the creditors in an amalgamation. The Director does not have the discretionary power to refuse an amalgamation just because it fails to adequately protect the shareholders.[9]

An affidavit from a director or officer of each amalgamating corporation is submitted to the Director which states that the amalgamated corporation will be able to pay its liabilities as they become due, that the realizable value of the amalgamated corporation's assets will not be less than the sum of its liabilities and stated capital of all of its share classes, and that no creditor will be prejudiced by the amalgamation. In addition, the Director may require that a *pro forma* balance sheet for the amalgamated corporation be submitted, and perhaps even the written consent to the amalgamation from certain creditors.

AMENDING ARTICLES

The articles of the company may be amended by a special resolution of the shareholders. Amending the articles may implement a number of changes. The name of the company, the restrictions on the businesses it may carry on, the number of share classes, the rights and restrictions placed on its shares, the minimum and maximum number of its directors, and the restrictions on share transfer, can all be changed by amending the articles.

These items are normally set out in the initial articles when the company is first incorporated. Upon incorporation, the articles, along with the by-laws and any unanimous shareholder agreement, represent the company's charter or "constating documents". Shareholders attempting to understand the company's governance need to be familiar with these documents as well as the CBCA, and should be aware that a proposed amendment to the articles may significantly affect how the company is governed.

The holders of a class or series of shares may vote separately as a class or series on a proposed amendment if such amendment will adversely affect the preferences, priorities or rights of their shares, whether or not their class or series is otherwise entitled to vote.[10]

While a number of changes to the articles may be proposed at the same time, it is not necessary to pass a separate special resolution in respect of each change. All the changes may be authorized in one resolution and included in one set of articles of amendment.

AUDITORS

Right to Appoint Auditor

At each annual meeting of shareholders, the shareholders are generally required to appoint by ordinary resolution an auditor to hold office until the close of the next annual meeting.[11] However, the shareholders of a private company (but not of a distributing corporation) may resolve not to appoint an auditor. But that resolution is only valid if it receives the unanimous consent of the shareholders, whether they are entitled to vote or not, and even then the resolution is valid only until the next annual meeting.[12]

Right to Remove Auditor

The shareholders may remove the company's auditor by an ordinary resolution at a special meeting unless the auditor was court appointed, and the vacancy then created may be filled at the same meeting.[13]

BY-LAWS

If the directors have made, amended or repealed any by-law, the shareholders are entitled to confirm, reject or amend it at their next shareholder meeting by an ordinary resolution.[14] Any by-law rejected by the shareholders ceases to be effective.

By-laws generally govern the company's internal procedures and are different from resolutions which approve specific acts of the directors or shareholders, such as the declaration of dividends or authorization of a particular contract. Most of the by-laws governing a private company are contained in a comprehensive "general" by-law which is made at the time the company is incorporated and organized, and then amended from time to time thereafter to respond to various changes which may have occurred.

Since the by-laws are part of the company's charter as mentioned above, they have an impact upon how the shareholders are not only able to enforce their rights but also to become aware and participate in the governance of the company should they choose to do so. What follows

immediately below is a summary of some of the matters ordinarily addressed in the company's general by-law.

The general by-law is often divided into a number of parts, each part
dealing with a separate topic. One part may address certain operational
issues, such as when the company's financial year should end, or who
should be authorized to sign company contracts, carry out the company's
banking arrangements or vote the company's shares in other corporations. Another part may specify what borrowing may take place and
whether security over the company's assets may be given without having
to obtain the consent of the shareholders.

The general by-law will set out in another part the various rules applicable to the directors. It will likely stipulate their qualifications to serve,
the length of their terms, how they may be elected or removed, and how
a vacancy on the board may be filled or additional directors appointed. It
may also provide where their meetings are to be held, how meetings are
called and notice given, what quorum is required, who may chair a meeting, whether the meetings may be held by telephone, how many votes
will decide a particular matter, what conflict of interest rules should be
observed, and what director remuneration and expense reimbursement
may be paid.

Another part may identify the board committees that may be established, and a further part may describe the powers and duties of various
officer positions, along with the conflict of interest rules applicable to
them. An additional part may stipulate the various circumstances under
which a director or officer may be entitled to indemnification by the
company for certain losses and expenses incurred, and may provide for
the purchase of insurance to support the company's indemnification
obligations.

The procedures and conditions relating to the issuance and transfer of
company shares may appear in another part of the general by-law. The
rules for registration, certificate issuance, joint and deceased shareholders, and any lien for indebtedness to the company may all be prescribed
in this part. The rules for the declaration and payment of dividends may
be found in another part.

Shareholder meetings will comprise an additional part of the general
by-law. How annual and special meetings may be called, where they may
take place, whether shareholders may participate by electronic means,
who may chair a meeting, who may attend, how joint shareholders are

to be treated, the quorum required, and the rules for depositing and voting by proxy, may all be addressed. Furthermore, this part may prescribe the votes to govern a particular matter, the rules for a show of hands and ballots, and how a meeting may be adjourned.

The final part of the general by-law will likely deal with the giving of notices. It may stipulate the acceptable methods for giving notice, how notice periods are calculated, the effect of undeliverable notices, and how joint shareholders are to be notified.

CONTINUANCE

Any application by the company to continue in another corporate jurisdiction, whether provincial or foreign, as if it had been incorporated under the laws of that other jurisdiction must be approved by a special resolution of the company's shareholders. This continuation is often described as an "export" continuance. Each company share carries the right to vote on the continuance whether or not it otherwise carries the right to vote,[15] but there are no separate class votes.

In contrast to an export continuance, an "import" continuance describes a corporation governed by the laws of another jurisdiction continuing under the CBCA. An importing corporation must first satisfy the requirements of its own jurisdiction in authorizing its application for continuance under the CBCA, upon which it may then be discontinued in that jurisdiction.

The special resolution approving an export continuance ordinarily allows the directors to abandon the continuance without further shareholder approval if difficulties arise in the other jurisdiction. Since shareholders have dissent and appraisal rights in connection with export continuances, the special resolution may also allow the directors to abandon the continuance if difficulties arise from the exercise of such rights.

Even if the export continuance is approved by a special resolution of the shareholders, it must still be approved by the Director appointed under the CBCA who must be satisfied that the continuance will not adversely affect the company's creditors or shareholders. The application to the Director should contain an affidavit from a company officer or director stating that the shareholders have received full disclosure of the effect of the continuance on their rights and interests. The application should also contain a statement that the company will honour the rights of dissenting shareholders and that it has adequate funds to pay them.

Where there are complaints by persons who feel they are being adversely affected or oppressed, the Director may refuse the continuance.

DIRECTORS

Right to Elect Directors
At each annual meeting of shareholders, the shareholders are required to elect directors to hold office for a term expiring not later than the close of the third following annual meeting.[16] The election is by ordinary resolution, which usually approves the group of directors or "slate" presented to the meeting. Shareholders may vote in favour of the slate or withhold their vote, but they do not vote against the slate or any particular candidate.

They may be able to follow a "cumulative voting" procedure instead if provided in the company's articles.[17] Cumulative voting in the election of directors gives a shareholder the right to cast a number of votes equal to the number of voting shares she holds, multiplied by the number of directors to be elected. She may then cast all such votes in favour of one candidate or distribute them among the various candidates in any proportion she chooses. This type of voting enables those holding just a minority of company shares to elect one or more directors.

Right to Remove Directors
The shareholders may remove any director or directors from office at any special meeting of shareholders, and may fill the resulting vacancy at that meeting. If the holders of any particular class or series of shares have the exclusive right to elect one or more directors, such directors may only be removed by a resolution of those shareholders.[18]

Since the holding of a special meeting may involve some expense to the company, the shareholders may prefer to simply wait until the expiry of the director's term (which is usually at the next annual meeting) and then elect at that meeting another candidate whom the shareholders would rather have as a director.

Right to Restrict Directors' Powers
As part of their rights to amend the articles and confirm the by-laws of the company, the shareholders may authorize various provisions in the

articles or by-laws which restrict the powers of the directors.[19] Such restrictions may apply, for example, to the kinds of company business which may be carried on, the issuance and repurchase of shares, the conduct of director meetings, the appointment of officers and their remuneration, and the borrowing of money.

LIQUIDATION AND DISSOLUTION

The shareholders may by a special resolution authorize the dissolution of the company, or its liquidation and dissolution, provided that the company is not insolvent or bankrupt.[20] If the company has issued more than one class of shares, a special resolution of the holders of each class is required, whether or not they are otherwise entitled to vote.[21]

Upon approval by the shareholders, a statement of intent to dissolve is submitted to the Director appointed under the CBCA. The Director then issues a certificate of intent to dissolve, which starts the liquidation process requiring the company to cease business operations, although the company continues to exist. The company must then notify its creditors, and then proceed to dispose of its properties and discharge its obligations, after which it may then distribute its remaining property among the shareholders according to their respective rights.

Property which cannot be distributed to shareholders because they cannot be located is to be converted into cash and paid to the Receiver General of Canada.[22] Once the liquidation has been completed, articles of dissolution may be filed with the Director who in turn may issue a certificate of dissolution, upon which the company will cease to exist.

SHAREHOLDER SQUEEZE-OUT

If the company wishes to implement what it is called a "squeeze-out" transaction, a majority of the holders of each class of shares that are affected by the transaction must approve it, voting separately as a class. A squeeze-out involves an amendment to the company's articles which results in the termination of the holder's share interest without her consent and without substituting company shares of equivalent value with equal or greater rights.[23]

Approval of the transaction is subject to what is often described as a "majority of the minority" requirement, since those shareholders who will receive after the transaction greater consideration or superior rights or privileges than other shareholders are not entitled to vote. A special resolution of all of the shareholders is also required to approve the amendment to the articles.

Squeeze-out transactions are usually carried out by way of either consolidation of the company's shares or amalgamation with another corporation, and are intended to eliminate a small number of shareholders holding a small number of shares.

Although such transactions result in the expropriation of minority interests, the expropriation is not without compensation, since the minority shareholders are entitled to exercise their dissent and appraisal rights described in the previous chapter. Normally the company or its controlling shareholder will offer a fair price to the shareholders being squeezed-out, given the relatively small percentage of the outstanding shares involved.

In a share consolidation, the outstanding shares are consolidated so that the minority shareholders receive only a fractional interest in a share which may be eliminated by a cash payment rather than permit the receipt of a fractional certificate. For example, with a consolidation on a 1000 to 1 basis, holders of less than 1000 shares would cease to hold shares, leaving a majority shareholder who held more than 1000 shares prior to the consolidation as the only shareholder afterwards. Alternatively, the company may issue scrip certificates for the fractional shares which may be redeemed by the holder for cash within a certain time period. Holders of scrip certificates may not vote or receive dividends.[24]

In an amalgamation squeeze-out, the majority shareholders will transfer their company shares to a newly formed "temporary" corporation which then amalgamates with the company. The amalgamation agreement provides that the holders of all of the company's shares except for the temporary corporation will receive redeemable preferred shares of the amalgamated corporation, whereas the shareholders of the temporary corporation will receive common shares of the amalgamated corporation. The preferred shares are then redeemed, thereby forcing out the original minority shareholders and leaving the company's original majority shareholders as the only shareholders of the amalgamated corporation.

STATED CAPITAL

The company is required to maintain a separate "stated capital" account for each class and series of shares issued. When shares are issued, the full amount of the consideration received by the company for such shares is to be added to the appropriate stated capital account, although less than the full amount may be added in the case of certain transfers between non-arm's length parties, arrangements and amalgamations.[25]

Right to Increase Stated Capital

The shareholders must approve by special resolution any addition to a stated capital account if the amount to be added was not received by the company as consideration for the issuance of shares and the company has at least two classes or series of outstanding shares. An exception exists when there are just two classes outstanding which represent convertible shares.[26]

Right to Reduce Stated Capital

The shareholders may reduce the stated capital of the company by means of a special resolution. Although the stated capital may be reduced for any reason, it is often reduced in order to permit a return of capital to the shareholders, or to reflect a decline in value of the company's realizable assets. This right to reduce the stated capital is subject to a statutory solvency test.[27]

Since a company's capital has traditionally be regarded as a "cushion" for creditors, allowing them to risk possible non-payment of amounts they may be owed by the company, the reduction of capital has certain implications for the company's perceived creditworthiness. A company's capital is more frequently reduced through its purchase or redemption of its outstanding shares.

TRANSFER OF ALL OF THE ASSETS

A sale, lease or exchange of all or substantially all of the property of the company other than in the ordinary course of business requires the approval of the holders of each class or series by way of special resolution. The notice of the meeting requesting approval is to include the agreement for the transaction or a summary of it. Each share of the company carries the right to vote for this purpose whether or not it is otherwise a voting share.

The holders of a particular class or series of shares are entitled to vote separately as a class or series only if their class or series is affected differently by the transaction than another class or series. The shareholders may authorize the directors to fix any of the terms and conditions of the transaction.[28]

In determining whether the property being transferred constitutes substantially all of the company's property in order to require a special resolution, the transfer is to be looked at "qualitatively", assessing whether the nature of the company's business will be fundamentally changed should the property be transferred, and not "quantitatively" by just looking at its value.[29]

Since shareholders have dissent and appraisal rights in connection with the transaction, the special resolution may allow the directors to abandon the transaction without further approval from the shareholders in case problems are created through the exercise of such rights.

Shareholder Meetings

As described in the previous two chapters, it is the shareholders who elect the directors and it is the shareholders who must approve certain company actions before such actions may be carried out. Traditionally such elections and approvals have taken place at a meeting of shareholders which allowed the shareholders to attend and present their views on the various matters put before the meeting and to raise other issues which they felt were relevant to the success of the company.

Many of the shareholder statutory rights may only be exercised at a shareholder meeting, unless it is practicable for a written resolution to be signed by all of the shareholders instead.[1]

For a private company with a relatively large number of shareholders, or whose shareholders are unlikely to act unanimously by way of written resolution, a shareholder meeting will likely be called at least once a year.

This chapter will focus on how a shareholder meeting is called and conducted, but will not address the statutory basis for the rights being exercised at the meeting. Many of the specific individual statutory rights given to a shareholder under the CBCA which relate to shareholder meetings and which have been described in the *Shareholder Statutory Rights – Part I* chapter will not be repeated here. These include the rights to requisition a meeting, solicit proxies, submit proposals, and vote, either in person or by proxy. Neither will the collective statutory rights described in the previous chapter be repeated in this chapter.

This chapter will generally look at shareholder meetings called by the directors, although meetings may also be called by requisition of certain shareholders, or by court order as described in the *Dispute Resolution and Shareholder Remedies* chapter. The calling of a meeting by court order does not necessarily indicate the existence of disputes between the directors and shareholders, but may simply reflect the inability to satisfy the company's quorum requirements, which may be varied or dispensed with at the meeting if the court permits.[2]

ANNUAL MEETINGS

The directors are required to call an annual meeting not later than 18 months after the company comes into existence and then not later than 15 months after the last preceding annual meeting. An annual meeting should be held not later than 6 months after the company's preceding financial year.[3]

An annual meeting ordinarily covers a number of matters prescribed by the CBCA. It should allow for the consideration of the company's financial statements,[4] appointment of auditors,[5] election of directors,[6] and confirmation of any by-laws enacted during the past year.[7] Though not a statutory requirement, it may also receive the directors' report on the company's operations and confirm all acts of the directors taken in the past year.

SPECIAL MEETINGS

The directors may also call a special meeting for the transaction of any "special" business. Special business is any business other than the consideration of the financial statements and auditor's report, election of directors and reappointment of the incumbent auditor.[8]

PLACE OF MEETINGS

A shareholder meeting is to be held within Canada at the place specified in the company's by-laws, or at the place determined by the directors if not specified in the by-laws. It may, however, be held outside Canada if the company's articles designate such a place or if all of the shareholders agree. Any shareholders attending the meeting outside Canada are deemed to agree unless they are attending to specifically object to the meeting being held.[9]

A meeting does not have to be held "face-to-face" at a common physical location, and may be held by means of an "electronic or other communication facility" unless the company's by-laws otherwise provide.[10]

NOTICE OF MEETING

Notice of the time and place of a shareholder meeting is to be sent not fewer than 21 days and not more than 60 days[11] before the meeting unless the by-laws or articles of the company provide for a shorter period.[12] The by-laws normally allow the directors to determine the exact time and place of the meeting.

While notice of the meeting is to be sent to every shareholder entitled to vote, every director and the auditor, notice is not required to be sent to shareholders who were not registered on the company's records on the "record date". A record date is the date used for determining the shareholders entitled to receive notice of the meeting, which may be fixed by the directors in advance of giving the notice. If no record date is fixed, it is deemed to be the day before the notice is given. Failure to receive a notice does not deprive a shareholder of the right to vote at the meeting.[13]

The notice must identify the items to be discussed at the meeting. The items normally identified in a notice for an annual meeting include the consideration of the financial statements and auditor's report, election of directors and reappointment of the incumbent auditor. Any other items, to be transacted as special business at a special meeting, are to be identified in the notice in sufficient detail to permit the shareholders to form a reasoned judgment on them, along with the text of any resolution to be submitted to the meeting.[14] Often just one notice of an annual and special meeting combining all of these items will be given.

The company's by-laws are likely to provide that any accidental omission to notify a particular shareholder will not invalidate the business of the meeting. A written waiver of notice of the meeting signed by all of the shareholders or their proxies will normally correct any irregularities in the notice. Usually the company secretary will certify at the meeting the proper mailing of notices and his certificate will be placed in the company's records for the meeting. However, if a meeting is held without proper notice and if even just one shareholder does not sign a proxy or waiver or otherwise consents to the business conducted, the business may be declared invalid.[15]

ADJOURNMENT OF MEETING

The by-laws are also likely to provide that the chair, upon convening the meeting, with the consent of the meeting and subject to any conditions as the meeting may decide, may adjourn the meeting from time to time and place to place.

If the meeting is adjourned for fewer than 30 days, there is no need to give a further notice of the adjourned meeting unless the by-laws so require. If it is adjourned by one or more adjournments totaling 30 days or more, then notice of the adjourned meeting must be given as if an original meeting.[16]

PREPARATION FOR A MEETING

In preparing for a shareholder meeting, especially an annual meeting which will be dealing with special business, the chair's agenda is drafted well in advance of the meeting. The agenda will often attempt to include additional items which may arise at the meeting, scheduling the essential items for early in the meeting and deferring more contentious items until later.

The number of contentious items expected to be discussed, and the number of shareholders entitled to attend and vote, will influence the extent of the preparation undertaken. Ballots may have to be produced in anticipation that a poll will be called for instead of a show of hands on certain matters, and independent scrutineers may have to be appointed to oversee the voting process. It may be expedient for routine motions to be read by "movers" and "seconders" who have been selected beforehand. The chair will usually be well coached to answer a variety of questions which may asked by the shareholders.

The chair is most likely to be the officer designated in the by-laws to chair the meeting, often the company's president. If no chair has been designated, the shareholders present may select one of their number to chair the meeting.

CONDUCT OF THE MEETING

Upon calling the meeting to order, the chair will attempt to ascertain whether a quorum is present. If the holders of a majority of the shares entitled to vote at the meeting are present in person or represented by proxy, there will be a sufficient quorum to proceed regardless of the number of persons actually present, unless the by-laws stipulate otherwise.[17] It may be necessary to involve scrutineers to make this determination.

Once quorum has been established, the chair will then declare that the meeting may proceed. Even if quorum is lost at any time throughout the meeting, the meeting may continue on unless the by-laws provide to the contrary. If a quorum cannot be established at the outset, the meeting may be adjourned by the shareholders present but they may not transact any other business.[18]

The meeting then commences with a reading of the notice of the meeting and a tabling of the secretary's certificate that the notice, financial statements and other documents have been properly sent as required. The minutes of the previous shareholder meeting may then be read, or more likely, a motion will be requested for the minutes to be taken as read. The minutes may then be signed, or corrected and then signed if an amendment is requested.

Each item set out in the meeting agenda will then by dealt with by the chair requesting that a motion in respect of the item be made, seconded, and then submitted to the shareholders for their discussion, possible amendment and vote. The chair normally decides upon any questions regarding the meeting's procedures but must act fairly to all the shareholders present and comply with any rules of procedure prescribed in the company's by-laws. However, the chair must ensure that the business identified in the notice of the meeting is completed, and may therefore be required to cut short those speakers wandering off topic.

If an amendment to any motion is proposed, it should only vary the original motion in some detail. The chair should refuse to allow an amendment to be proposed if it introduces an essentially new item or is completely negative to the original motion, and call for a new motion instead. If the chair allows an amendment to be proposed, the amendment should be voted on first. If it loses, the original motion should then be put to the meeting. If the amendment wins, it should be included in the original motion and voted on again as a motion which supersedes the original motion. If the amended motion loses, the original motion is not revived.

The chair may end the discussion on any item and put that item to a vote if the meeting approves a motion to do so. A vote is ordinarily taken by a show of hands unless a ballot is demanded by a shareholder or proxyholder. However, where a resolution needs to be passed by a certain percentage of the shares held or votes cast, such as a special resolution which requires a majority of not less than two-thirds of the votes cast, a ballot should be taken. If scrutineers have been appointed, they will report the results of any ballot to the chair who will, in turn, announce the results to the meeting and declare whether or not the resolution has been adopted by the required majority. Their written report on the actual vote is ordinarily presented after the meeting and attached to the minutes of the meeting.

After completion of all of the items on the agenda, the chair usually asks the meeting if there is any other business. If new business is raised at that time, the chair has to decide if such business falls within the purpose for which the meeting was called before allowing it to be considered by the meeting. If no new business is raised, the chair may then adjourn the meeting with its consent.

Director Duties and Liabilities

While the owners and managers of a private company need to be aware of the rights enjoyed by the company's shareholders, they also need to be aware of the duties owed by the company's directors. After all, the owners and managers are likely directors of the company, so they should be familiar with the potential liabilities they may face when performing those duties, or more importantly, when performing them improperly or not performing them at all.

Previous chapters have stated that the directors have the statutory power and duty to manage, or supervise the management of, the company's business and affairs. Even though this general duty is subject to the rights granted to the shareholders under the CBCA and subject to a number of additional rights which the shareholders may acquire, the directors are still required to carry out a number of specific duties.

This chapter will describe some of these duties. As well as examining the overriding fiduciary duty and duty of care imposed upon the directors, it will set out a number of other duties which the directors are supposed to perform under the CBCA when managing the company's business. Some of the liabilities which the directors may face, the means of avoiding such liabilities, and their rights to be indemnified by the company, in carrying out their duties will also be discussed. The conduct of director meetings will be addressed as well.

However, this chapter will not describe the numerous duties imposed upon directors under other federal statutes or under the statutes of the various provinces in which the company may be operating. Numbering possibly in the hundreds if the company operates across Canada, these statutes affect most corporate functions and cover many areas, including taxation, competition, securities, employment insurance, health and safety, pensions, the environment, and many more.

While the directors are given the overall power to manage the company, they don't have to exercise all of this power together. They may delegate many of their powers to committees of directors or to a managing director.[1] Even their borrowing power can be delegated to a director or committee of directors, or to an officer.[2] However, a director may not act by a proxy or substitute.

The right to delegate is often exercised by relatively large boards which have difficulty convening frequent board meetings on short notice. Since committees have fewer members than the full board, they are often used to deal with urgent matters. As particular committees are usually comprised of directors with skills and interests in specific areas, they are also used to address matters within those areas.

However, not all matters may be delegated by the board to a committee or managing director. For example, filling a vacancy among the directors or in the office of auditor, issuing debt securities and shares, declaring dividends, acquiring and redeeming shares, paying commissions on the purchase of shares, approving financial statements and passing by-laws require the authority of the full board.[3] These particular matters are left to the full board since it may incur liability if they are improperly handled.

While relatively few private companies have more than just one or two committees of directors, if they have any committees at all, there is no shortage of committees which may be set up if the practices of some public companies are to be followed. The following chapter on *Governance* explores this topic in greater detail.

An executive committee is the most likely to be established. It is ordinarily delegated all of the powers which the full board has to conduct the ongoing business of the company, except for those matters referred to above which cannot be delegated.

An audit committee is also frequently appointed, comprised of directors with certain financial expertise, although its mandate often goes beyond strict financial matters. It may be expected to monitor the effectiveness of internal controls, risk management guidelines and management information systems. Audit committees required under the CBCA for distributing corporations must review the company's financial statements before being submitted to the board for approval, and they must have a majority of members who are not officers or employees.[4]

In addition to these two committees, the board may establish a compensation committee to set appropriate levels of management compensation and perhaps handle other matters relating to human resources, such as employee benefit plans. This committee is usually comprised of non-management directors. The board may also establish a nominating committee for the purpose of identifying possible directors, and depending upon the nature of the company's business, an environmental committee.

Some committees are established to serve on a temporary basis in order to investigate and consider a particular issue, and then either report to the board or take its own actions to resolve the issue. Sometimes these special committees appoint their own counsel and experts, whose advice they may then rely upon in the exercise of their own duty of care. Special committees are generally regarded as the preferred way to solve problems which the board, attempting to deal with them on its own, might address inappropriately and thereby incur legal liability.

If the board establishes a committee without any power to act on the board's behalf but to instead report back and recommend to the board on certain matters, such a committee need not be comprised of only directors.

Whether a particular matter is addressed by the full board or by a committee, any director participating in the discussions and ultimate resolution of such matter must be aware of her broad fiduciary duty and duty of care.

FIDUCIARY DUTY

The directors are required to act honestly and in good faith with a view to the best interests of the company when exercising their powers and discharging their duties.[5] Because this duty reflects the fiduciary relationship between each director and the company, the director is often described as a trustee of the company. However, the description is not entirely accurate, since company directors make decisions entailing a variety of business risks, whereas trustees are essentially engaged in the preservation of property.

This fiduciary duty is owed to the company and not to any particular group of stakeholders, such as the shareholders. Often the interests of the shareholders and other stakeholders are the same as the interests of the company, but if they conflict, the directors' duty is clearly to the company. The duty is not confined to short-term profit or share value, but to the company's long-term interests, assuming it remains a going concern. In determining how to proceed on any particular matter, the directors may ordinarily rely upon their own business judgment, in accordance with the business judgment rule described below.[6]

In order to act honestly and in good faith with regard to the company, the directors must respect the trust and confidence given to them to manage the company's assets. They must avoid conflicts of interest with the company. They must avoid abusing their director position to gain personal benefit. They must keep confidential the information they acquire because of their position.[7]

Disclosing Conflicts of Interest

Because the directors are in a fiduciary relationship with the company, they must not profit from any transactions involving the company without the knowledge and consent of the company. They must not be in a position where their personal interests will conflict with their duties as a director. However, they may deal with the company and keep any profit resulting from the transaction if they have made full disclosure to the company and the company has consented to it.

The CBCA requires a director to disclose in writing, or have recorded in the minutes of a meeting of directors, the nature and extent of any interest she may have in a material contract or transaction with the company, whether it is made or proposed. The director personally may be a party, or a director or officer of a party, or have a material interest in a party, to the contract or transaction.[8] There are no specific rules regarding the amount of detail which the director should disclose but the other directors should be sufficiently informed about the director's interest before they make a decision.

There are, however, specific rules for the timing of the director's disclosure.[9] Disclosure must be made at the meeting at which the proposed contract is first considered. If the director was not then interested, or becomes interested after the contract is made, disclosure must be made at the first meeting after she becomes interested. If an individual who is interested in a contract later becomes a director, disclosure must be made at the first meeting after she becomes a director.

If a material contract or transaction is one that would not ordinarily be presented to the board for approval, the director must still disclose her interest in it by notifying the board in writing or requesting that her interest be recorded in the minutes of the meetings of directors.[10]

A director having an interest in a material contract or transaction may not vote on it unless it relates primarily to her remuneration, or is for indemnity or insurance.[11]

In light of these requirements, many directors provide their board with a general declaration of interest which identifies all of the organizations of which they may be a director or officer or in which they have a material interest. This declaration is usually provided when the director is first appointed and then regularly updated, often annually.

Any contract or transaction requiring disclosure does not become invalid, and the director does not have to account for any profit made from it, just because the director had an interest in it, so long as three conditions are met. First, the director had to disclose her interest as required. Second, the other directors had to approve the contract or transaction. And third, the contract or transaction had to be reasonable and fair to the company at the time it was approved.[12]

This third condition can be difficult to satisfy, especially if the director's interest is attacked years later in a court proceeding and the board's approval is viewed in the light of subsequent events. Even if the contract or transaction has been approved by the shareholders by way of a special resolution, it may still not be saved if the court finds it was not reasonable and fair to the company when it was approved.[13]

Avoiding Misuse of Corporate Opportunity

Related to their duty to disclose their potential conflicts of interest and also arising out of their fiduciary relationship with the company, the directors should not take for themselves or divert to a related party a maturing business opportunity which the company is actively pursuing. The opportunity rightfully belongs to the company.[14]

Resigning from the board before taking up such an opportunity does not get around this prohibition if the resignation was prompted by the desire to take advantage of the opportunity. Even if the company could not have made a profit if it pursued the opportunity itself, the directors taking it up are still not relieved of their fiduciary obligations to the company. Only when the opportunity is a fresh initiative which is later acquired by the directors will they be permitted to pursue it.

Unless a director makes sufficient disclosure to the company and secures its consent before proceeding to take up the opportunity, she may well be liable to account to the company for her profits.

DUTY OF CARE

The directors are required to exercise the care, diligence and skill that a reasonably prudent person would exercise in comparable circumstances when exercising their powers and discharging their duties.[15] While boards are composed of directors with a variety of skills, no one director is expected to be skilled in all areas of the company's business.

However, in those areas where a director is not skilled, the director is expected to make diligent inquiries and perhaps seek outside advice. A director can comply with this duty of care by relying in good faith upon financial statements presented by the company's officers or contained in an auditor's report, or upon reports from professional advisers such as accountants, lawyers, valuation experts or engineers.[16]

Unlike the fiduciary duty described above which is owed solely to the company, this duty of care can be owed by the directors to the company's various stakeholders.[17] These may include the shareholders, employees, creditors, consumers, governments and the environment.

Because of the vast number of laws which govern a company's conduct, as well as impose responsibility upon the directors for seeing that such laws are complied with, the directors are often required to prove in any legal proceedings brought against them or the company under such laws that they have exercised care, diligence and skill by developing policies and procedures to ensure compliance with these laws by company personnel. Some form of reporting system should be put into place allowing the directors to monitor the ongoing effectiveness of their policies.

Business Judgment Rule

The possible liability which the directors face under their duty of care is influenced by the "business judgment rule" being applied by the courts. Under this rule, the courts have been deferential to board decisions so long as the directors have acted reasonably and fairly.[18]

Provided the directors have made a reasonable decision, though not necessarily a perfect decision, a court will not substitute its opinion for that of the board even though subsequent events have cast doubt on the board's determination. The board need only have selected from a number of reasonable alternatives.

Board decisions, in other words, will not be subject to microscopic examination, since the courts have generally been reluctant to interfere with the board's function to manage. They have generally recognized that a board decision must often be made under considerable time pressure when detailed information may not be available. The courts have also recognized that they may be ill-suited to make certain business decisions and shouldn't second-guess the application of the board's particular expertise.

However, the courts are capable of determining whether an appropriate degree of diligence has been exercised by a board. If a court finds the manner in which the board arrived at a decision to be lacking, the business judgment rule cannot be used to save the decision. If the board followed a flawed process in making a decision, perhaps by acting too quickly without due consideration of other alternatives, a board decision may be overturned.[19]

OTHER DIRECTOR DUTIES

Acquisition and Redemption of Shares

The directors may authorize the acquisition and redemption of the company's shares provided that the company is able to satisfy the statutory solvency tests.[20] If the company fails to meet these tests, the directors will be jointly and severally liable to restore to the company the funds that were improperly paid out.[21] However, the directors may then ask a court to compel any shareholder receiving an improper amount to pay such amount to the directors.[22]

Because solvency tests must be satisfied by the company in order for the directors to authorize share purchases and redemptions, as well as declare dividends as mentioned below, they are expected to have independent appraisals of the realizable value of the company's assets made available to them. Compliance with these tests cannot be ensured by referring to the company's financial statements alone, since the balance sheets may reflect only the historical cost of the assets, not their current realizable value.

Ordinarily the company's shares are cancelled upon acquisition, since the company is generally prohibited from holding its own shares, although there are a few limited exceptions. Even if the company is allowed to hold its own shares, such shares may not be voted unless held by the company as a legal representative for another party.[23]

Approval of Financial Statements

The company is required to send financial statements to each shareholder before the annual meeting unless the shareholder doesn't want to receive them.[24] Before the statements are mailed, they must be approved by the directors. Approval is usually evidenced by the signature of two directors authorized to sign.

Appointment of Officers

Officers may be appointed by the directors.[25] Often the directors appoint officers for the ensuing year at a meeting immediately following the annual shareholder meeting at which the directors are elected. However, apart from a managing director, there is no provision in the CBCA for the appointment of other officers, including a president or secretary.

Unless the articles, by-laws or unanimous shareholder agreement otherwise provide, the appointment of officers by the board is undertaken pursuant to its general power to manage the company's business and affairs. Yet any officers who are appointed are subject to the same fiduciary duty and duty of care as apply to the directors, as discussed above.[26]

Authorizing Payment of Commissions

The directors may authorize the company to pay a reasonable commission to anyone who procures buyers for the company's shares.[27] However, if the commissions are excessive, the directors will be jointly and severally liable to reimburse the company for the commissions that were improperly paid out.[28]

Borrowing

Without the authorization of the shareholders but subject to the articles, by-laws or unanimous shareholder agreement, the directors may borrow money on the credit of the company, issue or pledge debt obligations of the company, give company guarantees, and mortgage or pledge the company's property to secure any company obligations.[29]

Compliance with CBCA and Company Charter

The directors are required to comply with the CBCA and its regulations, the company's articles and by-laws, and any unanimous shareholder agreement. No provision in the articles or by-laws, or in any resolution or contract, may relieve a director of the duty to act in accordance with the CBCA and its regulations, nor relieve the director of liability for breach of either.[30]

An exception to this prohibition is made for unanimous shareholder agreements to the extent they transfer any duties from the directors to the shareholders.

Declaration of Dividends

The directors may declare dividends provided that the company can meet the statutory solvency test.[31] Even though sufficient profits exist to allow for the payment of dividends, a shareholder is not entitled to require the company to pay dividends. Although the company's general by-law is likely to provide that the directors may declare and pay dividends from time to time out of funds available for that purpose, the declaration of dividends is one of the board functions which may not be delegated to a committee of directors or to a managing director.[32]

Although dividends were traditionally payable only out of profits, they may be distributed out of other sources by the directors at their discretion so long as the solvency test can be met. For example, dividends may be paid even if the company has sustained a temporary loss, in order to satisfy the shareholders' long–standing expectations for regular dividends. They may also be paid out of the capital appreciation of company assets, whether such appreciation has resulted in realized gains or not, particularly when depreciation expenses have been taken for assets which effectively did not depreciate.

Furthermore, dividends may be paid out of surpluses even if the surpluses are invested in inventory or receivables and are not represented by cash balances. Although the directors may be reluctant to borrow in order to pay cash dividends, they may do so if the company meets the solvency test.

Directors who authorize payment of a dividend when the company fails to meet this test will be jointly and severally liable to restore to the company the funds that were improperly paid out.[33] However, the directors may then ask a court to compel any shareholder receiving an improper dividend to pay the amount of the dividend to the directors.[34] But the directors will not be liable if they exercised due diligence when authorizing the payment, perhaps by relying upon the company's audited financial statements.[35]

Subject to the dividend rights which attach to a particular class of shares, the directors may be given in the company's articles the discretion to declare different dividends on different classes of shares. For a private company with just a few shareholders, especially for a family-owed company whose shareholders are related to each other, the directors may then engage in "income splitting" by declaring the largest dividend on the class of shares held by the family member with the lowest income and marginal tax rate.[36]

In addition to declaring cash dividends, the directors may authorize payment of dividends in property or fully paid shares, subject to any restrictions in the company's articles or unanimous shareholder agreement. If the dividend is to be paid in property, the company must be able to satisfy the solvency test.[37]

If the dividend is to be paid in company shares, the declared amount of the dividend in money is to be added to the stated capital account for the shares. These stock dividends allow the company to distribute some of its surplus to the shareholders without using cash needed for company operations. Stock dividends may be issued as shares of the same class or as shares of another class.

When declaring dividends, the directors must be aware of any other restrictions on dividends which may be contained in the company's financing agreements. The company may have entered into debentures, mortgages, loan agreements or trust deeds which contain various covenants limiting the amount and frequency of dividends which may be paid, or prohibiting the payment of any dividends without the consent of the financing party unless they are mandatory under the terms of the shares.

Filling Director and Auditor Vacancies
The directors may fill a vacancy among the directors or in the office of auditor, or appoint additional directors.[38]

Fixing Remuneration
The directors may fix the remuneration of the directors, officers and employees of the company, subject to the articles, the by-laws or any unanimous shareholder agreement.[39]

Issuance of Shares

Shares of the company may be issued at such times, to such persons, and for such consideration as the directors may determine, even though such issuance may be opposed by certain shareholders. However, shares may not be issued until the consideration is paid in money, or in property or past services that are not less in value than the fair equivalent of the money the company would have received if the shares had been issued for money. The directors therefore have to determine the value of the property or past services received. Acceptable consideration does not include a promissory note or other promise to pay.[40]

If the directors issue shares for property worth less than the fair equivalent of money the company would have received, they will be jointly and severally liable to the company to make good the deficiency.[41] One exception to this prohibition is the issuance of stock dividends, as discussed above.

Passing By-laws

The directors may pass by-laws regulating the business and affairs of the company unless the articles, by-laws or a unanimous shareholder agreement provide otherwise. Any by-laws made by the directors are subject to the approval of the shareholders at the next shareholder meeting, at which time the by-laws may be confirmed, amended or repealed.[42]

DIRECTOR MEETINGS

Given the liabilities that directors potentially face when they serve on the board of a private company, they should pay some attention to the formal requirements relating to board meetings. While the boards of many private companies document their decisions by way of written resolutions[43] which are circulated and signed by all of the directors, some boards prefer to conduct their business at face-to-face meetings which are recorded by written minutes.

Notice of Meetings

Notice of the time and place of a board meeting must be given to all of the directors in accordance with the company's by-laws, and any business transacted at a meeting of directors which was not preceded by proper notice to all of the directors will be invalid unless those directors who are not given proper notice waive their right to notice.[44]

Most private company by-laws allow for notice to be sent to the directors by facsimile or e-mail, although the by-laws of older companies may not permit notice by such means. Some by-laws prescribe certain types of business that must be set out in the notice if such business is intended to be transacted at the meeting.[45]

Since the directors should not be taken by surprise at a board meeting, it is a common practice to circulate a proposed agenda of the meeting along with the notice as a means of informing the directors of those matters to be dealt with at the meeting.

Attendance at Meetings

Although board meetings may be attended only by the directors of the company, other persons may be admitted with the consent of the chair of the meeting or if given a right to attend under the by-laws. However, the attendance of "special guests" should be allowed with caution since only officers and directors have to keep company information confidential as part of their fiduciary duties as mentioned above, and outsiders attending board meetings are not under the same duties.

Despite every director being entitled to attend each board meeting, some directors are unable or unwilling to attend. However, because they may be liable for any decisions which are taken by the board in their absence, they should attempt to attend as many meetings as possible. An absent director has to provide a written dissent within seven days of receiving the minutes of the meeting she failed to attend if she is to avoid being deemed to have approved a particular matter.[46]

Because individual directors cannot delegate their duties to a third party, a director who is not able to attend a meeting may not send a proxy or alternate to attend instead, and any board resolution which is circulated among the directors for signature may not be signed on behalf of a particular director by power of attorney.

The right of a director to attend board meetings is generally unqualified. Subject to the requirements to disclose conflicts of interest as outlined above, a director may not be excluded from board meetings just because she appears unfit, or has allegedly engaged in improper conduct, or has business dealing with competitors of the company.

When certain issues to be addressed by the board appear to be extremely sensitive or contentious, some directors may prefer that they be addressed at an "in camera" meeting attended only by certain directors who may or may not constitute a quorum instead of being addressed by the full board at a duly called board meeting. For example, an in camera meeting may be attended by the company's outside directors without management present in an attempt to have a private, candid discussion amongst themselves about the affairs of the company. Regardless of the intentions behind such a meeting, decisions made in camera do not have any legal effect.

Unless the company's by-laws otherwise provide, a majority of the number of directors or minimum number of directors required by the company's articles constitutes a quorum at any meeting of directors, and if a quorum is not achieved at a board meeting, any resolution passed at that meeting will be invalid.[47]

Should certain directors refuse to attend board meetings and thereby frustrate the ability of the other directors to achieve quorum and conduct company business, it may be necessary for the shareholders to requisition a shareholder meeting[48] as previously described at which the shareholders may remove the refusing directors and replace them with more co-operative nominees.[49]

To get around this potential problem, some private companies include in their by-laws a provision deeming a director who fails to attend a certain number of board meetings within a specified period of time to have resigned and allowing the vacancy to be filled. Alternatively, the by-laws might provide that if a quorum is not constituted because of the absence of a director, a second board meeting may be called and proceed with the balance of the directors in attendance constituting a quorum.

Conduct of Meetings

Most private company by-laws designate who shall chair board meetings, but failing such a designation, a quorum of the board may elect someone present from among the directors to chair a particular board meeting.

The person chairing the meeting should preserve order and attempt to ascertain the consensus or "sense of the meeting", allow or disallow certain comments, and perhaps settle any contentious matter by exercising a second or casting vote if the by-laws so permit, while recognizing that all of the directors are entitled to participate and contribute to the decision-making.

The right to exercise a casting vote is generally meant to remedy the occasional tie vote at meetings and is not intended to deal with an ongoing board deadlock. It should be exercised in good faith. Even if the by-laws allow for a casting vote, the person chairing the meeting is not required to exercise it in the event of a tie, and may abstain from voting on any matter like any other director.

The director conflict of interest rules described above must be observed in connection with the meeting. In addition to making the required disclosure of any applicable conflict, a director having an interest in a material contract or transaction coming before the meeting may not vote on it unless it relates primarily to her remuneration, or is for indemnity or insurance.

In performing their board duties, the directors must spend sufficient time when considering the matters brought before them. As mentioned in the above discussion of the business judgment rule, that rule cannot be used to save a board decision if the board followed a flawed process in making the decision. The directors should ensure that they receive all necessary information on a timely basis, and that they have adequate time to obtain clarification if needed before finally deciding on a particular matter.

No specific method for voting at a board meeting is prescribed by statute, although voting is usually conducted by a show of hands, with each director having one vote. However, there may be occasions when a vote needs to be taken on a sensitive or contentious question, and a secret ballot may be used so that only the person chairing the board meeting upon counting the ballots will know how each director voted, assuming the directors' names appear on the ballots. But some of the secrecy associated with a secret ballot may be lost if a dissenting director insists that her dissent be recorded in the minutes of the meeting. The effect of a director's dissent is discussed below.

Minutes of Meetings

A private company is required to prepare and maintain records containing minutes of director meetings and resolutions,[50] and should take reasonable steps to prevent their loss or destruction. Although minutes of director meetings are generally considered to be confidential, any portions of them that contain disclosure of a director's conflict of interest may be reviewed by the company's shareholders.[51]

It is important that minutes of a board meeting be accurate, since proving in later legal proceedings that an event or resolution took place is made much more difficult if the minutes of the meeting are poorly drafted. The bases for director decisions on crucial matters should be reflected in the minutes, and the materials provided to the directors before and at the meeting should be attached to the minutes. The minutes should always be carefully reviewed by the directors before they are approved by the board.

Usually the minutes of a board meeting are signed by both the chair and secretary of the meeting, although there is no statutory requirement that the minutes of one meeting must be approved at a subsequent meeting, or that the minutes have to be signed in order to be valid. The two signatures on the minutes merely reflect that at least two persons in attendance at the meeting confirm what took place.

Although some directors may be inclined to make their own notes at a board meeting, such notes may later present a problem if the minutes of the meeting are challenged in subsequent proceedings and the notes conflict with the minutes. There should be only one record of the board's deliberations, and that record should be the minutes of the meeting that are approved and inserted into the company's minute book. Therefore, it is often a board's policy that any meeting notes kept by individual directors should be destroyed once the minutes of the meeting have been approved.

PROTECTION OF DIRECTORS

For an individual who is already a director of a private company, or who has been asked to become a director, the potential liabilities discussed above which a director faces and the possibility of the director's personal assets being used to satisfy such liabilities should cause a director to seriously consider how to protect herself.

A private company is specifically permitted under the CBCA to indemnify a director against all costs, charges and expenses, including any amount paid to settle an action or satisfy a judgment, reasonably incurred by the director in respect of any civil, criminal, administrative, investigative or other proceeding in which the director was involved because of her association with the company.[52] The company may even advance funds to the director for her costs, charges and expenses related to such proceedings.[53]

The main purpose of indemnification is to provide assurance to those willing to serve as directors that they will be compensated by the company for any adverse consequences arising from their well-intentioned commercial decisions made on behalf of the company. However, while attempting to encourage director entrepreneurism, the CBCA discourages director misconduct by prohibiting corporate indemnification in certain circumstances.

A director may not be indemnified, and may have to repay any funds advanced to her, unless she acted honestly and in good faith with a view to the best interests of the company. In the case of criminal or administrative proceedings enforced by a monetary penalty, she must also have had reasonable grounds for believing her conduct was lawful. If she meets these conditions, and is not judged by a court or other authority to have been at fault, she is entitled to be indemnified whether the company wishes to indemnify her or not.[54]

Determining whether a director is able to meet these good faith and lawful conduct requirements in order to qualify for indemnification can be difficult. A company may attempt to deny indemnification if the director was engaged in opportunistic or self-seeking behaviour, or if her conduct was inexplicable, perhaps reckless, giving rise to the inference that she was acting in bad faith.[55] It may also deny indemnification if the director's belief that her conduct was lawful was unreasonable given that such belief would be obviously erroneous to the "most untrained observer".[56]

In other words, the company can only indemnify its directors to the extent permitted under the CBCA. While indemnification may be mandatory in certain circumstances, in many other circumstances the company may choose to indemnify but it is not required to do so.

So what can a director do to protect herself and her assets? The remainder of this chapter suggests certain actions that the director might take. These recommended actions might also be taken by officers of the company who face similar liabilities.

Reviewing the Company's By-laws

The company's by-laws may well require director indemnification consistent with the foregoing CBCA provisions. But many private company by-laws not only replicate the indemnification provisions contained in the CBCA but also reword them to turn optional indemnification into mandatory indemnification.

Yet many by-laws, particularly those of older companies which may not have been updated for many years, may not reflect the broad forms of indemnification which are now permitted.

Since the broadest permitted indemnification in a company's by-laws is often considered to be the first layer of director protection, any individual who is a company director, or is thinking about becoming a company director, should insist that the company by-laws be amended unless they already provide for broad mandatory indemnification.

Obtaining an Indemnification Agreement

Even though a director or prospective director may take some comfort in the indemnification provisions of the company's by-laws, the by-laws can always be changed with appropriate board and shareholder approval.

To avoid the possibility that indemnification provided under the company's by-laws might be reduced or removed by subsequent by-law amendment, a director should obtain an indemnification agreement with the company which cannot be changed without the director's consent and which can be enforced by the director against the company as any other company contract.

This contractual indemnity should provide at least the same broad indemnification as would be provided in updated by-laws. It may also impose an obligation on the company to obtain and maintain a director and officer liability insurance policy, or D&O insurance, as described below.

For those directors who are serving on the company's board as nominees of a larger shareholder, they may also be protected by an indemnity agreement provided to them by that shareholder when they begin their term as a director.

Obtaining insurance

Despite the protection afforded to a director under the company's by-laws or under an indemnification agreement, such protection may not be available in the event the company becomes insolvent. In a company bankruptcy, a director with a claim for indemnity will rank only as an unsecured creditor.

For this reason, a director or prospective director may insist that the company obtain D&O insurance, because under such insurance, the insurance company or companies behind the policy pay the director indemnification. The company is allowed to purchase and maintain insurance for the benefit of the director in her capacity as a director.[57] Such insurance is often a director's only means of recovery if the company becomes insolvent and is unable to make any indemnity payments. Claims against directors generally increase when a company is insolvent.

Insurance coverage, however, is not necessarily available to every company on an affordable basis, and usually excludes certain areas of significant director exposure.

D&O policies vary considerably and are quite complicated, and a director or prospective director may need specialist professional advice when considering the adequacy of a company's D&O coverage. Those items deserving particular attention are addressed below.

The policy should cover former directors as well as anyone elected or appointed a director after the policy is in place, and anyone else who acts as a director for a company subsidiary or for any corporation at the request of the company.

Any exclusions from coverage should be examined, including those for dishonesty, fraud or criminal conduct. There should be an obligation on the part of the insurer to defend the director up until a matter has been adjudicated despite the third party allegations made.

If the company is covered under the policy in addition to the directors, and the company and the directors share the same coverage limit, the policy may be exhausted by claims against the company before the directors are indemnified. Separate coverage, or no coverage, for the company should be considered.

Termination of the policy by the insurer should be allowed only for non-payment of policy premiums. And coverage of all the directors should not be affected if coverage is denied to just one director. For example, a director's fraud should not disentitle the innocent directors from receiving coverage.

Because most D&O policies are "claims made" policies with often just one-year terms, it is crucial for directors facing a claim or potential claim to report it to the D&O insurer before the end of the term of the policy in place. While a policy may have been in place when the events leading to the claim occurred, it is necessary that the policy continues to be in place when the claim is reported in order for coverage to follow.

Claiming Due Diligence Defense

Many of the statutes which impose personal liability upon directors allow the directors to avoid liability if they can establish a defense of due diligence. As mentioned above in the discussion on the director's duty of care, a director needs to act responsibly at all times.

Consequently, each director should ensure that adequate controls are always in place, and should regularly receive reports and statements from the company's management. Directors should take the steps necessary to correct any problems or mistakes that arise, and all corrective action taken should be documented.

For example, to address the potential personal liability of directors for the failure of the company to withhold and remit various employee deductions[58] to the Canada Revenue Agency as described in the *Dealing with Employees* chapter, a director should obtain ongoing confirmation from management that the required remittances have been made.

Recording Dissents

Some of the statutes that impose personal liability on a director for a particular matter require that the director have voted for that matter, and a director attending a board meeting is deemed to have consented to all of the resolutions passed at that meeting unless the director records her dissent.[59]

A director wishing to dissent against a resolution passed at a board meeting which she attends should request the secretary of the meeting to have the minutes show the director's opposition to the resolution and the reasons given, if any, for such opposition. In addition to having her dissent recorded in the minutes, the director may send a letter confirming the dissent to the meeting's secretary.

As mentioned above, if she wishes to dissent against a resolution passed at a meeting which she did not attend, she has to provide a written dissent within seven days of receiving the minutes of the meeting to avoid being deemed to have approved the particular matter.[60]

A director's request to have her dissent recorded in the minutes of a board meeting in connection with a particular decision may allow the director to avoid personal liability for that decision, as may be the case with the improper payment of dividends or redemption of company shares. Recording her dissent may also encourage the other directors to reconsider their decision.

A director's abstention from voting on a matter is not the same as a director's dissent, and any director attempting to avoid liability on that matter should have her dissent properly recorded.

Relying on Experts

A director is entitled to rely upon the work of experts, including financial statements or reports provided by the company's management, or any reports provided by a lawyer, accountant, appraiser, engineer, or other professional person. The obligation of a director to exercise reasonable diligence and act in good faith can often be satisfied by the director's reliance on such statements and reports.[61]

If the board has to consider a complicated or contentious issue and none of the directors has sufficient skill and experience to adequately deal with the issue, the board may need to engage the services of an outside expert to assess and advise on possible actions that the board may take, thereby allowing the board to make a more informed decision which is less likely to be challenged.

Implementing a Unanimous Shareholder Agreement

As described in the *Shareholder Agreements* chapter, a unanimous shareholder agreement can be an effective way to shield a company's directors from liability in certain circumstances. If such an agreement restricts the powers of the directors to manage or supervise the management of the company's business, the directors are relieved of their duties and liabilities, which are then assumed by the shareholders.

While not appropriate for many private companies, a unanimous shareholder agreement may be quite appropriate for a private company whose directors do not really function as a board. If the shareholders are all corporations, the liability of an individual director of the company then becomes a corporate liability of each shareholder, consequently protecting the personal assets of the director. However, if the shareholders are individuals and not corporations, shifting director liabilities to them will expose their own personal assets to possible claims.

In those circumstances where a private company is a wholly-owned subsidiary of another corporation, a unanimous shareholder declaration[62] is often used to shift potential liabilities from the directors of the subsidiary to the parent company shareholder so that the assets of the individual directors are protected.

Resigning

If a director disagrees with a course of action to be taken by the board in a particular situation and records her dissent, and yet the situation gets worse, she may have to resign to avoid potential liability. Resignation is often considered when all else fails, although resignation will not protect the resigning director from any liabilities that arise from events which occurred while she was a director.

Resignation, like dissent, has to be carried out a certain way. It must be in writing, and becomes legally effective when it is received by the company[63] unless it specifies a later date. Ordinarily a resigning director will want her resignation to be effective as soon as possible, and she should ensure that it is delivered to a senior officer of the company by courier or registered mail if she does not deliver it personally.

It is important for a resigning director to have her resignation recorded[64] in the applicable public registry of company directors, preferably on or close to the day that her resignation was made effective. Proceedings against individual directors are often initiated on the basis of the public record, and it is not unusual for an individual to be sued as a company director long after she has resigned because her resignation was never publicly recorded.

The date of resignation can be crucial in determining liability, since many statutes imposing director liability contain certain limitation periods, often two years after a director resigns.[65]

Governance

In addition to the need for the owners and managers of a private company to understand the duties and liabilities of the directors, as discussed in the previous chapter, there is also a need for them to understand the importance of good governance for the company. In a way, good governance is good business.

Just as various duties and restrictions may be placed on the directors by way of the company's articles, by-laws, share conditions or unanimous shareholder agreement, the statutory power of the directors to generally manage the company may be affected by the governance procedures which the company may adopt.

Some shareholders may be in a position to insist that certain governance procedures be implemented as a condition of making their investment in the company. Other shareholders may be able to persuade the directors to adopt such procedures simply because such procedures are the hallmarks of a well-managed company.

Public companies are expected to voluntarily comply with recommended governance standards and are required to publicly disclose what governance structures they do have in place.[1] Private companies are not. But while many private companies may be unwilling or unable to conform to these higher standards, if they are even aware such standards exist, some may be better off if they try to conform as best they can. The failure to respect good governance may place the company at a competitive disadvantage in the marketplace, not only in selling its products and services but also in obtaining financing from outside sources.

Many private companies, especially those with just a few shareholders, lack effective governance structures. Their boards are often in place only to "rubber stamp" those decisions of management which need to have board approval to satisfy a request from a banker, supplier or other third party, or to meet a technical legislative requirement. And their boards are often comprised of only the major shareholder and his family members. Yet many of these private companies like it this way. After all, many feel the absence of governance is one of the benefits of being private, with little bureaucracy to slow things down.

BENEFITS OF GOOD GOVERNANCE

However, a board or board committee with a few members who are independent of the major shareholder and management can serve as more than just a comforting watchdog for the other shareholders, on the prowl for conflicts of interest and digging up personal expenses being disguised as business expenses.

In addition to keeping management "honest" by overseeing transactions that might benefit the major shareholder but not the company, such a board or committee can also serve as a vehicle for arriving at better informed decisions. The senior executive of a private company can often benefit from the objective review and advice of others who are familiar with the company though separate from it. Setting company strategy and planning for growth, as well as realistically assessing ongoing performance, can often be done more effectively with the help of outsiders having broader perspectives.

But not just better informed decisions can be made. Tough decisions can be made as well.

A board comprised of just the major shareholder and his family members may be less inclined to initiate changes which may threaten their own personal interests, even though such changes may be badly needed by the company in order to keep up with the competition. Removing unqualified family members from executive positions, putting in place a business succession plan, cutting long-standing ties with an underperforming supplier or loyal but non-paying customer, dropping an unprofitable product which was invented by the major shareholder, or taking away various perquisites like expensive cars and clubs, are more likely to be suggested by a board or committee consisting of a few outsiders.

In addition to enabling tough as well as better informed decisions to be made, more rigorous governance standards are supposed to provide greater transparency of the process followed in arriving at such decisions. They are also supposed to facilitate accountability of those making the decisions. It's not only the shareholders, but also the employees, creditors and other stakeholders of the company, who take some comfort in knowing who makes the decisions and how the decisions are made.

RESISTANCE TO GOOD GOVERNANCE

Despite the benefits that may be gained through the implementation of better governance structures, some private companies take the view that such structures just aren't for them. Many feel they are just too small, lacking the breadth of resources and operations which justify the maintenance of such structures. If they have only a few shareholders, all of whom are actively involved in management, they may feel there is no need for independent watchdogs, and that their decision-making process works just fine, with no need for a fix. They may feel that they are so "closely held" that they already have as much transparency and accountability as they want or need.

If they have never appointed an outside accounting firm to perform an audit in connection with their annual financial statements, how can they be convinced of the merits of appointing outside directors to serve on board committees? Why should they adopt a shareholder communication policy and feedback structure for just a few people? Why should they incur the time and expense in setting up and maintaining audit, nominating and compensation committees which may well turn out to be too unwieldy to deal quickly with fleeting opportunities?

Some of the benefits gained from governance structures recommended for public companies can be gained in the private company context by way of contract, without putting such structures into place. Subscription agreements and shareholder agreements can provide private company shareholders with ready access to information, and with rights to review and veto proposed transactions if they so choose, whether or not they sit on the company's board or on a board committee, and whether or not the board or its committees are comprised only of insiders. The shareholders of public companies don't ordinarily enjoy such contractual rights.

PRESSURES TO IMPLEMENT GOOD GOVERNANCE

The reluctance of a private company to implement more comprehensive governance structures may be understandable so long as it is financed by supportive family and friends. It may have to change its position, however, when it attempts to raise funds from other sources. Venture capitalists and other professional investors are starting to insist that the private companies they invest in adopt many of the governance practices now followed by public companies.

Not only do these investors want increased governance to ensure transparency, accountability and good decision making in order to protect their investment, they also want increased governance to protect their own nominees on the board who are under a director's duty to exercise care, diligence and skill. They also have to account to their own corporate and institutional shareholders, many of whom are under strict governance standards themselves. These standards often have to be observed by the professional investors and by the companies they invest in.

Since an initial public offering of the company, or a sale of the company to a third party, can provide an exit from their investment, professional investors often insist that increased governance be put into place when the company is private in order to make it easier for the company to either go public or be acquired by a public company.

RECOMMENDED GOVERNANCE STRUCTURES AND PRACTICES
Recommending one generic package of governance standards and practices to be adopted by each and every private company would be misguided. There are just too many variations of private company ownership. Some private companies have just one shareholder, but that shareholder may be an individual with little business expertise, or a large public corporation with operations around the world. While other private companies have a number of shareholders, the shareholders may all be full-time officers of the company, or they may have had nothing to do with the company since they invested in it years before. Some private companies have one controlling shareholder, others don't.

When a private company is prepared to put more comprehensive governance structures into place, either at its own instigation or upon the request of a professional investor as a condition to funding, it has a number of alternatives to consider. Most of the alternatives are conveniently included in the corporate governance guidelines recommended by the securities regulators for Canadian public companies. Some of the guidelines are inappropriate for certain kinds of private companies. Actually, some are even inappropriate for certain kinds of public companies.[2]

The guidelines recommended for public companies generally address the process a company should follow in selecting, orienting, compensating and assessing directors, and in promoting ethical business conduct, but don't address the specific tasks which should be assigned to the board or the decisions which require the board's prior approval. Although they recommend that the board assume responsibility for strategic planning, risk management, management succession planning, and corporate governance, the guidelines don't prescribe what goes on a board's agenda. They do, however, recommend the establishment of nominating and compensation committees of the board, in addition to the audit committee which is required for public companies by law.

Although "best" governance structures and practices will continue to evolve for all companies, both public and private, private companies evaluating their current governance structures have to start somewhere. Perhaps they should start by addressing what are often regarded as the fundamentals of corporate governance. These fundamentals include independent directors, nominating and compensation committees as well as an audit committee (assuming outside auditors are already engaged), a code of business conduct, director orientation and continuing education programs, and the regular assessment of director performance. These recommended structures and practices are described in more detail below.

The Board and Independent Directors

The board should have a majority of independent directors, and the chair of the board should be an independent director. If it's not appropriate for the chair to be independent, an independent director should be appointed to act as "lead director" to ensure that essential tasks make it onto the board's agenda. The independent directors should hold regularly scheduled meetings which members of management do not attend.

In order to be independent, a director must not have a relationship with the company, or with a subsidiary or parent of the company, which would be expected to interfere with the director's independent judgment.

Audit Committee

An audit committee should be established by the board, preferably with only independent directors who have a good grasp of financial statements. The audit committee should recommend to the board the external auditors to be nominated for appointment by the shareholders, and the compensation to be paid to the auditors. It should oversee the work of the external auditors and attempt to resolve any disagreements between the auditors and management over financial reporting.

The audit committee should also pre-approve all non-audit services to be provided to the company by the external auditors, and review the company's financial statements before being released generally to the shareholders or other stakeholders. It should have authority to communicate directly with both the company's internal and external auditors.

Nominating Committee

The board should create a nominating committee, preferably with only independent directors, to assist the board in nominating or appointing individuals to serve as board members or committee members.

The nominating committee should help the board identify what competencies and skills the board, as a whole, should possess, and assess what competencies and skills each existing director possesses. The nominating committee should determine what competencies and skills each new nominee should bring to the board, and should recommend individuals with such competencies and skills to be nominated as new directors at the next annual meeting of shareholders.

Compensation Committee

A compensation committee, preferably with only independent directors, should be set up by the board to review and approve the company's objectives which are relevant to the Chief Executive Officer's compensation, to evaluate the CEO's performance in light of the objectives, and to determine the CEO's compensation level based on the evaluation. The compensation committee should also make recommendations to the board regarding non-CEO officer and director compensation, incentive-compensation plans and equity-based plans.

Code of Business Conduct and Ethics

A written code of business conduct and ethics should be adopted by the board which applies to all of the company's directors, officers and employees. Designed to promote integrity and deter wrongdoing, it should address conflicts of interest, including transactions and agreements in which a director or executive officer has a material interest.

The code should prescribe the proper use and protection of corporate assets and opportunities, confidentiality of company information, compliance with laws and regulations, and reporting of any illegal or unethical behavior. It should also require that all of the company's security holders, customers, suppliers, competitors and employees are dealt with fairly.

The board should be responsible for monitoring compliance with the code, and only the board or a board committee should be able to permit non-compliance by an individual in particular circumstances.

Director Orientation and Continuing Education

All new directors should receive a comprehensive orientation so that they fully understand the role of the board and its committees, the contribution they are individually expected to make, and the nature and operation of the company's business. All directors should be provided with continuing education opportunities, not only to maintain or enhance their skills and abilities as directors, but also to ensure they remain current in their knowledge and understanding of the company's business.

Regular Board Assessments

The board, its committees and each individual director should be regularly assessed regarding their respective effectiveness and contribution to the company. The assessment of each individual director should be based upon the role that the director was expected to play on the board as well as upon the competencies and skills the director was expected to bring.

IMPLEMENTING GOOD GOVERNANCE

Once a private company has compared its current governance structures and practices with the above fundamentals and concludes a few things are missing, it then faces the decision of what to change and what to leave as is. For the company with professional investors as shareholders, it probably won't have much choice unless it is a start-up or early stage company. It is likely to be asked to put the fundamentals into place if it hasn't already done so, although there may be considerable overlap in the membership of its committees and the members themselves may not be fully independent.

For those private companies that have a choice, the decision of what's in and what's out is not easily made. Being convinced of the benefits of good governance is one thing, but having the time and resources to implement and maintain it is another.

Perhaps all that can be easily decided is that the fundamentals will not be put into place all at once. They are more likely to be phased in over time. While recruiting individuals who are truly independent to serve as directors is not an easy task, having at least one independent director is a good step to take. Having a code of business conduct is another. Nominating and compensation committees with only independent directors, or director performance reviews and continuing education, may follow later.

Dispute Resolution and Shareholder Remedies

Earlier chapters of this book have referred to the relationships the company may have with its employees, lenders and other creditors, and it is not unusual for these relationships to give rise to some dispute over time. Possible claims against the company by an employee for wrongful dismissal, or by a lender for arrears in interest and principal on a loan, may be just a few of the many claims which may be made against the company as it continues to grow and prosper. Even claims against the company for intellectual property infringement can occur.

The owners and managers of a private company may eventually also have to deal with any number of other complaints and disputes arising from its customers and suppliers, its distributors, agents and licensees, its landlord and even the government, in addition to its employees, lenders and other creditors.

But the company's shareholders may be the most difficult to deal with, especially when the company is closely-held and its shareholders are all related to each other.

Although private company shareholders may have the right to oversee the directors' management of the company by way of votes at shareholder meetings, they do not manage the company unless a unanimous shareholder agreement provides otherwise. Consequently their desires to be involved in company decision-making are often frustrated and their rights to challenge or overturn company actions are quite limited.

But they are not necessarily forced to rely upon shareholder meetings as their only forum for the scrutiny and criticism of the company. They may be able to take their disputes with management to the courts for adjudication in certain circumstances. Alternatively, they may have recourse to mediation and arbitration if they are party to a shareholder agreement which provides them with dispute resolution procedures.

As described earlier in this book, the CBCA provides that the directors, not the shareholders, are responsible for the company's management. In performing this role, the directors are under a fiduciary duty to act honestly and in good faith with a view to the best interests of the company. They are also under a duty of care to exercise the care, diligence and skill that a reasonably prudent person would exercise in comparable circumstances.[1]

Their fiduciary duty is owed to the company. In carrying out their fiduciary duty, the directors are supposed to look at the interests of the company's shareholders, as well as the interests of the employees, creditors, consumers, governments and the environment, when considering what is in the best interests of the company.[2] But their fiduciary duty is still to the company only, leaving open the possibility that they may disregard the interests of some of the shareholders.

However, a number of special remedies are available to protect shareholder interests. Traditionally only the beneficiary of a fiduciary duty was able to enforce it. If the company was the beneficiary, the directors managing the company were unlikely to sue themselves for breach of their own fiduciary duty. These special remedies get around that problem and provide the shareholders with recourse.

One of the remedies is the "derivative action" which allows shareholders to enforce the directors' duty to the company when the directors themselves are unwilling to do so. Shareholders are also able to bring a civil action for breach of the directors' duty of care, as well as an "oppression action" to seek compensation for the oppressive acts of the company or the directors. They may also apply to the courts for assistance in ordering that certain corporate action be taken.

Furthermore, court approval is required if the company intends to implement certain fundamental changes which affect the rights of shareholders. The shareholders are thereby able to argue before the court against any change proposed.

Some of these shareholder remedies and possible recourse to the courts are discussed in greater detail in this chapter. The use of mediation and arbitration, often prescribed in shareholder agreements as an alternative to involving the courts in resolving disputes between the shareholders themselves, is described first in this chapter.

Many of the shareholder rights referred to in this book are based not upon statute law but upon contract law, as may be set out in a subscription agreement or shareholder agreement. The remedies ordinarily associated with breach of contract, namely claims for damages or for specific performance of a contract, will not be discussed in this chapter.

MEDIATION AND ARBITRATION

Although alternative dispute resolution or "ADR" clauses in shareholder agreements come in many different forms, those reflecting a combination of mediation and arbitration are becoming more commonplace, with the disputing shareholders required to first try mediation. Only if their efforts at mediation fail, may they then proceed to arbitration to resolve their disagreement, rather than litigation. Unlike litigation which exposes a dispute to public scrutiny by way of court filings and proceedings, mediation and arbitration can be conducted in private.

Because the resolution of a dispute by mediation requires the consent of the parties to it, mediation alone as an ADR provision may not be very effective.

Many mediation clauses address how the mediator is to be appointed, which is often by mutual agreement. Failing such agreement, the clause may require that the mediator is to be appointed by a specific organization.[3] The clause may also stipulate which rules are to be followed for the mediation.[4] Often the place of the mediation will be specified as well as the language in which the mediation is to be conducted.

Any disputes remaining unsettled after mediation are then to be arbitrated, although the records of the mediation are to remain confidential and not to be introduced during the arbitration. As with the mediation clause, the arbitration clause will designate how the arbitrator is to be appointed and the rules the arbitration must follow,[5] along with the applicable location and language.

Some of these combined mediation and arbitration provisions fail to put a time limit on how long the mediation efforts may take, thereby allowing one of the parties, more likely the one at fault or facing a required payment, to frustrate the whole process.

Because the results of the arbitration are likely to be final and binding on the parties, with recourse to the courts thereafter only in very limited circumstances, the arbitration clause may provide more particular guidance to the parties than the mediation clause. The arbitration clause will generally outline the scope of the arbitration, identifying what issues may be arbitrated and what issues may not. However, the exclusion of certain issues can result in multiple proceedings.

In providing for the selection of impartial and neutral arbitrators, the arbitration clause will specify how many arbitrators are to be selected, and what skills or qualifications the arbitrators should possess. For a smaller company with a relatively low valuation, the arbitration clause in its shareholder agreement will probably require just one arbitrator. As three arbitrators definitely cost more, and involve more complicated proceedings, their involvement is more appropriate when the issues are quite complex and a significant amount of money is at stake. Yet under many sets of arbitration rules, three arbitrators is the default structure in the absence of the parties agreeing that only one arbitrator will be necessary. Ordinarily the costs of arbitration will be shared equally by the parties involved.

Some arbitration clauses will set out certain special rules which are intended to override the set of general rules otherwise selected. For example, the clause may address how and when documents are to be exchanged, when hearings are to take place, and the deadline for rendering any decision, all of which are otherwise normally determined in the discretion of the arbitrator under the general rules.

More importantly, some clauses restrict or expand upon the relief that the arbitrator may award under the general rules. They may address whether the arbitrator can or cannot award interim or permanent injunctions, or order a party to perform the agreement, or award monetary damages.

While most arbitration decisions are final, the arbitration clause may grant specific rights to appeal, whether to a court or to a second arbitration panel. It may also specify how a decision is to be enforced. The parties are often permitted to enter a decision with the courts in each jurisdiction where enforcement may be needed.

DERIVATIVE ACTION

A shareholder may generally take over a company lawsuit which the company is not prosecuting or defend a lawsuit which the company is not defending. With the permission or leave of the court, the shareholder may bring what is called a "derivative action" in the name and on behalf of the company or one of its subsidiaries to enforce a right of the company, or to intervene in an action to which the company or a subsidiary is a party, for the purpose of prosecuting, defending or discontinuing the action on behalf of the company or subsidiary.[6]

The need for leave of the court is to prevent frivolous or vexatious actions. The court has to be satisfied before granting leave that the shareholder has given the company directors at least 14 days notice of her intention to apply to the court, that she is acting in good faith, and that the action itself is in the interest of the company to be prosecuted, defended or discontinued. Obtaining leave is not easy, given that the shareholder may not be aware of all the relevant facts, and that the directors have already weighed the costs and benefits of the proposed action and decided not to pursue it.

In addition to authorizing the shareholder or some other party to control the conduct of the action, the court may order that any amount adjudged payable by a defendant in the action shall be paid directly to the company's current or former shareholders and not to the company, and may order that the company pay the legal expenses of the shareholder incurred in connection with the action.[7]

OPPRESSION REMEDY

The CBCA provides that a court may make an order to rectify the results of certain "oppressive" conduct. The conduct may be a specific act or omission of the company, or the manner in which the company has carried on business, or the manner in which the directors have exercised their powers. Conduct which is not oppressive but is still unfairly prejudicial or that unfairly disregards the interests of any security holder, creditor, director, or officer can give rise to a remedy. Rectification can also be ordered in respect of similar conduct involving the company's affiliates.[8]

The court is empowered to make any order it thinks fit. It may order, for example, the appointment of a receiver, the amendment of the company's articles, by-laws or unanimous shareholder agreement, the issue, exchange or purchase of securities, or the appointment or replacement of directors. It may also order the setting aside of a company transaction, provide for the compensation of aggrieved persons, or even require the liquidation and dissolution of the company.[9]

In examining the conduct complained of, the court generally first assesses whether the conduct breached the complainant's reasonable expectations, and then goes on to determine whether the conduct amounted to oppression, unfair prejudice or unfair disregard. Because an oppression action is regarded as an "equitable" remedy, the court looks at business realities, not simply narrow legalities, and attempts to enforce not what is just legal but also what is fair.

In deciding if a complainant's expectations are reasonable in the first place, a court will generally look at the facts of the particular case, the relationships involved, and the entire context in which the challenged conduct occurs, including the existence of any conflicting claims and expectations. Fair treatment is essentially what shareholders are entitled to reasonably expect.

There are a number of specific factors which a court may find useful in assessing the reasonableness of a complainant's expectations.[10]

Commercial practice is an important influence in the formation of a shareholder's expectations, and any departure from such practice which frustrates the exercise of the complainant's rights represents a significant factor to be considered by the court when deciding whether a remedy should be given.

The nature, size and structure of the company represent additional factors which are relevant in assessing the reasonableness of a complainant's expectations. The court may give more leeway to the directors of a small, closely-held company than to the directors of a larger, more widely-held company.

Reasonable expectations may also be influenced by the extent of any personal relationships between the complainant and others within the company. The court may apply a different standard if the expectations reflect relationships based on family or friendship ties rather than being between arm's length shareholders.

Past practice is another factor the court may use in deciding whether a complainant's expectations were reasonable, especially if such practice relates to the participation of the complainant in the company's profits and governance. However, the court will recognize that past practice may have to be changed for commercial reasons and that expectations should be altered accordingly.

The court may also look at whether the complainant was in a position to have taken steps to protect herself from the prejudice she claims to have suffered and whether she was influenced by any representations made in any correspondence or offering material when she became a shareholder. A shareholder agreement may also be viewed as forming the basis for reasonable expectations.

Once the court has determined that the complainant's expectations were reasonable, it then attempts to decide if the expectations were breached by conduct amounting to oppression, unfair prejudice or unfair disregard. While oppression is often taken to mean harsh and abusive conduct, unfair prejudice is often seen as less offensive. Examples might include squeezing out a minority shareholder, paying dividends without a formal declaration, failing to disclose related party transactions, paying directors' fees which are higher than the industry norm, or preferring some shareholders with management fees.[11]

Unfair disregard is seen as even less offensive. Improperly reducing a shareholder dividend or failing to deliver property belonging to the complainant are examples of unfair disregard.[12]

Once it decides that the complainant's reasonable expectations were breached by one of these three categories of wrongful conduct, the court may then fashion any remedy it think fits to properly rectify what took place.

Family Businesses

As mentioned above, family businesses may generate their own special shareholder expectations. Many private companies are established to hold family investments, serve as vehicles for estate freezes, or operate family businesses in which various family members actively participate. The oppression remedy provided by the CBCA has resulted in a growing number of cases involving family disputes arising out of these private companies.

While family tax planning may have been the primary reason for a private company to have been established, the ongoing power of the company's founder in maintaining the structure often creates tension and disharmony as the other family members wish to become more involved.

For example, under an estate freeze as discussed in the *Business Succession and Estate Freezes* chapter, the founder may wish to transfer the benefits of future growth of her company to her children in order to minimize taxes. While initially treating all of her children equally with the company issuing to all of them the same number of common or "growth" shares, she may later change her mind and wish for just one of them to carry on with the company as her successor. However, in having created a structure with all siblings being treated equally, any children no longer receiving equal treatment look to the possibility of commencing an oppression action to regain what they may have lost.

The prevalence of family businesses in the oppression cases involving private companies has influenced how estate freezes are now structured. In order to provide some flexibility to the freeze structure and allow the founder to change her mind or favour one child over another, the common or growth shares are issued instead to a family trust rather than to specific children directly. The trust can then empower the trustees to choose which children, as beneficiaries, should acquire the common shares from the trust when the appropriate time comes, which could be when the founder finally makes up her mind who is to succeed her as owner. The founder may not control the trust and is often just one of three trustees.

OTHER COURT APPLICATIONS

Appointment of Auditor
If a private company does not have an auditor, a shareholder may apply to the court for an order appointing and fixing the remuneration of an auditor for the company to hold office until an auditor is appointed by the shareholders. Such an order, however, may not be made if the shareholders have already resolved to dispense with an auditor, as described in the *Shareholder Statutory Rights – Part II* chapter.[13]

Calling of Meeting
If it is impracticable to call or conduct a shareholder meeting in the manner prescribed in the company's by-laws or articles or under the CBCA, a shareholder entitled to vote at a meeting may ask the court to order that a meeting be called and conducted in such manner as the court deems fit.[14]

Compliance with CBCA
If the company or any of its directors, officers, employees, agents or auditors fails to comply with any requirement of the CBCA or the company's articles, by-laws or unanimous shareholder agreement, a share-

holder may apply to the court for an order directing such person to comply or restraining any further non-compliance.[15]

Fix Fair Value of Shares

If the company fails to apply to a court to fix the fair value of a dissenting shareholder's shares when required to do so, the shareholder may apply to a court for the same purpose.[16]

Investigation of Company

A shareholder may apply to the court for an order directing that an investigation be made of the company and any of its affiliates. The investigation may be ordered if the business of the company or its affiliates has been carried on with intent to defraud any person, or has been oppressive or unfairly prejudicial, or has unfairly disregarded the interests of a shareholder. It may also be ordered if the company or any of its affiliates has been formed for a fraudulent or unlawful purpose or is being dissolved for such a purpose, or if persons connected with it have acted fraudulently or dishonestly.

The court's order may involve the appointment of an inspector to enter any premises, examine documents and records, carry out investigations, conduct hearings under oath, and eventually report to the court.[17]

Liquidation and Dissolution of Company

A shareholder may apply to the court to supervise the liquidation and dissolution of the company, or apply for an order that the company be dissolved, or liquidated and dissolved under the supervision of the court.[18] Dissolution may be ordered if the company has failed for two or more consecutive years to hold an annual meeting, or has denied the shareholder access to examine certain corporate records, or has failed to provide the shareholder with the required financial statements.

Dissolution may also be ordered if the court is satisfied that a unanimous shareholder agreement entitles the shareholder to demand dissolution after the occurrence of a specified event which has occurred, or that it would be "just and equitable" for the company to be dissolved.[19] Dissolution may be just and equitable if, in the absence of a shareholder agreement with at least some form of dispute resolution mechanism, a company with just two shareholders is deadlocked and cannot function properly because of an irresolvable shareholder dispute.

Rectification of Records

If a shareholder believes that her name has been wrongly entered in the company's share register or other record, or her name have been deleted or omitted, she may apply to the court for an order to have the register or record rectified. In addition to rectification, the court may order that a meeting or dividend payment not occur before the rectification, and even order that the shareholder be compensated for any loss.[20]

Removal of Auditor

A shareholder may apply to the court for an order declaring an auditor to be disqualified from serving and the office of auditor to be vacant.[21] A person is disqualified from serving as an auditor if she fails to be independent of the company, its affiliates, or their directors and officers. An auditor fails to be independent if, among other things, she or her business partner is a director, officer or shareholder of the company or an affiliate.

Restrain Holding of Meeting

Where a shareholder's proposal for any annual meeting has been refused by the company, the shareholder may apply to the court for an order to restrain the holding of the meeting at which the proposal was to be presented and to make any other order it thinks fit.[22]

Set Aside Contract

If any director or officer of the company fails to disclose her interest in any material contract with the company, a shareholder may apply to the court to have the contract set aside, or to require the director or officer to account to the company for any profit made on the contract.[23]

Settle Controversy over Elections

A shareholder may apply to the court to determine any controversy over the election or appointment of any director or auditor of the company. The court may make any order it thinks fit, including an order restraining a director or auditor from acting pending the determination of the dispute or declaring the result of a disputed election or appointment.

It may also order a new election or appointment, and provide directions for the management of the company's business in the meantime, as well as determine the voting rights of shareholders and of persons claiming to be shareholders.[24]

Conclusion

This book has attempted to describe some of the main legal and business issues which the owners and managers of private companies face from time to time. Dealing with these issues when they arise can sometimes create a difficult balancing act, as the interests and concerns of the company's many stakeholders may be in conflict and have to be reconciled.

Intended as a guide to help private company owners and managers prevent problems from occurring in the first place rather than just resolving them afterwards, this book encourages owners and managers to be more proactive and to plan for their company's future by being better informed and more aware of the rights and obligations surrounding the company's relationships with its stakeholders.

Whether the owners and managers are just starting up the company, or dealing with its employees, or trying to protect its intellectual property, or arranging its debt and equity financing, or implementing a business succession plan, or attempting some form of creditor proofing, or dealing with its shareholders, or improving its governance procedures, they should try to consider the interests of all of the stakeholders. For those who are company directors, they have a statutory duty of care to do so.[1]

Yet for the closely-held private company, especially one with only related family members as shareholders, the need to consider shareholder relationships can become an overriding concern. Although the oppression remedy described in the previous chapter may apply to most companies big or small, public or private, it seems that it's most frequently used in the context of smaller, closely-held companies if the number of reported decisions is a reliable indicator.[2]

And some shareholder disputes can prevent a company from being able to function at all.

The final third of this book has attempted to describe the various means available to the shareholders to become more involved in the company. It has attempted to explain how they may change things that they feel need to be changed, and it has attempted to describe what they can do other than simply wait around for the next annual meeting.

While they possess numerous individual and collective rights under the CBCA, and likely many additional rights under the terms of their shares or in the company's articles and by-laws, some of the most significant rights they enjoy may well come to them by way of contract, as may be set out in a shareholder agreement or subscription agreement.

However, even though the shareholders may be aware of their various rights, they may choose not to exercise them. They may simply not see any need to become more active as shareholders. Or when they do see a need, they may then feel that they're too late to do much about it. Or that it's not worth fighting for. Despite the many alternative actions described in the previous chapter, none may appear to be very attractive to a shareholder. The costs, delays and uncertainty associated with court applications may be a sufficient deterrent from pursing most of them.

Perhaps except for one. Getting out, or getting the other shareholders out, may be the only acceptable remedy to a shareholder who can't get along with the others.

In the absence of a public market for the company's shares, and in the absence of any buy-sell provisions in a shareholder agreement or separate buy-sell agreement, the shareholder may have to resort to the courts to achieve an exit from his investment. Even though the company may have a shareholder agreement, it may only allow shareholders to sell out to a third party if they have first offered their shares to the other shareholders and been turned down, and may say nothing about selling to the others in the absence of a third party offer.

If the company has just a few shareholders and is unable to properly function because they or their nominee directors are deadlocked and can't agree on anything, the shareholder may try to ask the court to wind up the company on the grounds that it would be "just and equitable" to do so. This is part of the liquidation and dissolution remedy described in the previous chapter. Alternatively, the shareholder may ask the court to order the others to buy his shares, or to sell their own shares to him, on the basis of the oppression remedy.

But by going to court in search of a way out, whether alleging that he has been oppressed by the company and the other shareholders, or asserting that the company is really a deadlocked partnership deserving of being wound up, he runs the risk that the court may prescribe a result he doesn't really want. If the court finds that he hasn't been treated all that badly by the others, he may end up worse off.

Although many cases have been reported involving these types of claims, looking at just a few may be useful reminders of what can happen when going the litigation route. The following four cases all involved companies with only a few shareholders, whose conduct towards each other was held not to be oppressive, and whose relationships were not subject to any buy-sell agreements. The shareholders concerned did nothing wrong and weren't at fault, but nonetheless found themselves without a clear way to change their circumstances.

One case[3] involved two brothers who owned 20 per cent of a cookie business. They were engaged in "a finger-pointing poisonous stand-off" with a husband and wife who owned the remaining 80 per cent. Both sides wanted out but had no mechanism for selling their shares. The court imposed one, by ordering that they establish a two button buzzer system that would identify the first side to push its button while the share price would be dropping every six seconds from a specified starting value. The side that did not fix the price would have the option of requiring the other to buy or sell at the fixed price, although the party required to buy could decline by selling at a 20 per cent discount. On appeal, this buzzer system was rejected, and the appeal court ordered the company to buy out the brothers' 20 per cent interest at a value to be determined by an independent valuator.

Yet the parties each experienced the feeling of having an unexpected solution imposed upon them.

Another case[4] concerned four brothers who each owned 25 per cent of a disposal services business. When the son of one them established a competing business, causing the "once harmonious relationship" among the brothers to be "irreparably broken down", the brother with the ambitious son asked the court to order the others to buy him out. The court refused, holding that their 20-year-old shareholder agreement would not be amended to include a buy-sell provision.

A further case[5] featured a father and son who jointly owned two-thirds of a pharmacy business, with another pharmacist owning the remaining third. While the father and son wanted to buy out the pharmacist, and the pharmacist wanted to buy out the father and son, neither side could agree on how to proceed. The pharmacist ended up asking the court to order that the entire business be sold by public auction. The court responded by ordering that his shares be purchased by the father and son at fair value.

And the last case[6] dealt with a husband and wife going through divorce proceedings who lacked a mechanism for allowing one of them to sell out of the professional conference business which they owned 50-50. In finding that the wife "justifiably lost confidence" in her husband as a business partner, the court ordered a transfer of the husband's shares to the wife at fair market value.

Had the parties in these four cases entered into buy-sell agreements with each other before they realized they wanted to get out, they may have been able to go their separate ways a lot faster. And maybe a lot more cheaply, depending on their legal fees and the court's award of costs. Because buy-sell agreements prescribe an exit mechanism that was lacking in the foregoing cases, the certainty they provide may be preferable to the uncertainty of going to court in search of a resolution.

While these cases illustrate to a shareholder the specific advantages of buy-sell provisions in a shareholder agreement or separate buy-sell agreement, they also illustrate the broader advantages of having his special expectations as a shareholder reduced to contractual form. Any benefits he expects to receive as a shareholder which do not flow directly from the individual or collective statutory rights described earlier in this book should be set out in an agreement with the company and the other shareholders as a way of avoiding some of the unexpected results reflected in these cases. The courts prefer to enforce contracts, not ignore them or re-write them, so long as the contracts have unambiguous terms.

But having contractual protection hardly guarantees a shareholder a predictable, let alone harmonious, experience as a private company shareholder. While comprehensive agreements may provide some comfort, they are still contracts which may prove their worth only as a last resort, when negotiation and moral suasion fail to achieve compliance and recourse to the courts in a lawsuit for damages or specific performance may be the only alternative.

Despite the advantages of having enforceable contracts, a shareholder may be as well or better served through the implementation of some of the recommended practices described in the *Governance* chapter. With proper governance structures and procedures in place, at least some of the behaviour within the company which might otherwise give rise to a breach of contract claim before a court might be avoided altogether.

Good governance might also help to reduce the possibility of a shareholder's rights and expectations being frustrated or ignored in the absence of any agreement with the shareholder. At least it may detect and deter the kinds of behaviour which can lead to claims of shareholder oppression.

For example, the failure to simulate arm's length transactions when dealing with related parties, or the lack of good faith on the part of the directors, or the benefiting of majority shareholders to the exclusion of minority shareholders, are more likely to be avoided when the company has a board and audit committee with independent directors and has a code of business conduct which addresses conflicts of interest.

As described earlier, it is often difficult to fully implement good governance in the private company context. But whatever governance structures and procedures the company decides to implement, it will nonetheless be influenced by what other private companies it competes with, perhaps ones it envies, are also doing at the same time.

Despite the cynical view some managers may have that the recommended structures and procedures are mere window-dressing, good governance may become commonplace. It may become an indicator of the well-managed private company. It won't be looked at as a quick-fix management technique that falls in and out of fashion. It will instead be looked at as having enduring value, respected for no better reason than it's just the way things are done.

For those who remain as shareholders of a private company, they should encourage good governance as well as good contracts as the way to avoid shareholder disputes, so that the motivations and expectations they had when they first became shareholders may continue to be met.

Endnotes

Chapter 1 – Introduction

1 R.S.C. 1985, c. C-44.

2 Section 2(1) of the CBCA Regulations defines a "distributing corporation" as a "reporting issuer" under certain provincial securities legislation, or if not a "reporting issuer", a corporation which has filed a prospectus or registration statement, or which has securities listed on a stock exchange, or which has amalgamated or been reorganized with a corporation which has done so.

3 See the definition of "private issuer" in section 2.4(1) of National Instrument 45-106 *Prospectus and Registration Exemption*. The number of shareholders is limited to 50, excluding employees and former employees.

4 See subsections 125(7) and 248(1) of the *Income Tax Act*, R.S.C. 1985, c. 1 (5th Supp.) (the "ITA").

5 Section 263 of the CBCA and section 5 of the CBCA Regulations.

6 Subsection 21(3) of the CBCA.

7 Subsection 102(1) of the CBCA.

8 Subsection 50(4) of the CBCA provides that the registration of the issue of shares in the register is complete and valid registration for all purposes. Subsection 51(1) of the CBCA provides that the company may treat the registered shareholder as the person exclusively entitled to vote, to receive notices, to receive any interest, dividend or other payments in respect of the shares, and otherwise to exercise all the rights and powers of an owner of the shares.

9 Subsection 25(1) of the CBCA.

10 Subsection 25(3) of the CBCA.

Chapter 2 – Starting Up the Company

1   A sole proprietorship is a business vehicle owned by one person but is not a legal entity separate from that person. Since the business being carried on is not legally separate, the owner owns the assets and receives the income of the business, and is liable for all of the debts and other obligations of the business. The owner's liability is unlimited, or at least to the extent that her liability is not covered by insurance, so that her personal assets as well as the assets of the business are at risk of being seized to satisfy the obligations of the business. While the owner may employ others in the business, she cannot employ herself, for a person cannot enter into a contract with herself.

2   A partnership is a business vehicle owned by two or more persons, and like a sole proprietorship, is not a separate legal entity at common law. Consequently a partner cannot be both a partner and an employee of the partnership. However, partners can sue or be sued in the name of the partnership, giving the appearance of a separate legal status for litigation purposes. A partnership is defined as a legal relationship between two or more persons "carrying on a business in common with a view to profit". However, an agreement to share gross returns does not of itself create a partnership, nor does the ownership of joint property of itself create a partnership, regardless of whether the profits from the property are shared by the owners or not. There can be general partnerships, limited partnerships, or limited liability partnerships. See generally the Ontario *Partnerships Act*, R.S.O. 1990, c.P.5 and *Limited Partnerships Act*, R.S.O. 1990, c. L.16.

3   The income earned by a sole proprietorship business is included, and all losses incurred by the business are deducted, when calculating the owner's income from all other sources during the year. The owner does not file a separate federal or provincial tax return for the business. If the business losses exceed the other income of the proprietor for the year, they may be carried back 3 years and carried forward 20 years to be offset against any other income in those years, pursuant to subsection 111(1) of the ITA.

4   A partnership is not a separate taxable entity, although any income or loss from the partnership business is calculated at the partnership level and then allocated amongst the partners as prescribed in their partnership agreement. Various expenses are first deducted from the partnership's revenues to arrive at the partnership's net income or loss. Then the partner's share of that net income or loss is included in the partner's income from all sources for tax purposes and taxed at her marginal tax rate, whether or not any of the

partnership's income is actually distributed to the partner. The partners file their own tax returns and pay tax on the partnership income allocated to them, whereas the partnership files only an information return. Certain sources of income and loss, such as those relating to capital gains or interest, retain their initial character and "flow though" to the partner to be used in calculating her overall income. Capital cost allowance must be claimed at the partnership level and therefore the partners must agree amongst themselves how much capital cost allowance they want the partnership to claim in any given year. They then receive their share of the amount claimed whether they can use it or not.

5   See subsection 45(1) of the CBCA. Shareholders are, however, liable to a certain extent in particular circumstances. For example, they are liable to repay any distributions they may have received as a return of capital when the corporation was insolvent, under subsection 38(4) of the CBCA, or to repay any distributions they may have received upon the corporation's dissolution to the extent of any amounts still owing to the corporation's creditors, under section 226 of the CBCA.

6   Subsection 24(3) of the CBCA.

7   Subsection 24(4) of the CBCA.

8   The creation of a class of preferred shares upon incorporation as part of the transfer of assets to the company in exchange for a number of preferred shares often takes place to accomplish the transfer on a tax deferred or "rollover" basis. This may be done in connection with an "estate freeze" which is discussed in greater detail in the *Business Succession and Estate Freezes* chapter.

9   This joint election is usually made under section 85 of the ITA. The tax payable on the accrued but unrealized gain on the transfer will be deferred until the company disposes of the transferred property or the founder disposes of the company shares.

10   The advantages of income splitting generally do not apply when shares are issued to the founder's children who are under 18, since the "kiddie tax" provided in section 120.4 of the ITA taxes dividends at the highest marginal tax rate.

11   The specific rules for calculating the capital gains deduction for qualified small business corporation shares can be found in subsection 110.6(2.2) of the ITA The exemption is available only to individuals resident in Canada, and shelters from tax a maximum of $800,000 (for 2014, and thereafter indexed to inflation) in capital gains arising from the disposition of the shares

of a qualified small business corporation, or QSBC. If the shareholder has already used her $100,000 ordinary capital gains exemption (before it was eliminated in 1994), she will only have a $700,000 capital gains exemption available. Her maximum entitlement in any one year can also be limited if she has a cumulative net investment loss balance or has previously deducted allowable business investment losses. The exemption is not available to the company upon the sale of any of the company's assets, nor is it available upon the redemption by the company of the company's shares. In order for the shares of a company to be QSBC shares, three tests (which are described in the definition of qualified small business corporation shares in subsection 110.6(1) of the ITA) generally need to be met: the company had to be a "small business corporation" on the disposition of the shares, which is defined in subsection 248(1) of the ITA, to be a Canadian-controlled private corporation carrying on an active business primarily in Canada; the shares cannot have been owned by anyone other than the person disposing of them or by a related person during the two year period preceding the disposition; and during those two years, at least 50% of the fair market value of the assets of the company had to be used principally in an active business carried on primarily in Canada by the company or a related company. A company which is winding down, selling off its assets and investing the sale proceeds, is not carrying on an active business.

12   Any dividends and capital gains which are distributed by the trust retain their original character for tax purposes and are taxed accordingly in the hands of the beneficiaries.

13   See subsection 122(1) of the ITA.

14   See section 104 of the ITA.

15   To use their personal lifetime capital gains exemptions, the family members would have to sell their shares in the family holding corporation, but the shares of that corporation may not qualify as QSBC shares as described in endnote 10 above.

16   See subsection 56(2) of the ITA.

17   See subsection 15(1) of the ITA.

18   For example, see *Unisource Canada Inc. v. Hongkong Bank of Canada* (2000), 131 O.A.C. 24 (Ont. C.A.), varying (1998), 43 B.L.R. (2d) 226 (Ont. Gen. Div.).

Chapter 3 – Dealing with Employees

1   For example, see section 23 of the Ontario *Employment Standards Act*, 2000, S.O. 2000, c.41.

2   For example, see subsection 81(4) of the Ontario *Employment Standards Act*, 2000.

3   For example, see subsection 33(1) of the Ontario *Employment Standards Act*, 2000, which requires an employer to give an employee at least two weeks vacation a year. This obligation cannot be avoided by simply paying vacation pay, and employers often limit the ability of an employee carrying forward unused vacation time in excess of the statutory minimum in order to manage the company's overall liability to provide vacation time.

4   In Ontario, the minimum is prescribed in section 57 of the Ontario *Employment Standards Act*, 2000, and is generally one week per year of employment up to eight weeks.

5   The common law does not provide a fixed measure of the amount of "reasonable" notice required upon termination, but some long-term, senior-level employees have been awarded compensation equivalent to more than two years' notice. A number of factors are usually considered by the courts, including the age of the employee, his length of service, his position within the company, and the likelihood of his finding employment elsewhere.

6   See subsection 13(3) of the *Copyright Act*, R.S.C. 1985, c. C-42.

7   See section 14.1 of the *Copyright Act*.

8   See subsection 14.1(2) of the *Copyright Act*.

9   See *RBC Dominion Securities Inc. v. Merrill Lynch Canada Inc.*, 2008 SCC 54, [2008] 3 S.C.R. 79 (S.C.C.).

10 See note 2 above.

11 In the case of copyright, in the absence of an assignment of intellectual property agreement, outside consultants generally retain copyright in works which they have authored while providing "services" to the company, in contrast to employees under a contract of "service" referenced in note 1 above.

12 See the *Employment Insurance Act*, S.C. 1996, c. 23.

13 See the *Canada Pension Plan*, R.S.C. 1985, c C-8.

14 See the ITA.

15 For example, see the Ontario *Workplace Safety and Insurance Act, 1997*, S.O. 1997, c. 16, Sched. A.

16 For example, see the Ontario *Employment Standards Act*, 2000.

17   For example, see Canada Revenue Agency Tax Guide *RC4110 – Employee or Self-Employed*.

18   See the exemption from prospectus requirements in section 2.24(1) of National Instrument 45-106 *Prospectus and Registration Exemption*. Participating in a distribution by an employee must be voluntary.

19   Of the numerous cases dealing with constructive dismissal, the Supreme Court of Canada decision of *Farber c. Royal Trust Co.*, [1997] 1 S.C.R. 846 (S.C.C.), if often recognized as a leading authority.

20   For example, section 58 of the Ontario *Employment Standards Act*, 2000 sets out "mass termination" obligations when 50 or more employees are terminated in any period of 4 weeks or less, and provides for a greater statutory notice period for each employee involved of between 8 to 16 weeks, depending upon the number of employees terminated, along with a report to the Ontario Ministry of Labour.

21   For example, see subsection 60(1) of the Ontario *Employment Standards Act*, 2000.

22   See *McKinley v. BC Tel*, 2001 SCC 38, [2001] 2 S.C.R. 161 (S.C.C.).

23   For example, see the Ontario *Occupational Health and Safety Act*, R.S.O.1990, c.O.1. Subsection 9(2) requires a joint health and safety committee, and subsection 32.0.1(1) requires an employer to prepare policies on workplace violence and harassment.

24   For example, see the Ontario *Workplace Safety and Insurance Act, 1997*.

25   For example, see the Ontario *Human Rights Code*, R.S.O.1990, c. H.19. Under subsection 5(1), "every person has a right to equal treatment with respect to employment without discrimination because of race, ancestry, place of origin, colour, ethnic origin, citizenship, creed, sex, sexual orientation, age, record of offences, marital status, family status or disability".

26   For example, see the *Personal Information Protection and Electronic Documents Act*, S.C. 2000, c.5, which applies in Ontario.

Chapter 4 – Protecting Intellectual Property

1   See the *Plant Breeders' Rights Act*, S.C. 1990, c. 20.

2   See the *Integrated Circuit Topography Act*, S.C. 1990, c. 37.

3   Although there is no comprehensive statute to protect personality rights, the "property" in one's own personality (often a person's image) continues to be defined by the common law following the leading Ontario case of *Krouse v. Chrysler Canada Ltd.* (1973), 1 O.R. (2d) 225, 40 D.L.R. (3d) 15 (Ont.

C.A.). Some commercial use or implied endorsement is necessary for misappropriation of personality to occur.

4 See *International Corona Resources Ltd. v. LAC Minerals Ltd.*, [1989] 2 S.C.R. 574 (S.C.C.).

5 The term "trade secrets" is more prevalent in the United States, given that many states have adopted the *Uniform Trade Secrets Act*, a model law drafted by the National Conference of Commissioners on Uniform State Laws.

6 For example, see the decision in *Martel Building Ltd. v. R.*, 2000 SCC 60, [2000] 2 S.C.R. 860 (S.C.C.).

7 The *Patent Act*, R.S.C. 1985, c. P-4.

8 See section 2 of the *Patent Act*, which defines "invention" as "any new and useful art, process, machine, manufacture or composition of matter, or any new and useful improvement in any art, process, machine, manufacture or composition of matter".

9 See section 28.3 of the *Patent Act*.

10 The one-year grace period provided under subsection 28.2(1) of the *Patent Act* applies to disclosures made by the applicant or anyone who has derived knowledge of the invention from the applicant. Generally speaking, if the Canadian Patent Office is satisfied that the invention was known or used anywhere in the world by another person before the inventor made his invention, the application will be rejected.

11 The PCT is administered by the World Intellectual Property Organization in Geneva, and provides a standardized international filing procedure that is shared by Canada's principal trading partners. Under the PCT, the company may file for a patent in as many of the member countries as it chooses through a single application filed in Canada. This procedure is simpler than filing separate applications and can give the company more time to conduct market research and, if necessary, raise capital. When the company files under the PCT, it will receive an international search report which checks its international application against other applications and patents, as well as an initial opinion on the patentability of the invention. The company may then correspond with an examiner about the possibility of amending its application, and will ultimately receive an international preliminary report on patentability. This report does not guarantee that a patent will be granted. Local patent offices in the countries designated reserve the right to conduct their own examinations, but some accept the results of the international preliminary report on patentability. The company will therefore receive a fairly reliable indication of whether it's worthwhile to file for multiple patents in the designated countries before patent application fees become payable. Eighteen

months after filing (or after the priority date, if there is one), the company's application will be made available to the public.

12   See section 3 of the *Copyright Act*, R.S.C. 1985, c. C-42.

13   See section 13 of the *Copyright Act*.

14   Protection may also be available under the *Integrated Circuit Topography Act*, S.C. 1990, c. 37, discussed elsewhere in this chapter.

15   The definition of "literary works" in section 2 of the *Copyright Act* includes "tables, computer programs, and compilations of literary works".

16   See section 6 of the *Copyright Act*.

17   See subsections 53(1) and 53(2) of the *Copyright Act*.

18   This notice was once required in order to receive copyright protection in the United States, but in countries respecting the Berne Convention, this is no longer the case.

19   See subsection 13(3) of the *Copyright Act*.

20   See the definition of "trade-mark" in section 2 of the *Trade-marks Act*, R.S.C. 1985, c. T-13.

21   See section 13 of the *Trade-marks Act* providing for the registration of a "distinguishing guise", which is defined in section 2 as a "shaping of wares or their containers", or "mode of packaging or wrapping wares".

22   See paragraph 7(b) of the *Trade-marks Act*, which attempts to codify the traditional common law tort of passing off.

23   See subsection 16(1) of the *Trade-marks Act*.

24   See subsection 12(1) of the *Trade-marks Act*.

25   See section 46 of the *Trade-marks Act*.

26   See section 53.2 of the *Trade-marks Act*.

27   See section 45 of the *Trade-marks Act*. Under subsection 45(1), "the Registrar may at any time and, at the written request made after three years from the date of the registration of a trade-mark by any person who pays the prescribed fee shall, unless the Registrar sees good reason to the contrary, give notice to the registered owner of the trade-mark requiring the registered owner to furnish within three months an affidavit or a statutory declaration showing, with respect to each of the wares or services specified in the registration, whether the trade-mark was in use in Canada at any time during the three year period immediately preceding the date of the notice and, if not, the date when it was last so in use and the reason for the absence of such use since that date". Under subsection 45(3), "by reason of the evidence furnished to the Registrar or the failure to furnish any evidence, it appears to the Registrar that a trade-mark, either with respect to all of the wares or services specified

in the registration or with respect to any of those wares or services, was not used in Canada at any time during the three year period immediately preceding the date of the notice and that the absence of use has not been due to special circumstances that excuse the absence of use, the registration of the trade-mark is liable to be expunged or amended accordingly".

28 See subsection 50(1) of the *Trade-marks Act.*
29 See subsection 50(2) of the *Trade-marks Act.*
30 See section 4 of the *Industrial Design Act*, R.S.C. 1985, c. I-9, relating to registration, and section 2, which defines an industrial design as "features of shape, configuration, pattern or ornament and any combination of those features that, in a finished article, appeal to and are judged solely by the eye".
31 See subsection 6(3) of the *Industrial Design Act.*
32 See subsection 12(1) of the *Industrial Design Act.*
33 See paragraph 4(1)(b) and subsection 7(3) of the *Industrial Design Act.*
34 See section 9 of the *Industrial Design Act.*
35 See section 10 of the *Industrial Design Act.*
36 See section 7 of the *Industrial Design Act.*
37 See section 15.1 of the *Industrial Design Act.*
38 See section 17 of the *Industrial Design Act.*
39 See section 13 of the *Trade-marks Act.*
40 See subsections 64(2) and 64(3) of the *Copyright Act.*

Chapter 5 – Creditor Proofing

1 Some doubt on the acceptability of creditor proofing plans in British Columbia has arisen because of the decision of the British Columbia Court of Appeal in *Abakhan & Associates Inc. v. Braydon*, [2009] B.C.J. No. 2315, 2009 BCCA 521. Leave to appeal this decision to the Supreme Court of Canada was refused, [2010] S.C.C.A. No. 26, File No. 33545. The *Abakhan* decision held that the contemplation of future creditors who may be hindered or delayed may be sufficient to void a transfer under the British Columbia *Fraudulent Conveyance Act*, R.S.B.C. 1996, chapter 163. In contrast to the *Abakhan* decision, the Ontario Superior Court decision in *Duca Financial Services Credit Union Ltd. v. Bozzo*, [2010] O.J. No. 2233, 2010 ONSC 3104, stated at paragraph 54 that "a person is not prevented from rearranging his affairs to isolate assets from future, as opposed to present, liabilities". Although future cases or legislative reform may be necessary to reconcile the different approaches in these two decisions, it is questionable whether a policy of

protecting future creditors is justified where there is no fraud, dishonesty or bad faith. A future creditor should be able to determine the asset base and creditworthiness of the borrower, and may not deserve protection if it fails to undertake a reasonable amount of due diligence.

2   R.S.C. 1985, c. C-46.

3   While transferring assets without accrued capital gains may be transferred to another corporation tax-free, many transfers rely upon the rollover provisions of section 85 of the ITA to defer any capital gains tax which might otherwise be payable upon the transfer.

4   See subsection 112(1) of the ITA.

5   The transfer of company shares to family members may have to take into account the impact of applicable provincial family law, such as the Ontario *Family Law Act*, R.S.O. 1990, c. F.3. Similar, though not identical, legislation exists in the other provinces. In short, if a family member acquiring company shares is married, his spouse may have certain rights relating to the value of those shares after the transfer in the event that he and his spouse separate. Any appreciation in the value of the shares once transferred to the family member may end up being subject to equal division between the spouses.

6   See paragraph 96(1)(b) of the *Bankruptcy and Insolvency Act*, R.S.C. 1985, c. B-3.

7   See subsection 69(1) the ITA which applies to gifts and transfers of property between persons who are not dealing with each other at arm's length. The owner is deemed to have disposed of the shares for fair market value where there is a gift or sale below fair market value. Where there is a gift or transfer above fair market value, the recipient is deemed to have acquired the shares at fair market value

8   Outright gifts or transfers below fair market value may trigger the attribution rules found in subsections 74.1(1) and 74.1(2) and sections 74.2 and 74.3 of the ITA which apply to gifts and transfers of property between family members if the consideration is less than fair market value. They are intended to prevent income and capital gains splitting between spouses and income splitting with related minors. If shares are transferred to the owner's spouse, common-law partner or the owner's children who are under 18 years of age, any distributions made to them under such shares may be attributed back to the owner and taxed in his hands at his own marginal tax rate

9   See generally section 85 of the ITA.

10   Under subsection 85(1) of the ITA, a number of conditions must be met in order for the transfer of the shares to the holding company to be tax-free,

including that the holding company must issue at least one share in its capital as consideration paid for the shares acquired, a joint election must be filed by the transferring shareholders and the holding company, and the elected amount is equal to the cost of the shares transferred. Instead of taking back shares in the holding company, the transferring shareholders could receive non-share consideration such as a promissory note without being subject to tax, provided the value of the note is equal to or less than the lower of the adjusted cost base and paid-up capital of the shares being transferred.

11 Subsection 112(1) of the ITA allows many inter-corporate dividends to be received tax-free. However, in certain circumstances, subsection 55(2) of the ITA converts a tax-free inter-corporate dividend into a taxable capital gain if the amount of the dividend exceeds the amount of "safe income" on hand in the paying corporation.

12 The transfer may be made pursuant to subsection 85(1) of the ITA as discussed in note 10 above, although a separate election may be possible under section 22 of the ITA in respect of the accounts receivable if substantially all of the operating company's assets are transferred to the subsidiary.

13 These transfers are made under subsection 85(1) of the ITA, as discussed in note 10 above.

14 The purchase and redemption of shares will give rise in each case to a deemed dividend under subsection 84(3) of the ITA, which will be received by each company as a tax-free inter-corporate dividend as discussed in note 11 above, unless converted to a taxable capital gain under subsection 55(2) of the ITA.

15 See the *Bankruptcy and Insolvency Act.*

16 For example, in Ontario, see the *Fraudulent Conveyances Act,* R.S.O.1990, c.F.29, *Assignments and Preferences Act*, R.S.O. 1990, c.A.33, and *Bulk Sales Act,* R.S.O. 1990, c.B.14. Legislation similar to the first two of these statutes exists in other provinces, although Ontario remains the only province with specific bulk sales legislation. Under the Ontario *Bulk Sales Act*, a sale in bulk may be set aside and the buyer may be held to account to the creditors of the seller for the value of the assets sold unless the buyer complies with this Act. Compliance can be achieved if the seller delivers to the buyer a statement of the seller's creditors and the buyer then elects to pay the sale proceeds to the seller if the seller has also sworn that all of the creditors have been paid in full or if the seller has made provision for payment of all of the creditors immediately after the sale, except for those creditors waiving their rights to immediate payment. Alternatively, if 60 per cent of the unsecured trade creditors consent and they have received the seller's statement, the buyer

may elect to pay the sale proceeds to a trustee appointed by the seller for further disbursement to all of the creditors in accordance with the priorities established under the *Bankruptcy and Insolvency Act.*

17 See section 95 of the *Bankruptcy and Insolvency Act.*

18 See section 96 of the *Bankruptcy and Insolvency Act.*

19 See section 101 of the *Bankruptcy and Insolvency Act.*

20 See for example section 2 of the Ontario *Fraudulent Conveyances Act.*

21 See for example section 3 of the Ontario *Fraudulent Conveyances Act.*

22 See for example subsection 4(1) of the Ontario *Assignments and Preferences Act.*

23 See for example subsections 4(3) and 4(4) of the Ontario *Assignments and Preferences Act.*

24 See for example subsection 5(1) of the Ontario *Assignments and Preferences Act.*

25 See section 34 of the CBCA and, for example, section 30 of the Ontario *Business Corporations Act*, R.S.O. 1990, c.B.16.

26 See section 36 of the CBCA and, for example, section 32 of the Ontario *Business Corporations Act.*

27 See section 42 of the CBCA and, for example, section 38 of the Ontario *Business Corporations Act.*

28 See subsection 118(2) of the CBCA and, for example, subsection 130(2) of the Ontario *Business Corporations Act.*

29 See section 241 of the CBCA and, for example, section 248 of the Ontario *Business Corporations Act.*

30 See section 392 of the *Criminal Code.*

31 See sections 366 to 368 of the *Criminal Code.*

32 Sec section 21 of the *Criminal Code.*

33 A more detailed description of the badges fraud can be found in Houlden and Morawetz, *Bankruptcy and Insolvency Law of Canada*, 4th ed. (Toronto: Carswell, 2009).

34 (2001) 54 O.R. (3d) 161 (C.A.).

35 *Sinclair v. Dover Engineering Services Ltd.* (1987), 11 B.C.L.R (2d) 176 (S.C.), affirmed (1988) 49 D.L.R. (4th) 297 (B.C.C.A.).

Chapter 6 – Leasing Commercial Property

1 See, for example, the Ontario *Commercial Tenancies Act*, RSO 1990, c. L.7 (the "Act").

2   See subsection 23(1) of the Act which states that in every lease "containing a covenant, condition or agreement against assigning, underletting, or parting with the possession, or disposing of the land or property leased without licence or consent, such covenant, condition or agreement shall, unless the lease contains an express provision to the contrary, be deemed to be subject to a proviso to the effect that such licence or consent is not to be unreasonably withheld". Therefore, in Ontario, a landlord may insist upon a right to unreasonably withhold consent so long as that right is expressly set out in the lease.

Chapter 7 – Acquiring a Franchise

1   Alberta, Manitoba, New Brunswick, Ontario and Prince Edward Island have special franchise legislation.

2   A certificate of trademark registration is issued by the Registrar of Trademarks pursuant to section 40 of the *Trade-marks Act*, R.S.C. 1985, c. T-13.

3   In Alberta, there is the *Franchises Act*, R.S.A. 2000, c. F-23. In Manitoba, there is *The Franchises Act*, C.C.S.M. c. F156. In New Brunswick, there is the *Franchises Act*, S.N.B. 2007, c. F-23.5. In Ontario, there is the *Arthur Wishart Act (Franchise Disclosure), 2000*, S.O. 2000, c.3. In Prince Edward Island, there is the *Franchises Act*, R.S.P.E.I. 1988, as amended by S.P.E.I. 2005, c. 36.

4   See subsection 1(1) of the Act.

5   An alternative definition, commonly known as the "business opportunities" definition, appears in subsection 1(1) of the Act and includes the right to sell or distribute goods or services supplied by the franchisor together with the provision of location assistance.

6   See section 11 of the Act.

7   See *1490664 Ontario Ltd. v. Dig This Garden Retailers Ltd.* (2005), 256 D.L.R. (4th) 451, [2005] O.J. No. 3040 (Ont. C.A.) and *6792341 Canada Inc. v. Dollar It Ltd.* (2009), 95 O.R. (3d) 291 (Ont. C.A.).

8   See subsection 5(1) of the Act.

9   See subsection 1(1) of the Act which defines a material fact as including "any information about the business, operations, capital or control of the franchisor or franchisor's associate, or about the franchise system, that would reasonably be expected to have a significant effect on the value or price of the franchise to be granted or the decision to acquire the franchise".

10   See subsection 5(4) of the Act.

11   See subsection 5(3) of the Act and the *Dig This Garden* decision referred in note 7 above.

12   See section 7 to the Regulations under the Act.

13   See section 1 and subsection 5(5) of the Act. A "material change" means a change in the business, operations, capital or control of the franchisor or franchisor's associate, a change in the franchise system or a prescribed change, that would reasonably be expected to have a significant adverse effect on the value or price of the franchise to be granted or on the decision to acquire the franchise and includes a decision to implement such a change made by the board of directors of the franchisor or franchisor's associate or by senior management of the franchisor or franchisor's associate who believe that confirmation of the decision by the board of directors is probable.

14   See section 3 of the Act.

15   See, for example, *Fairview Donut Inc. v. TDL Group Corp.*, 2012 ONSC 1252 (Ont. S.C.J.), affirmed 2012 CarswellOnt 15496 (Ont. C.A.), leave to appeal refused 2013 CarswellOnt 6050 (S.C.C.).

16   See section 4 of the Act.

17   See subsection 6(1) of the Act.

18   See subsection 6(2) of the Act.

19   See subsection 6(6) of the Act.

20   See subsection 7(1) of the Act.

21   See subsections 7(2) and (3) of the Act.

22   See subsection 50(1) of the *Trade-Marks Act*, R.S.C. 1985, c. T-13.

23   See subclause 5(7)(a)(iv) of the Act which provides that a franchisor does not need to provide a prospective franchisee with its disclosure document where "the grant of the franchise is not effected by or through the franchisor", and see subsection 5(8) of the Act which states that the grant of a franchise is not effected by or through a franchisor merely because "the franchisor has a right, exercisable on reasonable grounds, to approve or disapprove the grant". See also the Ontario Court of Appeal decision in *2189205 Ontario Inc. v. Springdale Pizza Depot Ltd.*, 2011 ONCA 467 (Ont. C.A.), which held that the franchisor in that case had some involvement in the negotiations for the agreement of purchase and sale of the assets of the business between the selling franchisee and the buying franchisee and that the franchisor was not merely a "passive participant" in the resale, and consequently should have provided a disclosure document to the buying franchisee.

24   See the *Letters of Intent, Due Diligence*, and *Purchase and Sale Agreements*

chapters in Mahaffy, A. Paul, *Business Transactions Guide*, (Toronto: Thomson Reuters Canada Limited, 2010).

25 Section 68 of the ITA allows the buyer and seller to elect what amount of the overall purchase price is to be allocated to specific classes of the assets being purchased. In an effort to minimize their respective tax liabilities resulting from the deal, the buyer and seller will attempt to allocate the purchase price amongst the various asset categories, while recognizing that a high value allocated to a particular category may be advantageous to one party and disadvantageous to the other. While the seller may be concerned about the tax implications of such values for the year of the sale, the buyer may be more concerned about the tax implications for those years following the sale and the extent of various deductions then available. For example, a high value allocated to depreciable property may provide the buyer with greater deductions for capital cost allowance in subsequent years, but may trigger a recapture of capital cost allowance for the seller in the year of the sale. The buyer may prefer to allocate high values to inventory, whereas the seller may prefer to allocate high values to non-depreciable capital property. Although the Canada Revenue Agency may be entitled to reallocate the purchase price among all of the purchased assets pursuant to section 68 if it deems the allocations made by the parties to be unreasonable, the allocations negotiated between arm's length parties are generally upheld. A special election is available to the buyer and seller under section 22 of the ITA regarding accounts receivable. They may jointly elect what value is to be allocated to the seller's accounts receivable in order to reduce the amount of tax which might otherwise be paid by the seller if the face amount of the receivables was taken into the seller's income. A purchase price allocation to receivables which is for less than their face value creates a loss for the seller which can be deducted from the seller's income, but which is included in the buyer's income.

Chapter 8 – Business Succession and Estate Freezes

1 For example, see the 2004 Literature Survey conducted by Derek Picard at http://cfib.org.

2 See subsections 70(5) and 70(6) of the ITA which deem the owner to have disposed of her property immediately prior to her death for proceeds equal to its fair market value, thereby making her estate liable for any unrealized capital gains which have accrued on such property up to the date of her death. These gains are subject to possible tax-free rollover treatment for

bequests to her spouse or common–law partner or a trust established for her spouse or common-law partner.

3 For example, see subsections 34(2) and 36(2) relating to the repurchase and redemption of shares, respectively, and section 42 relating to the payment of dividends, under the CBCA.

4 See subsection 69(1) the ITA which applies to gifts and transfers of property between persons who are not dealing with each other at arm's length. The current owner is deemed to have disposed of the shares for fair market value where there is a gift or sale below fair market value. Where there is a gift or transfer above fair market value, the recipient is deemed to have acquired the shares at fair market value.

5 The specific rules for calculating the capital gains deduction for shares of a qualified small business corporation, or QSBC, can be found in subsection 110.6(2.1) of the ITA. The exemption is available only to individuals resident in Canada, and shelters from tax a maximum of $800,000 (for 2014, and thereafter indexed to inflation) in capital gains arising from the disposition of the shares of a QSBC. It is not available to the company upon the sale of any of the company's assets, nor is it available upon the redemption by the company of the company's shares. If the owner has already used her $100,000 ordinary capital gains exemption (before it was eliminated in 1994), she will only have a $700,000 capital gains exemption available. Her maximum entitlement in any one year can also be limited if she has a cumulative net investment loss balance or has previously deducted allowable business investment losses. In order for the shares of a company to be QSBC shares, three tests generally need to be met: the company had to be a "small business corporation" on the disposition of the shares, which is defined to be a Canadian-controlled private corporation carrying on an active business primarily in Canada; the shares cannot have been owned by anyone other than the person disposing of them or by a related person during the two year period preceding the disposition; and during those two years, at least 50% of the fair market value of the assets of the company had to be used principally in an active business carried on primarily in Canada by the company or a related company. A company which is winding down, selling off its assets and investing the sale proceeds is not carrying on an active business.

6 See note 3 immediately above. To avoid this imbalance between the amount deemed to be received by the owner and the amount paid by the children, the transfer documentation may contain a "price adjustment clause" which states that if the Canada Revenue Agency decides that the fair market value

of the shares is greater than the price paid by the children, the price will be retroactively adjusted to the greater value if the parties agree.

7   See subparagraph 40(1)(a)(iii) of the ITA for a definition of an eligible reserve. The 10-year reserve is available under subsection 40(1.1) of the ITA when shares of a small business corporation are sold to a child who is resident in Canada.

8   Outright gifts or transfers below fair market value also may trigger the attribution rules found in subsections 74.1(1) and 74.1(2) and sections 74.2 and 74.3 which apply to gifts and transfers of property between family members if the consideration is less than fair market value. They are intended to prevent income and capital gains splitting between spouses and income splitting with related minors. If common shares under the freeze are issued to the owner's spouse, common-law partner or the owner's children who are under 18 years of age, any distributions made to them under such shares may be attributed back to the owner and taxed in her hands at her own marginal tax rate.

9   In addition to reducing the amount of tax payable on unrealized capital gains described in note 2, an estate freeze may reduce the amount of estate duties and probate fees by capping the size of the owner's estate.

10 This exchange of common shares for preferred shares is ordinarily accomplished on a tax-free rollover basis under section 51 or 86 of the ITA, which provide that the proceeds of disposition received by a person exchanging shares will be deemed to be equal to the adjusted cost base of the shares so that no capital gain or loss should arise on the share exchange transaction. The preferred shares usually have the following characteristics: (i) they are redeemable at the option of the holder; (ii) they carry voting rights on matters pertaining to such class of shares; (iii) they have a first preference in any distributions of assets on a liquidation, winding-up or dissolution; (iv) they have no restrictions on transferability other than required under corporate law; and (v) they restrict the company from paying dividends on other classes of shares if the company would end up with insufficient assets to redeem the preferred shares. The preferred shares may contain a "price adjustment clause" similar to the clause described in note 6 above in order to address the possibility that the Canada Revenue Agency determines that the fair market value of the company is different from the redemption amount of the preferred shares, so that the redemption amount is retroactively adjusted to avoid any capital gain arising on the freeze.

11 The owner might file an election under section 85 of the ITA designating specific proceeds of disposition and thereby crystallizing all or a portion of

the accrued gain on her shares. The amount designated also becomes her cost of the preferred shares received in exchange, so that the "bump" in her cost will result in a smaller taxable capital gain being realized when she later disposes of the preferred shares or are deemed to be disposed when she dies.

12 The transfer would be made by special election under section 85 of the ITA.

13 The owner's transfer of her common shares to the holding corporation would likely be accomplished pursuant to section 85 of the ITA on a tax-free rollover basis. So long as the holding corporation is a QSBC, the attribution rules described in note 8 may not apply.

14 See subsection 84(3) of the ITA, which provides for the taxation of the redemption proceeds as a dividend to the extent they exceed the paid-up capital of the shares.

15 See subsection 104(2) of the ITA.

16 However, before distributing any trust property (as opposed to income) to a beneficiary, the trustee should obtain a tax clearance certificate from the Canada Revenue Agency since the trustee is personally liable under subsection 159(3) of the ITA for any unpaid taxes, interest or penalties owing by the trust. However, the trustee's liability is limited to the value of the property distributed to the beneficiaries.

17 If the trust chooses to retain income in the trust for tax purposes and designates an amount for retention under subsection 104(13.1) of the ITA, such amount is not deductible by the trust and is not taxable to the beneficiary.

18 See subsection 69(1) of the ITA.

19 See subsection 75(2) of the ITA.

20 See subsection 73(1) of the ITA.

21 See section 69 of the ITA.

22 See section 104 of the ITA.

23 The distribution to beneficiaries can be accomplished on a tax-deferred basis if the trust qualifies as a "personal trust" as defined in subsection 248(1) of the ITA.

24 See subsection 107(2) of the ITA.

25 There are other ways the owner's children can be provided for differently using a family trust. For example, if the owner is unsure about whether a particular child deserves to have any entitlement as a beneficiary at the time the trust is being set up, that decision may be deferred to a later time by giving the owner a power of appointment to alter the trust's beneficiaries by deed or in her will. A power of appointment can also be used to give the

owner the right to alter the proportionate share of each beneficiary under the trust.

26   The comments made in this chapter relating to the application of provincial family law are based upon the Ontario *Family Law Act,* R.S.O. 1990, c. F.3, but similar, though not identical, legislation exists in the other provinces.

27   See subsection 4(2) of the Ontario *Family Law Act.*

Chapter 9 – Valuation

1   See section 190 of the CBCA.

2   In the context of the ITA, since fair market value is not defined in the ITA, the judicial definition often accepted by the courts in Canada is that of Cattanach J. in *Henderson v. Minister of National Revenue* (1973), (*sub nom.* Bank of New York v. Minister of National Revenue) 73 D.T.C. 5471 (Fed. T.D.), affirmed 1975 CarswellNat 189 (Fed. C.A.), affirmed 1975 CarswellNat 188 (Fed. C.A.), which states at page 5476 as follows: "The statute does not define the expression "fair market value", but the expression has been defined in many different ways depending generally on the subject matter which the person seeking to define it had in mind. I do not think it necessary to attempt an exact definition of the expression as used in the statute other than to say that the words must be construed in accordance with the common understanding of them. That common understanding I take to mean the highest price an asset might reasonably be expected to bring if sold by the owner in the normal method applicable to the asset in question in the ordinary course of business in a market not exposed to any undue stresses and composed of willing buyers and sellers dealing at arm's length and under no compulsion to buy or sell. I would add that the foregoing understanding as I have expressed it in a general way includes what I conceive to be the essential element which is an open and unrestricted market in which the price is hammered out between willing and informed buyers and sellers on the anvil of supply and demand."

3   Subsection 69(1) of the ITA applies to gifts and transfers of property between persons who are not dealing with each other at arm's length. For a gift or sale below fair market value, the current owner is deemed to have disposed of the shares for fair market value regardless of the stipulated purchase price. For a gift or transfer above fair market value, the recipient is deemed to have acquired the shares at fair market value.

4   The owner may have decided to pay less compensation to himself and greater

compensation to certain members of his immediate family who pay tax at a lower marginal rate than the owner's own marginal tax rate, thereby allowing the family to collectively pay a lower amount of personal taxes than would be paid by the owner alone.

5   Discretionary cash flows are normally calculated before payments of interest and principal on the company's debt are made, on the assumption that the costs and benefits of financing are incorporated into the discount rate which is applied to the discretionary cash flows.

6   For example, subsection 173(1) of the CBCA provides that an amendment to a company's articles requires authorization by a "special resolution", which is defined in subsection 2(1) as a resolution passed at a meeting of shareholders by at least two-thirds of the votes cast.

Chapter 10 – Debt Financing and Commitment Letters

1   Under section 427 of the *Bank Act*, S.C. 1991, c.46, a notice of intention to give such security must have been filed within three years prior to the making of the advances, and the lender must hold an application for credit and promise to give security, along with an assignment in the prescribed form.

Chapter 11 – Credit and Loan Agreements

1   Section 4 of the *Interest Act*, R.S.C 1985, c. I-15.

2   See the *Financial Administration Act*, R.S.C. 1985, c. F-11.

3   Under section 81.1 of the *Bankruptcy and Insolvency Act*, an unpaid supplier is allowed to reclaim goods supplied within 30 days of a bankruptcy or receivership of the borrower, so long as they remain in the possession of the borrower, have not been resold, and are identifiable and in the same state as they were supplied.

4   See the Supreme Court of Canada decision in *Ronald Elwyn Lister Ltd. v. Dunlop Canada Ltd.*, [1982] 1 S.C.R. 726 (S.C.C.). In addition to the requirement imposed upon the lender under the common law to give reasonable notice before exercising its rights upon default, section 244 of the *Bankruptcy and Insolvency Act* requires the lender to give 10 days notice to the borrower if the lender intends to enforce upon all or substantially all of an insolvent party's inventory, accounts or property.

5   See subsection 244(1) of the *Bankruptcy and Insolvency Act*.

6   See section 119 of the CBCA and notes 12 to 16 to Chapter 3.

7   These proceedings may be initiated by filing a notice of intention to make a proposal or by filing a proposal under the *Bankruptcy and Insolvency Act,* or by applying for an initial order under the *Companies' Creditors Arrangement Act*, R.S.C. 1985, c. C-36.

Chapter 12 – Security Agreements and Guarantees

1   The commentary in this chapter is based upon the Ontario *Personal Property Security Act*, R.S.O. 1990, c. P.10, which is similar to the personal property security legislation of the other provinces except for Quebec, but reference should be made to the applicable provincial statute because of certain variations.

2   See the *Trade-marks Act, Patent Act*, and *Copyright Act.*

3   See the *Financial Administration Act*, R.S.C. 1985, c. F-11.

Chapter 13 – Equity Financing and Term Sheets

1   See section 42 of the CBCA.

2   See subsections 34 (2) and 36 (2) of the CBCA.

3   This contractual right to vote as a separate class is in addition to the statutory right to vote as a separate class provided under subsection 176(1) of the CBCA in connection with certain changes to the company's articles.

Chapter 14 – Subscription Agreements

1   See subsection 25(3) of the CBCA.

2   See subsection 25(5) of the CBCA.

3   For example, see generally the Ontario *Securities Act*, R.S.O. 1990, c. S.5. Ordinarily any person trading in a security must be registered as a dealer or salesperson, and no distribution of securities may be conducted unless a preliminary prospectus and a prospectus have been filed with the Ontario Securities Commission. A prospectus is intended to provide full, true and plain disclosure of all material facts relating to the security.

4   See generally National Instrument 45-106 *Prospectus and Registration Exemption.*

5   See the definition of "private issuer" and the exemption in section 2.4 of National Instrument 45-106 *Prospectus and Registration Exemption*. The main advantage of this exemption is its ease of use, since it does not require

the payment of any fees or filing of any forms, and there is no limit on the amount of money that can be raised in reliance upon this exemption. To rely upon this exemption, the company must have restrictions on the transfer of its securities contained in its constating documents (such as its articles or shareholder agreement), must have no more than 50 securityholders (ex-cluding employees and former employees), and must issue its securities only to certain categories of purchasers, such as directors, officers, employees, their family members or close personal friends and business associates, "ac-credited investors" (see the following note), and persons who are not "mem-bers of the public". This last group is a catch-all category comprising those having "common bonds" with the company's directors, officers or share-holders, or who already have access to enough company information and don't need to receive a prospectus.

6   See the definition of "accredited investor" in section 1.1 and the exemption in section 2.3 of National Instrument 45-106 *Prospectus and Registration Exemption*. This exemption assumes that any purchaser falling into any of the specified categories has the ability to withstand possible financial loss along with the expertise to evaluate the investment opportunity, and there-fore does not need the protection afforded by a prospectus. There is no limit on the number of times this exemption may be used.

7   See paragraph 1.1.(m) of the definition in the previous note, which requires at least $5 million in net assets as shown on the most recently prepared financial statements of the party purchasing the securities.

8   For example, if the agreement is governed by Ontario law, the parties will consider Ontario's *Limitations Act, 2002*, S.O. 2002, c. 24 Sched. B, which provides that business agreements between parties who are not "consumers" (as defined in Ontario's *Consumer Protection Act, 2002*, S.O. 2002, c. 30, Sched. A) may vary or exclude a basic limitation period, and may vary an ultimate limitation period provided that it may be suspended or extended only if the relevant claim has been discovered.

Chapter 16 – Shareholder Agreements

1   Subsection 146(1) of the CBCA.

2   See for example *Motherwell v. Schoof*, [1949] 4 D.L.R. 812 (Alta. T.D.) and *Ringuet v. Bergeron*, [1960] S.C.R. 672, 24 D.L.R. (2d) 449 (S.C.C.).

3   Subsection 102(1) of the CBCA.

4   See *Duha Printers (Western) Ltd. v. R.*, (*sub nom.* Duha Printers (Western) Ltd. v. Canada) [1998] 1 S.C.R. 795 (S.C.C.).

5   Subsection 146(1) of the CBCA.

6   Subsection 6(3) of the CBCA.

7   Paragraph 49(8)(c) of the CBCA.

8   Subsection 146(2) of the CBCA.

9   Subsection 146(5) of the CBCA.

10 Section 119 of the CBCA.

11 Paragraph 122(1)(a) of the CBCA.

12 Subsection 84(3) of the ITA provides that a share repurchase by a corporation entails a deemed dividend to the seller of the shares for the amount paid in excess of the paid up capital on those shares. Because the amount is treated as a dividend and not as a capital gain, the amount cannot be included in the taxpayer's lifetime capital gains exemption. Section 54 of the ITA in defining "proceeds of disposition" excludes in subparagraph (j) "any amount that would otherwise be proceeds of disposition of a share to the extent that the amount is deemed by subsection 84(2) or (3) to be a dividend received and is not deemed by paragraph 55(2)(a) or subparagraph 88(2)(b)(ii) not to be a dividend".

13 See subsections 34(2) and 36(2) of the CBCA.

14 See *J.G. Collins Insurance Agencies v. Elsley*, [1978] 2 S.C.R. 916 (S.C.C.), *H.L. Staebler Co. v. Allan* (2008), 92 O.R. (3d) 107 (Ont. C.A.), leave to appeal refused 2009 CarswellOnt 816, 2009 CarswellOnt 817 (S.C.C.) and *KRG Insurance Brokers (Western) Inc. v. Shafron*, 2009 SCC 6 (S.C.C.). See also *Guay inc. c. Payette*, 2013 SCC 45 (S.C.C.), which distinguishes non-solicitation covenants from non-competition covenants, and holds that non-solicitation covenants do not generally require a territorial limitation.

15 The comments made in this chapter relating to the application of provincial family law are based upon the Ontario *Family Law Act*, R.S.O. 1990, c. F.3, but similar, though not identical, legislation exists in the other provinces.

Chapter 17 – Shareholder Statutory Rights – Part I

1   See section 2(1) of the CBCA Regulations, which defines a "distributing corporation" as a "reporting issuer" under certain provincial securities legislation, or if not a "reporting issuer", a corporation which has filed a prospectus or registration statement, or which has securities listed on a stock exchange,

or which has amalgamated or been reorganized with a corporation which has done so.

2   Subsection 45(1) of the CBCA provides shareholder immunity from the liabilities, acts and defaults of the company except for liability under subsections 38(4) [improper return of capital], 118(4) and (5) [improper distributions], 146(5) [directors' liabilities assumed under a unanimous shareholder agreement], and 226(4) and (5) [distributions made upon the company's dissolution if claims are made within 2 years following the dissolution]. The case law also provides certain exceptions from such immunity, as occurs when a shareholder (often the only shareholder) is the company's *alter ego* and the company is almost a sham used to perpetrate dishonest actions, or acts merely as the shareholder's agent.

3   Subsection 24(3) of the CBCA.
4   Section 27 of the CBCA.
5   Subsection 24(4) of the CBCA.
6   Subsection 21(1) of the CBCA.
7   Subsection 20(1) of the CBCA.
8   Subsection 120(6.1) of the CBCA.
9   Subsection 21(1) of the CBCA.
10   Subsection 21(2) of the CBCA.
11   Subsection 138(4) of the CBCA.
12   Subsection 21(3) of the CBCA.
13   Subsections 21(7) and (9) of the CBCA.
14   Subsection 21(6) of the CBCA.
15   Section 190 of the CBCA.
16   Subsection 157(2) of the CBCA.
17   Subsection 159(1) of the CBCA.
18   Part 8 of the CBCA Regulations.
19   Paragraph 24(3)(b) of the CBCA
20   Section 42 of the CBCA.
21   Subsection 43(1) of the CBCA.
22   Paragraph 24(3)(c) of the CBCA.
23   Subsection 226(4) of the CBCA.
24   Section 49 of the CBCA.
25   Section 80 of the CBCA.
26   Subsection 168(2) of the CBCA.
27   Section 143 of the CBCA.
28   Section 150 of the CBCA and sections 57, 63 and 64 of the CBCA Regulations.

29 Section 137 of the CBCA and Part 6 of the CBCA Regulations.

30 Subsection 149(2) of the CBCA.

31 Section 175 of the CBCA.

32 Section 140 of the CBCA.

33 Section 148 of the CBCA.

34 Section 141 of the CBCA.

35 Section 145.1 of the CBCA.

Chapter 18 — Shareholder Statutory Rights – Part II

1   Subsection 142(1) of the CBCA.

2   Subsection 2(1) of the CBCA.

3   Subsections 176(6) and 189(8) of the CBCA.

4   Section 183 of the CBCA.

5   Section 184 of the CBCA.

6   Section 181 of the CBCA.

7   Section 186 of the CBCA.

8   Subsection 182(1) of the CBCA.

9   See *Canada (Director appointed under s. 260 of the Business Corporations Act), Re* (1991), 3 O.R. (3d) 336, 80 D.L.R. (4th) 619 (Ont. C.A.).

10 Subsections 176(1) and (5) of the CBCA.

11 Subsection 162(1) of the CBCA.

12 Section 163 of the CBCA.

13 Section 165 of the CBCA.

14 Subsection 103(2) of the CBCA.

15 Section 188 of the CBCA.

16 Subsection 106(3) of the CBCA.

17 Section 107 of the CBCA.

18 Section 109 of the CBCA.

19 Sections 103 and 173 of the CBCA.

20 Any proceedings to dissolve or liquidate the company must be stayed if it is found to be insolvent under the *Bankruptcy and Insolvency Act*, R.S.C. 1985, c. B-3.

21 Sections 210 and 211 of the CBCA.

22 Section 227 of the CBCA.

23 Section 194 of the CBCA.

24 Subsection 49(18) of the CBCA.

25 Subsections 26(1) to (3) of the CBCA.

26   Subsection 26(5) of the CBCA.

27   Section 38 of the CBCA.

28   Subsections 189(3) to (9) of the CBCA.

29   See *Benson v. Third Canadian General Investment Trust Ltd.* (1993), 14 O.R. (3d) 493 (Ont. Gen. Div. [Commercial List]).

Chapter 19 – Shareholder Meetings

1   Section 142 of the CBCA.

2   Subsection 144(2) of the CBCA.

3   Subsection 133(1) of the CBCA, although the company may apply to the court for an order extending the time for calling an annual meeting.

4   Section 155 of the CBCA.

5   Section 162 of the CBCA.

6   Section 106 of the CBCA.

7   Section 103 of the CBCA.

8   Subsection 135(5) of the CBCA.

9   Section 132 of the CBCA.

10 Subsections 132(4) and (5) and 141(3) and (4) of the CBCA, and section 45 of the CBCA Regulations. A shareholder entitled to vote may vote by means of a telephonic, electronic or other communication facility if the facility enables the votes to be gathered in a manner that permits their subsequent verification and permits the tallied votes to be presented to the company without it being possible for the company to identify how each shareholder or group of shareholders voted.

11 Part 5 of the CBCA Regulations.

12 Subsection 135(1.1) of the CBCA.

13 Subsection 135(2) of the CBCA.

14 Subsection 135(6) of the CBCA.

15 See *Anderson Lumber Co. v. Canadian Conifer Ltd.* (1977), 77 D.L.R. (3d) 126 (Alta. C.A.), leave to appeal allowed (1977), 7 A.R. 88 (note) (S.C.C.).

16 Subsections 135(3) and (4).

17 Subsection 139(1) of the CBCA.

18 Subsections 139(2) and (3) of the CBCA.

Chapter 20 – Director Duties and Liabilities

1   Subsection 115(1) of the CBCA.

2 Subsection 189(2) of the CBCA.

3 Subsection 115(3) of the CBCA.

4 Section 171 of the CBCA.

5 Paragraph 122(1)(a) of the CBCA.

6 See *BCE Inc., Re*, 2008 SCC 69 (S.C.C.), at paras. 37, 38.

7 See *People's Department Stores Ltd. (1992) Inc., Re*, 2004 SCC 68, [2004] 3 S.C.R. 461 (S.C.C.).

8 Subsection 120(1) of the CBCA.

9 Subsection 120(2) of the CBCA.

10 Subsection 120(4) of the CBCA.

11 Subsection 120(5) of the CBCA.

12 Subsection 120(7) of the CBCA.

13 Subsections 120(7.1) and (8) of the CBCA.

14 See *Canadian Aero Service Ltd. v. O'Malley* (1973), [1974] S.C.R. 592 (S.C.C.), and *International Corona Resources Ltd. v. LAC Minerals Ltd.*, [1989] 2 S.C.R. 574 (S.C.C.).

15 Paragraph 122(1)(b) of the CBCA.

16 Subsection 123(4) of the CBCA.

17 See the *Peoples* decision in note 7.

18 See the *Peoples* decision in note 7, and *Pente Investment Management Ltd. v. Schneider Corp.* (1998), (*sub nom.* Maple Leaf Foods Inc. v. Schneider Corp.) 42 O.R. (3d) 177 (Ont. C.A.).

19 See *UPM-Kymmene Corp. v. UPM-Kymmene Miramichi Inc.*, 2002 CarswellOnt 2096, [2002] O.J. No. 2412 (Ont. S.C.J. [Commercial List]), additional reasons 2002 CarswellOnt 3579 (Ont. S.C.J. [Commercial List]), leave to appeal refused 2004 CarswellOnt 691 (Ont. C.A.), affirmed 2004 CarswellOnt 691 (Ont. C.A.).

20 Subsections 34(2), 35(3) and 36(2) and paragraph 115(3)(e) of the CBCA.

21 Paragraph 118(2)(a) of the CBCA.

22 Subsection 118(4) of the CBCA.

23 Sections 30 to 33 and subsection 39(6) of the CBCA.

24 Subsection 159(1) of the CBCA.

25 Section 121 of the CBCA.

26 Section 122 of the CBCA.

27 Section 41 of the CBCA.

28 Paragraph 118(2)(b) of the CBCA.

29 Subsection 189(1) of the CBCA.

30 Subsections 122(2) and (3) of the CBCA.

31 Section 42 of the CBCA.

32 Paragraph 115(3)(d) of the CBCA.

33 Paragraph 118(2)(c) of the CBCA.

34 Subsection 118(4) of the CBCA.

35 Subsection 123(4) of the CBCA.

36 See *McClurg v. Minister of National Revenue, (sub nom.* McClurg v. Canada) [1990] 3 S.C.R. 1020 (S.C.C.) and *Neuman v. Minister of National Revenue,* [1998] 1 S.C.R. 770 (S.C.C.).

37 Section 43 of the CBCA.

38 Paragraph 115(3)(b) of the CBCA.

39 Section 125 of the CBCA.

40 Paragraph 115(3)(c) and subsections 25(3) and (4) of the CBCA.

41 Subsection 118(1) of the CBCA.

42 Section 103 of the CBCA.

43 Subsection 117(1) of the CBCA provides that a resolution in writing, signed by all the directors entitled to vote on that resolution at a meeting of directors, is as valid as if it had been passed at a meeting of directors.

44 Subsection 114(6) of the CBCA.

45 See subsection 114(5) of the CBCA which provides that the notice of a board meeting need not specify the purpose of or the business to be transacted at the meeting unless the by-laws otherwise provide, except for those matters referred to in subsection 115(3) of the CBCA which include the issuance of securities, redemption or purchase of company shares, and declaration of dividends.

46 Under subsection 123(3) of the CBCA, a director is deemed to have consented to a resolution that was passed or action taken at a meeting she did not attend unless within seven days after becoming aware of the resolution, the director "causes a dissent to be placed with the minutes of the meeting" or "sends a dissent by registered mail or delivers it to the registered office of the corporation".

47 See subsection 114(2) of the CBCA which provides that notwithstanding any vacancy among the directors, a quorum of directors may exercise all the powers of the directors.

48 Section 143 of the CBCA.

49 Subsection 109(1) of the CBCA.

50 Subsections 20(1) and (2) of the CBCA.

51 Subsection 120(6.1) of the CBCA.

52 Subsection 124(1) of the CBCA.

53 Subsection 124(2) of the CBCA.

54 Subsections 124(3) and (5) of the CBCA.

55 See *Blair v. Consolidated Enfield Corp.*, [1995] 4 S.C.R. 5 (S.C.C.).

56 See *Bennett v. Bennett Environmental Inc.*, 2009 ONCA 198 (Ont. C.A.).

57 Subsection 124(6) of the CBCA.

58 See notes 12, 13 and 14 to Chapter 3.

59 Subsection 123(1) of the CBCA.

60 See note 46 above.

61 Subsections 123(4) and (5) of the CBCA.

62 Subsection 146(2) of the CBCA.

63 Subsection 108(2) of the CBCA.

64 Resignation of a director from a CBCA company is recorded upon the filing of Form 6 – Changes Respecting Directors with Industry Canada.

65 For example, see subsection 119(3) of the CBCA which relieves a director from liability under subsection 119(1) for unpaid employee wages if she is not sued within two years after ceasing to be a director.

Chapter 21 – Governance

1 See National Policy 58-201 *Corporate Governance Guidelines*, National Instrument 58-101 *Disclosure of Corporate Governance Practices*, and National Instrument 52-110 *Audit Committees*.

2 Public companies which are "venture issuers" as defined in National Instrument 58-101 are partially relieved from providing the governance disclosure required of larger listed companies.

Chapter 22 – Dispute Resolution and Shareholder Remedies

1 Subsection 122(1) of the CBCA.

2 *BCE Inc., Re*, 2008 SCC 69 (S.C.C.).

3 For example, the ADR Institute of Ontario.

4 For example, the National Mediation Rules of the ADR Institute of Canada, Inc.

5 For example, the National Arbitration Rules of the ADR Institute of Canada, Inc., or for shorter timelines and expedited procedures, the Simplified Arbitration Rules of the ADR Institute of Canada, Inc.

6 Section 239 of the CBCA.

7 Section 240 of the CBCA.

8   Section 241 of the CBCA.

9   See *The Canadian Oppression Remedy Judicially Considered: 1995-2001* (2004) 30 Queen's L.J., a survey of the oppression remedy conducted by Professors Ben-Ishai and Puri which includes the results of a second study for the period December 2001 to February 2004. Of the 71 cases considered in their first study, 92 per cent dealt with private, closely-held companies. The authors observed, at page 89, that the majority of the successful oppression actions in the period of the first study involved the diversion of corporate profits, personal use of corporate profits by those controlling the corporation, the exclusion of the applicant from the operations of the corporation, or the alteration of proportional shareholdings. The remedy most often granted was a share purchase, usually in the context of a closely-held corporation where the shareholders lost confidence in each other and could not continue to work together.

10   Paragraphs 73 to 80 of the *BCE Inc.* decision described in note 2.

11   Paragraph 93 of the *BCE Inc.* decision described in note 2.

12   Paragraph 94 of the *BCE Inc.* decision described in note 2.

13   Section 167 of the CBCA.

14   Subsection 144(1) of the CBCA.

15   Section 247 of the CBCA.

16   Subsection 190(16) of the CBCA.

17   Part XIX of the CBCA.

18   Subsections 211(8) and 213(3) of the CBCA.

19   Subsection 214(1) of the CBCA.

20   Section 243 of the CBCA.

21   Subsection 161(4) of the CBCA.

22   Subsection 137(8) of the CBCA.

23   Subsection 120(8) of the CBCA.

24   Section 145 of the CBCA.

Chapter 23 – Conclusion

1   See the *Peoples* decision in note 7 of the *Directors Duties and Liabilities* chapter.

2   See note 9 of the *Dispute Resolution and Shareholder Remedies* chapter.

3   See *Wittlin v. Bergman* (1995), 25 O.R. (3d) 761 (Ont. C.A.), reversing (1994), 19 O.R. (3d) 145 (Ont. Gen. Div.).

4   See *Lecce v. Lecce* (1990), 72 O.R. (2d) 540 (Ont. H.C.).

5   See *Footitt v. Gleason* (1995), 25 O.R. (3d) 729 (Ont. Gen. Div. [Commercial List]), additional reasons at 1995 CarswellOnt 4274 (Ont. Gen. Div. [Commercial List]), affirmed 1998 CarswellOnt 1040 (Ont. C.A.).

6   See *Belman v. Belman* (1995), 26 O.R. (3d) 56 (Ont. Gen. Div.).

Index

- demolition or sale, 73
- due diligence, 76
  - condition of the premises, 78
    - independent building search, 78
  - title search, 76
  - zoning compliance, 77
    - changing by-laws, 77
- environmental indemnity, 70
- exclusivity and other restrictions, 68
- gross lease v. net lease, 62
- indemnity, 70
- insurance, 70
- leasehold improvements, 69
- net lease v. gross lease, 62
- offer to lease, 62
- option to purchase and right of refusal, 67
- option to renew and right to extend, 65
- percentage rent, 63
- relocation, 71
- removal and restoration, 75
- subordination and attornment, 68

Liabilities, *see* Director duties and liabilities

M

Meetings, *see* Shareholder meetings

N

Negative covenants, 269
- enforcement of negative covenants, 271
- non-competition covenant, 271
- non-disclosure covenant, 270
- non-solicitation covenant, 270

O

Owners vs. managers, 3

Ownership, determining, 30

P

Patents, 34

Preferred shares, 9

Private company, 2

Protecting intellectual property, 29
- copyright, 37
- determining ownership, 30
- industrial design, 40
- maintaining ownership, 31
- patents, 34
- trade secrets and confidential information, 32
- trademarks, 38

R

Remedies, *see* Dispute resolution and shareholder remedies

Representations, *see* Warranties and representations

S

Security agreements and guarantees, 185
- conflicts with loan agreement, 185
- describing the obligations secured, 186
- general security, 188
- guarantees, 187
- postponement and assignment, 187
- priority of other security, 192
- special treatment of certain assets, 190
- specific security, 189

Shares, 9
- buy-back rights, 13
- class of, 8
- gift, 118
- issuing, 9
- payment for, 13
- preferred shares, 9
- sale, 119
- valuation of, 13

Shareholder, 4

Shareholder agreements, 249
- auction rights, 269
- bank financing and guarantees, 258